BUSINESS ENGLISH

BUSINESS ENGLISH

Fourth Edition

Mary Ellen Guffey

Los Angeles Pierce College

Wadsworth Publishing Company
Belmont, California
A Division of Wadsworth, Inc.

Student Edition ISBN: 0-534-92906-0
Instructor's Edition ISBN: 0-534-92907-9

Editor: Rolf Janke
Assistant Editor: Marnie Pommett
Production Coordinator: Pamela Rockwell
Manufacturing Coordinator: Marcia Locke
Interior Designer: Julia Gecha and Pamela Rockwell
Cover Designer: Outhouse Graphics
Typesetting: Grafacon, Inc.
Cover Printing: New England Book Components, Inc.
Printing and Binding: Courier Companies, Inc., Westford

Printed in the United States of America
93 94 95—10 9 8 7 6 5

CONTENTS

PREFACE

Mary Ellen Guffey

The bold new approach taken by the first edition of *Business English* in 1983 has continued to appeal to instructors and students. Many users have found that the three-level format permits flexibility in teaching the wide range of students currently enrolling in business English courses. The fourth edition of *Business English* retains its original broad goals:

1. To provide college students with comprehensive, up-to-date, and relevant instruction in the correct use of English grammar.
2. To develop proficiency in punctuation, capitalization, and number style skills.
3. To demonstrate realistic applications of current usage and style in the work world.
4. To furnish optional instruction in spelling, vocabulary development, and business writing skills.

Textbook Features

Three-Level Approach

Beginning with Chapter 4, the language concepts appear in levels. These levels progress from fundamental, frequently used concepts in Level I to more complex concepts in Level III. Each level has its own trial exercises as well as numerous relevant student reinforcement drills.

The three-level approach has three distinct advantages. First, the overall organization of the complex subject of English is immediately recognizable. Second, the three-level approach facilitates comprehension and promotes student confidence by providing small, easily mastered learning segments. Third, this strategy provides convenient blocks of material that allow individual instructors to tailor the content of the course to fit student abilities, institutional goals, and time constraints.

Hot Line Queries

One of the most popular features of *Business English* has been its questions and answers from grammar hot line services across the country. These authentic questions—and the author's suggested answers to them—illustrate everyday communication problems encountered in the work world. In easy-to-read question-and-answer format, important distinctions in English grammar, usage, style, and vocabulary are explained. New questions for the Fourth Edition have been collected from hot line services across the country, including those in Delaware, North Carolina, Alabama, Ohio, Indiana, Illinois, Arizona, and California.

Pretests and Posttests

Each chapter includes a brief pretest to preview concepts and to pique the interest of students, as well as a posttest to enable students to evaluate their learning.

Self-Check Exercises and Unit Reviews

The first student exercise in each level of each chapter is self-checked. Students are therefore able to determine immediately whether they comprehend the concepts just presented. At the end of each unit, a self-checked review exercise enables students to test their mastery of the unit.

Learning Objectives

Each chapter is introduced by a group of concisely stated learning objectives that summarize the concepts presented. Such overtly stated goals facilitate learning by stimulating a student mind-set favorable to the learning process.

N.B. Boxes

N.B. is an abbreviation of the Latin phrase *nota bene,* meaning "note well." Writers sometimes use it to call a reader's attention to an important passage. The N.B. boxes employed in *Business English* help students comprehend and retain language principles by suggesting memory devices, clues, hints, and other learning aids.

Spelling and Vocabulary

For students who desire them and for instructors who can find time to include them, optional spelling and vocabulary development materials are provided in separate appendixes. *Business English* includes spelling rules and a program for spelling improvement that can accompany each chapter if the instructor desires.

Writing Component

An extensive optional writing program—covering paragraphs, memos, and business letters—is available in Appendixes 3, 4, and 5. Transparency masters, available from the author, illustrate these appendixes. The Instructor's Edition includes ideas for incorporating this writing program in the business English course.

Reference Manual Coordination

Business English instructors recognize the importance of coordinating a classroom textbook with a general reference book. Although most conventions in English have become standardized, some minor usage recommendations may vary from book to book—and these variations cause students considerable confusion. Such confusion can be avoided if the textbook and reference manual are coordinated. The business English concepts and rules presented in this text coordinate with those presented in Clark and Clark's highly successful reference manual, *HOW 6: A Handbook for Office Workers.*

New to the Fourth Edition

In response to reviewers' and users' wishes, the fourth edition of *Business English* remains largely unchanged. The major addition to the entire package is that of software.

Computer Software

The author and Lois Wagner, Southwest Wisconsin Technical College, developed a set of reinforcement exercises in the form of a computer study guide. Included with each Instructor's Edition is a diskette containing 15 chapters of exercises correlated with the textbook. Each of the computer chapters has 30 true-false, multiple-choice, or fill-in questions progressing from simple to complex.

The questions focus on Level I and II concepts. The computer program provides two modes: (1) a self-test mode, to be used as a pretest or posttest, and (2) a study guide mode, with answers and feedback immediately available. Students who pilot tested the software overwhelmingly approved this alternative learning method. They liked being able to test themselves on the questions first and then repeat the questions in study mode, where they found ample explanations and feedback. The master diskette may be duplicated for each student once the book is adopted.

More Sentence Writing

At the suggestion of reviewers, more emphasis is being given to composition. An optional sentence-writing exercise now concludes each chapter. These skill-building opportunities encourage students to apply chapter principles in forming complete sentences. In addition, optional editing and composition unit tests (to supplement the objective tests) are available in the Instructor's Edition.

Transparency Acetates

A set of 116 transparencies illustrate major concepts from every level of every chapter (and some appendixes) in *Business English.* These transparencies are now fully prepared acetates—not masters. They may be ordered from Wadsworth Publishing Company, Belmont, California 94002.

Testing Materials

The Instructor's Edition includes a test bank with approximately 50 objective test items for each chapter. Also included in the Instructor's Edition are printed sets of unit tests (both objective and editing-composition tests) along with a final examination. For those instructors who wish to prepare tests on the computer, a test bank diskette may be obtained from Wadsworth Publishing Company, Belmont, California 94002.

Self-Help Exercises

Because business English students need many opportunities to try out their learning, they appreciate exercises in addition to those provided in their textbooks. Supplementary exercises for all levels of all chapters are provided in the Instructor's Edition. These self-checked exercises may be reproduced and distributed for self-paced reinforcement.

Pretest

Preceding Chapter 1 is a pretest designed to help students assess their business English strengths and weaknesses.

Teaching Suggestions

The Instructor's Edition contains a sample lesson plan and practical suggestions for developing a complete, effective business English course.

Acknowledgements

Many individuals have contributed to the success of *Business English,* and I am deeply grateful to them.

In developing the Hot Line Queries for the Fourth Edition, I extend thanks to the following language specialists for their service to their communities and for their contributions to this book: Jo Allen, The University Writing Center, East Carolina University, Greenville, NC; Carol Cauthen, Grammar Hotline, Jacksonville State University, Jacksonville, AL; Billie Miller Cooper, Cosumnes River College, Sacramento, CA; Hillard Hebda, Grammarphone, Triton College, River Grove, IL; Muriel Harris, Grammar Hotline, Writing Lab, Purdue University, West Lafayette, IN; Margaret P. Hassert, University Writing Center, University of Delaware, Newark, DE; J. J. Lamberts, Grammar Hotline, Tempe, AZ; Patricia Maddox, Grammarphone, Writing Lab, Amarillo College, Amarillo, TX; Phyllis A. Sherwood, Dial-a-Grammar, Raymond Walters College, Cincinnati, OH; Jeanne H. Simpson, Writing Center, Eastern Illinois University, Charleston, IL; and Margaret W. Taylor, Grammar Hotline, Cuyahoga Community College, Warrensville Township, OH.

Instructors across the country have sent me excellent ideas, constructive insights, and supportive comments. I am particularly grateful to Paige P. Baker, Trinity Valley Community College, Athens, TX; Charlotte Cohen, Monroe College, Bronx, NY; Judy Ehresman, Mercer County Community College, Trenton, NJ; Valerie Evans, Cuesta College, San Luis Obispo, CA; Donna R. Everett, Texas Tech University, Lubbock, TX; Marye B. Gilford, St. Philips College, San Antonio, TX; Margaret E. Gorman, Cayuga Community College, Auburn, NY; Kathy Green, Phoenix College, Phoenix, AZ; Ginger Guzman, J. Sargeant Reynolds Community College, Richmond, VA; Molly L. Harned, NEC-Allentown Business School, Allentown, PA; Marilyn Helser, Lima Technical College, Lima, OH; Janet L. Hough, Spokane Community College, Spokane, WA; Karen Howie, Northwestern Michigan College, Traverse City, MI; Marilynne Hudgens, Southwestern College, Chula Vista, CA; Ernestine A. Hunter, Rio Hondo College, Whittier, CA; Edna V. Jellesed, Lane Community College; Evelyn A. Katusak, Broome Community College, Binghamton, NY; Lydia J. Keuser, San Jose City College, San Jose, CA; Deborah Kitchin, Heald Business College, San Francisco, CA; Shelley Konishi, Kauai Community College, Lihue, HI; Linell Loncorich, Hutchinson Technical College, Hutchinson, MN; Barbara J. Malom, WITC, Rice Lake, WI; Jane Mangrum, Miami-Dade Community College; Edward J. Mautz, Los Angeles Trade Technical College; Darlene McClure, College of the Redwoods, Crescent City, CA; Timothy A. Miank, Lansing Community College, Lansing, MI; Carol Vermeere Middendorff, Clackamas Community College, Oregon City, OR; Cheryl Mueller, Northwestern Business College, Paul W. Murphey, Southwest Wisconsin Technical College, Fennimore, WI; Jaunett S. Neighbors, Central Virginia Community College, Lynchburg, VA; Jackie Ohlson, University of Alaska, Anchorage; Judith R. Rice, Chippewa Valley Technical College, Eau Claire, WI; Maria Robinson, Columbia College, Columbia, CA; Vilera Rood, Concordia College, Moorhead, MN; Evelyn Taylor, Cincinnati Bible College, Cincinnati, OH; Susan Uchida, Kauai Community College, Lihue, HI; June Uharriet, East Los Angeles Community College; Iva A. Upchurch, Ventura College, Ventura, CA; and Lois A. Wagner, Southwest Wisconsin Technical College, Fennimore, WI.

I consider myself fortunate to be teaching at Los Angeles Pierce College alongside extraordinary colleagues who not only provide encouragement but also are willing to share their deep fund of instructional expertise. My warm appreciation goes to Ellen Anderson, Kathleene Basil, Janet Horne, Leo Sirakides, and especially to Dr. Lyn Clark.

I commend the following dedicated professionals at PWS-KENT Publishing Company for their care, patience, and prowess in guiding *Business English* to its prominent position in the field: Managing Editor Rolf Janke, Senior Production Editor Pam Rockwell, Product Manager Robert Wolcott, and all the enthusiastic PWS-KENT sales representatives in the field.

Finally, for his wise counsel and inestimable assistance in the creation of *Business English,* I extend my heartfelt thanks and dedicate this book to my husband, Dr. George R. Guffey, Department of English, University of California—Los Angeles.

Instructor Networking

Each year I develop and distribute new classroom teaching materials, such as transparency teaching units and reinforcement exercises, to business communication instructors. Instructors tell me that they appreciate this continuing flow of classroom materials. They like the feeling that the author is "in the trenches" with them, rather than sitting in an ivory tower or reclining in a retirement rocker. To ensure that you receive notice of these free materials, please send me your name and address. I would also be delighted to read any comments regarding your course or suggestions for this book.

Dr. Mary Ellen Guffey
Los Angeles Pierce College
5942 Paseo Canyon
Malibu, CA 90265

Name ______________________

PRETEST

In the following sentences, defects of grammar, punctuation, capitalization, or number expression may appear. For each sentence underline any inappropriate form(s). Then write a corrected form in the space provided. *Clue:* one sentence at each level is correct.

EXAMPLE: The inheritance will be given to my brother and *myself* on our twenty-first birthdays. ___me___

LEVEL I

1. Mr. Cortez paid into the system for thirty years, then he retired and began to draw benefits. ______
2. The seminar in Boulder, Colorado in the spring sounds as if it will be worthwhile. ______
3. The announcement from our Personnel Services Department surprised the secretaries as much as I. ______
4. Jim and I certainly appreciate you answering the telephone when he and I are away from the office. ______
5. A set of guidelines were developed for him and the others. ______
6. Every classified employee, as well as every management and certified employee, is eligible for sales discounts. ______
7. For you Mrs. Alison, we have a one-year subscription to your favorite magazine. ______
8. Under the circumstances, we can give you only 90 days time in which to sell the house and its contents. ______
9. We normally hire only experienced operators; but on occasion we consider well-trained individuals who lack experience. ______
10. During the fall Lisa took courses in history, spanish, and accounting. ______

LEVEL II

11. All our customers names and addresses will be transferred to computer diskettes. ______
12. Either Mr. Harris or his assistant will be working at the shop on the next two Sunday's. ______

13. Of the 500 letters mailed, Mr. Turner's secretary reported that only five were returned. __________

14. If you want a three-week vacation, you must speak to the Personnel Manager. __________

15. The warehouse has been moved from 5th Street to 39th Street. __________

16. Chapter 15, which is entitled "Credit Buying," is one of the best chapters in *Today's Consumer.* __________

17. Before her trip to the East last summer, my mother purchased a Kodak Camera. __________

18. We need at least one hundred thirty-cent postage stamps. __________

19. Your account is now 90 days overdue, therefore, we are submitting it to an agency for collection. __________

20. I feel badly about your missing the deadline, but the application has been lying on your desk for fifteen days. __________

LEVEL III

21. The award will be made to whomever has the best record. __________

22. All letter styles must comply to those shown in the company style manual. __________

23. Iris Products is larger than any food processing plant on the West Coast. __________

24. The number of employees interested in attending the seminar are surprising. __________

25. The school's alumni are certainly different than its currently enrolled students. __________

26. She is one of those efficient, competent managers who is able to give sincere praise for work done well. __________

27. Because she looks like her sister, Mary is often taken to be her. __________

28. If I was him, I would call the Harrises' attorney at once. __________

29. Three employees were given merit raises, namely, Carol Chang, Tom Nelson, and Toni Simpson. __________

30. Surely it was he who left the package on the boss's desk. __________

UNIT ONE

Laying a Foundation

CHAPTER 1

Reference Skills

OBJECTIVES When you have completed the materials in this chapter, you will be able to do the following:

— *Describe three types of dictionaries.*
— *Use a dictionary confidently to determine spelling, meaning, pronunciation, syllabication, accent, word usage, and word history.*
— *Select a dictionary to suit your needs.*
— *Anticipate what information is included in dictionaries and what information is not.*
— *Understand the value of reference manuals.*

PRETEST

Each chapter will begin with a brief pretest. Answer the questions in the pretest to assess your prior knowledge of the chapter content and also to give you a preview of what you will learn. Compare your answers with those at the bottom of the page. When you complete the chapter, take the posttest to measure your improvement.

Write *T* (true) or *F* (false) after the following statements.

1. College students need a current unabridged dictionary for their daily use. _____
2. Dictionary guide words help readers pronounce words correctly. _____
3. The usage label *archaic* means that a word is very old. _____
4. All dictionaries present word definitions in the same order. _____
5. A reader should not expect to find the spelling of the plural form of *branch* in most dictionaries. _____

When Jennifer S. enrolled in business English, she did not plan to become an expert in the subject. When she finished the course, she didn't think of herself as an expert — although she had done well enough in the class. But when she started to work, she discovered that many of her fellow workers considered her an English expert. Most of them had never had any specific training in grammar—or they had studied it long ago, and their skills were very rusty. Jennifer found that even her boss asked her questions like, "What are they doing now about letter salutations?" Or, "Where do you think we

---

1. F, 2. F, 3. T, 4. F, 5. T

should put that apostrophe?" Everyone seemed to think that because she had just finished school, she would know all the answers. Jennifer didn't know all the answers. But she knew where to find them.

One of the goals of your education is to know where to find answers, as well as how to interpret the information you find. Experts do not know *all* the answers. Attorneys refer to casebooks. Doctors consult their medical libraries. And you, a student of the language, must develop skill and confidence in using reference materials. You will become a business English expert not only by learning from this textbook but also by learning where to find additional data when you need it.

Using reference books should become second nature. The need to verify words, punctuation, style, and usage is universal; the habit of verifying information is essential in achieving accurate, effective communication.

You can find information quickly and efficiently by having your own personal library of reference materials. At the minimum, a current desk or college dictionary and a good reference manual are needed. Another helpful reference book is a thesaurus, which is a collection of synonyms (words with similar meanings) and antonyms (words with opposite meanings). Specific career fields may require additional materials.

The dictionary is probably the most used and the most useful of all reference materials. Here are some suggestions for selecting and using a dictionary.

Dictionaries

Types

Dictionaries can be grouped into three categories: pocket, desk (college), and unabridged. In choosing one for yourself, consider your needs. A *pocket* dictionary is handy and efficient. However, since it usually has no more than 75,000 entries, it may prove inadequate for college reference homework.

A *desk* or *college-level* dictionary contains over 170,000 entries plus extra features. Both pocket and desk dictionaries are abridged; that is, they are condensed or shortened dictionaries. For college work you should own a current desk dictionary. The following list shows some of the best-known desk dictionaries. Notice that the titles of two dictionaries contain the name *Webster*. Because names cannot be copyrighted, any publisher may use the word *Webster* on its dictionary. Definitions and usage in this textbook are based on the *Webster's Ninth New Collegiate Dictonary*. Many publishers rely upon this dictionary as their standard. Some readers, however, prefer *The American Heritage Dictionary* because it provides more plural spellings, more usage labels, and more opinions about appropriate usage than other dictionaries.

Name	Approximate number of definitions
The American Heritage Dictionary	200,000
The Random House College Dictionary	173,000
*Webster's Ninth New Collegiate Dictionary**	200,000
Webster's New World Dictionary	170,000

Unabridged or complete dictionaries are large, heavy volumes that contain nearly all English words. Schools, libraries, newspapers, and business offices that are concerned with editing or publishing use unabridged dictionaries. One of the best-known unabridged dictionaries is *Webster's New International Dictionary*. It includes over 450,000 entries. Another famous unabridged dictionary is the *Oxford English Dictionary (OED)*. This 13-

**The standard dictionary for definitions and usage in this book.*

volume set shows the historical development of all English words; it is often used by professional writers, scholars of the language, and academics. A computer version on CD ROM is now available for easy access.

Copyright Date

If the copyright date of your current dictionary shows that the dictionary was published ten or more years ago, consider investing in a more recent edition. English is a responsive, dynamic language that admits new words and recognizes changes in meanings and usage of familiar words. These changes are reflected in an up-to-date dictionary.

Features

Before selecting a dictionary, check the features it offers in addition to vocabulary definitions. Many editions contain biographical and geographical data, abbreviations, standard measurements, signs, symbols, foreign words and phrases, lists of colleges and universities, given names, and information about the language.

Entry

This example from *The American Heritage Dictionary, Second College Edition,** illustrates some of the ten points we will discuss here to help you use your dictionary more effectively.

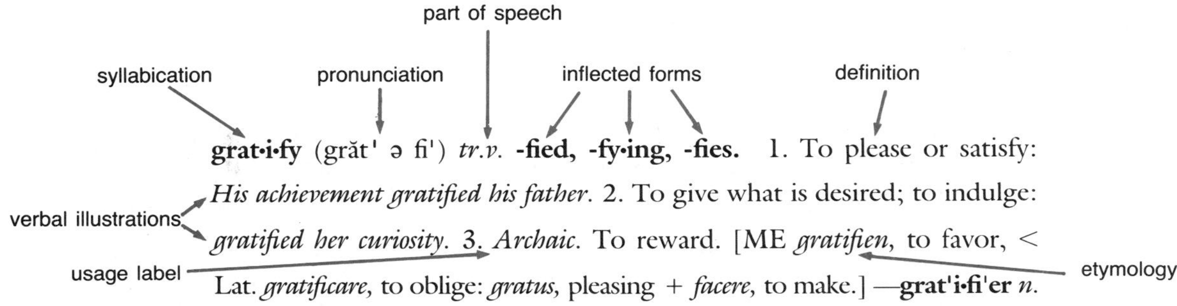

Dictionary Use

1. *Introduction.* Before using your dictionary, take a few moments to read the instructions located in the pages just before the beginning of the vocabulary entries. Pay particular attention to the order of definitions. Some dictionaries show the most common definitions first. Other dictionaries develop meanings historically; that is, the first known meaning of the word is shown first.

2. *Guide Words.* In boldface type at the top of each dictionary page are two words that indicate the first and last entries on the page. When searching for a word, look *only* at these guide words until you locate the desired page.

3. *Syllabication.* Most dictionaries show syllable breaks with a centered dot, as shown for the word *gratify*. Compound words are sometimes troublesome to dictionary users. If a compound word is shown with a centered dot, it is one word, as in *work•out* (workout). If a compound word is shown with a hyphen, it is hyphenated, as in *old-fashioned*. If two words appear without a centered dot or a hyphen, they should be written as two words, as in *work up*. If you find no entry for a word or phrase in a college-level dictionary, you may usually assume that the words are written separately, for example, *ball field*.

4. *Pronunciation.* Special symbols (diacritical marks) are used to help you pronounce words correctly. A detailed explanation of pronunciation symbols is found in the front of a dictionary; a summary of these symbols may appear at the bottom of each set of pages. If two pronunciations are possible, the preferred one is usually shown first.

5. *Accent.* Most dictionaries show accents with a raised stress mark immediately following the accented syllable, as shown for the syllable *grat* in our example. Other dictionaries use a raised stress mark immediately *preceding* the accented syllable (*'grat e fi*). Secondary stress may be shown in lighter print (as illustrated on the syllable *fi* from our example), or it may be shown with a *lowered* accent mark (*'grat e ˌfi*).

6. *Etymology.* College-level dictionaries provide in square brackets [ ] the brief history or etymology of the word. For example, the word *gratify* originated in Latin, and its meanings further developed in Old French and Middle English. Keys to etymological abbreviations may be found in the introductory notes in your dictionary. Do not confuse the etymological definition shown in brackets with the vocabulary entry definition(s).

7. *Part of Speech.* Following the phonetic pronunciation of an entry word is an italicized or boldfaced label indicating what part of speech the entry word represents. The most common labels are the following:

adj	(adjective)	*prep*	(preposition)
adv	(adverb)	*pron*	(pronoun)
conj	(conjunction)	*v* or *vb*	(verb)
interj	(interjection)	*vt* or *tr. v.*	(verb transitive)
n	(noun)	*vi* or *int. v.*	(verb intransitive)

Spelling, pronunciation, and meaning may differ for a given word when that word functions as different parts of speech. Therefore, check its grammatical label carefully. If the parts of speech seem foreign to you at this time, do not despair. Chapter 2 and successive chapters will help you learn more about the parts of speech.

8. *Labels.* Not all words listed in dictionaries are acceptable in business or other writing. Usage labels are used to warn readers about the use of certain words. In the dictionary entry for the word *gratify,* one meaning is labeled *archaic.* The following list defines *archaic* and other usage labels:

Label	Example
archaic: words surviving from a previous period	*knave* (meaning *male servant*)
obsolete: no longer in use	*miss* (meaning *a loss*)
colloquial or *informal**: used in casual writing or conversation	*shindig* (*festive party*)
slang: very informal but may be sparingly used for effect	*boonies* (*rural area*)
nonstandard and *substandard:* not conforming to usage among educated speakers	*hisself* (*himself*)
dialect, Brit., South, Scot, etc.: used in certain regions	*bodacious* (used in South to mean *remarkable*)

If no usage label appears, a word is considered standard; that is, it is acceptable for all uses. However, it should be noted that many lexicographers, those who make dictionaries, have substantially reduced the number of usage labels in current editions.

9. *Inflected Forms.* When nouns, verbs, adverbs, or adjectives change form grammatically, they are said to be *inflected,* as when *child* becomes *children.* Because of limited space, dictionaries usually show only irregular inflected forms. Thus, nouns with irregular or

**Some dictionaries no longer use the labels* colloquial *or* informal.

unusual plurals (*wife, wives*) will be shown. Verbs with irregular tenses or difficult spelling (*gratified, gratifying*) will be shown. Adverbs or adjectives with irregular comparatives or superlatives (*good, better, best*) will also be shown. But regular noun plurals, verb tenses, and comparatives generally will *not* be shown in dictionaries. Succeeding chapters will elucidate regular and irregular parts of speech.

10. *Synonyms and Antonyms.* *Synonyms,* words having similar meanings, are often provided after word definitions. For example, a synonym for *elucidate* is *explain.* Synonyms are helpful as word substitutes. *Antonyms,* words having opposite meanings, appear less frequently in dictionaries; when included, they usually follow synonyms. One *antonym* for *elucidate* is *confuse.* The best place to find synonyms and antonyms is in a *thesaurus.*

Reference Manuals

Reference Manual Versus Dictionary

In addition to one or more dictionaries, all writers and office workers should have a good reference manual or handbook readily available. In it one can find helpful information not available in dictionaries. Most reference manuals provide the following information:

1. *Punctuation.* Detailed explanations of punctuation rules are presented logically. A well-written manual will also provide ample illustrations of punctuation usage so that the reader can readily find solutions to punctuation dilemmas.

2. *Hyphenation.* Dictionaries provide syllable breaks. Words, however, cannot be divided at all syllable breaks. A reference manual will supply rules for, and examples of, word division. Moreover, a good reference manual will explain when compound adjectives like *up-to-the-minute* should be hyphenated.

3. *Capitalization.* Complete rules with precise examples illustrating capitalization style will be shown.

4. *Numbers.* Deciding whether to write a number as a figure or as a word can be very confusing. A reference manual will provide both instruction and numerous examples illustrating number and word styles.

Other topics covered in reference manuals are confusing words (such as *effect* and *affect*), abbreviations, contractions, literary and artistic titles, forms of address, and letter and report formats. In addition, some manuals contain sections devoted to English grammar and office procedures.

Reference Manual Versus Textbook

You may be wondering how a reference manual differs from a business English textbook such as the one you are now reading. Although content is similar, the primary difference is one of purpose. A textbook is developed *pedagogically,* that is, for teaching, so that the student understands and learns concepts. A reference manual is organized *functionally,* so that the reader finds accurate information efficiently. A well-written reference manual is complete, coherent, and concise.

Most of the language and style questions that perplex business people and students could be answered quickly by a trained person using a reliable dictionary and a well-written reference manual.

Complete now the reinforcement exercises on the following pages.

Name ______________________________

CHAPTER 1 **Reinforcement Exercises**

Note: At the beginning of every set of reinforcement exercises, a self-checked exercise is provided so that you will know immediately if you understand the concepts presented in the chapter. Do not look at the answers until you have completed the exercise. Then compare your responses with the answers shown at the bottom of the page. If you have more than three incorrect responses, reread the chapter before continuing with the other reinforcement exercises.

A. (Self-check) Write *T* (true) or *F* (false) after the following statements.

1. Students and office workers would find an unabridged dictionary handy to carry with them. ______
2. Guide words help a dictionary user to pronounce a word. ______
3. The label *colloquial* means that a word is informal and may be used in casual writing and conversation. ______
4. Most dictionaries use centered dots to indicate syllables. ______
5. All dictionaries show accented syllables with a raised stress mark preceding a syllable. ______
6. Dictionaries usually show noun plurals only if they are irregular. ______
7. Synonyms are words that are spelled alike or sound alike. ______
8. A reference manual is a small dictionary. ______
9. Rules for hyphenating compound adjectives may be found in a reference manual. ______
10. All dictionaries show definitions in historical order. ______

Check your answers at the bottom of the page.

Use a *current* desk or college-level dictionary to complete the following exercises. If you do not have a dictionary, use one at a library. The definitions, pronunciations, and usage in this book come from *Webster's Ninth New Collegiate Dictionary*.

B. Select the letter that provides the best definition or synonym for each word shown.

1. adversary (n) — (a) attorney, (b) advisor, (c) adulterer, (d) opponent ______
2. cacophony (n) — (a) poor handwriting, (b) harsh sounds, (c) rhythmic beat, (d) enormous wealth ______
3. entomology (n) — (a) study of words, (b) study of fossils, (c) study of insects, (d) love of outdoors ______

A. 1. F, 2. F, 3. T, 4. T, 5. F, 6. T, 7. F, 8. F, 9. T, 10. F

4. jeopardy (n) (a) game show, (b) adornment, (c) immunity, (d) danger ______
5. obtuse (adj.) (a) dull, (b) old, (c) fixed, (d) stubborn ______
6. peripatetic (adj.) (a) itinerant, (b) mutineer, (c) pacifist, (d) informer ______
7. prevaricate (v) (a) construct, (b) equivocate, (c) exemplify, (d) precede ______
8. query (n) (a) complaint, (b) question, (c) request, (d) baked custard pie ______
9. rampant (adj.) (a) morose, (b) irregular, (c) husky, (d) widespread ______
10. warrant (n) (a) caution, (b) rabbits, (c) authorization, (d) program ______

C. Write the correct form of the following words. Use a current dictionary to determine whether they should be written as one word or two words or whether they should be hyphenated.

EXAMPLE: print out (n) printout

1. cathode ray tube ______
2. double space (v) ______
3. in as much as ______
4. never the less ______
5. off spring ______
6. old fashioned ______
7. time clock ______
8. time honored ______

D. For each of the following words, write the syllable that receives the primary accent. Then give a brief definition or synonym of the word.

Word	Syllable	Definition or synonym
EXAMPLE: judicious	dic	prudent, exhibiting sound judgment
1. advertisement	______	______
2. antipathy	______	______
3. comparable	______	______
4. desert (n)	______	______
5. desert (v)	______	______
6. formidable	______	______
7. indefatigable	______	______
8. infamous	______	______
9. irrevocable	______	______
10. posthumous	______	______

E. If your dictionary shows usage labels for the following words, write them in the spaces provided. If no label appears for a word, which of the following labels would you consider giving it if you were a lexicographer? Put your initials next to the labels you suggest.

LABELS: archaic nonstandard colloquial or informal dialect slang

EXAMPLE: goober dialect

1. cheapskate ______
2. goodwife ______
3. petrol ______
4. poke (meaning "sack") ______

Name ______________________

5. irregardless ______________________ 6. sawbones ______________________

F. Select the letter that most accurately completes the sentence.

1. A proposal to construct a shopping center received *approbation* from city officials; therefore, the center will probably be
   (a) rejected (c) constructed
   (b) delayed (d) modified ____

2. The abbreviation *e.g.* stands for
   (a) for example (c) that is
   (b) extra good (d) eye glasses ____

3. If you have a *bibulous* uncle, he probably engages in too much
   (a) sleeping (c) talking
   (b) drinking (d) gambling ____

4. To stage a *boycott,* individuals might follow which of the following actions?
   (a) withhold their services (c) reduce their production
   (b) refuse to buy a product (d) refuse to cross picket lines ____

5. The word *eclectic* originated in what language?
   (a) Latin (c) French
   (b) Greek (d) Old English ____

6. Condominiums that provide more than one form of *egress* must have more than one
   (a) parking space (c) exit
   (b) level (d) mortgage ____

7. One meaning of *featherbedding* is
   (a) employing more workers than needed (c) producing lightweight mattresses
   (b) providing for oneself first (d) illegally reducing salaries ____

8. The word *FORTRAN* is derived from the words
   (a) fast operating translator (c) formula translation
   (b) future ordinal transfer (d) forms transfer ____

9. The abbreviation *i.e.* stands for
   (a) for example (c) in earnest
   (b) for instance (d) that is ____

10. What professional would most likely hold the *D.D.S.* degree?
    (a) dentist (c) banker
    (b) licensed broker (d) surgeon ____

11. The word *magazine* is derived from a French term meaning
    (a) ammunition (c) a periodical
    (b) a storehouse (d) a firearm compartment ____

12. *Nepotism* is derived from French, Italian, and Latin words suggesting
(a) pain (c) employment
(b) nephew (d) parent ______

13. An individual who is *quixotic* is
(a) idealistic (c) aggressive
(b) radical (d) patient ______

14. A business regulated by the *SEC* would probably be concerned with
(a) communication (c) securities
(b) transportation (d) energy ______

15. Which of the following is written correctly?
(a) unAmerican (c) un-American
(b) un-american (d) Un-American ______

G. Answer true (*T*) or false (*F*).

1. Pocket dictionaries are handy but may be insufficient for all one's needs. ______
2. If two pronunciations of a word are possible, most dictionaries show the preferred pronunciation first. ______
3. When searching for a word in a dictionary, look only at the guide words until you locate the desired page. ______
4. The abbreviations *v*, *vb*, *vi*, and *vt* may all indicate a verb. ______
5. Rules for capitalization would more likely be found in a dictionary than in a reference manual. ______

H. ***Optional Composition.*** Your instructor may ask you to complete this exercise on a separate sheet. Type or use a computer printer if possible. Write complete sentences using the following words: *unabridged dictionary, abridged dictionary, synonym, antonym, hyphenate, archaic, dialect,* and *colloquial.*

POSTTEST

Write *T* (true) or *F* (false) after the following statements. Compare your answers with those at the bottom of the page.

1. The best dictionary for a college student's assignments is a pocket dictionary. ______
2. When searching for a word in a dictionary, look only at the guide words until you locate the desired page. ______
3. The etymology of a word is usually contained within square brackets. ______
4. The usage label *colloquial* means that the word may be used in certain regions only. ______
5. A dictionary user could expect to find the spelling of the past tense of an irregular verb such as *build.* ______

1. F, 2. T, 3. T, 4. F, 5. T

CHAPTER 2

Parts of Speech

OBJECTIVES When you have completed the materials in this chapter, you will be able to do the following:

— *Define the eight parts of speech.*
— *Recognize how parts of speech function in sentences.*
— *Compose sentences showing words playing more than one grammatical role.*

PRETEST

Study the following sentence and identify selected parts of speech. Underline the best answer. Compare your answers with those at the bottom of the page.

Ann and I carefully completed our tax forms before April 15.

1. *and*	(a) preposition	(b) conjunction	(c) verb	(d) adverb
2. *carefully*	(a) preposition	(b) conjunction	(c) verb	(d) adverb
3. *completed*	(a) preposition	(b) conjunction	(c) verb	(d) adverb
4. *tax*	(a) adjective	(b) pronoun	(c) noun	(d) adverb
5. *before*	(a) preposition	(b) conjunction	(c) noun	(d) adverb

Business English is the study of the fundamentals of English grammar, current usage, and appropriate business style. Such a study logically begins with the eight parts of speech, the building blocks of our language. This chapter will provide a brief overview of the parts of speech; the following chapters will deal with these topics more thoroughly. The goal of this chapter is to help you develop a foundation vocabulary so that you will have the tools necessary to study the language and to improve your effectiveness in communication.

The Eight Parts of Speech

Nouns

In elementary school you probably learned that nouns are the names given to persons, places, and things. In addition, though, nouns name qualities, concepts, and activities.

---

1. b, 2. d, 3. c, 4. a, 5. a

Persons:	Maria, Mr. Hartman, president, Scott
Places:	Toledo, island, Canada, college
Things:	computers, stationery, motorcycle, chair
Qualities:	dependability, honesty, initiative
Concepts:	knowledge, freedom, friendship, happiness
Activities:	skiing, typing, management, eating

Nouns are perhaps the most important words in our language. Sentences revolve around nouns since nouns function both as subjects and as objects of verbs. In Chapter 4 (pp. 38–44) you will learn four classes of nouns and rules for making nouns plural.

N.B.* To determine if a word is really a noun, try using it with the verbs *is* or *are*. Notice that all the nouns listed above would make sense if used in this way: *Maria* is, *Toledo* is, *computers* are, and so on.

Pronouns

As substitutes for nouns, pronouns are used in our language for variety and efficiency. Compare these two versions of the same sentence:

Without pronouns — Elizabeth gave the book to John so that John could use the book to study.

With pronouns — Elizabeth gave the book to John so that *he* could use *it* to study.

In sentences pronouns may function as subjects (for example, *I, we, they*) or as objects of verbs (*me, us, them*). They may show possession (*mine, ours, his*), and they may act as connectors (*that, which, who*). Only a few examples are given here. More examples along with functions and classifications of pronouns will be presented in Chapters 6 and 7 (pp. 63–86).

Verbs

Verbs do two things: (a) they show the action of a sentence, or (b) they join to the subject of the sentence words that describe it. Some action verbs are *runs, studies, works, fixes*. Verbs that join descriptive words to the subject are called "linking" verbs. Some linking verbs are *am, is, are, was, were, be, being,* and *been*. Other linking verbs express the senses: *feels, appears, tastes, sounds, seems, looks*.

N.B. To test whether a word is truly a verb, try using it with a noun or pronoun, such as *George* runs, *she* seems, *it* is. *He* food doesn't make sense because *food* is not a verb.

**N.B.*, *or* nota bene *(pronounced* no tah BEAN ee*), is a Latin phrase meaning "note well." Writers use it to call a reader's attention to important passages. In this book the N.B. boxes will highlight grammar and usage principles by presenting memory devices, clues, hints, and learning aids to help you understand and remember significant points.*

Verbs will be treated more fully in Chapters 8 through 11. At this point it is important that you be able to recognize verbs so that you can determine whether sentences are complete. All sentences have at least one verb; many sentences will have more than one verb. Verbs may appear singly or in phrases.

Honeywell recently designed that massive computer system. (Action verb)

It is a computer that stores, processes, and retrieves data. (Linking and action verbs)

Our company definitely will be ordering a new computer system soon. (Verb phrase)

I feel bad because Karen worked so late last night. (Linking and action verbs)

Adjectives

Words that describe nouns or pronouns are called *adjectives*. They often answer the questions *what kind?*, *how many?*, or *which one?* The adjectives in the following sentences are italicized. Observe that the adjectives all answer questions about the nouns that they describe.

Small, independent businesses are becoming *numerous*. (What kind of businesses?)

Fourteen franchises were granted in *four* states. (How many franchises? How many states?)

That chain of hotels started as a *small* operation. (Which chain? What kind of operation?)

The president of *the profitable* company is *energetic*. (Which president? Which company?)

Adjectives usually precede nouns and pronouns. They may, however, follow the words they describe, especially when used with linking verbs, as shown in the first and last examples above.

Here is a brief list of words often used as adjectives.

successful	sensitive	effective
terrific	bright	small
helpless	long	wet

Three words (*a*, *an*, and *the*) form a special group of adjectives that are called *articles*.

Adverbs

Words that modify (describe or limit) verbs, adjectives, or other adverbs are *adverbs*. Adverbs often answer the questions *when? how? where?* and *to what extent?*

Today we must begin work. (Must begin when?)

Jones proceeded *rapidly* with the orders. (Proceeded how?)

He seemed *exceedingly* happy. (How happy?)

Did you see the schedule *there*? (Where?)

The prosecutor did not question him *further*. (Questioned him to what extent?)

Here are additional examples of adverbs:

now	evenly	commercially
very	only	really
rather	carefully	greatly

Many, but not all, words ending in *ly* are adverbs. Some exceptions are *friendly, costly,* and *ugly,* all of which are adjectives.

N.B. To remember more easily the definition of the word *adverb,* think of its two syllables: *ad* (its first syllable) suggests that you will be adding to or amplifying the meaning of a *verb* (its second syllable). Hence, adverbs usually modify verbs. But adverbs can also modify adjectives and other adverbs.

Prepositions

Prepositions join nouns and pronouns to other words in a sentence. As the word itself suggests (*pre* meaning "before"), a preposition is a word in a position *before* its object (a noun or pronoun). Prepositions are used in phrases to show a relationship between the object of the preposition and another word in the sentence. In the following sentence notice how the preposition changes the relation of the object (*Mr. Lee*) to the verb (*talked*):

Ellen often talked *with* Mr. Lee.
Ellen often talked *about* Mr. Lee.
Ellen often talked *to* Mr. Lee.

The most frequently used prepositions are *to, by, for, at, from, with,* and *of.* A more complete list of prepositions can be found in Chapter 13. Learn to recognize objects of prepositions so that you won't confuse them with sentence subjects.

Conjunctions

Words that connect other words or groups of words are conjunctions. The most common conjunctions are *and, or, but,* and *nor.* These are called *coordinating conjunctions* because they join equal (coordinate) parts of sentences. Other kinds of conjunctions will be presented in Chapter 15. Study the examples of coordinating conjunctions shown here:

Get the necessary information from IBM, Xerox, *or* Wang. (Joins equal words.)

Word processing systems reduce work for our employees *and* for management. (Joins equal groups of words.)

Interjections

Words expressing strong feelings are interjections. Interjections standing alone are followed by exclamation marks. When woven into a sentence, they are usually followed by commas.

Wow! Did you see the total of our bill?
Gosh, I hope I have my credit card!

Summary

The sentence below illustrates all eight parts of speech.

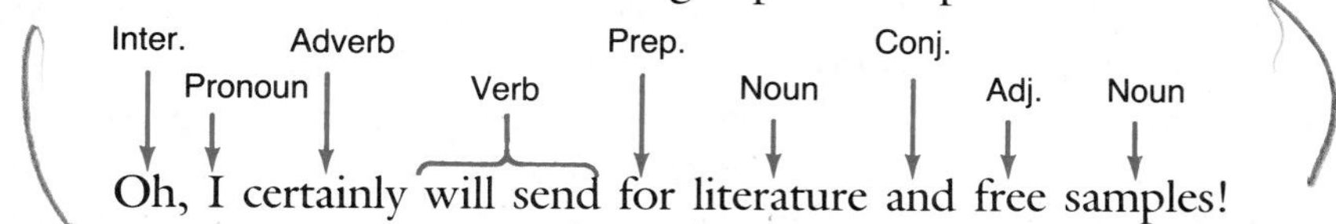

You need to know the functions of these eight parts of speech so that you will be able to understand the rest of this textbook and profit from your study of business English. The explanation of the parts of speech has so far been kept simple. This chapter is meant to serve as an introduction to later, more fully developed chapters. At this stage, you should not expect to be able to identify the functions of *all* words in *all* sentences.

A word of caution. English is a wonderfully flexible language. As we noted in using the dictionary, many words in our language can serve as more than one part of speech. Notice how flexible the word *mail* is in these sentences:

Our *mail* is late today. (Noun — serves as subject of sentence)

The knight's suit of *mail* protected him. (Noun — serves as object of preposition)

Mail the letter today. (Verb — serves as action word in sentence)

Your *mail* slot is full. (Adjective — used here to describe *slot,* which is the subject of sentence)

HOT LINE QUERIES

Business people are very concerned about appropriate English usage, grammar, and style. This concern is evident in the number and kinds of questions called in to grammar hot line services across the country.

Among the callers are business supervisors, managers, executives, secretaries, clerks, and word processing specialists. Writers, teachers, librarians, students, and other community members also request answers to language questions.

Some of the questions asked and appropriate answers to them will be presented in the following chapters. In this way, you, as a student of the language, will understand the kinds of everyday communication problems encountered in the work world.

The original questions in our Hot Line Queries came from the Los Angeles Pierce College Business English Hot Line. More recently, questions were selected from the following grammar hot line services: University of Delaware, Purdue University, Amarillo College, Triton College, East Carolina University, Arizona State University, Cuyahoga Community College, Raymond Walters College, Jacksonville State University, Eastern Illinois University, and Cosumnes River College. For a directory of grammar hot line services across the country, send a self-addressed, stamped envelope to the Grammar Hotline Directory, Writing Center Humanities Division, Tidewater Community College, Virginia Beach, VA 23456.

QUESTION: Help! How do I write *fax*? Small letters? Capital letters? Periods? And is it proper to use it as a verb, such as *May we fax the material to you?*

ANSWER: The shortened form of *facsimile* is *fax,* written in small letters without periods. Yes, it may be used as a verb, as you did in your sentence.

QUESTION: I saw this sentence recently in the newspaper: *At the movie premier the crowd scanned the limousines for glitterati.* Is *gliterrati* a real word?

ANSWER: A new noun to our vocabulary, *glitterati* means "celebrities or beautiful people." New words are generally considered legitimate when their use is clear and when they are necessary (that is, when no other word says exactly what they do). If educated individuals begin to use such words, the words then appear in dictionaries, and *glitterati* has made it.

QUESTION: Which word should I use in this sentence? *Our department will disburse or disperse the funds shortly.*

ANSWER: Use *disburse. Disperse* means "to scatter" or "to distribute" (*information will be dispersed to all divisions*). *Disburse* means "to pay out." Perhaps this memory device will help you keep them straight: associate the *b* in *disburse* with *bank* (*banks disburse money*).

QUESTION: How should I address a person who signed a letter *J. R. Henderson?*

ANSWER: Use *Dear J. R. Henderson.*

QUESTION: What's the difference between *toward* and *towards?*

ANSWER: None. They are interchangeable in use. However, it's more efficient to use the shorter word *toward.*

QUESTION: Is *every day* one word or two in this case? *We encounter these problems every day.*

ANSWER: In your sentence it is two words. When it means "ordinary," it is one word (*she wore everyday clothes*). If you can insert the word *single* between *every* and *day* without altering your meaning, you should be using two words.

QUESTION: I work in an office where we frequently send letters addressed to people on a first-name basis. Should I use a comma or a colon after a salutation like *Dear Mike?*

ANSWER: The content of the letter, not the salutation (greeting), determines the punctuation after the salutation. If the letter is a business letter, always use a colon. If the letter is totally personal, a comma may be used, although a colon would also be appropriate.

QUESTION: What is the name of a group of initials that form a word? Is it an abbreviation?

ANSWER: A word formed from the initial letters of an expression is called an *acronym* (pronounced *ACK ro nim*). Examples: *snafu,* from *situation normal, all fouled up,* and *DOS,* from *disk operating system.* Acronyms are usually pronounced as a single word and are different from abbreviations, such as *FBI* or *dept.*

Name ______________________

CHAPTER 2 **Reinforcement Exercises**

A. (Self-check) Complete these statements.

1. Used for variety and efficiency, pronouns substitute for
   (a) interjections (c) verbs
   (b) nouns (d) conjunctions ______

2. The part of speech that answers the question *what kind* is
   (a) adverb (c) interjection
   (b) adjective (d) conjunction ______

3. Names for persons, places, things, qualities, concepts, and activities are
   (a) verbs (c) nouns
   (b) adjectives (d) pronouns ______

4. Words that modify verbs, adjectives, and adverbs are
   (a) adverbs (c) pronouns
   (b) adjectives (d) conjunctions ______

5. *I, we, you,* and *he* are examples of
   (a) pronouns (c) verbs
   (b) nouns (d) adverbs ______

6. Action words in sentences are
   (a) nouns (c) adjectives
   (b) pronouns (d) verbs ______

7. *Beautifully, frankly,* and *smoothly* are examples of
   (a) adjectives (c) interjections
   (b) verbs (d) adverbs ______

8. Words that express strong feeling are
   (a) conjunctions (c) pronouns
   (b) adverbs (d) interjections ______

9. *And, or, nor,* and *but* are
   (a) conjunctions (c) interjections
   (b) verbs (d) adverbs ______

10. Words that join noun or pronoun objects to other words in sentences are
   (a) adverbs (c) interjections
   (b) prepositions (d) adjectives ______

Check your answers.

B. In each of the following groups of sentences, one word is used as an adjective, as a noun, and as a verb. For each sentence, indicate the part of speech for the italicized word.

A. 1. b, 2. b, 3. c, 4. a, 5. a, 6. d, 7. d, 8. d, 9. a, 10. b

EXAMPLE: Much *work* must be done. ________ noun

Can you *work* overtime? ________ verb

We need two *work* orders. ________ adjective

1. In what *time* zone do you live? ________
2. Do you have the *time*? ________
3. The coach will *time* the runners. ________
4. Our *stock* of canned goods is low. ________
5. The *stock* boy works tonight. ________
6. He will *stock* the shelves. ________
7. I like my *keyboarding* class. ________
8. *Keyboarding* is my best subject. ________
9. I am *keyboarding* my résumé. ________

Write complete sentences using the word *guard* as a noun, as an adjective, and as a verb.

1. (noun) ________________________________
2. (adjective) ________________________________
3. (verb) ________________________________

C. The underlined words in the following sentences are either prepositions or conjunctions. Write *C* for conjunction or *P* for preposition.

1. Technical skills are important for entry-level positions, but communication skills are necessary for promotion into management.
2. Writing sensitive letters and memos to customers creates goodwill for business organizations.
3. Neither large nor small service businesses maintain much merchandise in inventory because selling goods from stock is not their function.

for	________
but	________
into	________
and	________
to	________
for	________
nor	________
in	________
from	________

D. Read the following sentences and, taking into account the function of each word within each sentence, identify the part of speech of each word shown. Use a dictionary if necessary.

Hurriedly, she parked the small sports car and quickly raced to class.

Hurriedly ________	small ________	quickly ________
she ________	sports ________	raced ________
parked ________	car ________	to ________
the ________	and ________	class ________

Name ____________________

Six students qualified, but only one young woman came to the session.

Six	________	only	________	came	________
students	________	one	________	to	________
qualified	________	young	________	the	________
but	________	woman	________	session	________

E. Verbs in the following sentences have been italicized. Use a check mark to indicate whether each verb is a linking verb or an action verb.

	Linking verb	Action verb
EXAMPLE: We *are* the chief suppliers of film ribbons.	✓	____
1. The task of management *is* never an easy one.	____	____
2. Control Systems, Inc., *produces* components for computers.	____	____
3. The personnel manager *selected* four outstanding applicants.	____	____
4. Two employees' organizations *were* in operation ten years ago.	____	____
5. We *borrowed* three fourths of the necessary capital.	____	____
6. The manager and the personnel director *studied* the job descriptions carefully.	____	____
7. The first equipment proposal *was* quite adequate for our needs.	____	____
8. Our latest design *called* for a conveyer-belt operation.	____	____
9. Jim definitely *feels* better about his promotion prospects.	____	____
10. Last Sunday's advertisement *created* a large demand for portable copy machines.	____	____

F. Supply appropriate words for the blanks in these sentences. The words you supply should represent the part of speech shown for each blank. Use a single word for each blank.

EXAMPLE: Greg said (pronoun) knew the answer. he

1. In every business, whether large (conjunction) small, risks are involved. ____________

2. To most workers, the thought of owning one's own business (verb) very appealing. ____________

3. (Preposition) the way, the possibility of failure is significantly greater among small firms. ____________

4. Prospective business people must (verb) sufficient capital before starting a business. ____________

5. (Pronoun) must also have some experience in the proposed business. ____________

6. __(Adverb)__ are two ways to become an independent business person or entrepreneur.

7. You may buy an already established business or you may __(verb)__ your own new business.

8. Buying an existing business may be __(adjective)__ unless its earning record is well-known.

9. For numerous reasons, many people would prefer to start a completely new __(noun)__.

10. Starting a business involves a __(adjective)__ deal of hard work.

G. ***Optional Composition.*** Your instructor may ask you to complete this exercise on a separate sheet. Write eight sentences that illustrate these parts of speech: noun, pronoun, verb, adjective, adverb, conjunction, preposition, and interjection. Identify each part of speech by labeling it at the beginning of the sentence and underlining it within the sentence. If possible, type or print this exercise. Example: Noun: In this class I expect to improve my basic communication skills.

POSTTEST

Identify the parts of speech in this sentence by underlining the correct choice. Compare your answers with those at the bottom of the page.

Our manager explained the use of the new computer slowly.

1. *manager*	(a) noun	(b) pronoun	(c) preposition	(d) conjunction
2. *explained*	(a) adverb	(b) verb	(c) preposition	(d) conjunction
3. *of*	(a) noun	(b) pronoun	(c) preposition	(d) conjunction
4. *new*	(a) verb	(b) adverb	(c) adjective	(d) preposition
5. *slowly*	(a) verb	(b) adverb	(c) preposition	(d) conjunction

1. a, 2. b, 3. c, 4. c, 5. b

CHAPTER 3

Sentences: Elements, Patterns, Types

OBJECTIVES When you have completed the materials in this chapter, you will be able to do the following:

— *Recognize subjects and predicates.*
— *Convert fragments into complete sentences.*
— *Recognize basic sentence faults such as comma splices and run-on sentences.*
— *Complete sentences in three basic sentence patterns.*
— *Punctuate statements, commands, questions, and exclamations.*

PRETEST

Write *a, b, c,* or *d* after each of the numbered groups of words below to identify it.

(a) correctly punctuated sentence (c) comma splice
(b) fragment (d) run-on sentence

1. John, completing the training course in less than four weeks. _____
2. John works 30 hours this week, Martha works 32. _____
3. Across the street are the copy store and the print shop. _____
4. Some employees use the company van however others rely upon their own cars. _____
5. Although some people start at 6 a.m., which explains the empty parking lot. _____

Sentence Elements

Subjects and Predicates

Sentences are composed of two essential elements: subjects and predicates. The subject of a sentence is the person or thing being talked about, and the predicate tells what the subject is, what the subject is doing, or what is being done to the subject. Study the following sentence:

---

1. b, 2. c, 3. a, 4. d, 5. b

The new manager of the office — received our cooperation.

complete subject — complete predicate

The *complete subject* of the sentence includes the *subject* (in this case a noun) plus all the words that describe or limit the subject (its modifiers). The *complete predicate* includes the *verb* plus its modifiers.

The heart of the complete subject is the simple subject (*manager*), and the heart of the predicate is the simple predicate, or verb (*received*). The following sentences are divided into complete subjects and complete predicates, and the simple subjects and verbs are underlined.

Complete subjects	Complete predicates
All branches of the company	are connected by computer.
Our largest department store	will be having a sale.
The economic recovery program	is improving business.
Chain store executives	conduct traffic counts.

Notice in the previous sentences that the verbs may consist of one word or several. In a verb phrase the principal verb is the final one; the other verbs are *helping* or *auxiliary* verbs. The most frequently used helping verbs are *am, is, are, was, were, been, have, has, had, must, ought, can, might, could, would, should, will, do, does,* and *did.*

N.B. As you probably observed, many linking verbs also serve as helping verbs. Please note that a verb phrase is considered to be *linking* only when the final verb is a linking verb, such as in the phrase *might have been.* The verb phrase *has been working* does not, however, function as a linking verb because the final verb (*working*) is not a linking verb.

Sentence Sense

In addition to a subject and a predicate, a group of words must possess one additional element to qualify as a sentence: the group of words must make sense. Observe that two of the groups of words that follow express complete thoughts and make sense; the third does not.

Bradley built his business through personal contacts. (Subject plus predicate making sense = sentence.)

Efficient service ensured return business. (Subject plus predicate making sense = sentence.)

When Bradley started his own business (Subject plus predicate but not making sense = no sentence.)

In the third case, a reader or listener senses that the idea expressed is incomplete. We do not have a sentence; instead, we have a fragment.

Sentence Faults

Three typical sentence faults are fragments, comma splices, and run-on sentences.

Fragment

Fragments are often groups of words that are broken off from nearby sentences. They cannot function as complete sentences. Avoid fragments by making certain that each sentence contains a subject and a verb and makes sense by itself. In the examples below fragments are italicized. Notice how they can be revised to make complete sentences.

Fragment: We're looking for a potential mananger. *An individual who can accept responsibility and supervise other employees.*

Revision: We're looking for a potential manager who can accept responsibility and supervise other employees.

Fragment: My research report in business communications took a long time to prepare. *And then turned out badly.*

Revision: My research report in business communications took a long time to prepare and then turned out badly.

Fragment: Business letters should generate goodwill towards the writer and towards the organization. *Which explains why empathy is an important writing skill to develop.*

Revision: Business letters should generate goodwill towards the writer and towards the organization, which explains why empathy is an important writing skill to develop.

Comma Splice

A second basic sentence fault results when two sentences are incorrectly joined or spliced together with a comma. The sentences below show how comma splices could be revised into acceptable sentences.

Comma Splice: Let us show you how to improve your mail service, contact our local postal service representative.

Revision: Let us show you how to improve your mail service. Contact our local postal service representative.

Comma Splice: You must fill one more purchase order, then your work is finished.

Revision: You must fill one more purchase order. Then your work is finished.

Comma Splice: Many applicants responded to our advertisement, however only one had the proper training.

Revision: Many applicants responded to our advertisement; however, only one had the proper training. (Semicolons will be treated in Chapters 14 and 17.)

Run-on Sentence

A third basic sentence fault is the run-on sentence. Avoid constructing sentences that run together two complete thoughts without proper punctuation. Notice how the run-on sentences below can be corrected by dividing the two thoughts into separate sentences.

Run-on sentence: The work ethic in America is not dead it is deeply ingrained in most people.

Revision: The work ethic in America is not dead. It is deeply ingrained in most people.

Run-on sentence: Employees want to keep their jobs they will work hard for promotions.

Revision: Employees want to keep their jobs. They will work hard for promotions.

Sentence Patterns

Three basic word patterns are used to express thoughts in English sentences.

Pattern No. 1: Subject–Verb

In the most basic sentence pattern, the subject is followed by its verb. No additional words are needed for the sentence to make sense and be complete.

Subject	Verb
We	worked.
Everyone	is studying.
She	might have called.
All the employees	are being informed.

Pattern No. 2: Subject–Action Verb–Object

In this kind of sentence, the subject is followed by an action verb and its direct object. The object usually answers the question *what?* or *whom?*

Subject	Action verb	Object
Most students	brought	supplies.
The manager	praised	the worker.
Mrs. Stevenson	supervised	them.

This basic sentence pattern may also employ an indirect object that usually answers the question *to whom?*

Subject	Action verb	Indirect object	Direct object
Our company	offers	employees	excellent benefits.
Tiffany	gave	him	the book.

Pattern No. 3: Subject–Linking Verb–Complement

In the third kind of sentence, the subject is followed by a linking verb and its complement. A complement is a noun, pronoun, or adjective that renames or describes the subject. A complement *completes* the meaning of the subject.

Subject	Linking verb	Complement	
The author	was	Mr. Arnold.	(Noun complements)
Our customers	are	friends.	
Your supervisor	is	she.	(Pronoun complements)
The callers	might have been	they.	
These data	are	accurate.	(Adjective complements)
His report	is	excellent.	

The sentences shown here have been kept simple so that their patterns can be recognized easily. Although most speakers and writers expand these basic patterns with additional phrases and clauses, the basic sentence structure remains the same. Despite its length, the following sentence follows the basic subject-verb-object order:

Many large *companies,* as well as small companies with sizable real estate holdings, *employ* specialized risk *managers* to handle their insurance problems. (The simple subject is *companies,* the verb is *employ,* and the object is *managers.*)

Inverted Order

In some sentences the elements appear in inverted order, with the verb preceding the subject.

In front is Doreen.
Last was the dessert.

In questions the verb may precede the subject or may be interrupted by the subject.

What is the shipment number?
Have the letters been filed?

In sentences beginning with *here* or *there,* the normal word order is also inverted.

Here are the applications.
There is a demand for accountants.

To locate the true subject in any inverted sentence, mentally rearrange the words. Place them in the normal subject-verb order.

Doreen is in front.
The shipment number is what?
The applications are here.

Four Sentence Types

Statements

Statements make assertions and end with periods.

Laws require truth in advertising.
Manufacturers today must label the contents of packages.

Questions

Direct questions are followed by question marks.

Where will we place the new equipment?
Does this machine require a hood?

Commands

Commands end with periods or, occasionally, with exclamation points. Note that the subject in all commands is understood to be you. The subject you is not normally stated in the command.

Shut the door. ([You] shut the door.)
Insure your home against fire loss. ([You] insure your home.)

Exclamations

Showing surprise, disbelief, or strong feelings, exclamations may or may not be expressed as complete thoughts. Both subject and predicate may be implied.

> Oh! Static electricity gave me a shock!
> What a remarkable employee she is!
> How extraordinary [that is]!

Complete the reinforcement exercises.

HOT LINE QUERIES

QUESTION: This sentence doesn't sound right to me, but I can't decide how to improve it: *The reason I'm applying is because I enjoy electronics.*

ANSWER: The problem lies in this construction: *the reason . . . is because. . . .* Only nouns or adjectives may act as complements following linking verbs. In your sentence an adverbial clause follows the linking verb and sounds awkward. One way to improve the sentence is to substitute a noun clause beginning with *that: The reason I'm applying is that I enjoy electronics.* An even beter way to improve the sentence would be to make it a direct statement: *I'm applying because I enjoy electronics.*

QUESTION: My friend says that this sentence is correct: *Jill will first duplicate all the letters, then she will prepare the envelopes.* I think something is wrong, but I'm not sure what.

ANSWER: You're right. This sentence has two short independent clauses, and some writers attempt to join them with a comma. But this construction produces a comma splice. The adverb *then* cannot function as a conjunction, such as *and,* to join these two clauses. Start a new sentence or use a semicolon between the clauses.

QUESTION: My boss dictated a report with this sentence: *Saleswise, our staff is excellent.* Should I change it?

ANSWER: Never change wording without checking with the author. You might point out, however, that the practice of attaching *-wise* to nouns is frowned upon by many language experts. Such combinations as *budgetwise, taxwise,* and *productionwise* are considered commercial jargon. Suggest this revision: *On the basis of sales, our staff is excellent.*

QUESTION: At the end of a letter I wrote: *Thank you for attending to this matter immediately.* Should I hyphenate *thank you?*

ANSWER: Do not hyphenate *thank you* when using it as a verb (*thank you for writing*). Do hyphenate it when using it as an adjective (*I sent a thank-you note*). It is also hyphenated when used as a noun (*I sent four thank-yous*). Since *thank you* is used as a verb in your sentence, do not hyphenate it. Notice that *thank you* is never written as a single word.

QUESTION: A fellow worker insists on saying, *I could care less.* Seems to me that it should be *I couldn't care less.* Who is right?

ANSWER: The phrase *I couldn't care less* has been in the language a long time. It means, of course, "I have little concern about the matter." Recently, though, people have begun to use *I could care less* with the same meaning. Most careful listeners realize that the latter phrase says just the opposite of its intent. Although both phrases are clichés, stick with *I couldn't care less* if you want to be clear.

Name ____________________

CHAPTER 3 **Reinforcement Exercises**

A. (Self-check) Indicate whether the following statements are true (*T*) or false (*F*).

1. The verbs *are, may,* and *have* are examples of auxiliary or helping verbs. ____
2. A group of words with a subject and a predicate is automatically a complete sentence. ____
3. The complete subject of a sentence includes a noun or pronoun and all its modifiers. ____
4. Two sentences joined together by a comma create a *comma splice.* ____
5. In questions, the verb may appear before the subject. ____
6. The complete predicate of a sentence tells what the subject is, what the subject is doing, or what is being done to the subject. ____
7. Sentences that show strong feeling are usually concluded with question marks. ____
8. The verb phrase *could have been* is considered to be a linking verb. ____
9. Sentences that begin with *here* or *there* follow normal subject-verb order. ____
10. Complements may follow either action verbs or linking verbs. ____

Check your answers.

B. Study the examples shown below. Then fill in the words necessary to complete the three sentence patterns.

Pattern No. 1: Subject–Verb

EXAMPLE: The boss ___called___.

1. The telephone ____________.
2. Our computer ____________.
3. Students ____________.
4. Salespeople ____________.
5. Senators ____________.
6. Secretaries ____________.
7. Scissors ____________.
8. Money ____________.

Pattern No. 2: Subject–Action Verb–Object

EXAMPLE: Secretaries type ___letters___.

9. Kelly answered the ____________.
10. The mailcarrier delivered ____________.
11. Salespeople sold ____________.
12. Investors bought ____________.
13. The carpenter built a ____________.
14. Stock pays ____________.
15. Students threw a ____________.
16. Congress passes ____________.

A. 1. T, 2. F, 3. T, 4. T, 5. T, 6. T, 7. F, 8. T, 9. F, 10. F

Pattern No. 3: Subject–Linking Verb–Complement

Fill in noun or pronoun complements.

EXAMPLE: The manager is John.

17. The applicant was __________.
18. Tina is the new __________.
19. The caller could have been __________.
20. The president is __________.

Fill in adjective complements.

EXAMPLE: The salary is good.

21. My investment was __________.
22. New York is __________.
23. Ice cream is __________.
24. The report could have been __________.

C. The following sentences do not follow normal word order. To help you locate subjects, invert these sentences so that the subject comes first. Then underline the simple subject once and the simple predicate twice.

EXAMPLE: Here are some of the materials we need.
Some of the materials we need are here.

1. There are two telephone numbers listed for that organization.
2. Here is the agenda for the Tuesday board meeting.
3. Where is the Gibson contract?
4. Across from our office is the subway station.
5. What is the name of your local dealer?

D. From the list below select the letter that accurately describes each of the following groups of words. If a group of words requires an end punctuation mark, add it.

(a) fragment (c) command (e) exclamation
(b) statement (d) question

EXAMPLE: The resources of that country, although never fully developed — a

1. School and work holidays should always be scheduled on Mondays and Fridays. _____
2. Do employers and workers contribute jointly to the retirement fund? _____
3. If there is mutual agreement to all contract terms _____
4. Analyze the gross national product for the past ten years. _____

Name ______________________

5. Although Singapore flourishes as a center of banking, shipbuilding, offshore-oil technology, refining, aircraft maintenance, electronics manufacturing, and international trade ______
6. What a splendid view we have from the observatory on the tenth floor! ______
7. In Europe where most countries are joining the European Community ______
8. Do you know if Tom Truong received the purchase order? ______
9. Turn off the power, close the windows, and lock the doors before you leave. ______
10. The smell of freshly cut grass and the sight of blooming tulips and daffodils ______

E. The following groups of words may be complete sentences. If so, add appropriate punctuation marks, but if a group is incomplete, add any appropriate words to create a complete sentence.

1. If I had just won the lottery and had collected over $50 million, ______________________
2. The Internal Revenue Service, although I promised to make an appointment to meet with them soon, ______________________
3. All the helicopters, including those flying to Catalina Island, ______________________
4. To be able to record the minutes of a meeting, you must be able to listen carefully and to summarize topics. ______________________
5. Since we plan to update all equipment in the office, ______________________

F. Write *a, b, c,* or *d* after each of the following groups of words to indicate whether it represents a correctly punctuated sentence, a fragment, a comma splice, or a run-on sentence.

(a) fragment (c) comma splice
(b) correctly punctuated sentence (d) run-on sentence

EXAMPLE: Which can save you valuable time. a

1. Almost everyone in business today needs to know something about computers. b
2. Our corporate headquarters will be moved next year, then I expect to be transferred. c
3. Although we have a powerful printer capable of producing high-quality graphics. a
4. Karen wanted a practical spreadsheet program she just didn't know what to purchase. d

5. Morning seems to be better than afternoon for catching business executives in their offices. b

6. Mr. Harrington arrived at the airport on time, however his flight was overbooked. c

7. Some banks may require in-depth personal investigations. b

8. Particularly if you are a married woman and want to open a credit account in your own name. a

9. We have tried to collect this account in a friendly manner, our efforts, however, have failed to secure your cooperation. c

10. Some employers weigh education and grades heavily they look at transcripts carefully. d

11. References are a personnel selection tool, they are written by previous employers, co-workers, or acquaintances. c

12. Although a contract cannot be valid if the action agreed to is illegal. a

13. Sales jobs are best for people with a strong need for achievement. b

14. Research suggests that job stress is linked to mental problems stress is also associated with ulcers and heart disease. d

15. Next Monday is Veterans Day, hence all branch offices will be closed. c

For class discussion: In the preceding exercise, how could each of the incorrectly punctuated groups of words be made acceptable?

G. ***Optional Composition.*** Your instructor may ask you to complete this exercise on a separate sheet. Write sentences that illustrate each of the following forms: a statement, a question, a command, an exclamation, a sentence with a pronoun complement, and a sentence in inverted order. Identify each sentence.

POSTTEST

Write *a, b, c,* or *d* to identify each of the numbered lines below.

(a) correctly punctuated sentence (c) comma splice
(b) fragment (d) run-on sentence

1. The computer was installed Monday the printer is expected shortly. ______
2. Outside the front office is the receptionist's desk. ______
3. Since the contract was mailed Monday but not received until late Friday. ______
4. On Monday the mail is picked up early, on Friday it's not picked up until 3 p.m. ______
5. Because Celeste, who is one of our best workers, was ill last week. ______

1. d, 2. a, 3. b, 4. c, 5. b

Name ______________________

UNIT 1 REVIEW **Chapters 1–3 (Self-Check)**

Begin your review by rereading Chapters 1 through 3. Then check your comprehension of those chapters by writing *T* for true or *F* for false in the blanks below. Compare your responses with those at the end of the review.

1. All dictionaries use the same plan for showing the order of definitions. ______
2. Usage labels such as *obsolete, archaic,* and *informal* warn dictionary users about appropriate usage. ______
3. The etymology code helps you to pronounce a word correctly. ______
4. Because the English language changes very little, the publication date of a dictionary is unimportant. ______
5. Most dictionaries show noun plurals only if the plurals are irregular, such as the word *children.* ______
6. A thesaurus is a collection of words and their definitions. ______
7. Accent marks may appear before or after stressed syllables. ______
8. The usage label *nonstandard* means that a word is no longer in use. ______
9. The terms *desk* and *college-level* refer to the same kind of dictionary. ______
10. A summary of diacritical marks is often found at the bottom of dictionary pages. ______

Read the following sentence carefully. Identify the parts of speech for the words as they are used in this sentence.

He looked quickly at the page and then scribbled two answers.

11. He	(a) noun	(b) pronoun	(c) adverb	(d) adj	______
12. looked	(a) conj	(b) prep	(c) verb	(d) adverb	______
13. quickly	(a) conj	(b) prep	(c) adj	(d) adverb	______
14. at	(a) conj	(b) prep	(c) adj	(d) adverb	______
15. page	(a) noun	(b) pronoun	(c) conj	(d) adverb	______
16. and	(a) noun	(b) pronoun	(c) conj	(d) prep	______
17. then	(a) noun	(b) adverb	(c) conj	(d) prep	______
18. scribbled	(a) verb	(b) adverb	(c) conj	(d) prep	______
19. two	(a) verb	(b) adverb	(c) adj	(d) prep	______
20. answers	(a) noun	(b) pronoun	(c) adj	(d) prep	______

For each of the following statements, determine the word or phrase that correctly completes that statement and write its letter in the space provided.

21. In the sentence *Clean white paper is needed for this job,* the simple subject is (a) clean, (b) white, (c) paper, (d) job. ______

22. In the sentence *Here are the sheets,* the simple subject is (a) Here, (b) are, (c) sheets, (d) you. ______

23. In the sentence *I feel bad,* the verb *feel* is considered a (a) linking verb, (b) helping verb, (c) subject, (d) predicate. ______

24. The sentence *She typed a letter* represents what sentence pattern: (a) subject-verb, (b) subject-action verb-object, (c) subject-linking verb-complement, (d) subject-linking verb-object. ______

Use (a), (b), (c), (d), or (e) to describe the groups of words below.

(a) command
(b) complete sentence
(c) fragment
(d) comma splice
(e) run-on sentence

25. I must call one more person, then I will be ready to evaluate his record. ______

26. Whenever Mr. Jackson calls to confirm the shipping date. ______

27. Bring more paper and pens when you come back to the office. ______

28. That company's products are excellent their service is somewhat slow. ______

29. Many employees are interested in the proposed in-service training. ______

30. Although you will be on vacation when your check is issued. ______

31. Complete the form and send it with your check. ______

32. This computer is powerful, I'm not sure I need that much power. ______

33. The letter arrived today the package should be here next week. ______

34. Many companies today feature profit-sharing plans, but some employees are reluctant to participate in them. ______

35. After you read the contract, sign and return it. ______

Hot Line Review

Select the word or phrase that correctly completes each statement and write its letter in the corresponding blank.

36. (a) Thankyou, (b) Thank-you, (c) Thank you for providing me with the application. ______

37. Informative literature and coupons will be (a) dispersed, (b) disbursed at the beginning of our promotion. ______

38. It is possible to have deliveries (a) everyday, (b) every day (c) every-day if we make arrangements in advance. ______

39. The reason I am late is (a) because, (b) that my car stalled. ______

40. In a business letter the salutation *Dear Frank* should be followed by a (a) semicolon, (b) comma, (c) colon, (d) space. ______

---

1. F, 2. T, 3. F, 4. F, 5. T, 6. F, 7. T, 8. F, 9. T, 10. T, 11. b, 12. c, 13. d, 14. b, 15. a, 16. c, 17. b, 18. a, 19. c, 20. a, 21. c, 22. c, 23. a, 24. b, 25. d, 26. c, 27. a, 28. e, 29. b, 30. c, 31. a, 32. d, 33. e, 34. b, 35. a, 36. c, 37. a, 38. b, 39. b, 40. c.

UNIT TWO

Knowing the Namers

CHAPTER 4

Nouns

OBJECTIVES When you have completed the materials at this level, you will be able to do the following:

Level I — *Recognize four kinds of nouns.*

Level II — *Spell troublesome plural nouns ending in* y, o, *and* f.

— *Form the plurals of compound nouns, numerals, letters, degrees, and abbreviations.*

Level III — *Recognize and use correctly foreign plural nouns and selected special nouns*

— *Create sentences using plural personal titles.*

PRETEST

Underline any incorrectly spelled noun in the following sentences. Write a correct spelling in the space provided.

1. Three children put their books on the bottom shelfs. ________
2. At the market she purchased some tomatoes and potatos. ________
3. Several attornies requested tax write-offs for books. ________
4. Our two CPAs both asked for leave of absences in June. ________
5. Based on all the criterion, several diagnoses were given. ________

This business English textbook treats the study of our language *selectively*. We will not consider *all* the rules and conventions of English. Instead, this book will focus on those aspects of the language that have proved troublesome. Therefore, in this chapter on nouns, the principal concern will be the forming and spelling of plural nouns — an area of confusion for many business writers.

Beginning with this chapter, concepts will be presented in levels, progressing from basic, frequently used concepts at Level I to more complex and less frequently used concepts at Level III.

---

1. shelves, 2. potatoes, 3. attorneys, 4. leaves of absence, 5. criteria or criterions

As you will recall from Chapter 2 (p. 13), nouns *name* persons, places, things, qualities, and concepts.

Forms

Concrete and Abstract Nouns

Concrete nouns name specific objects that can actually be seen, heard, felt, tasted, or smelled. Abstract nouns name qualities and concepts. Because concrete nouns are precise and forceful, they are more effective in writing and talking than abstract nouns.

Concrete nouns		Abstract nouns	
jetliner	transcriptionist	freedom	happiness
stapler	jasmine	diligence	accuracy
lemonade	affidavit	memory	personality
microcomputer	coffee	truth	love

Common and Proper Nouns

Common nouns name *generalized* persons, places, and things. Proper nouns, on the other hand, name *specific* persons, places, and things. They are always capitalized. Rules for capitalization are presented in Chapter 19.

Common nouns		Proper nouns	
document	dog	Touch-Tone telephone*	United Nations
organization	computer	Manhattan Island	Xerox Corporation
student	telephone	American Can Company	Rex Montgomery
photocopier	company	Apple computer*	Bill of Rights

Basic Plurals

Singular nouns name *one* person, place, or thing. Plural nouns name *two* or more. At Level I you will learn basic rules for forming plurals. At Level II you will learn how to form the plurals of nouns that create spelling problems.

Regular nouns form the plural with the addition of *s* or *es*.

Add s to most nouns:

desk, desks	advantage, advantages	Tom, Toms†

Add es to nouns ending in s, x, z, ch, or sh:

brush, brushes	business, businesses	bunch, bunches
tax, taxes	wrench, wrenches	Sanchez, Sanchezes†

A few nouns form the plural by changing the spelling of the word.

man, men	foot, feet	mouse, mice
goose, geese	child, children	ox, oxen, or oxes

* *Note that common nouns following proper nouns are not capitalized.*

† *Proper nouns are made plural in the same way that common nouns are made plural except for proper nouns ending in y. See the explanation in 1-b in the following section.*

Most dictionaries do *not* show plurals of *regular* nouns. Thus, if you look up the plural of *ranch,* you probably will not find it. Dictionaries *do* show the plurals of nouns that might be confusing or difficult to spell. (*The American Heritage Dictionary* is exceptional in that it shows the plurals of nearly all nouns.)

N.B. Apostrophes (') are *not* used to form most plural nouns.
Wrong: Management *executive's* have highly developed communication skills.
Right: Management *executives* have highly developed communication skills.

Now complete the reinforcement exercises for Level I.

LEVEL II

Spelling Troublesome Noun Plurals

Your ability to spell certain troublesome nouns can be greatly improved by studying the following rules and examples.

1. *Common nouns ending in y* form the plural in two ways.
   a. When the *y* is preceded by a vowel (*a, e, i, o, u*), the plural is formed with the addition of *s* only.

valley, valleys	journey, journeys	money, moneys*
turkey, turkeys	attorney, attorneys	Harvey, Harveys

   b. When the *y* is preceded by a consonant (all letters other than vowels), the plural is formed by changing the *y* to *ies.*

country, countries	quality, qualities	city, cities
currency, currencies	company, companies	secretary, secretaries

(This rule does *not* apply to the plural forms of proper nouns: *Amy, Amys; February, Februarys; Kelly, Kellys*)

3. *Nouns ending in f or fe* follow no standard rules in the formation of plurals. Study the examples shown here, and use a dictionary when in doubt.

Add *s*	Change to *ves*	Both forms recognized[†]
safe, safes	shelf, shelves	calves, calfs
sheriff, sheriffs	wife, wives	dwarfs, dwarves
staff, staffs	knife, knives	wharves, wharfs
cliff, cliffs	leaf, leaves	scarves, scarfs
brief, briefs	half, halves	
Wolf, Wolfs	wolf, wolves	

* *Preferred form;* monies *also recognized.*

[†]*Preferred form shown first.*

N.B. Do not confuse nouns with verbs. He *saves* (verb) his money in two *safes* (noun).

Nouns: beliefs, proofs, leaves, loaves   Verbs: believes, proves, leafs, loafs

3. *Nouns ending in o* may be made plural by adding *s* or *es*.
   a. When the *o* is preceded by a vowel, the plural is formed by adding *s* only.

      studio, studios   curio, curios   radio, radios

   b. When the *o* is preceded by a consonant, the plural is formed by adding *s* or *es*. Study the following examples and, again, use your dictionary whenever you are in doubt.

Add *s*	Add *es*	Both forms recognized*
auto, autos	veto, vetoes	commandos, commandoes
patio, patios	echo, echoes	mosquitoes, mosquitos
memo, memos	potato, potatoes	tornadoes, tornados
ratio, ratios	tomato, tomatoes	volcanos, volcanoes
portfolio, portfolios	embargo, embargoes	zeros, zeroes
Alvarado, Alvarados	hero, heroes	cargoes, cargos

N.B. Musical terms ending in *o* always form the plural with the addition of *s* only.

solo, solos   cello, cellos   banjo, banjos
alto, altos   piano, pianos   contralto, contraltos

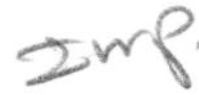

4. *Compound nouns* may be written as single words, may be hyphenated, or may appear as two words.
   a. When written as single words, compound nouns form the plural by appropriate changes in the final element.

      salesperson, salespeople   payroll, payrolls
      stepchild, stepchildren   bookshelf, bookshelves

   b. When written in hyphenated or open form, compound nouns form the plural by appropriate changes in the principal noun.

      mothers-in-law   editors in chief
      runners-up   leaves of absence
      lookers-on   boards of directors
      mayors-elect   bills of lading

**Preferred form shown first.*

c. If the compound noun has no principal noun at all, the final element is made plural.

write-offs
trade-ins
no-shows
know-it-alls
cure-alls
show-offs

d. Some compounds form plurals in two recognized ways. In the list below, the preferred way is shown first.

attorneys general, attorney generals
cupfuls, cupsful
teaspoonfuls, teaspoonsful
courts-martial, court-martials
notaries public, notary publics

5. *Numerals, alphabet letters, isolated words, and degrees* are made plural by adding *s, es,* or *'s*. The modern trend is to use the *'s* only when necessary for clarity.

a. Numerals and uppercase letters (with the exception of *A, I, M,* and *U*) require only *s* in plural formation.

Price trends from the *1980s* are expected to continue into the *1990s*.
Her new calculator was not printing *7s* and *9s*.
Brian received all *Bs* and *Cs* on his grade report.

b. Isolated words used as nouns are made plural with the addition of *s* or *es,* as needed for pronunciation.

The president took a count of *yeses* and *noes* on the measure.
Numerous *ands, ahs,* and *you knows* made his speech ineffective.

c. Degrees are made plural with the addition of *s*.

Dr. Helstrum holds two *Ph.D.s* in related fields.
Graduates with *M.B.A.s* are being heavily recruited.

d. Isolated lowercase letters and the capital letters *A, I, M,* and *U* require *'s* for clarity.

Unless she writes more legibly, her *o's* may be mistaken for *a's*.
In preparing the notice for the marquee yesterday, we ran out of *A's* and *I's*.

6. *Abbreviations* are usually made plural by adding *s* to the singular form.

yr., yrs.	mgr., mgrs.	dept., depts.	wk., wks.
c.o.d., c.o.d.s	CPA, CPAs	IOU, IOUs	No., Nos.

The singular and plural forms of abbreviations for units of measurement are, however, often identical.

deg. (degree or degrees)	in. (inch or inches)
ft. (foot or feet)	oz. (ounce or ounces)

Some units of measurement have two plural forms.

lb. or lbs.   yd. or yds.   qt. or qts.

Complete the reinforcement exercises for Level II.

Special Plural Forms

1. *Nouns borrowed from foreign languages* may retain a foreign plural. A few, however, have an Americanized plural form, shown in parentheses below. Check your dictionary for the preferred form.

Singular	Plural
analysis	analyses
basis	bases
crisis	crises
diagnosis	diagnoses
hypothesis	hypotheses
parenthesis	parentheses
thesis	theses
criterion	criteria (or criterions)
bacterium	bacteria
phenomenon	phenomena
memorandum	memoranda (or memorandums)
curriculum	curricula (or curriculums)
datum	data*
erratum	errata
alumna (*feminine*)	alumnae (pronounced *a lum′nee*)
alumnus (*masculine*)	alumni (pronounced *a lum′nī*)
stimulus	stimuli
alga	algae (or algas)
formula	formulae (or formulas)
larva	larvae
genus	genera

2. *Personal titles* may have both formal and informal plural forms.

Singular	Formal plurals	Informal plurals
Miss	the Misses Smith	the Miss Smiths
Mr.	Messrs.[†] Kahn and Lee	Mr. Kahn and Mr. Lee
Mrs.	Mmes.[‡] Davis and Klein	Mrs. Davis and Mrs. Klein
Ms.	Mses.[§] Freiden and Allen	Ms. Freiden and Ms. Allen

3. *Special nouns,* many of which end in *s,* may normally be *only* singular *or* plural in meaning. Other special nouns may be considered *either* singular *or* plural in meaning.

Usually singular	Usually plural	May be singular or plural
genetics	clothes	corps
mathematics	goods	deer
measles	scissors	Vietnamese
economics	statistics	sheep
news	thanks	politics

**See discussion on p. 43.*

[†]*Pronounced Mĕs′ərz (abbreviation of* Messieurs)

[‡]*Pronounced Mā dam′ (abbreviation of* Mesdames)

[§]*Pronounced Mz′ez*

N.B. Practice these special nouns by using them with the singular verb *is* or the plural verb *are.* Genetics *is* fascinating (sing.). Scissors are useful (plural).

4. *Single-letter abbreviations* may be made plural by doubling the letter.

pp. (pages)	See pp. 18–21. (pages 18 through 21)
ff. (and following)	See pp. 18 ff. (page 18 and following pages)

Complete the reinforcement exercises for Level III.

HOT LINE QUERIES

QUESTION: It seems to me that the meaning of the word *impact* has changed. I thought it meant "an effect." But now I hear this use: *How does this policy impact on the Middle East?* What's happening to this word?

ANSWER: In our language nouns often become verbs (to *bridge* the gap, to *corner* a market, to *telephone* a friend). Whether a noun-turned-verb is assimilated into the language seems to depend upon its utility, its efficiency, and the status of the individuals who use it. Skilled writers, for example, avoid the word *prioritize* because it is inefficient and sounds bureaucratic. Transformation of the noun *impact* into a verb would appear to be unnecessary, since the word *affect* clearly suffices in most constructions (*how does this program affect the Middle East?*). Although we hear *impact* used frequently as a verb today, many language specialists find it offensive.

QUESTION: Could you help me spell the plural of *do* and *don't?*

ANSWER: In forming the plural of isolated words, the trend today is to add *s* and no aprostrophe. Thus, we have *dos* and *don'ts.* Formerly, apostrophes were used to make isolated words plural. However, if no confusion results, make plurals by adding *s* only.

QUESTION: One member of our staff consistently corrects our use of the word *data.* He says the word is plural. Is it never singular?

ANSWER: The word *data* is indeed plural; the singular form is *datum.* Through frequent usage, however, *data* has recently become a collective noun. Collective nouns may be singular or plural depending upon whether they are considered as one unit or as separate units. For example, *These data are much different from those findings.* Or, *This data is conclusive.*

QUESTION: I don't have a dictionary handy. Can you tell me which word I should use in this sentence: *A [stationary/stationery] circuit board will be installed.*

ANSWER: In your sentence use *stationary,* which means "not moving" or "permanent" (*the concrete columns are stationary*). *Stationery* means "writing paper" (*his stationery has his address printed on it*). You might be able to remember the word *stationery* by associating *envelopes* with the *e* in *stationery.*

QUESTION: My mother is always correcting me when I say, *I hate when that happens.* What's wrong with this? I hear it on TV all the time.

ANSWER: Your mother wants you to speak standard English, the written and spoken language of educated people. Hearing an expression on TV is no assurance that it's acceptable. The problem with an expression like *I hate when that happens* is that an adverbial phrase (*when that happens*) is used as the object of a verb (*hate*). Only nouns, noun clauses, or pronouns may act as object of verbs. Correction: *I hate it when that happens,* or *I hate this to happen.*

QUESTION: As a sportswriter, I need to know the plural of *hole-in-one.*

ANSWER: Make the principal word plural, *holes-in-one.*

Name ______________________

CHAPTER 4 **Reinforcement Exercises**

LEVEL I

Note: At the beginning of each level, a self-check exercise is provided so that you may immediately check your understanding of the concepts in this chapter. Do not look at the answers until you have finished the exercise. Then compare your responses with the answers shown at the bottom of the page. If more than three of your answers do not agree with those shown, reread the chapter before continuing with the other reinforcement exercises.

A. (Self-check) Write the plural forms of the singular nouns shown in parentheses.

EXAMPLE: The (Finch) have purchased an office building on Ventura Boulevard. Finches

1. Some (business) are formed as limited partnerships. businesses ✓
2. Traps were set to catch the many (mouse) recently seen in the building. mice ✱
3. The toy manufacturer invited many (child) to test its new products. Children ✓
4. After four lengthy (speech), boredom overcame the audience. Speeches ✓
5. Neil made two (batch) of chocolate chip cookies after school. batches ✓
6. The condition will not change unless Congress passes a law with (tooth) in it. teeth ✓
7. One administrative secretary may serve six (boss). bosses ✓
8. The (Morris) are planning to move to Delaware as soon as their escrow closes. Morrisses ✱
9. How many (sandwich) did you say he ate? Sandwiches ✓
10. The (Gregory) have three children enrolled in college. Gregorys ✓

Check your answers.

B. Correct any errors in the use of plural nouns in the following sentences by underlining the incorrect form and writing the correct form in the space provided. If the sentence is correct as it stands, write *C*.

EXAMPLE: The advertising agency submitted several <u>sketch</u> of the design. sketches

---

A. 1. businesses, 2. mice, 3. children, 4. speeches, 5. batches, 6. teeth, 7. bosses, 8. Morrises, 9. sandwiches, 10. Gregorys

1. Several men and woman were being considered for the vacant position. Women
2. Anderson was one of the writer's working on the screenplay. Writers
3. The customers of two other business share our parking lot. businesses
4. Bunchs of spectators gathered outside the stock exchange. Bunches
5. Mrs. Hollingsworth secured the door with two latchs. Latches
6. Because three Brian's are employed in that department, surnames are used. Brians
7. Each employee received two free pass's to the exhibit. passes
8. Kelly used two different lens for her photography assignment. lenses
9. Last year the losses of Datapro exceeded its profits. profits
10. Have the Finchs submitted this year's income tax return? Finches
11. The reception room has four benchs and two upholstered chairs. benches
12. Mr. Burtness and his two stepchilds attended the reunion. stepchildren
13. Sharing ownership in the venture are the Joneses and the Garveys. Jonesses
14. Only two news dispatchs were released concerning the stock split. dispatches
15. Swans, ducks, and gooses live in the sanctuary during the winter. gees

C. Write plural forms for the nouns listed.

1. employee employees
2. watch watches
3. Lynch Lynches
4. franchise franchises
5. quartz quartzes
6. rich riches
7. mile miles
8. Thompson Thompsons
9. tax taxes
10. Lorna Lornas
11. hunch hunches
12. sketch sketches
13. cassette Cassettes
14. Lohman Lohmans
15. service Services
16. gas gases
17. area areas
18. absence absences
19. pamphlet pamphlets
20. Ramirez Ramirezes

Name ______________________

LEVEL II

A. (Self-check) Provide the correct plural form of the words shown in parentheses.

1. Many (attorney) now advertise their services in local newspapers. ______________
2. Upper (shelf) contain less frequently used company files. ______________
3. Small businesses can afford few administrative (luxury). ______________
4. For the past three (January), the directors voted dividends. ______________
5. Students had to show their (ID) before they were admitted. ______________
6. Two (bill of lading) were missing from the shipment. ______________
7. Deciduous trees drop their (leaf) in the autumn. ______________
8. Our organization is prepared to deal in foreign (currency). ______________
9. Few orchestras have more than seven (cello) in the string section. ______________
10. The committee debated the (pro and con) of decentralization. ______________

Check your answers.

B. Write the correct plural form of the singular expression shown in parentheses.

1. All that remains standing after the fire are blackened (chimney). ______________
2. The liquidity (ratio) of the two companies were compared. ______________
3. A total of 243 (CEO) of major corporations responded to the survey. ______________
4. President Farley wanted a manager with conservative (belief). ______________
5. Both (Lisa) are outstanding customer service representatives. ______________
6. More graduates with (M.B.A.) are available than ever before. ______________
7. Do the (Wolf) subscribe to *Business Week*? ______________
8. City Council awarded medals to the fire (hero). ______________
9. After the lecture three (hanger-on) remained at the lectern. ______________
10. Congress established the Small Business Administration in the (1950). ______________
11. Computer users must distinguish between zeros and (O). ______________
12. We will tabulate all (yes and no) before releasing the vote. ______________
13. The two (board of directors) voted to begin merger negotiations. ______________

A. 1. attorneys, 2. shelves, 3. luxuries, 4. Januarys, 5. IDs, 6. bills of lading, 7. leaves, 8. currencies, 9. cellos, 10. pros and cons

14. President Lincoln had four (brother-in-law) serving in the Confederate Army.

15. At least two employees have taken (leave of absence) this month.

C. Write plural forms for the nouns listed. Use a dictionary if you are unsure of the spelling.

1. editor in chief
2. half
3. bill of sale
4. 1990
5. subsidiary
6. TV
7. July
8. balance of trade
9. Shelley
10. safe
11. company
12. 7
13. turkey
14. banjo
15. port of entry
16. cure-all
17. L.V.N.
18. C
19. No.
20. governor-elect
21. if
22. avocado
23. RSVP
24. dept.
25. q
26. Ph.D.
27. Emory
28. don't
29. Fox
30. in and out

D. Write sentences using the plural form of the nouns shown in parentheses.

1. (trade-in)
2. (Moreno)
3. (up and down)
4. (R.N.)
5. (CPA)

Name ______________________

LEVEL III

A. (Self-check) Write the preferred plural form for each sentence.

1. Moving lights and other (stimulus) affect the human eye. ____________
2. Black holes are but one of the (phenomenon) of astronomy. ____________
3. The collection of art illustrates varying (emphasis) of the museum directors. ____________
4. Friends and (alumnus) of Michigan State University attended. ____________
5. Formal invitations were sent to (Mrs.) Wagner, Phillips, and Wang. ____________
6. You will find the index on (p.) 116–120. ____________
7. Experts presented conflicting (analysis) of the problem. ____________
8. Greg's family was troubled by numerous (crisis). ____________
9. The announcement reported that (Mr.) Spinello and Busch had formed a partnership. ____________
10. Our office manager ordered new stationery for (memorandum). ____________

Check your answers.

B. Write the plural form in the space provided.

1. Researchers collected substantial (datum) to support their hypothesis. ____________
2. The girls' school will honor its illustrious (alumna). ____________
3. References to hydraulic lifts may be found on pp. 25 (and following pages). ____________
4. Dr. Hersh revealed the two startling (hypothesis) in a press conference. ____________
5. All variant spellings are shown in sets of (parenthesis). ____________
6. Several (genus) were recently reclassified by experts. ____________
7. Jack asked for information about two related (curriculum). ____________
8. Our catalog shows real estate courses on (p.) 226–231. ____________
9. Her disorder has resulted in several different (diagnosis). ____________
10. Betty's master's and doctor's (thesis) were both in the library. ____________

A. 1. stimuli, 2. phenomena, 3. emphases, 4. alumni, 5. Mmes., 6. pp., 7. analyses, 8. crises, 9. Messrs., 10. memoranda or memorandums

C. Complete the sentences below, selecting the proper singular or plural verb to agree with the nouns.

1. Genetics (is, are) an exciting field of study. ____________
2. Curricula (is, are) currently being developed in word processing. ____________
3. (Is, Are) the proceeds to be donated to charity? ____________
4. Leo said the scissors (is, are) on the desk. ____________
5. Economics (is, are) a field with career potential. ____________
6. The statistics on crime (is, are) staggering. ____________
7. Thanks (is, are) due to our committee chairs. ____________
8. Several Vietnamese (is, are) enrolled in this class. ____________
9. News of the stock merger (is, are) rocking the market. ____________
10. Insect larvae (is, are) responsible for the damage. ____________

D. ***Optional Composition.*** Your instructor may ask you to complete this exercise on a separate sheet. Write complete sentences using the plural forms of the following nouns: *phenomenon, datum, tooth, CEO, shelf, attorney, business, company, Mr. and Mrs. Lopez, father-in-law.*

POSTTEST

Underline any incorrectly spelled noun. Write a correct form.

1. All the children were warned to be careful of the sharp knifes. ____________
2. Three bunches of red tomatos look ripe enough to eat. ____________
3. Grey wolves are reported to live in the two vallies. ____________
4. In the 1980s many companys were searching for M.B.A.s. ____________
5. After several business crises, we hired two attornies. ____________

1. knives, 2. tomatoes, 3. valleys, 4. companies, 5. attorneys

CHAPTER 5

Possessive Nouns

OBJECTIVES When you have completed the materials at this level, you will be able to do the following:

Level I
- — *Distinguish between possessive nouns and noun plurals.*
- — *Follow five steps in using the apostrophe to show ownership.*

Level II
- — *Use apostrophe construction for animate nouns.*
- — *Distinguish between descriptive nouns and possessive nouns.*
- — *Pluralize compound nouns, combined ownership nouns, organization names, and abbreviations.*
- — *Understand incomplete possessives.*
- — *Avoid awkward possessives.*

Level III
- — *Determine if an extra syllable can be pronounced in forming a possessive.*
- — *Make proper nouns possessive.*

PRETEST

Underline any incorrect possessive forms. Write correct versions in the spaces provided.

1. Only two employees applied for workers compensation. ____________
2. Michael's output this month is greater than Jeffreys. ____________
3. Both accounts were credited with two months interest. ____________
4. Mr. Ross real talent lies in the electronics field. ____________
5. The Horowitzs daughters are both married. ____________

Thus far you have studied four kinds of nouns (concrete, abstract, common, and proper), and you have learned how to make nouns plural. In this chapter you will learn how to use the apostrophe in making nouns possessive.

---

1. workers', 2. Jeffrey's, 3. months', 4. Mr. Ross' or Ross's, 5. Horowitzes'

Showing Possession With Apostrophes

Notice in the following phrases how possessive nouns show ownership, origin, authorship, or measurement:

Jack's typewriter (ownership)
Alaska's citizens (origin)
Vonnegut's writings (authorship)
three years' time (measurement)

In expressing possession, speakers and writers have a choice. They may show possession with an apostrophe construction, or they may use a prepositional phrase with no apostrophe:

the typewriter of Jack
the citizens of Alaska
the writings of Vonnegut
the time of three years

The use of a prepositional phrase to show ownership is more formal and tends to emphasize the ownership word. The use of the apostrophe construction to show ownership is both more efficient and natural, especially in conversation. In writing, however, placing the apostrophe can be perplexing. Here are five simple but effective steps that will help you write possessives correctly.

Five Steps in Using the Apostrophe Correctly

1. *Look for possessive construction.* Usually two nouns appear together. The first noun shows ownership of (or special relationship to) the second noun.

the man['s] book
the children['s] games
a year['s] time
both doctors['] offices
the musicians['] instruments

2. *Reverse the nouns.* Use the second noun to begin a prepositional phrase. The object of the preposition is the ownership word.

book of the *man*
games of the *children*
time of a *year*
offices of both *doctors*
instruments of the *musicians*

3. *Examine the ownership word.* To determine the correct placement of the apostrophe, you must know whether the ownership word ends in an *s* sound (such as *s, x,* or *z*).

4. *If the ownership word does not end in an* s *sound, add an apostrophe and* s.

the man's book
the children's games
a year's time

5. *If the ownership word does end in an s sound, usually add only an apostrophe.*

both doctors' offices
musicians' instruments

A word of caution. Once students begin to study apostrophes, they tend to use a shotgun approach on passages with words ending in *s,* indiscriminately peppering them with apostrophes. Do *not* use apostrophes for nouns that simply show more than one of something. In the sentence *These companies are opening new branches in the West,* no apostrophes are required. The words *companies* and *branches* are plural; they are not possessive. In addition, be careful to avoid changing the spelling of singular nouns when making them possessive. For example, the *secretary's* desk (meaning one secretary) is *not* spelled *secretaries'.*

Pay particular attention to the following possessive constructions. Perhaps the explanations and hints in parentheses will help you understand and remember these expressions.

a day's work (the work of one single day)
three days' work (the work of three days)
a dollar's worth (the worth of one single dollar)
your money's worth (the worth of your money)
today's weather (there can be only one *today*)
tomorrow's work (there can be only one *tomorrow*)
the stockholders' meeting (we usually assume that a meeting involves more than one person)

The guides for possessive construction presented thus far cover the majority of possessives found in business writing.

Complete the reinforcement exercises for Level I.

LEVEL II

Problem Possessive Constructions

1. *Animate versus inanimate nouns.* As a matter of style, some careful writers prefer to reserve the apostrophe construction for people and animals. For other nouns use prepositional phrases or simple adjectives.

roof of the car, or car roof (better than *car's roof*)
color of the desk, or the desk color (better than *desk's color*)
heat of the motor, or motor heat (better than *motor's heat*)

2. *Descriptive versus possessive nouns.* When nouns provide description or identification only, the possessive form is *not* used. Writers have most problems with descriptive nouns ending in *s,* such as *Claims* Department. No apostrophe is needed, just as none is necessary in *Personnel* Department.

Sales Department (not Sales' Department)
the electronics industry (not electronics' industry)
Los Angeles Dodgers (not Los Angeles' Dodgers)

3. *Compound nouns.* Make compound words possessive by adding an apostrophe or an *'s* to the final element of the compound.

his father-in-law's property
onlookers' interest
notary public's seal

4. *Incomplete possessives.* When the second noun in a possessive noun construction is unstated, the first noun is nevertheless treated as possessive.

You'll find bond paper at the stationer's [store].
Let's meet at Patrick's [home] after the game.
This year's sales are higher than last year's [sales].

5. *Separate or combined ownership.* When two names express separate ownership, make both names possessive. When two names express combined ownership, make only the *second* name possessive.

Separate ownership	Combined ownership
landlords' and tenants' rights	the husband and wife's business
Mike's and Sam's stereos	my aunt and uncle's house

N.B. Look at the object owned (*business, house,* etc.). If that object is singular, ownership is usually combined.

6. *Names of organizations.* Organizations with possessives in their names may or may not use apostrophes. Follow the style used by the individual organization. (Consult the organization's stationery or a directory listing.)

Malibu West Homeowners Assn.	Stuckey's
State Teachers' Retirement System	Sears

7. *Abbreviations.* Make abbreviations possessive by following the same guidelines as for animate nouns.

AMA's ruling	all R.N.s' credentials
NBC's coverage	May Co.'s advertisement

8. *Awkward possessives.* When the addition of an apostrophe results in an awkward construction, show ownership by using a prepositional phrase.

Awkward	Improved
my brothers-in-law's opinions	opinions of my brothers-in-law
your neighbor's doctor's telephone	telephone of your neighbor's doctor
my professor, Dr. Aller's, office	office of my professor, Dr. Aller

Complete the reinforcement exercises for Level II.

LEVEL III

You have now learned to follow five steps in identifying possessive constructions and in placing the apostrophe correctly. The guides presented thus far cover most possessive constructions. The possessive form of a few nouns, however, requires a refinement of Step 5.

Additional Guideline

Let us briefly review the five-step plan for placing the apostrophe in noun possessives. Having done so, we will then add a refinement to the fifth step.

1. Look for possessive construction. (Usually, but not always, two nouns appear together.)
2. Reverse the nouns.
3. Examine the ownership word.
4. If the ownership word does *not* end in an *s* sound, add an apostrophe and *s*.
5. If the ownership word *does* end in an *s* sound, usually add just an apostrophe. *However, if an extra syllable can be easily pronounced in the possessive form, most writers will add an apostrophe and an s to singular nouns.*

Singular noun ending in an *s* sound; extra syllable can be easily pronounced	Add apostrophe and *s*
menu of the waitress[s]	waitress's menu
desk of the boss[s]	boss's desk
den of the fox[s]	the fox's den

Making Difficult Proper Nouns Possessive

Of all possessive forms, individuals' names — especially those ending in *s* sounds — are the most puzzling to students, and understandably so. Even experts don't always agree on the possessive form for singular proper nouns.

Traditionalists, as represented in *The Chicago Manual of Style* and *The Modern Language Association Style Manual,* prefer adding *'s* to troublesome *singular proper* nouns that end in *s* sounds. On the other hand, writers of more popular literature, as represented in *The Associated Press Stylebook and Libel Manual,* prefer the simpler style of adding just an apostrophe to singular proper nouns. You may apply either style, but be consistent. Please note in the examples below that the style choice applies *only* to singular names ending in *s* sounds. Plural names are always made possessive with the addition of an apostrophe only. Study the examples shown here.

Singular name	Singular possessive-traditional	Singular possessive-popular	Plural possessive
Mrs. Jones	Mrs. Jones's	Mrs. Jones'	the Joneses'
Mr. Morris	Mr. Morris's	Mr. Morris'	the Morrises'
Mrs. Lopez	Mrs. Lopez's	Mrs. Lopez'	the Lopezes'
Mr. Horowitz	Mr. Horowitz's	Mr. Horowitz'	the Horowitzes'

N.B. Here's a summary of the possessive rule that should be easy to remember. If an ownership word does not end in an *s*, add an apostrophe and *s*. If the ownership word does end in an *s*, add just an apostrophe — unless you can easily pronounce an extra syllable. If you can pronounce that extra syllable, add an apostrophe and *s*.

N.B. The word *the* preceding a name is a clue that the name is being used in a plural sense. For example, *the* Rosses means the entire Ross family.

HOT LINE QUERIES

QUESTION: Where should the apostrophe go in *employee's handbook?*

ANSWER: This is tricky because the writer of that phrase must decide whether he considers the handbook from one employee's point of view or from all employees' points of view. Depending upon the point of view, the apostrophe could be justified for either position. The trend today seems to favor the singular construction (*employee's handbook*).

QUESTION: I'm addressing a letter to the American Nurses Association. What salutation shall I use? One person in our office suggested *Gentlewomen.* Is this being used?

ANSWER: I recommend that you use *Ladies and Gentlemen* since both male and female nurses are members of the association. In fact, this salutation is appropriate for any organization in which men and women may be represented in management. I would not use *Gentlewomen* because it sounds stilted and artificial. In response to the women's movement, many businesses and individuals are trying to avoid sexism in language. Salutations such as *Dear Sir* and *Gentlemen* are no longer used automatically. Today we are more sensitive to women as employees, managers, and executives. The use of awkward terms like *Gentlewomen* or *Gentlepersons,* however, is an overreaction and should be avoided. To solve the problem of sexism in letter salutations, consider using the AMS (American Management Society) simplified letter style. It substitutes a subject line for the salutation. (See Figure 3 in Appendix 6.)

QUESTION: Should *undercapitalized* be hyphenated? I can't find it in my dictionary.

ANSWER: The prefixes *under* and *over* are not followed by hyphens.

QUESTION: Is there an apostrophe in *Veterans* Day, and if so, where does it go?

ANSWER: *Veterans Day* has no apostrophe, but *New Year's Day* does have one.

QUESTION: My boss has dictated, *I respectfully call you and your client's attention to* . . . . What's wrong with this? How can I make *you* possessive?

ANSWER: The best way to handle this awkward possessive is to avoid using the possessive form and use a prepositional phrase instead (*I respectfully call to the attention of you and your client* . . .).

QUESTION: Here at the Cancer Society we have a bureau of speakers. Where should the apostrophe go when we use the possessive form of the word *speakers?*

ANSWER: *Speakers' bureau.*

Name ______________________

CHAPTER 5 **Reinforcement Exercises**

LEVEL I

A. (Self-check) Rewrite the following phrases avoiding the use of the apostrophe. Use a prepositional phrase. Does the ownership word end in an *s* sound?

	Revision	Does ownership word end in *s* sound?
EXAMPLE: the trainee's hours	hours of the trainee	No
1. the sheriff's posse		
2. the lady's voice		
3. three men's suggestions		
4. our company's policy		
5. your money's worth		
6. a beginner's luck		
7. two years' time		
8. all drivers' engines		
9. the children's books		
10. six months' interest		

Check your answers.

B. Using apostrophes, change the following prepositional phrases into possessive constructions. Ownership words are underlined.

EXAMPLE: compensation of <u>women</u>	women's compensation
1. records of my <u>accountant</u>	
2. wages of all <u>employees</u>	
3. permit for a <u>seller</u>	
4. sales for six <u>months</u>	Six months' sales
5. addresses of <u>customers</u>	
6. stock of this <u>company</u>	
7. prices of <u>competitors</u>	
8. duties of the <u>secretary</u>	

A. 1. No, 2. No, 3. No, 4. No, 5. No, 6. No, 7. Yes, 8. Yes, 9. No, 10. Yes

9. delay of a month
10. meeting of stockholders

C. Underline the errors in the following sentences. Write the correct form at the right. If the sentence is correct as it stands, write *C.*

EXAMPLE: Some students cars were ticketed. students'

1. Several womens organizations offer career counseling.
2. Customers expect a dollars worth of value for a dollar spent.
3. In todays mail we received three orders.
4. Both clerks salaries will be upwardly adjusted next quarter.
5. More than 100 foreign countries currently trade with the U.S.
6. Most students difficulties lie in recognizing possessives.
7. Many management firms will tailor their services and charges to a producers needs.
8. Several bakeries in our neighborhood provide excellent products.
9. Three months interest will be due in four days.
10. Success depends upon a companies capacity to deliver.
11. The four astronomers theories created international news.
12. Not a single customers complaint will be ignored.
13. For many years all brokerage firms charged a uniform commission.
14. An inventors patent protects his invention for seventeen years.
15. At each stereo buyers expense, high-quality speakers may be substituted.
16. You have exactly four days in which to find new fire and liability insurance policies for the buildings.
17. All taxpayers returns are checked by the computer.
18. Only one customers telephone could not be installed.
19. Davids salary is higher than that of the other clerks because he has greater responsibilities.
20. When the bill receives the Governors signature, it will become law.

Name ____________________

LEVEL II

A. (Self-check) For each of the following sentences, underline any possessive construction that could be improved. Write an improved form in the space provided. If the sentence is acceptable as it stands, write *C*.

EXAMPLES: Our office's roof is leaking. — The roof of our office
The meeting Friday is at Ellens. — Ellen's

1. This pencil's point is dull. ____________
2. The St. Louis' Cardinals are having a good season. ____________
3. Lisa's and Bill's new home is close to the city. ____________
4. This company's product line is superior to that companys. ____________
5. The first runner-ups trophy will also be awarded tonight. ____________
6. Small aircraft sales were stimulated by the FAAs ruling. ____________
7. All teachers contribute to the State Teacher's Retirement System. ____________
8. Our editor in chiefs suggestions are always followed. ____________
9. Most ladies and mens raincoats are reduced in price. ____________
10. Is your sister-in-laws job downtown? ____________

B. For each of the following sentences, underline any possessive construction that could be improved. Write an improved form in the space provided. If the sentence is acceptable as it stands, write *C*.

1. What is that sticky substance on the typewriter's keys? ____________
2. The King and Queen's limousine approached slowly. ____________
3. On the second floor is the chief of staffs office. ____________
4. Many manufacturer's representatives displayed equipment. ____________
5. All beneficiaries names are entered on the third line. ____________
6. NASAs budget may be cut drastically. ____________
7. Duplicate forms were sent to the Claims Department. ____________
8. This month's production figures are lower than last months. ____________
9. Numerous employees personnel folders will be reviewed. ____________
10. Several new roses were described in news releases. ____________
11. Both the husband's and wife's signatures must be secured before the sale is valid. ____________

A. 1. The point of this pencil or pencil point, 2. St. Louis, 3. Lisa, 4. company's, 5. runner-up's, 6. FAA's, 7. Teachers', 8. chief's, 9. ladies', men's, 10. sister-in-law's

12. Most of this companys customers are concentrated nearby. ______

13. At least a dozen buyers and sellers finances were scrutinized. ______

14. Some air-freight lines and all bus lines are subject to the ICCs latest regulation. ______

15. Your totals for the last three columns are certainly different from Carols. ______

16. Because of the gravity of the offense, the district attorneys staff is investigating. ______

17. Lyon & Co.s annual sale is scheduled to begin in three days. ______

18. Frank's and Pam's new car has a two-year warranty. ______

19. Although I'm interested in the electronics' field, I have not settled on a definite career. ______

20. We expect our team's total sales to greatly exceed their teams. ______

C. Rewrite these sentences to remedy awkward or incorrect possessives.

EXAMPLE: My brother's friend's car is available. The car of my brother's friend is available. (Hint: Start your sentence with the word that is owned.)

1. His company's accountant's suggestions are wise. ______

2. Brent Harris, my lawyer's, practice is flourishing. ______

3. Were both your sisters-in-law's cars ticketed on the same day? ______

4. Mr. Freed's secretary's replacement will be able to remain with us for one more week. ______

5. My friend's brothers' motorcycles were always parked in the driveway. ______

Name ______________________

LEVEL III

A. (Self-check) Select an acceptable possessive form.

1. Miss (a) Betz' or Betz's, (b) Betzes' vacation is scheduled for April. ________
2. We can't locate (a) Guses', (b) Gus' or Gus's application. ________
3. Is that a realtor's sign on the (a) Harrises's, (b) Harrises' home? ________
4. That (a) actress's, (b) actress' performance was excellent. ________
5. Cheryl took Dr. (a) Fox' or Fox's, (b) Foxes' prescription to a pharmacy. ________
6. All (a) creditor's, (b) creditors' claims will be honored. ________
7. A few (a) waitress's, (b) waitresses' stations were eliminated. ________
8. Please verify Mrs. (a) Lopezes', (b) Lopez's or Lopez' hours ________
9. Have you noticed that the (a) Horowitzes, (b) Horowitzes' have a new car? (Tricky!) ________
10. Have you noticed the (a) Harris' or Harris's, (b) Harrises' new car? ________

B. Fill in the singular possessive forms for the two styles shown below.

Name	Traditional style	Popular style
EXAMPLE: [Mr. Jones] suit	Mr. Jones's suit	Mr. Jones' suit
1. [Ms. Burns] purse		
2. [Russ] car		
3. [Mr. Harris] desk		
4. [Dr. Cortez] office		
5. [Miss Metz] letter		
6. [Lois] computer		
7. [Mr. Fields] book		

When you complete this exercise, check your local newspaper for its possessive style. Which does it use? Bring an example of a singular possessive proper noun ending in *s* from your newspaper (like the ones above) to class when you discuss this exercise.

C. Review of Levels I, II, and III. Each of the following sentences has one error in the use of a possessive. Write the corrected form in the space provided.

1. I believe that Russ letter is on the top of the pile. ________________
2. His landlord said that four months rent was due. ________________
3. Mrs. Lopez salary warrant did not reflect the deduction. ________________

A. 1. a, 2. b, 3. b, 4. a, 5. a, 6. b, 7. b, 8. b, 9. a, 10. b

4. We were all invited to the party at the Thomas. ______________

5. Despite a weeks delay the package finally arrived. ______________

6. Mr. Gross investments were carefully selected. ______________

7. All city council representatives were invited to the homeowners meeting. ______________

8. Our records show that Mr. Murray account has an error. ______________

9. After seven years time the property reverts to state ownership. ______________

10. One witnesses testimony was questioned. ______________

11. The Horowitz sons are enrolled in a Washington college. ______________

12. Do you feel that you got your moneys worth? ______________

13. After three days practice all trainees qualified. ______________

14. Today's weather is much better than yesterday. ______________

15. We were told to report to Mr. Norris office. ______________

D. ***Optional Composition.*** Your instructor may ask you to complete this exercise on a separate sheet. Write sentences that illustrate the possessive forms of the following words: *Tiffany, two years, driver, Jason and Ann, waitress, one month, customers, company, editor in chief, the Cosbys.* Underline the possessive form in each sentence.

POSTTEST

Underline any incorrect possessive forms. Write correct versions.

1. New dividends were announced at the stockholders meeting. ______________
2. This month's sales figures were better than last months. ______________
3. In just two years time, your profits will likely double. ______________
4. Mrs. Betz secretary located all the accounts receivable. ______________
5. The three witnesses testimony required seven court days. ______________

---

1. stockholders', 2. last month's, 3. years', 4. Betz' or Betz's, 5. witnesses'

CHAPTER 6

Personal Pronouns

OBJECTIVES When you have completed the materials in this chapter, you will be able to do the following:

Level I — *Use personal pronouns correctly as subjects and objects.*

— *Distinguish between personal possessive pronouns (such as* its*) and contractions (such as* it's*).*

Level II — *Choose the correct pronoun in compound constructions, comparatives, and appositives.*

— *Use reflexive pronouns correctly.*

Level III — *Use nominative case pronouns with subject complements.*

— *Select the correct pronouns for use with the infinitive* to be.

PRETEST

Underline the correct pronouns. Compare your answers with those at the bottom of the page.

1. The contract was signed by Mr. Lee and (I, me, myself) last week.
2. (Us, We) employees receive additional health benefits in September.
3. Only one of the job applicants can keyboard as fast as (her, she).
4. Are you sure it was (he, him) who called me yesterday morning?
5. Good workers like you and (he, him) are difficult to locate.

As you will remember from Chapter 2 (p. 14), pronouns are words that substitute for nouns and other pronouns. They enable us to speak and write without awkward repetition. Grammatically, pronouns may be divided into seven types (personal, relative, interrogative, demonstrative, indefinite, reflexive, and reciprocal). Rather than consider all seven pronoun types, this textbook will be concerned only with those pronouns that cause difficulty in use.

---

1. me, 2. We, 3. she, 4. he, 5. him

Personal Pronouns

The personal pronouns indicate the person speaking, the person spoken to, or the person or object spoken of. Notice in the following table that the personal pronouns change their form (or *case*) depending upon who is speaking (called the *person*), how many are speaking (the *number*), and the sex (or *gender*) of the speaker. For example, the third person feminine objective singular case is *her*. Most personal pronoun errors by speakers and writers involve faulty usage of case forms. Study this table to avoid errors in personal pronoun use:

	NOMINATIVE CASE*		OBJECTIVE CASE		POSSESSIVE CASE	
	Sing.	Plural	Sing.	Plural	Sing.	Plural
First person (person speaking)	I	we	me	us	my, mine	our, ours
Second person (person spoken to)	you	you	you	you	your, yours	your, yours
Third person (person or thing spoken of)	he, she, it	they	him, her, it	them	his, her, hers, its	their, theirs

Basic Use of the Nominative Case

Nominative case pronouns are used primarily as the subjects of verbs. Every verb or verb phrase, regardless of its position in a sentence, has a subject. If that subject is a pronoun, it must be in the nominative case.

I thought *he* had left the office.
They asked if *we* had valid passports.

Basic Use of the Objective Case

Objective case pronouns most commonly are used in two ways:

1. *Object of a Verb.* When pronouns act as direct or indirect objects of verbs, they must be in the objective case.

Give *them* a building map.
Bob asked *her* for help.

2. *Object of a Preposition.* The objective case is used for pronouns that are objects of prepositions.

Supplies were sent to *them*.
An excellent report was given by *him*.
Just between *you* and *me,* profits are slipping.

**Some authorities prefer the term* subjective case.

N.B. When the words *between, but, like,* and *except* are used as prepositions, errors in pronoun case are likely to occur. To avoid such errors, isolate the prepositional phrase, and then use an objective case pronoun as the object of the preposition. Example: *Every employee [but Tom and him] completed the form.*

Basic Use of the Possessive Case

Possessive pronouns show ownership. Unlike possessive nouns, possessive pronouns require no apostrophes. Study these five possessive pronouns: *hers, yours, ours, theirs, its.* Notice the absence of apostrophes. Do not confuse possessive pronouns with contractions. Contractions are shortened (contracted) forms of subjects and verbs, such as *it's* (for *it is*), *there's* (for *there is*), and *they're* (for *they are*). In these examples the apostrophes indicate omitted letters.

Possessive pronouns	Contractions
Theirs is the first car in line.	*There's* no stationery left.
The cat is cleaning *its* fur.	*It's* a dangerous situation.

N.B. Whenever you become confused and are unable to choose between *its* and *it's,* substitute *it is* for the form in question. For example: *it's unusual; it is unusual.* If *it is* makes sense, use the apostrophe. If not, use the pronoun *its.*

Complete the reinforcement exercises for Level I.

LEVEL II

Problems in Using Personal Pronouns

Compound Subjects and Objects

When a pronoun appears in combination with a noun or another pronoun, special attention must be given to case selection. Use this technique to help you choose the correct pronoun case: ignore the extra noun or pronoun and its related conjunction, and consider separately the pronoun in question to determine what the case should be.

Laura asked [you and] *me* for advice. (Ignore *you and.*)

[Larry and] *he* enrolled in the class. (Ignore *Larry and.*)

Will you permit [Tony and] *them* to join you? (Ignore *Tony and.*)

Notice in the first sentence, for example, that when *you and* is removed, the pronoun *me* must be selected because it functions as the object of the verb.

Comparatives

In statements of comparison, words are often implied but not actually stated. To determine pronoun case in only partially complete comparative statements introduced by *than* or *as,* always mentally finish the comparative by adding the implied missing words.

Each month Jon saves as much as they. (Jon saves as much as *they* — not *them* — save.)

Lisa spells better than he. (. . . better than *he* — not *him* — spells.)

Tardiness annoys Mr. Britton as much as *me*. (. . . as much as it annoys *me* — not *I*.)

Appositives

Appositives explain or rename previously mentioned nouns or pronouns. A pronoun in apposition takes the same case as that of the noun or pronoun with which it is in apposition. In order to determine more easily what pronoun case to use for a pronoun in combination with an appositive, temporarily ignore the appositive.

We [consumers] are protected by laws. (Ignore *consumers*.)

Precautions were taken by *us* [neighbors]. (Ignore *neighbors*.)

Reflexive (or Compound Personal) Pronouns

Reflexive pronouns which end in *-self* emphasize or reflect back upon the antecedents (the nouns or pronouns previously mentioned).

The president *himself* presented the award. (Emphasizes *president*.)

The matter should resolve *itself*. (Reflects back upon *matter*.)

Errors result when reflexive pronouns are used instead of personal pronouns. If no previously mentioned noun or pronoun is stated in the sentence, use a personal pronoun instead of a reflexive pronoun.

Bring the proposed agenda to either Bradley or *me*. (Not *myself*.)

Mr. Stewart and *I* analyzed the numerous possibilities. (Not *myself*.)

Please note that *hisself* is substandard and should always be avoided.

Complete the reinforcement exercises for Level II.

LEVEL III

Advanced Uses of Nominative Case Pronouns

Subject Complement

As we have already seen earlier in this chapter, nominative case pronouns usually function as subjects of verbs. Less frequently, nominative case pronouns also perform as subject complements. A pronoun that follows a linking verb and renames the subject must be in the nominative case. Be especially alert to the linking verbs *am, is, are, was, were, be, being,* and *been.*

> It *was I* who placed the order.
> I'm sure it *is she* who usually answers the telephone.
> If you *were I,* what would you do?

When a verb of several words appears in a phrase, look at the final word of the verb. If it is a linking verb, use a nominative pronoun.

> It *might have been they* who made the bid.
> The driver *could have been he.*
> If the teacher *had been she,* my grade might have been higher.

N.B. In conversation it is common to say, *It is* me, or more likely, *It's* me. Careful speakers and writers, though, normally use nominative case pronouns after linking verbs. If the resulting constructions sound too "formal," revise your sentences appropriately. For example, instead of *It is I who placed the order,* use *I placed the order.*

Infinitive *to be* Without a Subject

Infinitives are the present forms of verbs preceded by *to;* for example, *to sit, to run,* and *to walk.* Nominative pronouns are used following the infinitive *to be* when the infinitive has no subject. In this instance the infinitive joins a complement (not an object) to the subject.

> Her twin sister was often taken to be *she.* (The infinitive *to be* has no subject; *she* is the complement of the subject *sister.*)
> Darrell was mistakenly thought to be *I.* (The infinitive *to be* has no subject; *I* is the complement of the subject *Darrell.*)
> Why would Jennifer want to be *she*? (The infinitive *to be* has no subject; *she* is the complement of the subject *Jennifer.*)

Advanced Applications of Personal Case Pronouns

Infinitive *to be* With a Subject

When the infinitive *to be* has a subject, any pronoun following it will function as an object. Therefore, the pronoun following the infinitive will function as its object and take the objective case.

> The teacher believed Jennifer to be *her.* (The subject of the infinitive *to be* is

Jennifer; therefore, the pronoun functions as an object. Try it another way: *The teacher believed her to be Jennifer.* You would not say, *The teacher believed she to be Jennifer.*)

John expected the callers to be *us.* (The subject of the infinitive *to be* is *callers;* therefore, the pronoun functions as an object.)

Colonel Dunn judged the winner to be *him.* (The subject of the infinitive *to be* is *winner;* therefore use the objective case pronoun *him.*)

Whenever you have selected a pronoun for the infinitive *to be* and you want to test its correctness, try reversing the pronoun and its antecedent. For example, *We thought the winner to be her* (*We thought her* [*not she*] *to be the winner*) or *Cheryl was often taken to be she* (*She* [*not her*] *was often taken to be Cheryl*).

N.B. This memory device may help you to remember the correct pronoun form to use with the infinitive *to be:* No subject, then *no*minative. That is, if the infinitive *to be* has no subject, supply a nominative pronoun. For example, *I was thought* to be she.

Summary

The following table summarizes the uses of nominative and objective case pronouns.

Nominative case	Objective case
Subject of the verb: *They* are sky divers.	Direct or indirect object of the verb: Give *him* another chance.
Subject complement: That is *he.*	Object of a preposition: Send the order to *him.*
Infinitive *to be* without a subject: Ed pretended to be *he.*	Object of an infinitive: Ann hoped to call *us.*
	Infinitive *to be* with subject: We thought the guests to be *them.*

Complete the reinforcement exercises for Level III.

Types of Pronouns

For students of the language interested in a total view, here is a summary of the seven types of pronouns, with sentences illustrating each type. This list is presented for your interest alone, not for potential testing.

1. *Personal pronouns* replace nouns or other pronouns.

Nominative case:	I, we, you, he, she, it, they
Objective case:	me, us, you, him, her, it, them
Possessive case:	my, mine, our, ours, your, yours, his, hers, its, their, theirs.

Mr. Benton said *he* put *his* signature on *it* yesterday.

2. *Relative pronouns* join subordinate clauses to antecedents: who, whose, whom, which, that, whoever, whomever, whichever, whatever.

He is the candidate *whom* we all admire.

3. *Interrogative pronouns* replace nouns in a question: who, whose, whom, which, what.

Whose seat is this?

4. *Demonstrative pronouns* designate specific persons or things: this, these, that, those.

This must be the work request we need.

5. *Indefinite pronouns* replace nouns: everyone, anyone, someone, each, everybody, anybody, one, none, some, all, etc.

Everybody needs adequate nourishment.

6. *Reflexive pronouns (compound personal)* emphasize or reflect back upon antecedents: myself, yourself, himself, herself, itself, oneself, etc.

The president *himself* answered that letter.

7. *Reciprocal pronouns* indicate mutual relationship: each other, one another.

All three chief executive officers consulted *one another* before making the announcement.

HOT LINE QUERIES

QUESTION: On the radio I recently heard a talk-show host say, *My producer and myself* . . . . A little later that same host said, *Send any inquiries to the station or myself at this address.* This sounded half right and half wrong, but I would have trouble explaining the problem. Can you help?

ANSWER: The problem is a common one: use of a reflexive pronoun (*myself*) when it has no preceding noun on which to reflect. Correction: *My producer and I* and *Send inquiries to the station or me.* Reflexive pronouns like *myself* should be used only with obvious antecedents, such as *I, myself, will take the calls.* Individuals in the media often misuse reflexive pronouns, perhaps to avoid sounding egocentric with overuse of *I* and *me*.

QUESTION: I have a question about the use of *etc.* in this sentence: *We are installing better lighting, acoustical tile, sound barriers, and* etc. Should I use two periods at the end of the sentence, and does a comma precede *etc.?*

ANSWER: Although the use of *etc.* (meaning "and so forth") is generally avoided, do not, if it is to be used, include the redundant word *and*. When *etc.* is found at the end of a sentence, one comma should precede it. When *etc.* appears in the middle of a sentence, two commas should set it off. For example, *Better lighting, acoustical tile, and sound barriers, etc., are being installed. Never* use two periods at the end of a sentence, even if the sentence ends with an abbreviation such as *etc.*

QUESTION: We're having a disagreement in our office about the word *healthy*. Is it correct to write *Exercise is healthy?*

ANSWER: Strictly speaking, *healthy* means "to have or possess good health." For example, *The rosy-cheeked schoolchildren look healthy*. The word *healthful* means "to promote or be conducive to good health." Your sentence should read: *Exercise is healthful.*

QUESTION: Should a hyphen be used in the word *dissimilar*?

ANSWER: No. Prefixes such as *dis, pre, non,* and *un* do not require hyphens. Even when the final letter of the prefix is repeated in the initial letter of the root word, no hyphens are used: *disspirited, preenroll, nonnutritive.*

QUESTION: I thought I knew the difference between *to* and *too,* but could you provide me with a quick review?

ANSWER: *To* may serve as a preposition (*I'm going to the store*), and it may also serve as part of an infinitive construction (*to sign his name*). The adverb *too* may be used to mean "also" (*Andrea will attend too*). In addition, the word *too* may be used to indicate "to an excessive extent" (*the letter is too long*).

QUESTION: I have a lot of trouble with the word *extension,* as in the expressions *extension* cord and telephone *extension*. Is the word ever spelled *extention*?

ANSWER: You are not alone in having trouble with *extension*. No, it is never spelled with the familiar suffix *tion*. Perhaps you could remember it better if you associate the word *tension* with *extension*.

Name ______________________

CHAPTER 6 **Reinforcement Exercises**

LEVEL I

A. (Self-check) Select the correct form.

1. We are sure that (he, him) graduated from the University of Illinois. he ✓
2. All the students except (she, her) took the final exam. her ✓
3. Send the letter to (they, them) at their Florida address. them ✓
4. (They, Them), as well as some other employees, volunteered for the project. They ✓
5. It seems strange that someone like (he, him) could be given the assignment. him ✓
6. Please discuss it with Michael and (she, her) before proceeding. her ✓
7. Purchases made by (she, her) were billed incorrectly. her ✓
8. Are you sure (there's, theirs) time to complete the form? there's ✓
9. Melvin said that (its, it's) your turn next. it's ✓
10. Don is certain that nobody but (he, him) can open the lock. him ✓

Check your answers.

B. In the spaces provided, list five personal pronouns that can be used as subjects of verbs and five that can be used as objects of verbs or objects of prepositions.

Personal pronouns that can be used as subjects	Personal pronouns that can be used as objects
1. He 2. she 3. I	1. me 2. us 3. you
4. we 5. they	4. him 5. them

C. In this set of sentences, all the omitted pronouns serve as subjects of verbs. Write the correct pronoun for each sentence.

1. The project director and (she, her) worked on the program budget. she
2. I know that James Naylor and (he, him) will be purchasing the franchise as a joint venture. he

A. 1. he, 2. her, 3. them, 4. They, 5. him, 6. her, 7. her, 8. there's, 9. it's, 10. him

3. After the series of interviews, only (she, her) was asked to submit additional recommendations. ____________
4. When the new product was introduced, other salespeople and (they, them) attended four training sessions. ____________
5. We are pleased to learn that (he, him) will be transferred to our division. ____________

In the next set of sentences, all the omitted pronouns serve as objects of verbs or as objects of prepositions. Selected prepositions have been underlined to help you recognize them. Write the correct pronoun for each sentence.

6. Mr. Jacobson asked if the terms of the agreement were satisfactory to (we, us). ____________
7. Capital for the enterprise was subscribed by (he, him). ____________
8. Send Mrs. Jordan and (I, me) your latest pricing figures for the Model T-S40. ____________
9. Everyone but (they, them) invested in growth stocks. ____________
10. After that group finishes, please give the register to (we, us). ____________

D. In the spaces provided, write *A, B,* or *C* to indicate how the italicized pronouns function in these sentences.

A = Subject of a verb B = Object of a verb C = Object of a preposition

EXAMPLE: Please ask *her* for the number. B

1. Mrs. Bates asked *me* for the assignment. ______
2. Cheryl and *she* were late for their counseling appointments. ______
3. When Mike completed the difficult task, the supervisor praised *him*. ______
4. The secret agreement between Harper and *him* was not revealed. ______
5. *They* made an offer to purchase the four-acre plot. ______

E. Select the correct pronoun.

1. Please have (he, him) notarize this document. ____________
2. Our sales team can take pride in (it's, its) sales record. ____________
3. Nobody but (he, him) has been authorized to use the premises. ____________
4. Are you sure that this apartment is (there's, theirs, their's)? ____________
5. Between you and (I, me), who will be our next company president? ____________
6. We have already sent the parts to (they, them) for inspection. ____________
7. (It's, Its) roof may collapse under the weight of the wet snow. ____________
8. As Mr. Hadley and (he, him) discussed the matter, new information was revealed. ____________

Name ______________________

LEVEL II

A. (Self-check) Select the correct pronoun and write it in the space provided.

1. A profit-sharing plan was offered to (we, us) employees in place of cost-of-living raises. ______
2. No one made more profit in that transaction than (he, him). ______
3. His counselor and (he, him) worked out a schedule of classes. ______
4. Both girls, Alicia and (she, her), will be able to work this weekend. ______
5. (Us, We) delegates stayed in the Hotel Dupar during the convention. ______
6. Miss Ferguson and (myself, I, me) received new job classifications. ______
7. Proposals submitted by (her and me, she and I) were considered. ______
8. No one but my friend and (I, me) spoke up during the discussion. ______
9. Separate planes were taken by the business manager and (I, me). ______
10. The tragedy shocked Dr. Callihan as much as (I, me). ______

Check your answers.

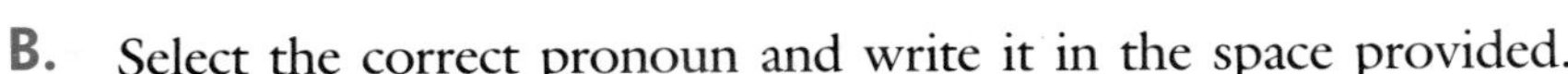

B. Select the correct pronoun and write it in the space provided.

1. Her friend and (she, her) ordered double-dip Dutch chocolate ice cream cones. ______
2. It appears that Carrie is much taller than (she, her). ______
3. An attorney is in charge of (we, us) trainees. ______
4. There are no employees quite like Steve and (he, him). ______
5. Idle gossip disturbs Mrs. Bronski as much as (I, me). ______
6. He has no one but (hisself, himself) to blame. ______
7. It's interesting that (us, we) accountants were audited this year. ______
8. The production manager told a reporter and (he, him) that computerization had virtually eliminated the need for paperwork. ______
9. The co-pilots, Turner and (he, him), requested permission to land. ______

A. 1. us, 2. he, 3. he, 4. she, 5. We, 6. I, 7. her and me, 8. me, 9. me, 10. me

10. A serious disagreement between the management and (he, him) caused his termination. him

11. Mr. Jefferson and (I, me, myself) will make the announcement very soon. I

12. No one knows that problem better than (I, me). I

13. News of the merger upset President Davis as much as (I, me). me

14. All employees but Mr. Herzog and (I, me) agreed to the economy measures. me

15. Several of (we, us) salespeople surpassed our monthly selling goals. us

16. Do you think Theresa can complete the work more quickly than (he, him)? he can complet he

17. Campaign literature was sent to (we, us) homeowners prior to the elections. us

18. The signatures on the letter appear to have been written by you and (she, her). her

19. Contracts were sent to the authors, Mrs. Richards and (she, her). her

20. Everyone except two drivers and (he, him) has checked in with the dispatcher. him

C. Write complete sentences that begin with the words shown. Supply a pronoun where indicated.

EXAMPLE: Mr. Paulson and (pronoun) Mr. Paulson and he agreed to market their invention.

1. My friend and (pronoun) ________________

2. The two students, Don and (pronoun), ________________

3. Just between you and (pronoun), ________________

4. Except for Mr. Sanders and (pronoun), ________________

See pp. 76-77 for additional Level I and II exercises.

Name ______________________

LEVEL III

A. (Self-check) Select the correct pronoun and write it in the space provided.

1. We wondered if it was (they, them) who sent the gift. ______________
2. At a glance his younger brother could be taken to be (he, him). ______________
3. Ramco asked my partner and (I, me) to design a logo. ______________
4. If I were (he, him), I would withdraw my endorsement. ______________
5. Gilbert said that it was (he, him) who used the microcomputer last. ______________
6. Sherilyn is often taken to be (her, she). ______________
7. It might have been (she, her) who called in the alarm. ______________
8. The audience didn't discover that Marcelle was (she, her) until after the performance. ______________
9. They thought Marcelle to be (she, her). ______________
10. I was asked to contact you and (they, them). ______________

Check your answers.

B. Select the correct pronoun.

1. When Frank answered the telephone, he said, "This is (he, him)." ______________
2. If you were (I, me), would you reenlist? ______________
3. The officer told Paul and (I, me) to report for duty Monday. ______________
4. Nearly everyone mistook the statuesque blonde to be (her, she). ______________
5. Surely it was (they, them) who left the package last night. ______________
6. An attempt was made to reach (he, him) and her in Geneva. ______________
7. There is some doubt whether the supervisor will be (he, him). ______________
8. I'm sure that it was (she, her) who called this morning. ______________
9. The lifeguard credited with the rescue was thought to be (he, him). ______________
10. If the newly elected council member had been (he, him), our worst fears might have been realized. ______________
11. Dr. Meza judged the winner to be (her, she). ______________

A. 1. they, 2. he, 3. me, 4. he, 5. he, 6. she, 7. she, 8. she, 9. her, 10. them

12. The committee invited Professor Basil and (he, him) to speak at the conference. ____________

13. Adam was certain it was not (they, them) who created the shortage. ____________

14. The intruder was taken to be (he, him)? ____________

15. When Jack opened the door, he expected to see you and (he, him). ____________

16. It must have been (they, them) who reported the missing funds. ____________

17. We hope to include Mrs. McGovern and (she, her) in our next series of interviews. ____________

18. If the caller is (he, him), please get his telephone number. ____________

19. The office staff expected the new manager to be (she, her). ____________

20. Are you certain it was (she, her) who called this morning? ____________

C. ***Review of Levels I and II.*** (Self-check) Some of the following sentences have errors in pronoun usage. For each sentence, underline the error and write a correct form in the space provided. If a sentence is correct as it stands, write *C* in the space. Then check your answers.

1. We have asked Mrs. Anderson and she to serve on the consumer panel. ____________

2. If the matter is kept just between you and him, no negative publicity should result. ____________

3. The basement of the house is satisfactory, but it's roof needs repair. ____________

4. There is no one else who can perform that function faster than him. ____________

5. Not all of we students agree with the action taken at the last meeting. ____________

6. Samples of our printing will be sent to Mr. Lowe and he as soon as we receive the special typeface. ____________

7. Two of our engineers, Dick and he, will be assigned to the project. ____________

8. It appears that everyone except Ramon and he will be reassigned. ____________

9. My partner and me will come right out to give an estimate on building the new addition. ____________

10. I am very concerned that Bill and her may have the wrong address. ____________

11. I don't believe that anyone could complete the entire task as well as he. ____________

C. 1. her, 2. C, 3. its, 4. he, 5. us, 6. him, 7. C, 8. him, 9. I, 10. she, 11. C, 12. us (workers), 13. C, 14. C, 15. C, 16. C, 17. she.

Name ______________________

12. A number of we workers on the night shift feel that we deserve additional benefits. ______________

13. Please send all inquiries to our Customer Relations Department or to me. ______________

14. A few employees, like Kevin and him, will take their vacations next week. ______________

15. Many of the proposals prepared by Mrs. Szabo and her were ultimately ratified. ______________

16. Next week all participants except you and him should be here at 6 p.m. ______________

17. We are trying to find a replacement who can keyboard as fast as her. ______________

D. ***Review of Levels I, II, and III.*** (Self-check) Select the correct pronoun.

1. The personnel director and (he, him) discussed job enrichment programs that would benefit our employees. ______________

2. If the task had been given to anyone but (she, her) to do, I would have less apprehension. ______________

3. Do you know (whose, who's) working on the final version of the Ramco proposal? ______________

4. A convincing sales talk was given by (she, her) when she met with their chief executive officer. ______________

5. One of our principal concerns about the motor is (it's, its) tendency to overheat. ______________

6. The wage discussions between Mr. O'Donnell and (they, them) appear to be progressing smoothly. ______________

7. I'm not sure whether this ruler is (yours, your's) or mine. ______________

8. We believe that no one is more familiar with the situation than (he, him). ______________

9. (We, Us) investors, of course, expect to make at least a minimal profit. ______________

10. No one could have been more surprised at the announcement than (we, us). ______________

11. Jensen assumed it was (they, them) who made the initial report. ______________

12. It's strange that Martin is sometimes taken to be (he, him). ______________

13. The insurance salespeople, Mr. Stalls and (her, she), made several appointments for evening interviews. ______________

D. 1. he, 2. her, 3. who's, 4. her, 5. its, 6. them, 7. yours, 8. he, 9. We, 10. we, 11. they, 12. he, 13. she, 14. me, 15. he

14. Everyone except the broker and (I, me) claimed a share of the commission. __________

15. The inventor credited with the idea was thought to be (he, him). __________

E. ***Optional Composition.*** Your instructor may ask you to complete this exercise on a separate sheet. Write sentences that illustrate pronouns with the following functions: subject of verb, object of verb, object of prepostion, and complement of subject. Label each pronoun and its function. In addition, write sentences using these words: *there, theirs, its, it's,* and *yours.*

POSTTEST

Underline the correct pronouns.

1. My friend and (I, me, myself) will be traveling together.
2. The questionnaires were addressed to (we, us) homeowners.
3. I'm convinced that no one will try harder than (she, her).
4. James said it was (they, them) who picked up the order today.
5. Just between you and (I, me), which is the better investment?

1. I, 2. us, 3. she, 4. they, 5. me

CHAPTER 7

Pronouns and Antecedents

OBJECTIVES When you have studied the materials in this chapter, you will be able to do the following:

Level I — *Make personal pronouns agree with their antecedents in number and gender.*
— *Understand the traditional use of common gender and be able to use its alternatives with sensitivity.*

Level II — *Make personal pronouns agree with subjects joined by* or *or* nor.
— *Make personal pronouns agree with indefinite pronouns, collective nouns, and organization names.*

Level III — *Understand the functions of* who *and* whom.
— *Follow a three-step plan in selecting* who *or* whom.

PRETEST

Underline the correct word.

1. Every one of the girls was surprised by (her, their) picture.
2. Before voting, the committee took a poll of (its, their) members.
3. Either of the departments may send (its, their) manager to the meeting.
4. (Who, Whom) would you recommend for the supervisory position?
5. Send the brochures to (whoever, whomever) requested them first.

LEVEL I

Fundamentals of Pronoun-Antecedent Agreement

The use of pronouns allows efficient and economical communication. Pronouns are ineffective, however, if the words to which they refer, their antecedents, are unclear. When pronouns

1. her, 2. its, 3. its, 4. whom, 5. whoever

substitute for nouns, the pronouns must agree with their antecedents in number (either singular or plural) and gender (either masculine, feminine, or neuter). Here are suggestions for using pronouns effectively.

Making Pronoun References Clear

Do not use a pronoun if your listener or reader might not be able to identify the noun it represents.

Unclear:	Robin told Lisa that *she* should verify the balance.
Clear:	Robin told Lisa to verify the balance.
Unclear:	In that theater *they* do not allow *you* to smoke.
Clear:	The theater management does not allow its patrons to smoke. *Or:* Smoking is not allowed in that theater.
Unclear:	Kevin's boss said that *he* deserved a raise.
Clear:	Kevin's boss said that Kevin deserved a raise.

Making Pronouns Agree With Their Antecedents in Number

Pronouns must agree in number with the nouns they represent. For example, if a pronoun replaces a singular noun, that pronoun must be singular.

Michelangelo felt that *he* was a failure. (Singular antecedent and pronoun.)

Great *artists* often doubt *their* success. (Plural antecedent and pronoun.)

If a pronoun refers to two nouns joined by *and*, the pronoun must be plural.

The *president* and the *stockholders* discussed *their* differences. (Plural antecedent and pronoun.)

Warren and *James* asked that suggestions be sent to *them*. (Plural antecedent and pronoun.)

Pronoun-antecedent agreement can be complicated when words or phrases come between the pronoun and the word to which it refers. Disregard phrases such as those introduced by *as well as, in addition to,* and *together with*. Find the true antecedent and make the pronoun agree with it.

The *general,* together with the chiefs of staff, is considering *his* strategy carefully. (Singular antecedent and pronoun.)

The *chiefs* of staff, along with the general, have submitted *their* plans. (Plural antecedent and pronoun.)

A female *member* of the group of protesting students demanded that *she* be treated equally. (Singular antecedent and pronoun.)

Making Pronouns Agree With Their Antecedents in Gender

Pronouns exhibit one of three genders: masculine (male), feminine (female), or neuter (neither masculine nor feminine):

John read *his* assignment. (Masculine gender.)
Nancy studied *her* notes. (Feminine gender.)
The idea had *its* limits. (Neuter gender.)

Concept of Common Gender. The English language has no all-purpose singular pronoun that can represent or refer to nouns of doubtful gender. For this reason over the years using masculine, or common-gender, pronouns to refer to nouns that may be either masculine or feminine had become an accepted practice. For example, in the sentence "A student has *his* rights," the pronoun *his* refers to the word *student,* which might name either a feminine or masculine person.

Today, however, sensitive writers and speakers have become increasingly uncomfortable about the use of common-gender pronouns and indeed about the use of all "sexist" pronouns. To automatically refer to a student of unknown gender, who may be either male or female, as *he* may be misleading or even offensive. Equally misleading, given the increasing number of male nurses, might be an automatic reference to a nurse as *she.* A sensitive writer may at times find it necessary to rewrite sentences in order to avoid misleading or common-gender pronouns. Here are some suggested alternatives:

Common gender: An employee has *his* job to do.
Alternative No. 1: Employees have *their* jobs to do.
Alternative No. 2: An employee has *a* job to do.
Alternative No. 3: An employee has *his* or *her* job to do.

In Alternative No. 1 the subject has been made plural to avoid the need for a singular common-gender pronoun. In Alternative No. 2 the pronoun is omitted, and an article is substituted for it, although at the cost of making the original meaning less emphatic. In Alternative No. 3 both masculine and feminine references (*his* or *her*) are used. Because the latter construction is wordy and clumsy, frequent use of it should be avoided.

Some language experts continue to defend the use of common-gender pronouns. They insist that common-gender pronouns have always referred to both men and women and that everyone using them has always been clear about their meaning. Sensitive writers alert to modern trends, however, generally avoid sexist language.

Exercise your own judgment about using or not using such pronouns. If possible, determine your reader's preference. Do not, however, attempt to solve the problem by using a plural pronoun to refer to a singular antecedent: *An employee has their job to do* is wrong.

Complete now the reinforcement exercises for Level I.

LEVEL II

Problems With Pronoun-Antecedent Agreement

Antecedents Joined by *or* or *nor*

When antecedents are joined by *or* or *nor,* the pronoun should agree with the antecedent closer to it.

Either Alice or *Vicki* left *her* coat in the office.
Neither the manager nor the *employees* objected to *their* salary cuts.

N.B. You may be wondering why antecedents joined by *and* are treated differently from antecedents joined by *or/nor.* The conjunction *and* joins one plus one to make two antecedents; hence a plural pronoun is used. The conjunctions *or/nor* require a choice between Antecedent No. 1 and Antecedent No. 2. Always match the pronoun to the closer antecedent.

Indefinite Pronouns as Antecedents

Pronouns such as *anyone, something,* or *anybody* are called indefinite because they refer to no specific person or object. Some indefinite pronouns are always singular; others are always plural.

Always singular		Always plural
anybody	everything	both
anyone	neither	few
anything	nobody	many
each	no one	several
either	nothing	
everybody	somebody	
everyone	someone	

When indefinite pronouns function as antecedents of pronouns, make certain that the pronoun agrees with its antecedent. Do not let prepositional phrases obscure the true antecedent.

Somebody in the men's league left *his* lights on.
Each of the corporations had *its* own home office.
Few of the vendors missed the show to demonstrate *their* equipment.
Several of our branches communicate *their* documents electronically.

The words *either* and *neither* can be confusing. When these words stand alone and function as pronoun subjects, they are always considered singular. When they are joined with *or* or *nor* to form conjunctions, however, they may connect plural subjects. These plural subjects, then, may act as antecedents to plural pronouns.

Has *either* of the women made *her* selection? (*Either* is a pronoun and functions as the subject of the sentence.)
Either the woman *or* her friends left *their* packages. (*Either/or* is used as a conjunction; *friends* is the pronoun antecedent.)

Collective Nouns as Antecedents

Words such as *jury, faculty, committee, union, team,* and *group* are called *collective* nouns because they refer to a collection of people, animals, or objects. Such words may be either singular or plural depending upon the mode of operation of the collection to which they refer. When a collective noun operates as a unit, it is singular. When the elements of a collective noun operate separately, the collective noun is plural.

Our *staff* reaffirmed *its* position on bargaining. (*Staff* operating as one unit.)

The management *team* of Rosen and Ross, Inc., is planning *its* strategy. (*Team* operating as one unit.)

The *jury* were divided in *their* opinions. (*Jury* operating as individuals.)

However, if a collective noun is to be used in a plural sense, it can often be made to sound less awkward by the addition of a plural noun, such as "the jury *members* were divided in their opinions."

Company and Organization Names as Antecedents

Company and organization names are generally considered singular. Unless the actions of the organization are attributed to individual representatives of that organization, pronouns referring to organizations should be singular.

Sears is having *its* biggest annual sale ever.

The United Nations, in addition to other organizations, is expanding *its* campaign to fight hunger.

Smith, Felker & Johnson, Inc., plans to move *its* corporate headquarters.

The Antecedents *each, every,* and *many a*

If the limiting adjectives *each, every,* or *many a* describe either noun or both nouns in a compound antecedent, that antecedent is considered singular.

Every player and coach on the men's team has *his* assigned duties.

Many a daughter and mother will receive *her* award at the banquet.

Complete the reinforcement exercises for Level II.

LEVEL III

Advanced Pronoun Uses

The Problem of *who* and *whom*

The use of *who* and *whom* presents a continuing dilemma for speakers and writers. In conversation the correct choice of *who* or *whom* is often especially difficult because of the mental gymnastics necessary in locating subjects and objects. In writing, however, an author has ample time to analyze a sentence carefully and make a correct choice — if the author understands the traditional functions of *who* and *whom*. *Who* is the nominative case form. Like other nominative case pronouns, *who* may function as the subject of a verb or as the subject complement of a noun following the linking verb. *Whom* is the objective case form. It may function as the object of a verb or as the object of a preposition.*

* Whom *may also function as the subject or object of an infinitive. Since little confusion results from these constructions, they will not be discussed.*

Who do you think will be chosen to direct the play? (*Who* is the subject of *will be chosen*.)

Jerry asked *who* your friend is. (*Who* is the complement of *friend*.)

Whom should we hire? (*Whom* is the object of *should hire*.)

She is the one to *whom* I spoke. (*Whom* is the object of *to*.)

How to Choose Between *who* or *whom*

The choice between *who* or *whom* becomes easier if the sentence in question is approached according to the following procedure:

1. Isolate the *who/whom* clause.
2. Invert the clause, if necessary, to restore normal subject-verb-object order.
3. Substitute the nominative pronoun *he* (*she* or *they*) for *who*. Substitute the objective pronoun *him* (*her* or *them*) for *whom*. If the sentence sounds correct with *him*, replace *him* with *whom*. If the sentence sounds correct with *he*, replace *he* with *who*.

Study the following sentences and notice how the choice of *who* or *whom* is made:

Here are the records of those (who/whom) we have selected.

Isolate:	________ we have selected
Invert:	we have selected ________
Substitute:	we have selected __him__
Equate:	we have selected __whom__
Complete:	Here are the records of those *whom* we have selected.

Do you know (who/whom) his doctor is?

Isolate:	________ his doctor is
Invert:	his doctor is ________ (*or* ________ is his doctor)
Substitute:	his doctor is __he__ (*or* __he__ is his doctor)
Equate:	his doctor is __who__ (*or* __who__ is his doctor)
Complete:	Do you know *who* his doctor is?

In choosing *who* or *whom,* ignore parenthetical expressions such as *I hope, we think, I believe,* and *you know*.

Edward is the candidate (who/whom) we believe is best.

Isolate:	________ we believe is best
Ignore:	________ [we believe] is best
Substitute:	__he__ is best
Equate:	__who__ is best
Complete:	Edward is the candidate who we believe is best.

Examples: *Whom* do you think we should call? (Invert: you do think we should call him/*whom*)

The person to *whom* the article referred was Mr. Stein. (Invert: the article referred to him/*whom*)

Do you know *who* the manager is? (Invert: the manager is he/*who*)

Whom would you like to see appointed to that position? (Invert: you would like to see him/*whom* appointed to that position)

The Use of *whoever* and *whomever*

Whoever, of course, is nominative and *whomever* is objective. The selection of the correct form is sometimes complicated when *whoever* or *whomever* appears in clauses. These clauses may act as objects of prepositions, objects of verbs, or subjects of verbs. Within the clauses, however, you must determine how *whoever* or *whomever* is functioning in order to choose the correct form. Study the following examples and explanations.

> Give the surplus to *whoever needs it*. (The clause *whoever needs it* is the object of the preposition *to*. Within the clause itself, *whoever* acts as the subject of *needs* and is therefore in the nominative case.)
>
> Special provision will be made for *whoever* meets the conditions. (The clause *whoever meets the conditions* is the object of the preposition *for*. Within the clause, *whoever* acts as the subject of *meets* and is therefore in the nominative case.)
>
> We will accept the name of *whomever they nominate*. (The clause *whomever they nominate* is the object of the preposition *of*. Within the clause, *whomever* is the object of *they nominate* and is therefore in the objective case.)

Complete the reinforcement exercises for Level III.

HOT LINE QUERIES

QUESTION: My friend insists that the combination *all right* is shown in her dictionary as one word. I say that it's two words. Who's right?

ANSWER: *All right* is the only acceptable spelling. The listing *alright* is shown in many dictionaries to guide readers to the acceptable spelling, *all right*. Do not use *alright*. By the way, some individuals can better remember that *all right* is two words by associating it with *all wrong*.

QUESTION: I don't seem to be able to hear the difference between *than* and *then*. Can you explain it to me?

ANSWER: The conjunction *than* is used to make comparisons (*your watch is more accurate than mine*). The adverb *then* means "at that time" (*we must complete this task; then we will take our break*), or "as a consequence" (*if all the angles of the triangle are equal, then it must be equilateral as well*).

QUESTION: What is the order of college degrees and which ones are capitalized?

ANSWER: Two kinds of undergraduate degrees are commonly awarded: the associate's degree, a two-year degree; and the bachelor's degree, a four-year degree. There are a variety of graduate degrees. The most frequently awarded are the master's degree and the doctorate. Merriam Webster dictionaries do not capitalize the names of degrees: associate of arts degree, bachelor of science, master of arts, doctor of philosophy. However, when used with an individual's name, the abbreviations for degrees are capitalized: Bruce Gourlay, M.A.; Cynthia L. Phillips, Ph.D.

QUESTION: Why does the sign above my grocery market's quick-check stand say *Ten or less items*? Shouldn't it read *Ten or fewer items*?

ANSWER: Right you are! *Fewer* refers to numbers, as in *fewer items. Less* refers to amounts or quantities, as in *less food.* Perhaps the markets prefer *less* because it has fewer letters.

QUESTION: If I have no interest in something, am I *disinterested*?

ANSWER: No. If you lack interest, you are *uninterested.* The word *disinterested* means "unbiased" or "impartial" (*the judge was disinterested in the cases before him*).

QUESTION: Everyone says "consensus of opinion." Yet, I understand that there is some objection to this expression.

ANSWER: Yes, the expression is widely used. However, since *consensus* means "collective opinion," the addition of the word *opinion* results in a redundancy.

QUESTION: I'm disgusted and infuriated at a New York University advertisement I just saw in our newspaper. It says, *It's not just who you know* . . . . Why would a leading institution of learning use such poor grammar?

ANSWER: Because it sounds familiar. But familiarity doesn't make it correct. You're right in recognizing that the proper form is *whom* (isolate the clause *you know him* or *whom*). The complete adage — or more appropriately, cliché — correctly stated is *It's not what you know but whom you know.*

Name ______________________

CHAPTER 7 **Reinforcement Exercises**

LEVEL I

A. (Self-check) Select the correct word(s) to complete the following sentences.

1. When a student completes the course, (his, her, his or her, their) grade is recorded immediately. ______
2. In addition to other family members, the winner was sent tickets for (his, her, his or her, their) personal use. ______
3. The visiting scientist and our resident engineer had (his, their) problems finding the control center. ______
4. No veterinarian assistant will be assigned to that task until (he is, he or she is, they are) trained. ______
5. One of the members of the boys' choir lost (his, their) robe. ______
6. After a contractor signs, (he is, he or she is, they are) responsible for fulfilling the terms of the contract. ______
7. One of the women asked how many sick days (she, they) had accumulated. ______
8. All flight attendants must have (her, their) uniforms cleaned regularly. ______
9. Mr. Simon, after consulting the production staff and others, made (his, their) pricing decision. ______
10. No employee must automatically retire when (he reaches, he or she reaches, they reach) the age of 65. ______

Check your answers.

B. Select the correct word(s) to complete the following sentences.

1. Workers in the four plants asked that (his, their) working conditions be improved. ______
2. An office manager, as well as the other members of management, must do (his, his or her, their) best to promote good employee relations. ______
3. A judge often feels that (he, he or she, they) should review the charges for the jury. ______

A. 1. his or her, 2. his or her, 3. their, 4. he or she is, 5. his, 6. he or she is, 7. she, 8. their, 9. his, 10. he or she reaches

4. Mrs. Alonzo and Miss Reese have given (her, their) approval. their
5. Lisa Lee, one of the clerks in the front office, asked that (her, their) vacation be changed. her
6. In that theater (you, customers) aren't allowed to smoke. Customers
7. Unless care is exercised, an employee might not get all the retirement benefits to which (he is, he or she is, they are) entitled. he/she
8. Mr. Tomkins and Mr. Ramos were not eager to have (his, their) complaints discussed in public. their
9. If the insured party causes an accident, (he, he or she, they) will be charged an additional fee in future premiums. he/she
10. The personnel manager advised each candidate of (his, his or her, their) opportunities for advancement within the organization. his/her

C. Rewrite the following sentences to avoid the use of common-gender pronouns. Show three versions of each sentence.

1. A homeowner must have *his* home inspected before selling it.
   a. ______
   b. ______
   c. ______
2. Be sure that each new employee has received *his* orientation packet.
   a. ______
   b. ______
   c. ______

D. Rewrite these sentences to make the pronoun references clear.

1. The article reported that Comcard had acquired Datacard and that it had sold its foreign subsidiaries. ______
2. They make you wear shoes and shirts in that restaurant. ______
3. Because Mr. Redman was replaced by Mr. Carlos, his parking space was changed. ______
4. Speer was Hitler's companion until the final days of the war when he turned against him. ______

Name ______________________

LEVEL II

A. (Self-check) Select the correct word to complete the following sentences, and write it in the space provided.

1. It looks as if somebody left (his, her, his or her, their) lights on. ______
2. We cannot believe that either the memorandum or the letters had (its, their) contents proofread. ______
3. Gold, Steinmetz & Burns, Inc., held an open house in honor of (its, their) anniversary. ______
4. Someone on the girls' team lost one of (her, their) shoes. ______
5. Each man, woman, and child in the club made (his, her, his or her, their) own contribution to the paper drive. ______
6. Either Mrs. Wall or Mrs. Snyder will offer (her, their) home for the meeting. ______
7. Nobody in the boisterous crowd could hear (his, her, his or her, their) name when called. ______
8. The President has asked for budget cuts, and Congress has indicated (its, their) willingness to legislate some of them. ______
9. Neither of the men had signed (his, their) salary warrant. ______
10. The Small Business Administration has (its, their) own offices to aid business executives. ______

Check your answers.

B. For each sentence below, select the appropriate pronoun and write it in the space provided.

1. Every worker and supervisor was notified when (his, her, his or her, their) yearly physical examination was due. ______
2. Dun and Bradstreet bases (their, its) financial ratings on business accounting reports. ______
3. As directed, the committee submitted (its, their) annual report. ______
4. Not one of the creditors would allow (his, her, his or her, their) claims to be decreased. ______
5. Did someone say that (his, her, his or her, their) test copy was illegible? ______

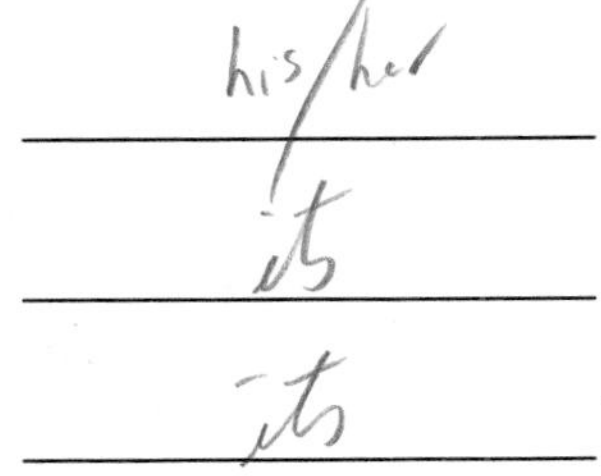

A. 1. his or her, 2. their, 3. its, 4. her, 5. his or her, 6. her, 7. his or her, 8. its, 9. his, 10. its

6. The Interstate Commerce Commission has had (its, their) jurisdiction broadened over the years. its
7. Every one of the drawers had (its, their) contents dumped. its
8. Most certainly the inspection team will have (its, their) decision on your desk Monday. its
9. Neither the glamour nor the excitement of the job had lost (its, their) appeal. its
10. Any new subscriber may cancel (his, her, his or her, their) subscription within the first ten days. his/her
11. The union members elected (its, their) officers by mailed ballot. their
12. Has everybody in the girls' team had (her, their) picture taken? her
13. Either of the companies may move (its, their) headquarters to Irvine. its
14. Every renter and homeowner should exercise (his, her, his or her, their) right to vote. his/her
15. If anyone needs assistance, Mr. Torres will help (him, her, him or her, them). him/her
16. Our staff agreed that (its, their) stand must be unified. its
17. *Better Homes and Gardens* announced a plan to change (their, its) method of marketing. its
18. Each of the supermarkets featured (its, their) advertisements on Thursday. its
19. Every one of the girls was pleased with (her, their) internship program. her
20. Neither the father nor his sons wanted (his, their) stocks to be sold. their

C. Revise the following sentences to avoid the use of common-gender pronouns. Show three versions of each sentence. Use your imagination.

1. Somebody left his lights on in the parking lot.

   a. ______________________

   b. ______________________

   c. ______________________

2. Has anyone picked up his tickets yet?

   a. ______________________

   b. ______________________

   c. ______________________

Name ______________________

LEVEL III

A. (Self-check) Select the correct word and write it in the space provided.

1. I know perfectly well (who, whom) you are. ______
2. Did you meet Juan, (who, whom) seems to be very interested in the job? ______
3. The contract will be awarded to (whoever, whomever) submits the lowest bid. ______
4. (Who, Whom) do you think we should interview for the newsletter? ______
5. She is the investment counselor of (who, whom) I spoke. ______
6. When I return the call, for (who, whom) should I ask? ______
7. (Who, Whom) did you say would drop by? ______
8. Will you recommend an attorney (who, whom) can handle this case? ______
9. To (who, whom) were these messages sent? ______
10. Give the job to (whoever, whomever) they select. ______

Check your answers.

B. Select the correct word and write it in the space provided.

1. Do you know (who, whom) the telephone caller is? who
2. He is a salesman (who, whom) we believe represents his company well. who
3. The position will be filled by (whoever, whomever) the manager hires. whomever
4. Mr. Brooks said that Mrs. Harris, (who, whom) starts next Monday, is an excellent accountant. who
5. (Who, Whom) have you asked to head the advertising campaign? whom
6. For (who, whom) does the bell toll? whom
7. I have a pizza for (whoever, whomever) placed the telephone order. whoever
8. The economics expert to (who, whom) the professor referred was Milton Friedman. whom

A. 1. who, 2. who, 3. whoever, 4. Whom, 5. whom, 6. whom, 7. Who, 8. who, 9. whom, 10. whomever

9. Mr. Stewart is the one (who, whom) we think should be made supervisor. ____________

10. Evans is the player against (who, whom) offensive interference was called. ____________

11. You'll never guess (who, whom) we saw in town. ____________

12. Do you know (who, whom) will be taking your place? ____________

13. Dr. Song will see (whoever, whomever) is next in line. ____________

14. I wonder (who, whom) the speaker is talking about. ____________

15. In making introductions, who should be introduced to (who, whom)? ____________

16. Mrs. Silver asked us (who, whom) we think should train Kelly. ____________

17. Please direct my inquiry to (whoever, whomever) is in charge of quality control. ____________

18. Tom Garcia is the graduate (who, whom) applied first. ____________

19. (Who, Whom) shall I say is calling? ____________

20. (Who, Whom) would you like to work with? ____________

21. Mr. Rodman, (who, whom) we thought should be appointed, was not among the final candidates. ____________

22. For (who, whom) is this book being ordered? ____________

23. Please send us the name of (whoever, whomever) you suggest for the opening. ____________

C. ***Optional Composition.*** Your instructor may ask you to complete this exercise on a separate sheet. Write sentences with the following words that function as subjects: *either, everyone, many, somebody, staff, committee,* and *McDonald's*. In each of the preceding sentences, the verb should be either *is* or *are*. You may add phrases for clarity, such as *Either of the two choices* . . . . In addition, write sentences showing *who* as the subject of a verb, *whom* as the object of a preposition, and *whoever* as the subject of a clause. Label each sentence.

POSTTEST

Underline the correct word.

1. Did anyone on the boys' team leave (his, their) shoes in the gym?
2. The entire faculty sent (its, their) support to the president.
3. Neither of the companies could identify (its, their) equipment.
4. (Who, Whom) would you like to see as the next department manager?
5. Give the prize to (whoever, whomever) earned the most points.

1. his, 2. its, 3. its, 4. Whom, 5. whoever

Name ______________________

UNIT 2 REVIEW **Chapters 4–7 (Self-Check)**

Begin your review by rereading Chapters 4 through 7. Then test your comprehension of those chapters by filling in the blanks in the exercises that follow. Compare your responses with those provided at the end of this review.

LEVEL I

1. I understand that the (a) Ramirezes, (b) Ramirez, (c) Ramirez's are opening a copy service on Fifth Street in Costa Mesa. ______
2. Every political campaign is filled with wordy (a) speechs, (b) speeches. ______
3. From the present group of four (a) foreman (b) foremen, (c) foremans, one will be promoted to supervisor. ______
4. After just two (a) years, (b) year's, (c) years' time, you may expect to earn a 25 percent return. ______
5. We are giving careful consideration to that (a) company's, (b) companies' (c) companys' stock. ______
6. Many of our (a) students', (b) students, (c) student's have difficulty with possessive constructions. ______
7. The committee completed (a) it's, (b) its work last week. ______
8. Just between you and (a) me, (b) I, what do you think? ______
9. All employees except Paul and (a) he, (b) him agreed to the reorganization. ______
10. Ask both of the designers when (a) she, (b) he, (c) he or she, (d) they can give us estimates. ______
11. When a customer makes a complaint, (a) he, (b) she, (c) he or she, (d) they must be treated courteously. ______

LEVEL II

12. The defendant hired two (a) attorneys, (b) attornies, (c) attornies', (d) attorneys' to represent him. ______
13. Mrs. Hale consulted her three (a) sister-in-laws, (b) sister-in-law's, (c) sisters-in-law before making her decision. ______
14. The (a) pro's and con's, (b) pros and cons of merging the two departments were discussed heatedly. ______
15. (a) Steve and Leslie's, (b) Steve's and Leslie's new home is located in Agoura Highlands. ______
16. I certainly hope that today's weather is better than (a) yesterdays. (b) yesterday's. ______

17. Brad hoped to find a job in the (a) electronics, (b) electronic's, (c) electronics' industry.

18. Insincerity irritates Mr. Sanchez as much as (a) I, (b) me.

19. The chairman and (a) I, (b) me, (c) myself will answer all questions.

20. Neither the mother nor her children wanted (a) her, (b) their savings accounts to be changed.

21. Every clerk and every secretary elected to exercise (a) his, (b) her, (c) his or her, (d) their voting rights.

22. Marsten, Davis, and Jackson, Inc., plans to move (a) it's, (b) its, (c) their offices to a new location.

LEVEL III

23. Following several financial (a) crisis, (b) crises, (c) crisises, the corporation was forced to declare bankruptcy.

24. Because of its excellent work, thanks (a) is, (b) are in order for our organizing committee.

25. We read an announcement that the (a) Harris', (b) Harris's, (c) Harrises, (d) Harrises' son won a scholarship.

26. I'm certain that my (a) bosses, (b) boss's, (c) bosses' signature will be forthcoming.

27. The IRS is checking Mr. (a) Gross's, (b) Gross', (c) Grosses' return.

28. The employee credited with the suggestion was thought to be (a) he, (b) him.

29. If I were (a) her, (b) she, I would decline the offer.

30. To (a) who, (b) whom did you send your application?

31. (a) Who, (b) Whom has been asked to head the commission?

32. Give the extra supplies to (a) whoever, (b) whomever needs them.

33. (a) Who, (b) Whom would you prefer to see in that job?

34. You'll never guess (a) who, (b) whom I saw today.

35. It could have been (a) her, (b) she who called you.

Hot Line Review

36. Professor Breuer said it was (a) to, (b) too early to sign up for these classes.

37. Check your (a) owner's, (b) owners' warranty carefully.

38. Daily exercise is recommended because it is (a) healthful, (b) healthy.

39. (a) Less, (b) Fewer people came to the event than were expected.

40. If it's (a) alright, (b) all right, (c) allright with you, I'll call the technician.

---

1. a, 2. b, 3. b, 4. c, 5. a, 6. b, 7. b, 8. a, 9. b, 10. d, 11. c, 12. a, 13. c, 14. b, 15. a, 16. b, 17. a, 18. b, 19. a, 20. b, 21. c, 22. b, 23. b, 24. b, 25. d, 26. b, 27. a or b, 28. a, 29. b, 30. b, 31. a, 32. a, 33. b, 34. b, 35. b, 36. b, 37. a, 38. a, 39. b, 40. b

UNIT THREE

Showing the Action

CHAPTER 8

Verbs: Kinds, Voices, Moods

OBJECTIVES When you have completed the materials in this chapter, you will be able to do the following:

Level I — *Distinguish between transitive and intransitive verbs.*
— *Identify at least ten linking verbs.*

Level II — *Recognize active and passive voice verbs.*
— *Convert sentences written in the passive voice to sentences in the active voice.*

Level III — *Recognize sentence constructions requiring the subjunctive verb mood.*
— *Create sentences using the subjunctive mood correctly.*

PRETEST

Underline the appropriate answers.

1. In the sentence *Maria listened to the instructions,* the verb *listened* is (a) transitive, (b) intransitive, (c) linking.
2. In the sentence *Written instructions were provided,* the verb phrase *were provided* is in the (a) active voice, (b) passive voice, (c) subjunctive mood, (d) intransitive mood.
3. In the sentence *Barbara Benesch taught the class,* the verb *taught* is in the (a) active voice, (b) passive voice, (c) subjunctive mood, (d) intransitive mood.
4. Jackie acts as if she (a) was, (b) were the professor.
5. Della Jones moved that a vote (a) is, (b) be taken.

A verb is a word that expresses action or a state of being. In relation to subjects, verbs tell what the subject is doing or what is being done to the subject. They may also link to the subject words that describe the subject or identify it.

The verb is the most complex part of speech. A complete treatment of its forms and uses would require at least a volume. Our discussion of verbs will be limited to four chapters.

---

1. b, 2. b, 3. a, 4. b, 5. b

In our discussion of sentences in Chapter 3, you became familiar with three basic sentence patterns: subject-verb, subject–active verb–object, and subject–linking verb–complement. Sentence patterns are determined by their verbs. You have already learned to identify active and linking verbs. Let's now consider how these verbs actually function.

First we'll deal with active verbs. They express their action either transitively or intransitively. When active verbs are transitive, they may create subject–active verb–object sentence patterns. When active verbs are intransitive, they may create subject-verb sentence patterns.

LEVEL I

Kinds of Verbs

Transitive Verbs

A verb expressing an action directed toward a person or thing is said to be transitive. An action verb used transitively needs, in addition to its subject, a noun or pronoun to complete its meaning. This noun or pronoun functions as the direct object of the transitive verb. Notice in the following sentences that the verbs direct action toward objects.

The directors demanded improved profits.
Yesterday the president called him.
We sold the stock at a profit.

Objects usually answer the questions *what?* or *whom?* In the first example, the directors demanded *what?* The object is *profits.* In the second example, the president called *whom?* The object is *him.*

Intransitive Verbs

An action verb that does not require an object to complete its action is said to be intransitive.

Ralph typed in the personnel office last summer.
Business grows rapidly at this time of the year.
Tanya listened carefully to the directions.

Notice that the verbs in these sentences do not express actions directed toward persons or things. Prepositional phrases (*in the personnel office, at this time, of the year, to the directions*) and adverbs (*rapidly, carefully*) do not receive the action expressed by the verbs. Therefore, prepositional phrases and adverbs do not function as objects of verbs.

Linking Verbs

You will recall that linking verbs *link* to the subject words that rename or describe the subject. A noun, pronoun, or adjective that renames or describes the subject is called a *complement* because it *completes* the meaning of the subject.

Angie is the manager. (*Manager* is a noun complement that completes the meaning of the sentence by renaming *Angie*.)

Her salary is excellent. (*Excellent* is an adjective complement that completes the meaning of *salary*.)

The caller was he. (*He* is a pronoun complement that completes the meaning of *caller*.)

Notice in the preceding sentences that the noun, pronoun, or adjective complements following these linking verbs do not receive action from the verb; instead, the complements *complete* the meaning of the subject.

You are already familiar with those linking verbs that are derived from the *to be* verb form: *am, is, are, was, were, be, being, been*. Other words that often serve as linking verbs are *feels, appears, tastes, seems, sounds, looks,* and *smells*. Notice that many of these words describe sense experience.

> N.B. Here's a mnemonic (memory) device to help you remember the verbs of the senses. Call them the FATS verbs, an acronym (word formed of initials) made from the first letters of *feel, appear, taste,* and *seem*.

Verbs expressing sense experience may be followed by complements just as the *to be* linking verbs often are.

They feel bad about the sale of the company. (*Bad* is an adjective complement following the linking verb *feel*. An adjective — not the adverb *badly* — is needed here to describe the senses.)

Settlement of the strike appears imminent. (*Imminent* is an adjective complement following the linking verb *appears*.)

The use of adjectives following such verbs will be discussed more completely in Chapter 12.

The function of a verb in a sentence determines its classification. The verb *typed*, for example, is intransitive when it has no object (*Ralph typed*). The same verb is transitive when an object follows (*Ralph typed a letter*). The verb *felt* is linking when it is used to connect a complement describing the subject (*Maria felt marvelous*). The same verb is transitive when it directs action to an object (*Maria felt the wet desk*). To distinguish between classifications, study carefully the constructions in which the verbs appear.

To review briefly:

1. Action Verbs — two kinds:
   a. Transitive: need objects to complete their meaning
   b. Intransitive: do not need objects to complete their meaning
2. Linking Verbs: form a link to words that rename or describe the subject

Complete the reinforcement exercises for Level I.

LEVEL II

Verb Voices

A verb expressing an action directed toward a person or thing is said to be transitive. Transitive verbs fall into two categories depending upon the receiver of the action of the verbs.

Active Voice

When the verb expresses an action directed by the subject toward the object of the verb, the verb is said to be in the *active* voice.

Alison answered the telephone. (Action directed to the object, *telephone.*)

Verbs in the active voice are direct and forceful; they clearly identify the doer of the action. For these reasons, writing that frequently uses the active voice is vigorous and effective. Writers of business communications strive to use the active voice; in fact, it is called the *voice of business*.

Passive Voice

When the action of the verb is directed toward the subject, the verb is said to be in the *passive* voice. Compare the two groups of sentences shown below:

Active voice	Passive voice
We use computers daily.	Computers are used daily.
Mr. Chavez is selling the machines.	The machines are being sold by Mr. Chavez.
The accountant made three errors in the report.	Three errors were made in the report.

Because the passive voice can be used to avoid mentioning the performer of the action, the passive voice is sometimes called the *voice of tact*. Notice how much more tactful the passive version of the last example shown above is. Although directness in business writing is generally preferable, in certain instances the passive voice is used when indirectness is desired.

N.B. In the passive voice, verbs always require a *helper,* such as *is, are, was, were, being,* or *been.* For example, *Repairs* were *made by the manufacturer.*

Complete the reinforcement exercises for Level II.

LEVEL III

Verb Moods

Three verb moods are available to enable a speaker or writer to express an attitude toward a subject: (1) the indicative mood is used to express a fact; (2) the imperative mood is used to express a command; (3) the subjunctive mood is used to express a doubt, a conjecture, or a suggestion. The subjunctive mood usually causes speakers and writers difficulty and therefore demands special attention.

Subjunctive Mood

Although the subjunctive mood is seldom used today, it is, however, still employed by careful individuals in the following constructions.

1. ***If and wish clauses.*** When a statement that is doubtful or contrary to fact is introduced by *if, as if,* or *wish,* the subjunctive form *were* is substituted for the indicative form *was.*

If Lori *were* here, we could proceed. (Lori is *not* here.)

She acts as if she *were* the boss. (She is *not* the boss.)

George wishes he *were* able to type. (George is *not* able to type.)

But if the statement could possibly be true, use the indicative form.

If Chris *was* in the audience, I missed him. (Chris might have been in the audience.)

2. ***That clauses.*** When a *that* clause follows a verb expressing a command, recommendation, request, suggestion, or requirement, the subjunctive verb form *be* is used.

The doctor recommended that everyone *be* inoculated.

Our manager ordered that all reports *be* proofread twice.

3. ***Motions.*** When a motion is stated, a subjunctive verb form should be used in the *that* clause in the sentence.

Gary moved that a vote *be* taken.

It has been seconded that the meeting *be* adjourned.

Caution: In a sentence without *that* clauses, do not mix subjunctive and indicative verbs.

Right:	If she *were skilled,* she *would receive* job offers. (Both verbs subjunctive.)
Right:	If she *is skilled,* she *will receive* job offers. (Both verbs indicative.)
Wrong:	If she *were skilled,* she *will receive* job offers. (One subjunctive verb and one indicative verb.)

N.B. Although the frequency of use of the subjunctive mood is declining, one should be well aware that no educated person today would say, *If I* was *you* . . . . It is a sign of your education, good or bad, to use the subjunctive correctly or incorrectly.

Complete the reinforcement exercises for Level III.

HOT LINE QUERIES

QUESTION: Which is better: *The truck carried canisters of highly flammable or inflammable liquid?*

ANSWER: Actually, both *flammable* and *inflammable* mean "easily set on fire." Either would be correct in your sentence. However, *flammable* is preferred because its meaning is less likely to be confused. Since the prefix *in* often means "not," the word *inflammable* could be misunderstood. Therefore, use *flammable* in technical matters, particularly if you wish to suggest a warning. You may use *inflammable* or its derivatives for nontechnical descriptions, such as *Her words were inflammatory.*

QUESTION: I have a sentence that begins *Beside(s) providing financial aid. . . .* Is there any real difference between *beside* and *besides?*

ANSWER: Yes, indeed! *Beside* is a preposition meaning "by the side of" (*come sit beside me*). *Besides* is an adverb meaning "in addition to" (*besides paper we must order ribbons*). In your sentence use *besides.*

QUESTION: I have looked and looked, but I cannot find this word in a dictionary. I'll pronounce it phonetically for you: *per-rog-a-tive.* I know it exists. What am I doing wrong?

ANSWER: You, like many other people, are mispronouncing it. The word is *pre-rog-a-tive,* meaning "a right or privilege" (*it is your prerogative to join a union*).

QUESTION: I received a magazine advertisement recently that promised me a *free gift* and a *15 percent off discount* if I subscribed. What's wrong with this wording?

ANSWER: You've got a double winner here in the category of redundancies. The word *gift* suggests *free;* therefore, to say *free gift* is like saying *I'm studying English English.* It would be better to say *special gift.* In the same way, *15 percent off discount* repeats itself. Omit *off.*

QUESTION: When do you use *may* and when do you use *can?*

ANSWER: Traditionally, the verb *may* is used in asking or granting permission (*yes, you may use that desk*). *Can* is used to suggest ability (*you can succeed in business*). In informal writing, however, authorities today generally agree that *can* may be substituted for *may.*

QUESTION: I just checked the dictionary and found that *cooperate* is now written as one word. It seems to me that years ago it was *co-operate* or *coöperate.* Has the spelling changed?

ANSWER: Yes, it has. And so has the spelling of many other words. As new words become more familiar, their spelling tends to become more simplified. For example, *per cent* and *good will* are now shown by most dictionaries as *percent* and *goodwill.* By the same token, many words formerly hyphenated are now written without hyphens: *strike-over* is now *strikeover, to-day* is *today, editor-in-chief* is *editor in chief, vice-president* is *vice president,* and *passer-by* is now *passerby.* Current dictionaries reflect these changes.

QUESTION: On my computer I'm using a program that checks the writer's style. My problem is that it flags every passive voice verb and tells me to consider using active voice verbs. Are passive voice verbs totally forbidden in business writing?

ANSWER: Of course not! Computer stylecheckers capitalize on language areas that can be detected mechanically, and a passive voice verb is easily identified by a computer. Although active voice verbs are considered more forceful, passive voice verbs have a genuine function in business writing. Because they hide the subject and diffuse attention, passive verbs are useful in sensitive messages where indirect language can develop an impersonal, inconspicuous tone. For example, when a lower-level employee must write a persuasive and somewhat negative message to a manager, passive voice verbs are quite useful.

QUESTION: What's the correct verb in this sentence? *Tim recognized that, if his company (was or were) to prosper, it would require considerable capital.*

ANSWER: The verb should be *were* because the clause in which it functions is not true. Statements contrary to fact that are introduced by words like *if* and *wish* require subjunctive mood verbs.

Name ______________________

CHAPTER 8 **Reinforcement Exercises**

LEVEL I

A. (Self-check) In the spaces provided indicate whether the italicized verbs are transitive (*T*), intransitive (*I*), or linking (*L*).

EXAMPLE: Elvira *is* the supervisor in that department. L

1. Despite medication, Ann *feels* worse. ____
2. The United States *exports* products to numerous foreign countries. ____
3. After dinner the delegates *returned* to their rooms. ____
4. Mr. Rose *is* the one on whom we all depend. ____
5. Mary *expects* Mr. Partington to return to the office soon. ____
6. It *was* he who devised the current work schedule. ____
7. The production manager *called* over four hours ago. ____
8. Shari *feels* certain that the calendar date is clear. ____
9. Well-written business letters *get* results. ____
10. We *sent* a replacement order to you as soon as we received your letter. ____

Check your answers.

B. Each of the following sentences contains a verb that is either transitive or intransitive. If the verb is intransitive, underline it and write *I* in the space provided. If the verb is transitive, underline it, write *T* in the space provided, and also write its direct object.

EXAMPLES: After his presentation the salesman left. I
Workers brought their lunches. T (lunches)

1. Insurance agents certify claims. ____
2. Traffic stopped. ____
3. We considered solar energy. ____
4. Our suppliers raised their prices. ____
5. Storm clouds gathered. ____
6. Over the years our assets increased. ____
7. Mr. Bateson often wrote business letters. ____
8. The telephone rang. ____
9. Gregory answered it. ____
10. Secretaries use their dictionaries. ____

A. 1. L, 2. T, 3. I, 4. L, 5. T, 6. L, 7. I, 8. L, 9. T, 10. T

Linking verbs are followed by complements that identify, rename, or describe the subjects. The most common linking verbs are the forms of *be* (*am, is, are, was,* etc.) and the verbs of the senses (*feels, appears, tastes, smells,* etc.) The following sentences all contain linking verbs. For each sentence underline the linking verb or verb phrase and write its complement in the space provided.

EXAMPLES: Joanna feels good about her project. good
Our current director is Ms. Abzug. Ms. Abzug

11. Most employees are satisfied.
12. The budget report is very long.
13. The flowers on her desk smell fragrant.
14. Over the telephone his voice sounds resonant.
15. It was she who called you earlier.
16. Mr. Flores was the committee representative last year.
17. This sweater feels warm and comfortable today.
18. The manager of that department might be Mr. Dorsey.
19. That table will be fine.
20. It seems unusually cold in here today.

C. In the following sentences selected verbs have been italicized. For each sentence indicate whether the italicized verb is transitive (*T*), intransitive (*I*), or linking (*L*). In addition, if the verb is transitive, write its object. If the verb is linking, write its complement.

EXAMPLES: The new employee *is* Janet Oso. L (Janet Oso)
Our computer *prints* the mailing list. T (list)

1. My top assistant on the project *is* Margaret McHenry.
2. Traffic *moves* from the suburbs along three major arteries.
3. General Motors *offered* a warranty on certain engine parts.
4. It *is* he who is responsible for processing all equipment requests.
5. Please *lay* the keys on the desk when you finish with them.
6. Her report *appears* accurate, but some data must be verified.
7. Mitchell *feels* marvelous about his recent promotion.
8. Producers *move* goods to market to meet seasonal demands.
9. It *must have been* they who made the anonymous gift.
10. The economy *appears* bright after the recent drop in interest rates.
11. Mr. Borman *is* the person whom you should call.
12. Despite vigorous consumer protests, the government *ended* the service.
13. Please *raise* the window before you leave.
14. Your report *is lying* over there.
15. All of us *feel* bad about her transfer.

Name ____________________

LEVEL II

A. (Self-check) Transitive verbs in the following sentences have been italicized. For each sentence write *active* or *passive* to indicate the voice of the italicized verb.

EXAMPLE: Two important omissions in the report *were found* by the committee. passive

1. Letters *were filed* at the end of the day by the file clerks. ____
2. The copy machine *produces* sharp, clean copies when it is operating properly. ____
3. Shorthand and transcription skills *were required* by some companies advertising for secretaries. ____
4. Other companies *required* only typing skills. ____
5. Our insurance company *is* now *offering* a new method of premium payment on life insurance. ____
6. The new plan *was devised* to make premium payment completely automatic. ____
7. Jennifer *sent* E-mail messages to all employees. ____
8. E-mail messages *were sent* to all employees. ____
9. Funds for the youth campaign *were collected* from private donors. ____
10. Private donors *made* contributions to the campaign because they believed in the worth of the project. ____

Check your answers.

B. In the spaces provided, write *active* or *passive* to indicate the voice of the italicized verbs in the following sentences.

1. Ms. Davis *prepared* the certified check. ____
2. The certified check *was prepared* by Ms. Davis. ____
3. Word processing and data processing functions *are being combined* in many companies. ____
4. You *withdrew* the funds in question on May 29. ____
5. From his gross income, Harrison *deducts* medical expenses and contributions. ____
6. Jim Perez *was told* to visit the personnel department. ____
7. Contract arbitration *will be conducted* by the union and the manufacturer. ____

A. 1. passive, 2. active, 3. passive, 4. active, 5. active, 6. passive, 7. active, 8. passive, 9. passive, 10. active

C. Careful writers strive to use the active voice in business communications. This is an important skill for you to develop. To give you practice in developing this skill, rewrite the following sentences changing their passive voice verbs to active voice. Normally you can change a verb from passive to active voice by making the doer of the action — usually contained in a *by* phrase — the subject of the sentence.

EXAMPLE: *Passive:* Production costs must be reduced by *manufacturers.*
Active: Manufacturers must reduce production costs.

1. Pollution was greatly reduced by General Motors when the company built its new plant. (Hint: *Who* greatly reduced pollution? Start your sentence with that name.) ________
____
____

2. Funds for the multipurpose shopping complex were contributed by federal, state, and private groups. ____
____
____

3. Massive short-term financing is used by Nike to pay off its production costs during its slow season. ____
____
____

D. Some sentences with passive-voice verbs do not identify the doer of the action. Before these sentences can be converted, a subject must be provided.

EXAMPLE: *Passive:* New subscribers will be offered a bonus. (By whom?—by *Time, Inc.*)
Active: Time, Inc., will offer new subscribers a bonus.

In each of the following sentences, first answer the question *By whom?* Then rewrite the sentence, beginning with your answer as the subject.

1. Our office was recently reorganized to increase efficiency and production. (By whom?)
____
____

2. Net income before taxes must be calculated carefully when you fill out your tax return. (By whom?) ____
____
____

3. Only a few of the many errors and changes were detected during the first proofreading. (By whom?) ____
____

Name ______________________

LEVEL III

A. (Self-check) Select the correct word and write it in the space provided.

1. If Mr. Cortez (was, were) our manager, he would not have approved these work rules. ______
2. Do we have a motion that the meeting (is, be) adjourned? ______
3. If I (was, were) you, I'd get a new alarm clock. ______
4. Did your instructor suggest that you (be, are) excused from class? ______
5. If Mr. McHenry (was, were) at the opening session, he did not announce himself. ______
6. His supervisor suggested that everyone (is, be) informed of the availability of the training seminar. ______
7. If you were in my place, I'm sure you (will, would) agree. ______
8. Mrs. Woodruff recommended that additional chairs (are, be) set up for the afternoon session. ______
9. He acts as if he (was, were) the only employee who had to work overtime. ______
10. It is extremely important that all applications (are, be) completed by the 15th of the month. ______

Check your answers.

B. Underscore the verbs that are incorrectly used in the following sentences. Write the correct forms in the spaces provided. Mark *C* if correct.

1. Mr. Harris wished that Vicki was happier about her work. ______
2. I move that Natalie is appointed acting secretary for the remainder of this year. ______
3. President Atkins asked that all salaried workers be made eligible for health care benefits. ______
4. If a better employee benefit program was available, recruiting would be easier. ______
5. A stockholder moved that dividends are declared immediately. ______
6. If he were in my place, he will be more understanding. ______
7. I wish the telephone was working so that I could make my call. ______
8. Miss McGinley suggested that antiglare shields are installed. ______

A. 1. were, 2. be, 3. were, 4. be, 5. was, 6. be, 7. would, 8. be, 9. were, 10. be

9. Michael said he wished that you were able to accompany him. ______________

10. If Carlos were in the office that day, I did not see him. ______________

C. ***Optional Composition.*** Your instructor may ask you to complete this exercise on a separate sheet. Write sentences that illustrate the following: a transitive verb, an intransitive verb, a linking verb, an active voice verb, a passive voice verb, and a verb in the subjunctive mood. Label each sentence.

POSTTEST

Underline the appropriate answers. Compare your answers with those at the bottom of the page.

1. In the sentence *Billie Scott wrote the memo,* the verb *wrote* is (a) transitive, (b) intransitive, (c) subjunctive, (d) passive.
2. In the sentence *Lucy Williams hired four employees,* the verb *hired* is in the (a) active voice, (b) passive voice, (c) subjunctive mood, (3) intransitive mood.
3. In the sentence *Ken Clouse was given the award,* the verb phrase *was given* is in the (a) active voice, (b) passive voice, (c) subjunctive mood, (3) intransitive mood.
4. If Clara Smith (a) was, (b) were the instructor, the class would be full.
5. Professor St. Clair recommended that students (a) be, (b) are admitted free.

---

1. a, 2. a, 3. b, 4. b, 5. a

CHAPTER 9

Verb Tenses and Parts

OBJECTIVES When you have completed the materials in this chapter, you will be able to do the following:

Level I — *Write verbs in the present, past, and future tenses correctly.*
— *Use the emphatic tense correctly.*

Level II — *Recognize and use present and past participles.*
— *Write the correct forms of sixty irregular verbs.*

Level III — *Supply correct verb forms in the progressive and perfect tenses.*

PRETEST

Underline the correct verb.

1. Anthony and she (came, come) over last night to use my computer.
2. After they had (gone, went), I was able to do my own homework.
3. When last seen, the papers were (laying, lying) near the desk.
4. The value of our stock has been steadily (raising, rising) all day.
5. The condominium project has (set, sat) there untouched for a year.

English verbs change form (inflection) to indicate number (singular or plural), person (first, second, or third), voice (active or passive), and tense (time). In contrast to French and German, English verbs are today no longer heavily inflected; that is, our verbs do not change form extensively to indicate number or person.

To indicate precise time, however, English employs four rather complex sets of tenses: primary tenses, emphatic tenses, perfect tenses, and progressive tenses. Level I will focus on the primary and emphatic tenses. Level II will consider participles and irregular verbs. Level III will treat the perfect and progressive tenses.

---

1. came, 2. gone, 3. lying, 4. rising, 5. sat

Primary Tenses

Present Tense

Verbs in the present tense express current or habitual action. Present tense verbs may also be used in constructions showing future action.

We *order* office supplies every month. (Current or habitual action.)

He *flies* to Washington tomorrow. (Future action.)

Past Tense

Verbs in the past tense show action that has been completed. Regular verbs form the past tense with the addition of *d* or *ed.*

Mr. Pasternak *needed* the forms yesterday.

Our vendor *provided* ribbon cartridges.

Future Tense

Verbs in the future tense show actions that are expected to occur at a later time. Traditionally, the helper verbs *shall* and *will* have been joined with principal verbs to express future tense. In business writing today, however, the verb *will* is generally used as the helper to express future tense. Careful writers continue to use *shall* in appropriate first-person constructions (*I/we shall attend the meeting*).

Andy *will need* office supplies next week.

You *will receive* your order on Thursday.

Problems With Primary Tenses

Most adult speakers of our language have few problems using present, past, and future tense verbs. A few considerations, however, merit mention:

1. Present tense verbs are used to express "timeless" facts, even if these verbs occur in sentences with other past tense verbs.

What did you say his duties *are?* (Not *were,* if he continues to perform these duties.)

We were told often that a penny saved *is* a penny earned. (Not *was.*)

What did you say the caller's name *is?* (Not *was.*)

2. A dictionary should be used to verify spelling of verbs that change form. One must be particularly careful in spelling *y*-ending verbs (*hurry, hurries, hurried*) and verbs for which the final consonant is doubled (*occurred, expelled*).

Summary of the Primary Tenses

The following table summarizes the various forms employed to express the primary tenses:

	Present tense		Past tense		Future tense	
	Singular	Plural	Singular	Plural	Singular	Plural
First person:	I need	we need	I needed	we needed	I will need	we will need
Second person:	you need	you need	you needed	you needed	you will need	you will need
Third person:	he, she, it, needs	they need	he, she, it needed	they needed	he, she, it will need	they will need

N.B. Singular third person verbs require an *s* ending (he needs) and plural third person verbs do *not* (they need). Ending a singular verb with an *s* is difficult for some writers and speakers because they associate *s* endings with the plural form of nouns.

Emphatic Tenses

To express emphasis, place *do, does,* or *did* before the present tense form of a verb.

She claims that she *does have* the necessary permission. (Present emphatic tense.)

I *do believe* you. (Present emphatic tense.)

The president *did authorize* the audit. (Past emphatic tense.)

You *did say* you were coming. (Past emphatic tense.)

Complete the reinforcement exercises for Level I.

LEVEL II

Present and Past Participles

To be able to use all the tenses of verbs correctly, you must understand the four principal parts of verbs: present, past, present participle, and past participle. You have already studied the present and past forms. Now, let's consider the participles.

Present Participle

The present participle of a regular verb is formed by adding *ing* to the present part of the verb. When used in a sentence as part of a verb phrase, the present participle is always preceded by some form of the helping verb *to be* (*am, is are, was, were, be, been*).

Betty *is changing* the ribbon.

You *are doing* a fine job.

Past Participle

The past participle of a regular verb is usally formed by adding a *d* or *t* sound to the present part of the verb. Like present participles, past participles may function as parts of verb phrases.

> Brian *has checked* his homework.
> His homework *has been checked* by Brian.
> Mr. Andrews *should have built* the factory earlier.
> New roads to the building *should have been built.*

Irregular Verbs

Up to this point, we have considered only regular verbs. Regular verbs form the past tense by the addition of a *d* or *ed* sound to the present tense form. Many verbs, however, form the past tense and the past participle irregularly. (More specifically, irregular verbs form the past tense by a variation in the root vowel and, commonly, the past participle by the addition of the *en* sound.) A list of the more frequently used irregular verbs follows. Learn the forms of these verbs by practicing in patterns such as this:

Present tense: Today I __drive.__
Past tense: Yesterday I __drove.__
Past participle: In the past I have __driven.__

Irregular Verbs

Present	Past	Past participle
arise	arose	arisen
be (am, is, are)	was, were	been
bear (to carry)	bore	borne
become	became	become
begin	began	begun
bite	bit	bitten
blow	blew	blown
break	broke	broken
bring	brought	brought
build	built	built
choose	chose	chosen
come	came	come
do	did	done
draw	drew	drawn
drink	drank	drunk
drive	drove	driven
eat	ate	eaten
fall	fell	fallen
fly	flew	flown
forbid	forbade	forbidden
forget	forgot	forgotten *or* forgot
forgive	forgave	forgiven
freeze	froze	frozen
get	got	gotten *or* got

Present	Past	Past participle
give	gave	given
go	went	gone
grow	grew	grown
hang (to suspend)	hung	hung
hang (to execute)	hanged	hanged
hide	hid	hidden *or* hid
know	knew	known
lay (to place)	laid	laid
leave	left	left
lie (to rest)	lay	lain
lie (to tell a falsehood)	lied	lied
pay	paid	paid
prove	proved	proved *or* proven
raise (to lift)	raised	raised
ride	rode	ridden
ring	rang	rung
rise (to move up)	rose	risen
run	ran	run
see	saw	seen
set (to place)	set	set
shake	shook	shaken
shrink	shrank	shrunk
sing	sang	sung
sink	sank	sunk
sit (to rest)	sat	sat
speak	spoke	spoken
spring	sprang	sprung
steal	stole	stolen
strike	struck	struck *or* stricken
swear	swore	sworn
swim	swam	swum
take	took	taken
tear	tore	torn
throw	threw	thrown
wear	wore	worn
write	wrote	written

N.B. The past participle should *not* be substituted for the past tense form.
Wrong: He come over last night.
Right: He came over last night.
Wrong: We seen them recently.
Right: We saw them recently.

Three Pairs of Frequently Misused Irregular Verbs

The key to the correct use of the following pairs of verbs lies in developing the ability to recognize the tense forms of each and to distinguish transitive verbs and constructions from intransitive ones.

Lie–Lay

These two verbs are confusing because the past tense of *lie* is spelled in exactly the same way that the present tense of *lay* is spelled. Memorize these verb forms:

	Present	Present participle	Past	Past participle
Intransitive:	lie (to rest)	lying	lay	lain
Transitive:	lay (to place)	laying	laid (not *layed*)	laid

The verb *lie* is intransitive; therefore, it requires no direct object to complete its meaning.

Today I *lie* down. (Note that *down* is not a direct object.)
"*Lie* down," he told his dog. (Commands are given in the present tense.)
Yesterday I *lay* down for a nap. (Past tense.)
The papers are *lying* on the desk. (Present participle.)
They have *lain* there for some time. (Past participle.)

The verb *lay* is transitive and must have a direct object to complete its meaning.

Lay the bricks over there. (Command in the present tense.)
The mason is *laying* bricks. (Present participle.)
He *laid* the bricks in a row. (Past.)
He has *laid* bricks all his life. (Past participle.)

Sit–Set

Less troublesome than *lie–lay,* the combination of *sit–set* is nevertheless perplexing because the sound of the verbs is similar. The intransitive verb *sit* (past tense, *sat;* past participle, *sat*) means "to rest" and requires no direct object.

Do you *sit* here often? (Used intransitively; *here* is not an object.)
Are you *sitting* here tomorrow? (Present participle.)

The transitive verb *set* (past tense, *set;* past participle, *set*) means "to place" and must have a direct object.

Letty usually *sets* her books there. (*Books* is the direct object.)
She is *setting* her books here today. (Present participle.)

Rise–Raise

The intransitive verb *rise* (past tense, *rose;* past participle, *risen*) means "to go up" or "to ascend" and requires no direct object.

The sun *rises* every morning in the east. (*Every morning* is an adverbial phrase, not an object.)
Our elevator is *rising* to the seventh floor. (Present participle.)
The bread dough *rose* nicely. (Past tense.)
Prices have *risen* substantially. (Past participle.)

The transitive verb *raise* (past tense, *raised;* past participle, *raised*) means "to lift up" or "to elevate" and must have a direct object.

> Please *raise* the window. (*Window* is a direct object.)
> Datamax is *raising* prices next month. (*Prices* is a direct object.)

> N.B. A tip to help you remember which of these troublesome verbs are intransitive and which are transitive. Look at the second letter of each of the intransitive verbs:
> l*i*e, lay; s*i*t, set; r*i*se, raise.
> Remember that the present-tense intransitive forms all have *i*'s for their second letters.

Complete the reinforcement exercises for Level II.

LEVEL III

Progressive and Perfect Tenses

Thus far in this chapter you have studied the primary tenses, the emphatic verb tenses, and irregular verbs. The remainder of this chapter focuses on two additional sets of verb tenses: the perfect tenses and the progressive tenses. Most native speakers and writers of English have little difficulty controlling these verb forms because they have frequently heard them used correctly. For individuals who are not native speakers and for those who are eager to study the entire range of verb tenses, this largely descriptive section is thus presented.

Progressive Tense

Present progressive tense

	First person	Second person	Third person
Active:	I am hearing we are hearing	you are hearing	he, she, it is hearing they are hearing
Passive:	I am being heard we are being heard	you are being heard	he, she, it is being heard they are being heard

Past progressive tense

	First person	Second person	Third person
Active:	I was hearing we were hearing	you were hearing	he, she, it was hearing they were hearing
Passive:	I was being heard we were being heard	you were being heard	he, she, it was being heard they were being heard

Future progressive tense

Active:	I will be hearing we will be hearing	you will be hearing	he, she, it will be hearing they will be hearing

Passive:	I will be being heard we will be being heard	you will be being heard	he, she, it will be being heard they will be being heard

We *are exporting* grain to numerous countries. (Present progressive tense expresses action in progress.)

Many textile companies *were sending* delegates to the government conference. (Past progressive tense indicates action begun in the past.)

They *will be receiving* the announcement shortly. (Future progressive indicates action in future.)

Perfect Tense

Present perfect tense

	First person	Second person	Third person
Active:	I have heard we have heard	you have heard	he, she, it has heard they have heard
Passive:	I have been heard we have been heard	you have been heard	he, she, it has been heard they have been heard

Past perfect tense

Active:	I had heard we had heard	you had heard	he, she, it had heard they had heard
Passive:	I had been heard we had been heard	you had been heard	he, she, it had been heard they had been heard

Future perfect tense

Active:	I will have heard we will have heard	you will have heard	he, she, it will have heard they will have heard
Passive:	I will have been heard we will have been heard	you will have been heard	he, she, it will have been heard they will have been heard

He has just *heard* the news. (Present perfect tense expresses action just completed or *perfected.*)

The check *had cleared* the bank before I canceled payment. (Past perfect tense shows an action finished before another action in the past.)

The polls *will have been closed* two hours when the results are telecast. (Future perfect tense indicates action that will be completed before another future action.)

Summary of Verb Tenses

Primary tenses	Emphatic tenses
Present	Present emphatic
Past	Past emphatic
Future	

Progressive tenses	Perfect tenses
Present progressive	Present perfect
Past progressive	Past perfect
Future progressive	Future perfect

Complete the reinforcement exercises for Level III.

HOT LINE QUERIES

QUESTION: I'm embarrassed to ask this because I should know the answer—but I don't. Is there an apostrophe in this: *its relevance to our program?*

ANSWER: No. Use an apostrophe only for the contraction *it's,* meaning *it is* (*it's a good plan*). The possessive pronoun *its,* as used in your example, has no apostrophe (*the car had its oil changed*).

QUESTION: How do you spell *Honolulu*? I looked in the dictionary but it isn't there.

ANSWER: *Honolulu* and other names are not in all dictionaries. Some dictionaries include proper nouns in the main entries; others have separate sections with biographical and geographical entries. You might also look up place names in a zip-code directory or a telephone book if you have no other reference book handy.

QUESTION: I thought I knew the difference between *principal* and *principle,* but now I'm not so sure. In a report I'm typing I find this: *The principal findings of the research are negative.* I thought *principal* always meant your "pal," the school principal.

ANSWER: You're partly right and partly wrong. *Principal* may be used as a noun meaning *chief* or *head person.* In addition, it may be used as an adjective to mean *chief* or *main.* This is the meaning most people forget, and this is the meaning of the word in your sentence. The word *principle* means a *law* or *rule.* Perhaps it is easiest to remember *principle-rule.* All other uses require *principal:* the *principal* of the school, the *principal* of the loan, the *principal* reason.

QUESTION: Even when I use a dictionary, I can't tell the difference between *affect* and *effect.* What should the word be in this sentence? *Changes in personnel (affected/effected) our production this month.*

ANSWER: No words generate more calls to the Hot Line than do *affect/effect.* In your sentence use *affected.* Let's see if we can resolve the *affect/effect* dilemma. *Affect* is a verb meaning "to influence" (*smoking affects health; government policies affect citizens*). *Affect* may also mean "to pretend or imitate" (*he affected a British accent*). *Effect* can be a noun or a verb. As a noun, it means "result" (*the effect of the law is slight*). As a verb, (and here's the troublesome part) *effect* means "to produce a result" (*small cars effect gasoline savings; GM effected a new pricing policy*).

QUESTION: I'm editing a screenplay for a studio, and I know something is grammatically wrong with this sentence: *The old man left the room hurriedly after discovering a body laying near the window.*

ANSWER: As you probably suspected, the verb *laying* should be *lying. Lay* means "to place" and requires an object (*he is laying the report on your desk now*). *Lie* means "to rest" and requires no object (*the document is lying on your desk*).

QUESTION: As the holiday season approaches, I'm wondering whether it's *Season's Greetings* or *Seasons' Greetings.*

ANSWER: If you are referring to one season, it's *Season's Greetings.*

QUESTION: I learned that the verb *set* is transitive and requires an object. If that's true, how can we say that the sun *sets* in the west?

ANSWER: Good question! The verb *set* is generally transitive, but it does have some standardized intransitive uses, such as the one you mention. Here's another: *Glue sets up quickly*. I doubt that anyone would be likely to substitute *sit* in either of these unusual uses. While we're on the subject, the verb *sit* also has some exceptions. Although generally intransitive, *sit* has a few transitive uses: *Sit yourself down,* and *The waiter sat us at Table 1.*

Name ____________________

CHAPTER 9 **Reinforcement Exercises**

LEVEL I

A. (Self-check) Select the correct verb. Use your dictionary to verify spelling if necessary.

1. Workers (applyed, applied) two coats of paint. ____________
2. What did you say your friend's name (is, was)? ____________
3. The machine (jamed, jammed) when conflicting instructions were entered. ____________
4. Mr. Milne said that the distance between Madison and Milwaukee (is, was) 90 miles. ____________
5. We (hurryed, hurried) through the rehearsals. ____________
6. Shirley's maiden name (is, was) Eiseman. ____________
7. He was (refered, referred) to the Motor Vehicle Department. ____________
8. They (studyed, studied) past midnight. ____________
9. The salespeople who called this morning said that they (are, were) with Halston, Inc. ____________
10. He (write, writes) about a dozen business letters a week. ____________

Check your answers.

B. In the following sentences, verbs have been italicized. Provide three tenses for each italicized verb.

EXAMPLE: I *arrive* at the office at 7:45 a.m.
Past arrived Future will arrive Present Emphatic do arrive

1. The nation's tax system *needs* to stimulate investment.
   Past ____________ Future ____________ Present Emphatic ____________
2. The corresponding secretary *will copy* from the handwritten manuscript.
   Present ____________ Past ____________ Past Emphatic ____________
3. Lori *hurries* to catch the bus.
   Past ____________ Future ____________ Present Emphatic ____________
4. You *will apply* the same standards in judging your own success.
   Present ____________ Past ____________ Past Emphatic ____________

A. 1. applied, 2. is, 3. jammed, 4. is, 5. hurried, 6. is, 7. referred, 8. studied, 9. are, 10. writes

5. Professor Williams *covered* the same material.

   Present ____________ Future ______________ Past Emphatic ____________

6. Monsanto *will label* its plastic soft-drink bottle.

   Present ____________ Past ______________ Present Emphatic ____________

7. Donald *plans* to major in business management.

   Past ____________ Future ______________ Past Emphatic ____________

8. Corporations *use* their profits for investing in new equipment.

   Past ____________ Future ______________ Present Emphatic ____________

9. The Prime Minister *fires* her navy minister today.

   Past ____________ Future ______________ Past Emphatic ____________

10. Questionnaires *will sample* customers' reactions to our new product.

    Past ____________ Present ______________ Present Emphatic ____________

C. Compose sentences using the verbs shown.

1. (Past emphatic tense of *work*) ____

2. (Present emphatic tense of *try*) ____

3. (Future tense of *study*) ____

4. (Past tense of *cancel*) ____

5. (Past emphatic tense of *learn*) ____

Name ____________________

LEVEL II

A (Self-check) Write the correct verb. Do not add a helper verb.

EXAMPLE He wished he had (eat) before he left. ____eaten____

1. Several of his friends (come) over yesterday. ________
2. Have you (see) the film before? ________
3. That helicopter has (fly) over the intersection twice. ________
4. Yesterday Lon (swim) the length of the pool. ________
5. Three poems were (write) by Mrs. Shapiro. ________
6. This morning's mild earthquake (shake) the dishes in the cabinet. ________
7. Over the past year Dr. Crowley (give) freely of his services. ________
8. Have you (speak) with the supervisor yet? ________
9. I wish Scott had (know) about the scholarship earlier. ________
10. All employees should have (go) to the computer demonstration. ________

Check your answers.

B. Underline any verb errors you find in the following sentences. Write the correct forms in the spaces provided. Do not add helper verbs. Write *C* if the sentence is correct as it stands.

EXAMPLE Janet said she <u>seen</u> the accident. ____saw____

1. Because it was washed in hot water, the sweater has shrank. ____shrunk____
2. Maureen set a record when she swam the Channel. ____C____
3. The office staff must chose a new letterhead stationery. ____choose____
4. Fiberglass was blown into the ceiling for insulation. ____C____
5. Leslie and Ross have went to the lecture in Royce Hall. ____gone____
6. Her friend asked if she had ate dinner yet. ____eaten____
7. His car was stole over the weekend. ____stolen____
8. Coach Meyer has worn the same lucky shirt to three games. ____C____
9. The water bill was not payed last month. ____Paid____
10. Is that the dog that has bit two passersby? ____bitten____
11. An agreement binding both parties was recently wrote. ________
12. The telephone has rang only twice in the past hour. ________
13. In lieu of the month's vacation to Tahiti, Mrs. Ferguson choose a foreign sports sedan. ____chose____

A. 1. came, 2. seen, 3. flown, 4. swam, 5. written, 6. shook, 7. gave, 8. spoken, 9. known, 10. gone

14. Prices on the stock exchange sunk to a new low. Sank

15. The first pitch of the season was thrown out by the President. C

C. *Lie–lay.* Write the correct forms of the verb.

Present	Present participle	Past	Past participle
lie (to rest):	Lying	Lay	lain
lay (to place):	Lay	Laid	Laid

Select the correct verb.

1. Mr. Gilson told his dog to (lay, lie) down.
2. She (layed, laid) the papers on Mrs. Betz's desk.
3. The papers had been (lying, laying) there for some time.
4. In fact, they had (laid, lain) there over a week.
5. Every day at 2 p.m. he (lies, lays) down to rest.

D. *Sit–set; rise–raise.* Write the correct forms of the verbs.

Present	Present participle	Past	Past participle
sit (to rest):	Sit	Sat	Sat
set (to place):	Set	Set	Set
rise (to go up):	rise	rose	[illegible]
raise (to lift):	raise	raised	raised

Select the correct verb.

1. Please (raise, rise) the windows to let in fresh air.
2. We'll never finish if Roland (sits, sets) there all day.
3. Automated typewriters (raise, rise) the temperature in a room.
4. The temperature (raises, rises) rapidly in a room filled with automated equipment.
5. Managers are (sitting, setting) goals for the production and sales staff.
6. The value of gold (rises, raises) or falls in relation to the dollar.
7. Miss Tibari (raised, rose) the question of retroactive benefits.
8. Julie and Tom Ringel always (sit, set) near the door.
9. The employee parking lot (sits, sets) some distance away.
10. Consumer prices have (risen, raised) faster than consumer income.

Name ______________________

LEVEL III

A. (Self-check) Verbs in the following sentences have been italicized. In the space provided, indicate the tense of each of these verbs. Refer to the text to guide you.

EXAMPLE: Your credit cards *had been recovered* by the time you reported the loss. — past perfect, passive

1. You *will have heard* the news before we have heard it. ______
2. Those orders *are being sent* to your San Diego branch. ______
3. Mr. Adams' case *will have been heard* in six weeks. ______
4. I cannot believe what I *am hearing*. ______
5. Charles *had been told* to report at once. ______
6. We *have* just *seen* your product advertised on television. ______
7. The manager's suggestions for reduced paper use *have been followed* by all employees. ______
8. You *will be seeing* an announcement of our price reduction shortly. ______
9. The Birches *have lived* in that neighborhood for years. ______
10. We *are* now *experiencing* the effects of the last cutback. ______

Check your answers.

B. Write the proper verb form.

EXAMPLE: They (drive) all night before they found a motel. (Past perfect) — had driven

1. Before the office announcement was made, we (hear) rumors about layoffs. (Past perfect) — had heard
2. When the fire alarm sounded, Miss Waters (help) James. (Past progressive) — was helping
3. By next April, Rayco (open) four branch outlets. (Future perfect) ______
4. I'm sure they (tell) about their trip when they return. (Future progressive) — will be telling
5. Plans (develop) to reduce administrative costs. (Present progressive, passive) — are been developed

---

A. 1. future perfect; 2. present progressive, passive; 3. future perfect, passive; 4. present progressive; 5. past perfect, passive; 6. present perfect; 7. present perfect, passive; 8. future progressive; 9. present perfect; 10. present progressive

6. Our department (think) about installing more modern information processing equipment. (Present progressive) ______
7. We are certain they (receive) the price quotation by now. (Present perfect) ______
8. By 5 p.m. the task (finish) and dropped in the mail. (Past perfect, passive) ______
9. Before next Monday he (paint) all the exterior and trim on the house. (Future perfect) ______
10. Did you say that you (live) in the same house all your life? (Present perfect) ______

C. ***Optional Composition.*** Your instructor may ask you to complete this exercise on a separate sheet. Write sentences using the following verbs: *given, chose, begun, lying (resting), raise, seen, comes, laid, spoke,* and *driven.*

POSTTEST

Underline the correct verb.

1. After we (saw, seen) the advertisement, we bought the machine.
2. Your telephone has (rung, rang) only twice while you were gone.
3. The contracts have (laid, lain) on your desk for over a week.
4. Soil temperatures will slowly (raise, rise) during the spring.
5. Mr. Jones has (worn, wore) the same suit every day this week.

1. saw, 2. rung, 3. lain, 4. rise, 5. worn

CHAPTER 10

Verb and Subject Agreement

OBJECTIVES When you have completed the materials in this chapter, you will be able to do the following:

Level I — *Locate the subjects of verbs despite intervening elements and inverted sentence structure.*

— *Make verbs agree with true subjects.*

— *Make verbs agree with subjects joined by* and.

Level II — *Make verbs agree with subjects joined by* or *and* nor.

— *Select the correct verbs to agree with collective nouns and indefinite pronouns.*

Level III — *Make verbs agree with quantities, fractions, portions, clauses, and* a number/the number.

— *Achieve subject-verb agreement within* who *clauses.*

PRETEST

Underline the correct verb.

1. One of our plans for reducing costs (require, requires) considerable capital.
2. The manager, along with the office secretary and accountant, (was, were) invited to the conference.
3. Neither the wholesaler nor his clients (is, are) satisfied with the level of service.
4. Behind this building (lies, lie) the parking lot and swimming pool.
5. The number of books yet to be sold (is, are) decreasing daily.

Subjects must agree with verbs in number and person. Beginning a sentence with "He don't . . ." damages a speaker's credibility and limits a communicator's effectiveness.

If an error is made in subject-verb agreement, it can generally be attributed to one of three lapses: (1) failure to locate the subject, (2) failure to recognize the number

1. requires, 2. was, 3. are, 4. lie, 5. is

(singular or plural) of the subject after locating it, or (3) failure to recognize the number of the verb. Suggestions for locating the true subject and determining the number of the subject and its verb follow.

LEVEL I

Locating Subjects

Prepositional Phrases

All verbs have subjects. Locating these subjects can be difficult, particularly if a prepositional phrase comes between the verb and its subject. Subjects of verbs are not found in prepositional phrases.* Therefore, you must learn to ignore such phrases in identifying subjects of verbs. Some of the most common prepositions are *of, to, in, from, for, with, at,* and *by.* Notice in these sentences that the prepositional phrases do not contain the subjects of the verbs.

> Only one *of the company executives* has insurance. (The verb *has* agrees with its subject *one.*)
>
> We wonder if the invoice *for the two shipments* is lost. (The verb *is* agrees with its subject *invoice.*)
>
> The range *of tasks and skill requirements* allows for upward growth potential. (The verb *allows* agrees with the subject *range.*)

Some of the less easily recognized prepositions are *except, but, like,* and *between.* In the following sentences, distinguish the subjects from the italicized prepositional phrases:

> All employees *but Tom* are to report early. (The verb *are* agrees with its subject *employees.*)
>
> Everyone *except the Harrises* is able to attend. (The verb *is* agrees with its subject *everyone.*)

Intervening Elements

Groups of words introduced by *as well as, in addition to, such as, including, together with,* and *other than* do *not* contain sentence subjects.

> The priceless book, *as well as other valuable documents,* was lost in the fire.

In this sentence the writer has elected to emphasize the subject *book* and to deemphasize *other valuable documents.* The writer could have given equal weight to these elements by writing: The priceless book *and* other valuable documents were lost in the fire. Notice that the number (singular or plural) of the verb changes when both *book* and *documents* are given equal emphasis. Here are additional examples involving intervening elements:

> Our president, *together with her entire staff of employees,* sends her greetings. (The singular subject *president* agrees with the singular verb *sends.*)
>
> Other pianists *such as Pennario* appear on the program. (The plural subject *pianists* agrees with the plural verb *appear.*)

**Occasionally a prepositional phrase may help to determine whether an indefinite pronoun, portion, or fraction is singular or plural; but the object of the preposition does not function as the subject of a verb. Further explanation appears later in this chapter.*

The Adverbs *there, here*

In sentences beginning with *there* or *here,* look for the true subject *after* the verb.

> There are four candidates for the position. (The subject *candidates* follows the verb *are*.)
>
> Here is the fuel oil consumption report. (The subject *report* follows the verb *is*.)

N.B. As adverbs, *here* and *there* cannot function as subjects.

Inverted Sentence Order

Look for the subject after the verb in inverted sentences and in questions.

> Attending the conference are salespeople from four states. (Verb precedes subject.)
>
> Have the product specifications been submitted? (Subject separates verb phrase.)

Basic Rules for Verb-Subject Agreement

Once you have located the sentence subject, decide whether the subject is singular or plural and select a verb that agrees in number.

Subjects Joined by *and*

When one subject is joined to another by the word *and,* the subject is plural and requires a plural verb.

> Carolyn and her brother work at Baker's.
>
> The proposed law and its amendment are before the legislature.

Company Names and Titles

Even though they may appear to be plural, company names and titles of publications are singular; therefore, they require singular verbs.

> *Better Homes and Gardens* makes an excellent gift.
>
> Continental Airlines is advertising the lowest fare to Hawaii.
>
> Richards, Bateman, and Richards is offering the bond issue.

N.B. The selection of the correct verb is often made easier by the temporary substitution of the word *it* for a singular subject or the word *they* for a plural subject. It is then easier to recognize true subject-verb agreement. For example, *The Three Musketeers is a classic.* Substitute *it* for the title; the singular verb *is* now sounds right.

Complete the reinforcement exercises for Level I.

Rules for Verb-Subject Agreement

Subjects Joined by *or* or *nor*

When two or more subjects are joined by *or* or *nor,* the verb should agree with the closer subject.

> Neither the supervisor nor the clerks know the order number.
> Either Leslie or you are in charge of ordering supplies.
> The manufacturer or the distributors carry spare parts.

N.B. Remember that, unlike subjects joined by *and,* subjects joined by *or/nor* require a choice between Subject No. 1 and Subject No. 2.

Indefinite Pronouns as Subjects

As you recall from Chapter 7 (pp. 79–92), some indefinite pronouns are always singular; and some indefinite pronouns are always plural. In addition, some may be singular or plural depending upon the words to which they refer.

Always singular	Always plural	Singular or plural
anyone, anybody, anything,	both	all
each, either, every, everyone,	few	more
everybody, everything, many a,	many	most
neither, nobody, nothing, someone,	several	some
somebody, something		any
		none*

> *Either* of the two applicants *is* satisfactory.
> *Everybody* in the lottery *has* an equal chance.
> A *few* of the workers *are* applying for stock shares.
> *Neither* of the dictionaries *is* available.
> *Most* of the letters *are* finished. (*Most* is plural because it refers to *letters.*)
> *Most* of the work *is* completed. (*Most* is singular because it refers to *work.*)

N.B. Indefinite pronouns such as *all, more,* and *most* provide one of the few instances when prepositional phrases become important in determining agreement. Although the prepositional phrase does not contain the subject of the sentence, it does contain the noun to which the indefinite pronoun refers.

See discussion on p. 131.

If the indefinite pronouns *each, every,* or *many a* are used to describe two or more subjects joined by *and,* the subjects are considered separate. Therefore, the verb is singular.*

> Many a semicolon and colon *is* misused.
>
> Every man, woman, and child *is* affected by the tax cut.

The indefinite pronouns *anyone, everyone,* and *someone* should be spelled as two words when followed by *of* phrases.

> *Any one* of the officers is available.
>
> *Every one* of the candidates has a campaign committee.

Collective Nouns as Subjects

Words such as *faculty, committee,* or *council* may be singular or plural depending upon their mode of operation. When a collective noun operates as a single unit, its verb should be singular. When the elements of a collective noun operate separately, the verb should be plural.

> Our faculty *has approved* the proposal. (*Faculty* is operating as a single unit.)
>
> The council *were* sharply *divided* over appropriations. (*Council* members were acting separately. While technically correct, the sentence would be less awkward if it read, "The council *members* were sharply . . . .")

Complete the reinforcement exercises for Level II.

LEVEL III

Rules for Verb-Subject Agreement

The Distinction Between *the number* and *a number*

When the word *number* is the subject of a sentence, its article (*the* or *a*) becomes significant. *The* is specific and therefore implies *singularity; a* is general and therefore implies *plurality*.

> *The number* of stenographers *is* declining. (Singular.)
>
> *A number* of orders *were* lost. (Plural.)

Quantities, Measures

When they refer to *total* amounts, quantities and measures are singular. If they refer to individual units that can be counted, quantities and measures are plural.

> Twenty dollars *is* more than I can afford. (Quantity as a total amount.)
>
> Three working days *are* required to repair your car. (Quantity as individual units.)

Fractions, Portions

Fractions and portions may be singular or plural depending on the nouns to which they refer.

> Two thirds of the cassettes *are* satisfactory.
>
> Over half of the contract *was* ratified.
>
> A majority of employees *agree* with the proposal.
>
> A minimum of work *is* required to receive approval.

**This use of a singular verb for two or more subjects joined by* and *is the only exception to the general rule presented in Level I.*

Part of the delegates *are* in favor of the plan.
Part of the proposal *is* ambiguous.

Who Clauses

Verbs in *who* clauses must agree in number and person with the nouns to which they refer. In *who* clauses introduced by *one of,* the verb is usually plural because it refers to a plural antecedent. In *who* clauses introduced by *the only one of,* the verb is singular.

Mrs. Stephens is *one of* those managers who always support the employees.
John is *one of* those people who are late sleepers.
Margaret is *the only one of* the girls who is prepared.

N.B. To facilitate selection of the correct verb in *one of those who* clauses that do not include the word *only,* begin reading with the word *of: Of those people who are late sleepers,* John is one. (Remember, if you know the number of a subject but still have difficulty selecting the proper verb, temporarily substitute *they* for the subject if it is plural and *he* or *it* if the subject is singular.)

Verbs must agree in person with the nouns or pronouns to which they refer.

It is you who are responsible for security.
Could it be I who am to blame?

Phrases, Clauses as Subjects

Use a singular verb when the subject of a sentence is a phrase or clause.

To learn about the stock market is fascinating.
That verbs must agree with subjects is accepted.

Subject Complements

In Chapter 8 you learned that linking verbs are followed by complements. Although a complement may differ from the subject in number, the linking verb should always agree with the subject.

The best part of the show is the singing and dancing. (The singular subject *part* agrees with the singular verb *is* despite the plural complement *singing and dancing*.)

The reason for the bankruptcy is poor investments in stocks.

To avoid awkwardness, it may be better to reconstruct such sentences so that the plural element is first: *The singing and dancing are the best part of the show.*

Complete the reinforcement exercises.

HOT LINE QUERIES

QUESTION: My uncle insists that *none* is singular. My English book says that it can be plural. Who's right?

ANSWER: Times are changing. Thirty years ago *none* was almost always used in a singular sense. Today, through usage, *none* may be singular or plural depending upon what you wish to emphasize. For example, *None are more willing than we.* But, *None of the students is* (or *are* if you wish to suggest many students) *failing.*

QUESTION: When do you use *all together*, and when do you use *altogether*?

ANSWER: *All together* means "collectively" or "all the members of a group" (*we must work all together to reach our goal*). *Altogether* means "entirely" (*he was altogether satisfied*).

QUESTION: Please help me with this sentence that I'm transcribing for a medical laboratory. *A copy of our analysis, along with our interpretation of its results, (has or have) been sent to you.*

ANSWER: The subject of your sentence is *copy;* thus the verb must be *has.* Don't let interrupting elements obscure the real sentence subject.

QUESTION: After looking in the dictionary, I'm beginning to wonder about this: *We have alot of work yet to do.* I can't find the word *alot* in the dictionary, but it must be there. Everyone uses it.

ANSWER: The two-word phrase *a lot* is frequently used in conversation or in very informal writing (*the copier makes a lot of copies*). *Alot* as one word does not exist. Don't confuse it with *allot* meaning "to distribute" (*the company will allot to each department its share of supplies*).

QUESTION: Should *reevaluate* be hyphenated?

ANSWER: No. It is not necessary to use a hyphen after the prefix *re* unless the resulting word may be confused with another word (*to re-mark the sales ticket, to re-cover the chair*).

QUESTION: I'm totally confused by job titles for women today. What do I call a woman who is a *fireman,* a *policeman,* a *chairman,* or a *spokesman?* And what about the word *mankind?*

ANSWER: As more and more women enter nontraditional careers, some previous designations are being replaced by neutral titles. Here are some substitutes:

firefighter	for fireman
mail carrier	for mailman
police officer	for policeman
flight attendant	for steward or stewardess
reporter or journalist	for newsman

On the other hand, some authorities argue that words like *chairman*, *spokesman*, and *mankind* have always been used universally to refer to both men and women. Alternate terms such as *chair, chairperson, spokesperson,* and *humankind* are awkwardly conspicuous. Unless an organization officially designates an individual as a *chairperson*, it's probably best to avoid the term. Although the treatment of the sexes should be fair and free from prejudice, one must use good judgment before neutralizing the language with unsatisfactory substitutions. The neutral term *chair* seems to be gaining acceptance.

QUESTION: I'm never sure how to handle words that are used to represent quantities and proportions in sentences. For example, what verb is correct in this sentence: *A large proportion of voters (was or were) against the measure.*"

ANSWER: Words that represent fractional amounts (such as *proportion, fraction, minimum,* and *majority*) may be singular or plural depending on the words they represent. In your sentence *proportion* represents *voters,* which is plural. Therefore, use the plural verb *were.*

Name ______________________

CHAPTER 10 **Reinforcement Exercises**

LEVEL I

A. (Self-check) Select the correct word to complete each sentence below. Write it in the space provided.

1. Everyone except Jan and two other workers (is, are) parking in the company lot. ____________
2. The copy machine in our department, along with those on the second and third floors, (need, needs) servicing. ____________
3. Here (is, are) one of the reasons we are having reception difficulties. ____________
4. (Has, Have) any of our work orders been completed yet? ____________
5. No one but Kim and her cousins (has, have) seen the ranch. ____________
6. The keyboard and the screen, along with the printer, (cost, costs) less than we expected. ____________
7. Addressing the sophomore class (is, are) members of the class of '80. ____________
8. We understand that Eastern Airlines (is, are) interviewing flight attendants. ____________
9. A set of guidelines to standardize input and output (was, were) developed. ____________
10. *Word Processing Fundamentals* by Shirley Waterhouse (appear, appears) to be our departmental selection. ____________

Check your answers.

B. For each of the following sentences, cross out any phrases that separate a verb from its subject. Then choose the correct verb and write it in the space provided.

EXAMPLES: The supervisor, ~~together with two of his assistants~~, (is, are) here. ____is____
Our catalog ~~of gift ideas~~ (is, are) being sent to you. ____is____

1. Our company's full range of products and services (is, are) available through our local dealers. ____is____
2. A description of the property, along with several other legal documents, (was, were) filed with my attorney. ____Was____

A. 1. is, 2. needs, 3. is, 4. Have, 5. has, 6. cost, 7. are, 8. is, 9. was, 10. appears

3. Everyone except the mailing room and shipping department workers (is, are) being trained on the new computer. __________

4. The list of vendors providing leased machines (was, were) recently revised. __________

5. All cooperatives except the Lemon Growing Exchange (has, have) been able to provide supplies at reduced prices. __________

6. Although the economy is improving, only one of the major automobile manufacturers (is, are) showing profits. __________

7. Outstanding salespeople like Mrs. Love (has, have) helped make our company a leader in the field. __________

8. One of your duties, in addition to the tasks already described, (is, are) the budgeting of funds for both departments. __________

C. If the following phrases served as sentence subjects, would their verbs be singular or plural?

	Singular	Plural
EXAMPLE: the controller and the treasurer		✓
1. a list of management objectives		
2. the instructor, together with his students		
3. other services such as dry cleaning		
4. the production cost and the markup of each item		
5. one of the most interesting books on all the lists		
6. current emphasis on product safety and consumer protection		
7. Madison, Lee & Cassidy, an executive placement service		
8. the tone and the wording of the letter		

D. Select the correct verb and write it in the space provided.

1. Here (is, are) the full list of names and addresses. __________

2. Seated next to the Alvarados (is, are) Joe Miranda. __________

3. There (is, are) two things you must do immediately. __________

4. He (doesn't, don't) mind working extra hours this weekend. __________

5. Our president, along with the general manager and three salesmen, (plan, plans) to attend the conference. __________

6. Not one of our four customer service representatives (is, are) available. __________

7. Western Airlines (is, are) featuring a low fare to San Diego. __________

8. Lying on my desk (is, are) my itinerary and plane tickets. __________

9. Kerr, McClellan, and Horn, a legal firm in Oklahoma City, (specializes, specialize) in corporate law. __________

10. Considerable time and money (was, were) spent on the final product. __________

Name ____________________

LEVEL II

A. (Self-check) Write the correct form.

1. ~~A~~ committee of four men and five women (is, are) to be appointed. ____________
2. Either Eric Leibeler or Lily Chow (has, have) the room key. ____________
3. The inventory and the report (is, are) being prepared. ____________
4. Each of the classifications (contains, contain) four parts. ____________
5. The union members (has, have) to vote on the proposed contract. ____________
6. Nothing but catalogs and bulletins (is, are) in this box. ____________
7. Many a clerk and receptionist (has, have) complained about the switchboard. ____________
8. (Everyone, Every one) of the wills can be produced on word processing equipment. ____________
9. All that work (is, are) yet to be logged in. ____________
10. Each clerk, secretary, and word processing specialist (was, were) asked to complete a questionnaire. ____________

Check your answers.

B. Write the correct form.

1. The Council on Consumer Prices (has, have) taken a firm position. has
2. Neither Mr. Rossi nor Mrs. Hahn (is, are) afraid of hard work. is
3. (Everyone, Every one) of the surgical reports required careful editing. Every One
4. Several of the proposals (contain, contains) complex formulas. Contain
5. Either the judge or the attorneys (has, have) asked for a recess. have
6. The group of players, coaches, and fans (is, are) booking a charter flight. is
7. Either of the two companies (is, are) satisfactory. is
8. Something about these insurance claims (appear, appears) questionable. appears
9. Neither the president nor the faculty members (favor, favors) a tuition increase. favor

need to have a subject

Subject

A. 1. is, 2. has, 3. are, 4. contains, 5. have, 6. is, 7. has, 8. Every one, 9. is, 10. was

10. Abstracts and affidavits (is, are) the principal typing in this office. __________

11. (Was, Were) any of the members of the organization present that afternoon? __________

12. (Is, Are) either of the letters ready for signature? __________

13. The jury (has, have) announced its verdict. __________

14. Somebody (is, are) to blame for these garbled messages. __________

15. Either of the photocopies (is, are) acceptable for our purposes. __________

16. A map showing the homes of celebrities (is, are) sold in Hollywood. __________

17. Either a book or an article (has, have) to be read as part of the assignment. __________

18. Our program, along with the efforts of other civic-oriented businesses, (is, are) aimed at urban renewal. __________

19. Any one of the stockholders (has, have) the right to delegate his or her proxy. __________

20. Some of the statistical report (is, are) almost illegible. __________

C. Complete the sentences that are started.

1. The staff (is, are) __________

2. Our city council (has, have) __________

3. Not one of the plans (was, were) __________

4. Some of the jury members (believe, believes) __________

5. Somebody in the bus filled with students (was, were) __________

Name ______________________

LEVEL III

A. (Self-check) For each sentence write the correct verb in the space provided.

1. The number of applicants (is, are) greater than expected. ______
2. Part of the loss of customers (is, are) the result of poor service. ______
3. Our company president is one of those executives who (is, are) able to delegate responsibility. ______
4. Fourteen feet of pipe (is, are) not enough for this job. ______
5. Didn't you know it is you who (is, are) to be honored at the ceremony? ______
6. There (is, are) a number of problems yet to be resolved. ______
7. She is the only one of the technicians who (operate, operates) all the equipment. ______
8. Whomever you name for the job (has, have) my approval. ______
9. About one third of the books (is, are) stored on microfiche. ______
10. The hardest part of the job (is, are) the bending and lifting. ______

Check your answers.

B. Select the correct verb.

1. Thirty-five dollars (is, are) required as a deposit before one can rent a tandem bicycle. is
2. Our latest advertisements featuring our spring clothing line (is, are) an example of the campaign. are
3. Is it he who (is, are) the new account representative? is
4. Carole is the only one of the lab assistants who (was, were) able to repair the malfunctioning machine. was
5. Vacations for employees who are entitled to three or more weeks (is, are) the next item on the agenda. are
6. Sixty days (is, are) the period of the loan. is
7. At the rear of the building complex (is, are) the quality control lab and the science department. are
8. Only a fraction of the conference delegates (was, were) unable to find accommodations in the Royal Manor. were
9. Serving in the student senate (is, are) a representative from each of the twenty departments on campus. is

A. 1. is, 2. is, 3. are, 4. is, 5. are, 6. are, 7. operates, 8. has, 9. are, 10. is

10. Over 80 percent of the individuals attending the lecture series (is, are) residents of nearby communities. ______

11. Steve is one of those people who always (get, gets) along well with fellow workers. ______

12. The reason for his wealth (is, are) wise investments in oil. ______

13. Neither the staff nor the students (think, thinks) that higher fees will solve the budget crisis. ______

14. Representing our office (is, are) several men and women with many years of experience. ______

15. Heinlein, Fagan & Ross, Inc., with headquarters in Chicago, (has, have) been chosen for the job. ______

16. One of the problems, in addition to those already mentioned, (seem, seems) to be resistance to change. ______

17. A chart showing all our management positions and responsibilities (was, were) prepared by the vice president. ______

18. Neither the defendant nor the plaintiffs (was, were) satisfied with the judgment. ______

19. Mr. Ornstein is one of those investors who (study, studies) a firm's annual report very carefully. ______

20. In our company the number of highly successful salespersons (is, are) steadily increasing. ______

C. ***Optional Composition.*** Your instructor may ask you to complete this exercise on a separate sheet. Write sentences using the following words as subjects of present tense verbs: *anyone, any one, everyone, every one, the number, a number, none, everything, council,* and *one of the managers*. Example: Anyone who joins is eligible for a gift.

POSTTEST

Underline the correct verb.

1. At least one of our accountants (suggest, suggests) using a tax-deferred plan.
2. The cost of supplies, along with service and equipment costs, (is, are) a major problem.
3. Either the administrative assistant or the engineers (has, have) to find the original copy.
4. Appearing next on the program (was, were) Raye Staples and Connie Aragun.
5. A number of surprising events (is, are) occurring in the stock market.

1. suggests, 2. is, 3. have, 4. were, 5. are

CHAPTER 11

Verbals

OBJECTIVES When you have completed the materials in this chapter, you will be able to do the following:

Level I — *Recognize gerunds and supply appropriate modifiers of gerunds.*
— *Identify and remedy split infinitives that result in awkward sentences.*

Level II — *Correctly punctuate introductory and other verbal phrases.*
— *Avoid writing awkward participial phrases.*

Level III — *Spot dangling verbal phrases and other misplaced modifiers.*
— *Rewrite sentences to avoid misplaced verbal phrases and modifiers.*

PRETEST

Write *a, b,* or *c* to describe the following sentences.

(a) contains no error
(b) contains error in use of verbal form
(c) contains error in punctuation of verbal form

1. Opening his book to the assigned chapter, the headings were read by Paul. _____
2. After considering the project carefully the vice president gave his approval. _____
3. To register by mail, return the enclosed application form. _____
4. Expertly trained in accounting techniques, the interviewer hired Kelly for the position. _____
5. To be finished on time the report required many hours of extra effort by the staff. _____

As you learned earlier, English is a highly flexible language in which a given word may have more than one grammatical function. In this chapter you will study verbals. Derived from verbs, verbals are words that function as nouns, adjectives, or adverbs. The three kinds of verbals are gerunds (verbal nouns), infinitives, and participles (verbal adjectives).

1. b, 2. c, 3. a, 4. b, 5. c

Gerunds

A verb form ending in *ing* and used as a noun is called a *gerund.*

Typing is fun. (Gerund used as the subject.)
Dale enjoys *computing.* (Gerund used as direct object.)

Using Gerunds Correctly

In using gerunds, follow this rule: Make any noun or pronoun modifying a gerund possessive, as Karen's *typing* or Dale's *computing.* Because we sometimes fail to recognize gerunds as nouns, we fail to make their modifiers possessive:

Wrong: The staff objects to Kevin *smoking.*
Right: The staff objects to Kevin's *smoking.*

The staff does not object to Kevin, as the first version states; it objects to his smoking. If we substitute a more easily recognized noun for *smoking,* the possessive form seems more natural: *The staff objects to Kevin's behavior. Behavior* is a noun, just as *smoking* is a noun; the noun or pronoun modifiers of both must be possessive.

Mr. Drake resented *his* (not *him*) calling during lunch. (The gerund *calling* requires the possessive pronoun *his.*)

We appreciate *your* (not *you*) bringing this matter to our attention.

Not all verbs ending in *ing* are, of course, gerunds. Some are elements in verb phrases and some act as adjectives.* Compare these three sentences:

I saw Monica typing. (The word *typing* functions as an adjective describing Monica.)

I admired Monica's typing. (As the object of the verb, *typing* acts as a gerund.)

Monica is typing. (Here *is typing* is a verb phrase.)

N.B. To distinguish between *ing* forms used as nouns and those used as adjectives, try the *what* question approach. In Sentence No. 1, for example, ask *I saw what?* Answer: I saw *Monica,* who happened to be typing. In Sentence No. 2, ask *I admired what?* Answer: I admired Monica's *typing,* not Monica.

Infinitives

When the present form of a verb is preceded by *to,* the most basic verb form results: the infinitive. The sign of the infinitive is the word *to.*

**Participles will be discussed in Level II of this chapter.*

Try *to sign* the papers immediately.

To write gracefully requires great skill.

Using Infinitives Correctly

In certain expressions infinitives may be misused. Observe the use of the word *to* in the following infinitive phrases. Do not substitute the conjunction *and* for the *to* of the infinitive:

Try *to call* when you arrive. (Not *try and call.*)

Be sure *to put* your initials on the letter. (Not *be sure and put.*)

Check *to see* when your appointment is. (Not *check and see.*)

When any word appears between *to* and the verb (*to* carefully *prepare*), an infinitive is said to be split. At one time split infinitives were considered great grammatical sins. Today most authorities agree that infinitives may be split if necessary for clarity and effect. Avoid, however, split infinitives that result in awkward sentences.

Awkward: Mr. Stokes wanted *to,* if he could find time, *recheck* his figures.

Better: If he could find time, Mr. Stokes wanted *to recheck* his figures.

Awkward: Our company has to, when the real estate market returns to normal, consider purchasing an office building.

Better: Our company has to consider, when the real estate market returns to normal, purchasing an office building.

Acceptable: *To* willfully *lie* under oath is perjury. (No awkwardness results from split infinitive.)

Acceptable: Mrs. Higgins expects you *to* really *work* hard. (No awkwardness results from split infinitive.)

Complete the reinforcement exercises for Level I.

LEVEL II

Participles

You have already studied the present and past forms of participles functioning as parts of verb phrases. You will recall that in such constructions present and past participles always require helping verbs: *is typing, was seen, had broken.*

In this chapter we will be concerned with a second possible function of participles. Participles can function as adjectives. As adjectives, participles modify nouns or pronouns, and they do not require helping verbs.

Participles used as adjectives have three tenses and two voices:

	Present tense	Past tense	Perfect tense
Active voice:	typing	—	having typed
Passive voice:	being typed	typed	having been typed

1. A participle in the present tense is used to show additional action occurring at the time of the action expressed by the main verb in the sentence (such main verbs may be present, past, or future).

Beth recognized the clerk *typing* the letter. (Present participle.)

2. A participle in the past or perfect tense is used to show other action completed *before* the action expressed by the main verb in the sentence.

Having completed the interview, Andrew felt relief. (Perfect participle used to show action completed prior to action of main verb *felt*.)

The *broken* chair had to be discarded. (Past participle shows that the chair was broken before it was discarded.)

Using Participles Correctly

Avoid using participial phrases that sound awkward, such as these:

Awkward: Pam's having been promoted to office manager was cause for celebration.

Better: Pam's promotion to office manager was cause for celebration.

Awkward: Being you have arrived early, may I leave now?

Better: Since you have arrived early, may I leave now?

Punctuating Verbal Forms

Determining whether verbal forms require commas often causes students difficulty. Let's try to clear up this difficulty with explanations and examples.

Punctuating Introductory Verbal Forms

When verbal forms are used in introductory words or expressions, there's no question about punctuating them. A comma should be placed between an introductory verbal form and the main clause of a sentence.

Astonished, the attorney turned to the jury. (Introductory verbal form.)

To improve product distribution, Burke hired a traffic manager. (Introductory verbal phrase.)

Filing the correspondence, Andy found the lost Harrison papers. (Introductory verbal phrase.)

After working forty-three years, Betty Bond retired. (Introductory verbal phrase.)

Not all verbal phrases that begin sentences, however, are considered introductory. If the verbal phrase represents the subject or part of the predicate of the sentence, *no* comma should separate it from the rest of the sentence.

Filing the correspondence is Andy's responsibility. (Verbal phrase used as subject; no comma.)

To change our budget at this time is almost impossible. (Verbal phrase used as subject; no comma.)

Located in the other building is our Shipping Department. (Verbal phrase used as part of predicate; no comma.)

Punctuating Nonessential Verbal Phrases*

Essential (restrictive) information is needed for the reader to understand the sentence. Verbal phrases often help identify the subject. These phrases require no commas. Nonessential information could be omitted without altering the basic meaning of the sentence; nonessential phrases are set off by commas.

Mrs. Ramirez, *working late at the office,* was able to meet the deadline.

**Many students find it easier to work with the words* essential *and* nonessential *than with the more traditional grammatical terms* restrictive *and* nonrestrictive*; therefore, the easier terminology is used here.*

(The verbal phrase *working late at the office* adds additional information, but it is not essential. The subject is fully identified by name. Use commas to set off the nonessential phrase.)

The woman *working late at the office* was able to meet the deadline. (In this sentence the verbal phrase *working late at the office* is essential; it is needed to identify the subject. *Which* woman was able to meet the deadline? The woman *working late at the office.* No commas separate this essential verbal phrase.)

First Federal Bank, *opening a new branch in Long Beach,* offered gifts to attract customers. (The verbal phrase is not essential because there is only one First Federal Bank, and it has been identified. Commas enclose this nonessential verbal phrase.)

A bank *opening a new branch in Long Beach* offered gifts to attract customers. (This verbal phrase is essential to identify *which* bank offered gifts. No commas are needed. Note: Even though you pause when you reach the end of the verbal phrase, don't be tempted to add a comma.)

Notice in the preceding sentences that whenever a nonessential verbal phrase interrupts the middle of a sentence, *two* commas set it off.

N.B. To help you understand the use of commas in dealing with nonessential (nonrestrictive) information, think of a window shade. Use commas to lower the window shade and cover the words enclosed. If words in a verbal phrase are not essential to the meaning of a sentence, use a comma window shade to obscure them.

Complete the reinforcement exercises for Level II.

LEVEL III

Avoiding Misplaced Verbal Modifiers

Introductory Verbal Phrases

Introductory verbal phrases must be followed by the words they can logically modify. Such phrases can create confusion or unintended humor when placed incorrectly in a sentence. Consider this sentence: *Sitting in the car, the mountains were breathtaking.* The introductory participial phrase in this sentence is said to *dangle* because it is not followed immediately by a word it can logically modify. The sentence could be improved by revising it to read: *Sitting in the car, we saw the breathtaking mountains.* Observe how the following illogical sentences have been improved:

Illogical: Slipping on the ice, his back was injured.

Logical: Slipping on the ice, *he* injured his back.

Illogical: Turning on the fan, papers flew about the office.

Logical: Turning on the fan, *I* caused papers to fly about the office.

Illogical: After answering the telephone, the doorbell began to ring insistently.
Logical: After answering the telephone, Jeremy heard the doorbell ring insistently.

Illogical: Skilled at typing and shorthand, the personnel director hired Kay.
Logical: Skilled at typing and shorthand, Kay was hired by the personnel director.

But: To ensure academic success, study diligently.
To ensure academic success, (you) study diligently. (In commands, the understood subject is *you*. Therefore, this sentence is correctly followed by the word to which it refers.)

N.B. After reading an introductory verbal phrase, ask the question *Who?* The answer to that question must immediately follow the introductory phrase. For example, *To find a good job, who.* To find a good job, *Derek* wrote to many companies.

Verbal Phrases in Other Positions

In other positions within sentences, verbal phrases must also be placed in logical relation to the words they modify.

Illogical: The missing purchase orders were found by Mrs. Seldon's secretary lying in her top desk drawer.
Logical: Mrs. Seldon's secretary found the missing purchase orders lying in her top desk drawer.

Illogical: Mr. South returned the envelope and its contents, recognizing his error.
Logical: Mr. South, recognizing his error, returned the envelope and its contents.

Complete the reinforcement exercises for Level III.

Hot Line Queries

QUESTION: Are there two meanings for the word *discreet?*

ANSWER: You are probably confusing the two words *discreet* and *discrete*. *Discreet* means "showing good judgment" and "prudent" (*the witness gave a discreet answer, avoiding gossip and hearsay*). The word *discrete* means "separate" or "noncontinuous" (*Alpha, Inc., has installed discrete computers rather than a network computer system*). You might find it helpful to remember that the *e*'s are separate in *discrete*.

QUESTION: Should I use *complimentary* or *complementary* to describe free tickets?

ANSWER: Use *complimentary,* which can mean "containing a compliment, favorable, or free" (*the dinner came with complimentary wine; he made a complimentary remark*). *Complementary* means "completing or making perfect" (*the complementary colors enhanced the room*). An easy way to remember *compliment* is by thinking "*I* like to receive a *compliment.*"

QUESTION: I confuse *i.e.* and *e.g.* What's the difference?

ANSWER: The abbreviation *i.e.* stands for the Latin *id est,* meaning "that is" (*the package exceeds the weight limit, i.e., 5 pounds*). Notice the use of a comma after *i.e.* The abbreviation *e.g.* stands for the Latin *exempli gratia,* meaning "for the sake of example" or "for example" (*the manufacturer may offer a purchase incentive, e.g., a rebate or discount plan*).

QUESTION: We're having an argument in our office about abbreviations. Can *department* be abbreviated *dep't*? How about *manufacturing* as *mf'g*? Where could we find a correct list of such abbreviations?

ANSWER: In informal writing or when space is limited, words may be contracted or abbreviated. If a conventional abbreviation for a word exists, use it instead of a contracted form. Abbreviations are simpler to write and easier to read. For example, use *dept.* instead of *dep't;* use *natl.* instead of *nat'l;* use *cont.* instead of *cont'd.* Other accepted abbreviations are *ins.* for *insurance; mfg.* for *manufacturing; mgr.* for *manager;* and *mdse.* for *merchandise.* Notice that all abbreviations end with periods. Some dictionaries show abbreviations of words along with their definitions. Other dictionaries alphabetize abbreviations within the main entries, so that a reader must know how to spell an abbreviation in order to be able to locate it. Reference manuals often have lists of abbreviations that are very helpful.

QUESTION: I'm not sure which word to use in this sentence: *They have used all (they're, their, there) resources in combating the disease.*

ANSWER: Use *their,* which is the possessive form of *they.* The adverb *there* means "at that place or at that point" (*we have been there before*). *There* is also used as an expletive or filler preceding a linking verb (*there are numerous explanations*). *They're* is a contraction of *they* and *are* (*they're coming this afternoon*).

QUESTION: In a letter written by my boss, how should we spell *there: We do not want an open invoice without there being justifiable reasons.*

ANSWER: *There* is spelled correctly, but its use creates an awkward verbal form. If your boss agrees, revise the sentence to read, *We do not want an open invoice without justification.*

Name ____________________

CHAPTER 11 Reinforcement Exercises

LEVEL I

A. (Self-check) In the following sentences gerunds are italicized. Other *ing* words that are not italicized are not functioning as gerunds. Select appropriate modifiers.

1. She is unhappy with (you, your) *handling* of the order. ____________
2. I saw (Mardi, Mardi's) changing the printwheel. ____________
3. (His, Him) *traveling* first class was questioned by the auditor. ____________
4. Did Gene tell you about (Gail, Gail's) *moving* to Alaska? ____________
5. The manager was upset about (Steve, Steve's) leaving early. ____________
6. The (clerk, clerk's) making the sale receives the commission. ____________
7. John suggested (you, your) *making* reservations early. ____________
8. I noticed Mrs. (Lee, Lee's) *handwriting* on the invoice. ____________
9. I appreciate (them, their) *answering* the telephone. ____________
10. The (salesperson, salesperson's) making the appointment is here. ____________

Check your answers.

B. Gerunds are again italicized. Choose the correct modifier.

1. Because of (you, your) *taking* responsibility, we are able to remain open. your
2. The (executive, executive's) submitting four cassettes forgot to sign his work request. exective
3. The accuracy of this report depends upon (him, his) *proofreading*. his
4. They said (you, your) *printing* of the brochures was excellent. your
5. The (firm, firm's) printing the forms went out of business. firm
6. Did the caller recommend (me, my) *returning* his call? my
7. The (customer, customer's) paying his bill complimented the service. customer
8. We are incredulous at (them, their) *winning* the series. their
9. The (player, player's) winning the final game takes the prize. player
10. (Him, His) *being* on time for the appointment is very important. his

A. 1. your, 2. Mardi, 3. His, 4. Gail's, 5. Steve's, 6. clerk, 7. your, 8. Lee's, 9. their, 10. salesperson

C. From each of the pairs of sentences shown, select the more acceptable version and write its letter in the space provided.

1. (a) Emilio was asked to, as soon as possible, record the lien due dates.
   (b) Emilio was asked to record the lien due dates as soon as possible. ______
2. (a) Happily, Mrs. Rodman began to open her birthday cards.
   (b) Mrs. Rodman began to happily open her birthday cards. ______
3. (a) Be sure and say hello for me.
   (b) Be sure to say hello for me. ______
4. (a) We wondered about his ordering so few office supplies.
   (b) We wondered about him ordering so few office supplies. ______
5. (a) The secretary started to, as the deadline approached, check the names and addresses.
   (b) As the deadline approached, the secretary started to check the names and addresses. ______
6. (a) Try to find when the meeting is scheduled.
   (b) Try and find when the meeting is scheduled. ______
7. (a) I think their being present at the hearing is crucial.
   (b) I think them being present at the hearing is crucial. ______
8. (a) Please check to see if the contract is ready.
   (b) Please check and see if the contract is ready. ______
9. (a) You may wish to, if you have time, contact your broker.
   (b) You may wish to contact your broker if you have time. ______
10. (a) The travel counselor recommended our traveling by train.
    (b) The travel counselor recommended us traveling by train. ______

D. Rewrite the following sentences to remedy any gerund or infinitive faults.

1. We plan to, if all the papers have been signed, initiate proceedings tomorrow.

2. Be sure and call to, if you haven't changed your mind, make your plane reservations.

3. I hope that you will inform your two agents that I appreciate them listening to my complaints.

4. When you are in Washington, try and visit the FBI exhibits.

Name ______________________

LEVEL II

A. Verbal phrases in the following sentences are shown in italics. All the sentences have been punctuated correctly. Study each sentence and select the letter that explains the reason for including or omitting commas.

(a) Introductory verbal phrase, comma necessary
(b) Essential verbal phrase, no commas necessary
(c) Nonessential verbal phrase, commas necessary
(d) Verbal phrase used as a subject; no commas necessary

EXAMPLES: *To settle the matter* is extremely difficult. ___d___
Mr. Manning, *to settle the matter*, flipped a coin. ___c___

1. *In preparing copies of her résumé,* Terri Mays used power equipment. ______
2. The student *looking for a parking place* was late to class. ______
3. Terri Mays, *preparing copies of her résumé,* used power equipment. ______
4. *Finding an earlier class* is very unlikely. ______
5. *Preparing copies of a résumé* is easy using power equipment. ______
6. *Consulting her astrologer,* Linda Starlet refused to set foot outside. ______
7. The person *consulting his astrologer* refused to set foot outside. ______
8. *Looking at the class schedule,* I see that I can take English. ______
9. Anyone *looking at a class schedule* can see what classes are available. ______
10. Professor Horne, *looking at a class schedule,* announced a change in our class time. ______

B. Selected verbal words and phrases have been italicized in the sentences below. Insert commas if needed. In the space provided at the right, write the number of commas that you insert for each sentence. If no commas are added, write *0*.

EXAMPLE: *To complete the job before the deadline*, we worked late. ___1___

1. *To introduce a new product successfully* manufacturers often depend upon advertising. ___1___
2. *Setting personal goals and objectives* is one important step in career planning. ___0___
3. *After studying the company's files* Mrs. Wohl recommended a more efficient records management system. ___1___
4. *Perplexed* the new owner of the retail outlet hired a financial expert for advice. ___1___
5. *Working in another office* are the legal secretaries who specialize in document production. ___0___
6. Composing memos and reports weekly the manager used a computer frequently. ___1___

A. 1. a, 2. b, 3. c, 4. d, 5. d, 6. a, 7. b, 8. a, 9. b, 10. c

7. *To improve the writing of government employees* consultants were hired. ______

8. *Startled* Jane Juralski dropped the letter folder. ______

9. *Beginning as a sole proprietor* H. J. Heinz eventually built a large corporation. ______

10. *Breaking down a job cycle into separate units of work* is the first task in a time-and-motion study. ______

C. Selected verbal phrases have been italicized in the following sentences. Insert commas if the phrases are nonessential. In the space provided, write the number of commas that you insert for each sentence. If no commas are added, write *0*.

1. Tommy Porter *sitting in the first seat of the third row* is next. ______
2. The student *sitting in the first seat of the third row* is next. ______
3. Sales Manager Everett *dictating into his portable unit* was able to keep up with his correspondence while traveling. ______
4. You may be interested to know that any student *enrolled in the college* has full library privileges. ______
5. The latest company contract enables employees *participating in our profit-sharing plan* to benefit from the stock split. ______
6. Jennifer Martin *striving to qualify for a promotion* enrolled in a Saturday course. ______
7. Anyone *striving to qualify for a promotion* should consider enrolling in college courses. ______

D. If needed, insert commas to punctuate verbal forms in the following sentences. In the space provided, indicate the number of commas added.

1. To plan effectively management must have a realistic picture of production. ______
2. General Motors facing unexpected competition from foreign suppliers decided to close the small fabrication plant. ______
3. After considering the matter carefully we have decided to implement your suggestion. ______
4. Reducing safety and health hazards is the primary function of OSHA (Occupational Safety and Health Administration). ______
5. Anyone possessing the necessary background may apply for the position. ______
6. Charles Brown possessing the necessary background and education immediately filled out an application. ______
7. Reducing safety and health hazards our division recently set a record for consecutive accident-free workdays. ______
8. Personnel Director Higgins hoping to help employees improve their job skills organized an in-service training class. ______
9. All employees interested in improving their job skills are invited to attend the in-service programs. ______
10. To enroll in any of the programs employees must sign up immediately. ______

Name ____________________________

LEVEL III

A. (Self-check) From each of the sets of sentences that follow, select the sentence that is stated in the most logical manner. Write its letter in the space provided.

1. (a) To locate precisely the right word, a thesaurus is often used.
   (b) To locate precisely the right word, one may often use a thesaurus. _____
2. (a) Sealed in an airtight crock, the Joneses savored the fine cheese.
   (b) Sealed in an airtight crock, the fine cheese was savored by the Joneses. _____
3. (a) To complete the accounting equation, one must add liabilities to equity.
   (b) To complete the accounting equation, it is necessary to add liabilities to equity. _____
4. (a) Before starting the project, permission must be obtained.
   (b) Before starting the project, one must obtain permission. _____
5. (a) In sorting the names and addresses, James discovered an error.
   (b) In sorting the names and addresses, an error was discovered by James. _____
6. (a) To graduate early, carry more units.
   (b) To graduate early, more units must be carried. _____
7. (a) After collecting author references on note cards, write the bibliography.
   (b) After collecting author references on note cards, the bibliography should be written. _____
8. (a) Having completed twenty years of service, Mr. White was presented a gold watch.
   (b) Having completed twenty years of service, a gold watch was presented to Mr. White. _____
9. (a) After seeing the job advertisement, a letter was sent by Miss Bruner.
   (b) After seeing the job advertisement, Miss Bruner sent a letter. _____
10. (a) To qualify for the certificate, perfect attendance must be maintained.
    (b) To qualify for the certificate, one must maintain perfect attendance. _____

Check your answers.

B. Each of the following sentences has an illogical introductory verbal phrase. Rewrite each sentence using that introductory phrase so that it is followed by a word it can logically modify. It may be necessary to add a subject. Keep the introductory verbal phrase at the beginning of the sentence.

EXAMPLE: Driving through Malibu Canyon, the ocean came into view.
Driving through Malibu Canyon, we saw the ocean come into view.

1. Answering the telephone on the first ring, goodwill is created by our staff. ____________
____
____

A. 1. b, 2. b, 3. a, 4. b, 5. a, 6. a, 7. a, 8. a, 9. b, 10. b

2. Comparing figures from four sources, the error in the balance sheet was finally discovered. ______________________________

3. To be binding, a consideration must support every contract. ______________________________

4. Repainted and completely reconditioned in every part, Laura was amazed at her old Volkswagen. ______________________________

The preceding sentences had misplaced introductory verbal phrases. The next sentences have misplaced verbal phrases in other sentence positions. Rewrite these sentences so that the verbal phrases are close to the words they can logically modify.

5. An autopsy revealed the cause of death to be strangulation by the coroner.

____

6. Noxious fumes made many office workers sick coming from the nearby auto paint shop.

____

C. ***Optional Composition.*** Your instructor may ask you to complete this exercise on a separate sheet. Write two sentences illustrating each of the following verb forms: gerund, infinitive, participle. Label each sentence.

POSTTEST

Write *a, b,* or *c* to describe the following sentences. Compare your answers with those at the bottom of the page.

(a) contains no errors
(b) contains error in use of verbal form
(c) contains error in punctuation of verbal form

1. Deciding that his first letter was unclear, a second letter was written by Mr. Holmes. _____
2. To supervise effectively a manager must have excellent communication skills. _____
3. To collect health benefits, fill out the long application. _____
4. Improving health and dental benefits for all employees is our primary goal. _____
5. Having submitted an application, benefits should be forthcoming immediately. _____

1. b, 2. c, 3. a, 4. a, 5. b

Name ______________________________

UNIT 3 REVIEW **Chapters 8–11 (Self-Check)**

Begin your review by rereading Chapters 8 through 11. Then test your comprehension of those chapters by completing the exercises that follow. Compare your responses with those provided at the end of this review.

LEVEL I

In the blank provided, write the letter of the word or phrase that correctly completes each of the following sentences.

1. In the sentence *He seems responsible*, the verb *seems* is (a) transitive, (b) intransitive, (c) linking. ______
2. In the sentence *She is the president*, the word *president* is a(n) (a) object, (b) linking verb, (c) complement. ______
3. A keyboard with 106 characters (a) has, (b) have been developed for your computer. ______
4. The president, together with her entire staff of employees, (a) send, (b) sends greetings to you. ______
5. The president and her entire staff (a) send, (b) sends greetings to you. ______
6. Be sure (a) to write, (b) and write the name and address legibly. ______
7. We certainly appreciate (a) him, (b) his handling of the program. ______
8. Davis, Crowley, and Kovacs, Inc., (a) is, (b) are expecting an increase in profits this quarter. ______
9. It appears that the shipping statement for the equipment and supplies (a) was, (b) were delayed. ______
10. Is there any possibility of (a) your, (b) you coming early? ______
11. Ms. Munoz and her partner Mr. Reese (a) appear, (b) appears to have submitted the lowest bid. ______

LEVEL II

Write the letter of the word or phrase that correctly completes each of the following sentences.

12. When converting a verb from the passive to the active voice, the writer must make the doer of the action the (a) subject, (b) object of the active-voice verb. ______
13. In the sentence *Three form letters were typed by Mary*, the verb is in the (a) active, (b) passive voice. ______

14. Many letters and packages have (a) laid, (b) lain, (c) lay on that desk for the past week. ______

15. The same burglar alarm has (a) rang, (b) rung twice today. ______

16. The contract (a) laying, (b) lying on your desk must be signed. ______

17. Neither the computer nor the printers (a) is, (b) are working. ______

18. We think that (a) anyone, (b) any one of our representatives will serve you well. ______

Insert commas where necessary in the next group of sentences. Indicate the number of commas that you added. Write 0 for none.

19. We were very pleased to see that Rebecca working until 10 p.m. was able to complete the job. ______

20. Storing thousands of customer files became physically possible when vertical file cabinets were installed. ______

21. Working until 10 p.m. Rebecca was able to complete the job. ______

LEVEL III

In the blank provided, write the letter of the word or phrase that correctly completes each sentence.

22. The problem would have been handled differently if I (a) was, (b) were in charge. ______

23. A motion was made that members (a) be, (b) are admitted free. ______

24. The number of employees participating in elective classes (a) is, (b) are steadily increasing. ______

25. It is you who (a) is, (b) are to do the judging tomorrow. ______

26. It looks as if three fourths of the brochures (a) has, (b) have yet to be assembled. ______

27. She is one of those executives who always (a) tell, (b) tells the truth. ______

For each sentence below, indicate whether (a) the sentence is written correctly or (b) the sentence has a verbal phrase placed illogically. Rewrite illogical sentences.

28. To qualify for the retirement incentive, applications must be made by January 1. ______

____

29. Skilled at programming computers, the personnel manager hired Joe instantly. ______

____

30. Driving to the office, two accidents were seen by Debbie. ______

____

1. c, 2. c, 3. a, 4. b, 5. a, 6. a, 7. b, 8. a, 9. a, 10. a, 11. a, 12. a, 13. b, 14. b, 15. b, 16. b, 17. b, 18. b, 19. 2, 20. 0, 21. 1, 22. b, 23. a, 24. a, 25. b, 26. b, 27. a, 28. b, 29. b, 30. b

UNIT FOUR

Modifying and Connecting Words

At your leisure
noun.
leisurely (adj or adverb)
not too many are adj or adverb.

taking a leisurel(ly) stroll.

CHAPTER 12

Modifiers: Adjectives and Adverbs

OBJECTIVES When you have completed the materials in this chapter, you will be able to do the following:

Level I — *Form the comparative and superlative degrees of regular and irregular adjectives and adverbs.*

— *Use articles correctly and avoid double negatives.*

Level II — *Use adjectives after linking verbs and use adverbs to modify verbs, adjectives, and other adverbs.*

— *Punctuate compound and successive independent adjectives correctly.*

Level III — *Compare degrees of absolute adjectives and make comparisons within a group.*

— *Place adverbs and adjectives close to the words they modify.*

PRETEST

Underline the correct word.

1. This is the (worse, worst) business report I've ever read.
2. It is (a, an) honor to be selected by the interviewing committee.
3. If you did (good, well) enough in the interview, you will be hired.
4. Our (six-year-old, six year old) lease must be renegotiated.
5. The (newly repaired, newly-repaired) copier seems to be working well.

LEVEL I

Both adjectives and adverbs act as modifiers; that is, they describe or limit other words. Since many of the forms and functions of adjectives and adverbs are similar and since faulty usage often results from the confusion of these two parts of speech, adjectives and adverbs will be treated together in this chapter.

1. worst, 2. an, 3. well, 4. six-year-old, 5. newly repaired

Basic Functions of Adjectives and Adverbs

What Do Adjectives and Adverbs Do?

Adjectives describe or limit nouns and pronouns. As you have already learned, they often answer the questions *what kind*? *how many*? or *which one*? Adjectives in the following sentences are italicized.

Short visits are *the best* visits.

Large government grants were awarded to *the eight top* institutions.

Adverbs describe or limit verbs, adjectives, or other adverbs. They often answer the questions *when*? *how*? *where*? or *to what extent*?

Yesterday our work went *slowly*.

He answered *quite decisively*.

Comparative Forms

Most adjectives and adverbs have three forms, or degrees: positive, comparative, and superlative. The examples below illustrate how the comparative and superlative degrees of regular adjectives and adverbs are formed.

	Positive	Comparative	Superlative
Adjective:	warm	warmer	warmest
Adverb:	warmly	more warmly	most warmly
Adjective:	careful	more careful	most careful
Adverb:	carefully	more carefully	most carefully

The positive degree of an adjective or an adverb is used in merely describing or in limiting another word. The comparative degree is used to compare two persons or things. The superlative degree is used in the comparison of three or more persons or things.

The comparative degree of short adjectives (nearly all one-syllable and most two-syllable adjectives ending in *y*) is formed by adding *r* or *er* (*warmer*). The superlative degree of short adjectives is formed by the addition of *st* or *est* (*warmest*). Long adjectives and those difficult to pronounce form the comparative and superlative degrees, as do adverbs, with the addition of *more* and *most* (*more careful, most careful*). The following sentences illustrate degrees of comparison for adjectives and adverbs.

Adjectives:	Sales are unusually *high*.	(Positive degree)
	Sales are *higher* than ever before.	(Comparative degree)
	Sales are the *highest* in years.	(Superlative degree)
Adverbs:	He drives *carefully*.	(Positive degree)
	He drives *more carefully* now.	(Comparative degree)
	He drives *most carefully* at night.	(Superlative degree)

N.B. Do not create a double comparative form by using *more* and the suffix *er* together (such as *more neater*) or by using *most* and the suffix *est* together (such as *most fastest*).

A few adjectives and adverbs form the comparative and the superlative degrees irregularly. Some irregular adjectives are *good* (*better, best*); *bad* (*worse, worst*); and *little* (*less, least*). Some irregular adverbs are *well* (*better, best*); *many* (*more, most*); and *much* (*more, most*).

Modifiers That Deserve Special Attention

Adjectives as Articles. The articles *a, an,* and *the* merit special attention. When describing a specific person or thing, use the article *the,* as in *the film.* When describing persons or things in general, use *a* or *an,* as in *a film* (meaning *any* film). The choice of *a* or *an* is determined by the initial sound of the word modified. *A* is used before consonant sounds; *an* is used before vowel sounds.

Before vowel sounds		Before consonant sounds	
an operator		a shop	
an executive		a plan	
an industry		a corporation	
an hour an honor	*h* is not voiced; vowel is heard	a hook a hole	*h* is voiced
an office an onion	*o* sounds like a vowel	a one-man show a one-week trip	*o* sounds like the consonant *w*
an understudy an umbrella	*u* sounds like a vowel	a union a unit	*u* sounds like the consonant *y*
an x-ray an M.D.	*x* and *m* sound like vowels		

N.B. The sound, not the spelling, of a word governs the choice between *a* and *an.* When the letter *u* sounds like a *y,* it is treated as a consonant: a *u*tility, a *u*sed car.

Adverbs and Double Negatives. When a negative adverb (*no, not, scarcely, hardly, barely*) is used in the same sentence with a negative verb (*didn't, don't, won't*) a substandard construction called a *double negative* results. At one time in the history of the English language, double negatives were acceptable. Today such constructions are considered to be illogical and illiterate. In the following examples, notice how eliminating one negative corrects the double negative.

Avoid: Calling her *won't* do *no* good.
Use: Calling her will do no good.
Or: Calling her won't do any good.

Avoid: We *couldn't hardly* believe the news report.
Use: We could hardly believe the news report.
Or: We couldn't believe the news report.

Avoid: Drivers *can't barely* see in the heavy fog.
Use: Drivers can barely see in the heavy fog.
Or: Drivers can't see in the heavy fog.

This/That, These/Those. The adjective *this,* and its plural form *these,* indicates something nearby. The adjective *that,* and its plural form *those,* indicates something at a distance. Be careful to use the singular forms of these words with singular nouns and the plural forms with plural nouns: *this shoe, that road, these accounts, those records.* Pay special attention to the nouns *kind, type,* and *sort.* Match singular adjectives to the singular forms of these nouns. For example, *this kind* of question, *that sort* of person; but *these kinds* of questions, *those sorts* of people.

Complete the reinforcement exercises for Level I.

LEVEL II

Problems With Adjectives and Adverbs

Confusion of Adjectives and Adverbs

Because they are closely related, adjectives are sometimes confused with adverbs. Here are guidelines that will help you avoid common adjective–adverb errors.

1. Use adjectives to modify nouns and pronouns. Note particularly that adjectives (not adverbs) should follow linking verbs.

> This orange tastes *sweet* (not *sweetly*).
> I feel *bad* (not *badly*) about the loss.*
> He looks *good* (not *well*) in his uniform.

2. Use adverbs to describe verbs, adjectives, or other adverbs.

> The engine runs *smoothly.* (Not *smooth.*)
> It runs *more smoothly* than before. (Not *smoother.*)
> Listen *carefully* to the directions. (Not *careful.*)
> The assignment went *easily.* (Not *easy.*)

It should be noted that a few adverbs have two acceptable forms: *slow, slowly; deep, deeply; direct, directly; close, closely.*

> Drive *slowly.* (Or, less formally, *slow.*)
> Pack the fruits *closely.* (Or, less formally, *close.*)

Compound Adjectives

Writers may form their own adjectives by joining two or more words. When these words act as a single modifier preceding a noun, they are temporarily hyphenated. If these same words appear after a noun, they are not hyphenated.

Words temporarily hyphenated before a noun	Same words not hyphenated after a noun
never-say-die attitude	attitude of never say die
eight-story building	building of eight stories
state-sponsored program	program that is state sponsored
a case-by-case analysis	analysis that is case by case

**Note: The misuse of* badly *for* bad *is one of the most frequent errors made by educated persons. Following the linking verb* feel, *use the adjective* bad, *not the adverb* badly.

high-performance computer	computer that has high performance
income-related expenses	expenses that are income related
four-year-old child	child who is four years old
out-of-warranty repair	repair that is out of warranty

Compound adjectives shown in your dictionary with hyphens are considered permanently hyphenated. Regardless of whether the compound appears before or after a noun, it retains the hyphens. Use a current dictionary to determine what expressions are always hyphenated. Be sure that you find the dictionary entry that is marked *adjective*. Here are samples:

Permanent hyphens before nouns	Permanent hyphens after nouns
first-class service	the service was first-class
up-to-date news	the news is up-to-date
old-fashioned attitude	attitude that is old-fashioned
short-term loan	loan that is short-term
well-known author	author who is well-known
well-rounded program	program that is well-rounded

Don't confuse adverbs ending in *ly* with compound adjectives: *newly decorated* office and *highly regarded* architect would not be hyphenated.

N.B. As compound adjectives become more familiar, they are often simplified and the hyphen is dropped. Some familiar compounds that are not hyphenated are these: *high school* student, *charge account* customer, *income tax* return, *home office* staff, *data processing* center.

Independent Adjectives

Two or more successive adjectives that independently modify a noun are separated by commas. No comma is needed, however, when the first adjective modifies the combined idea of the second adjective and the noun.

Two adjectives independently modifying a noun	First adjective modifying a second adjective plus a noun
confident, self-reliant woman	efficient administrative assistant
economical, efficient car	blue sports car
stimulating, provocative book	luxurious mobile home

N.B. To determine whether successive adjectives are independent, mentally insert the word *and* between them. If the insertion makes sense, the adjectives are probably independent and require a comma.

Special Cases

The following adjectives and adverbs cause difficulty for many writers and speakers. With a little study, you can master their correct usage.

farther (adv. — actual distance) How much *farther* is the market?
further (adv. — additionally) To argue the matter *further* is fruitless.
sure (adj. — certain) He is *sure* of victory.
surely (adv. — undoubtedly) He will *surely* be victorious.
later (adv. — after expected time) The contract arrived *later* in the day.
latter (adj. — the second of two things) Of the two options, I prefer the *latter*.
fewer (adj. — refers to numbers) *Fewer* requests for tours were granted this year.
less (adj. — refers to amounts or quantities) *Less* time remains than we anticipated.
real (adj. — actual, genuine) The *real* power in the company lies with the chairman of the board.
really (adv. — actually, truly) Jan wondered if she could *really* learn to operate the equipment in five hours.
good (adj. — desirable) A number of *good* plans were submitted.
well* { (adv. — satisfactorily) Robert did *well* on the test.
(adj. — healthy) She feels quite *well* since the operation.

Complete the reinforcement exercises for Level II.

LEVEL III

Other Uses of Adjectives and Adverbs

Absolute Modifiers

Adjectives and adverbs that name perfect or complete (absolute) qualities cannot logically be compared. For example, to say that one ball is more *round* than another ball is illogical. Here are some absolute words that should not be used in comparisons.

round	dead	complete
perfect	true	right
unique	correct	straight
perpendicular	endless	unanimous

It is possible, however, to compare degrees of perfection or completeness by using such words as *more nearly* or *most nearly*. Study the following sentences for various alternatives.

Illogical: A *truer* statement has never been spoken.
Logical: A *more nearly true* statement has never been spoken.

Illogical: This rose is the *most perfect* flower in our garden.
Logical: This rose is the *most nearly perfect* flower in our garden.

Illogical: A *straighter* route through the desert is Highway I-69.

**Note that* well *can be used as either an adjective or an adverb. As an adjective, it refers to conditions of health.*

Logical: A *more nearly straight* route through the desert is Highway I-69.

Comparisons Within a Group

When the word *than* is used to compare a person, place, or thing with other members of a group to which it belongs, be certain to include the words *other* or *else* in the comparison. This inclusion ensures that the person or thing being compared is separated from the group with which it is compared.

Illogical: Los Angeles is larger than any city in California. (This sentence suggests that Los Angeles is larger than itself.)
Logical: Los Angeles is larger than any *other* city in California.

Illogical: Our team had more points than any league team.
Logical: Our team had more points than any *other* league team.

Illogical: Alex works harder than anyone in the office.
Logical: Alex works harder than anyone *else* in the office.

Placing Adverbs and Adjectives

The position of an adverb or adjective can seriously affect the meaning of a sentence. Study these examples.

Only I can program this computer. (No one else can program it.)
I can *only* program this computer. (I can't do anything else to it.)
I can program *only* this computer. (I can't program any other computer.)

To avoid confusion, adverbs and adjectives should be placed close to the words they modify. In this regard, special attention should be given to the words *only, merely, first,* and *last.*

Confusing: He *merely* said that all soldiers couldn't be generals.
Clear: He said *merely* that all soldiers couldn't be generals.

Confusing: Seats in the five *first* rows have been reserved.
Clear: Seats in the *first* five rows have been reserved.

Complete the reinforcement exercises for Level III.

HOT LINE QUERIES

QUESTION: One of my favorite words is *hopefully,* but I understand that it's often used improperly. How should it be used?

ANSWER: Language purists insist that the word *hopefully* be used to modify a verb (*we looked at the door hopefully, expecting Mr. Gross to return momentarily*). The word *hopefully* should not be used as a substitute for *I hope that* or *We hope that.* Instead of saying, *Hopefully, interest rates will decline,* one should say, *I hope that interest rates will decline.*

QUESTION: I often find myself using this phrase: *I can't help but. . . .* Something's awkward about it, but I don't know exactly what.

ANSWER: The phrase sounds awkward because it involves a double negative (and double negatives are to be avoided). Another double negative is *can't hardly.* Eliminate one of the negatives. For example, *I can't help worrying* (instead of *I can't help but worry*). Use *I can hardly hear you* (instead of *I can't hardly hear you*).

QUESTION: Is it necessary to hyphenate a *25 percent* discount?

ANSWER: No. Percents are not treated in the same way that numbers appearing in compound adjectives are treated. Thus, you would not hyphenate a *15 percent* loan, but you would hyphenate a *15-year* loan.

QUESTION: Should hyphens be used in a *point-by-point analysis?*

ANSWER: Yes. When words are combined in order to create a single adjective preceding a noun, these words are temporarily hyphenated (*last-minute decision, two-semester course, step-by-step procedures*).

QUESTION: In my writing I want to use *firstly* and *secondly.* Are they acceptable?

ANSWER: Both words are acceptable, but most good writers prefer *first* and *second* because they are more efficient and equally accurate.

QUESTION: How many hyphens should I use in this sentence? *The three, four, and five year plans continue to be funded.*

ANSWER: Three hyphens are needed: *three-, four-, and five-year plans.* Hyphenate compound adjectives even when the parts of the compound are separated or suspended.

QUESTION: Why can't I remember how to spell *already*? I want to use it in this sentence: *Your account has already been credited with your payment.*

ANSWER: You — and many others — have difficulty with *already* because two different words (and meanings) are expressed by essentially the same sounds. The adverb *already* means "previously" or "before this time," as in your sentence. The two-word combination *all ready* means "all prepared," as in *The club members are all ready to board the bus.* If you can logically insert the word *completely* between *all* and *ready,* you know the two-word combination is needed.

QUESTION: I never know how to write *part time.* Is it always hyphenated?

ANSWER: The dictionary shows all of its uses to be hyphenated. *She was a part-time employee* (used as adjective). *He worked part-time* (used as adverb).

QUESTION: Here are some expressions that caused us trouble in our business letters. We want to hyphenate all of the following. Right? *Well-produced play, awareness-generation film, decision-making tables, one-paragraph note, swearing-in ceremony, commonly-used book.*

ANSWER: All your hyphenated forms are correct except the last one. Don't use a hyphen with an *ly*-ending adverb.

Name ______________________

CHAPTER 12 Reinforcement Exercises

LEVEL I

A. (Self-check) Select the correct forms.

1. This is undoubtedly the (worse, worst) coffee we have ever drunk. ____________
2. It is certainly (worse, worst) than yesterday's coffee. ____________
3. (This, These) sort of error could be prevented through more careful training. ____________
4. I can't think of a (better, more better) plan. ____________
5. We (can, can't) hardly work in this room without air conditioning ____________
6. Is Chris or Margaret the (better, best) person for the job? ____________
7. Examine closely the blades on (this, these) pair of scissors. ____________
8. Driving to the bank and back requires at least (a, an) hour's time. ____________
9. Rainfall for this year (has, hasn't) been barely ten inches. ____________
10. The outcome of the race between Connors and Morelli will determine the (faster, fastest) driver. ____________

Check your answers.

B. Select the correct forms.

1. (That, Those) sorts of businesses have been asked to restrict exports. ____________
2. Sheik Yamani is the (more, most) powerful of the cartel's members. ____________
3. Audrey keeps (a, an) umbrella in her office at all times. ____________
4. Ask the tailor if (this, these) pair of pants is ready. ____________
5. After paying his taxes, Wayne complained that he (has, hasn't) barely a dollar left. ____________
6. Health care and communications are two service industries growing at (a, an) unusually fast pace. ____________
7. Of the four brothers and sisters, he is the (younger, youngest). ____________
8. Which of these two colors is (better, best) for the hall? ____________

A. 1. worst, 2. worse, 3. This, 4. better, 5. can, 6. better, 7. this, 8. an, 9. has, 10. faster

C. Can you find 12 errors in this paragraph? Cross out the errors and write the correct form above the line. Hint: eight errors involve adverbs and adjectives.

In Beverly Hills a officer of a bank was involved in one of the worse embezzlement schemes in the ~~banks~~ bank's history. Because of lax bank controls, the embezzler was able to withdraw hundreds of thousands of dollars in a unprecedented banking loss. To avoid detection by the banks computer fraud defenses, the embezzler took advantage of his position as an bank officer. The scheme involved making debit and credit transactions in two offices, but the embezzler found the Beverly Hills office was best for withdrawals. As the size of the theft grew, the bank officer couldn't hardly conceal it any longer. The bank discovered it's loss when the embezzler made a error in filling out a credit slip instead of a debit slip. Embarrassed bank officials have announced there intention to set up new operational controls to prevent these kind of fraudulent scheme in the future.

D. Supply the proper article (*a* or *an*) for the following words.

EXAMPLE: __an__ adjustment

1. ____ number	7. ____ warehouse	13. ____ insult
2. ____ honor	8. ____ agency	14. ____ X-ray
3. ____ inventory	9. ____ combination	15. ____ illegible letter
4. ____ pattern	10. ____ idea	16. ____ one-year lease
5. ____ Hawaiian	11. ____ utility	17. ____ eight-year lease
6. ____ orange	12. ____ airplane	18. ____ oil embargo

E. In the space provided write the correct form of the adjective shown in parentheses.

EXAMPLE: Of the three filing systems, which is (good)? __best__

1. You must be (careful) the next time you write an order. ________
2. This is the (good) illustration submitted thus far. ________
3. Please send me the (current) figures you can find. ________
4. The 20-pound stationery is (heavy) than the 16-pound paper. ________
5. It appears that this plan is (costly) than our previous insurance coverage. ________
6. Of all the employees Richard is the (little) talkative. ________
7. Ms. Hansen is (businesslike) than the office manager she replaced. ________
8. Have you ever met a (kind) individual than Mr. Stevenson? ________
9. This is the (bad) winter we've had in years. ________
10. Which is the (interesting) of the two novels? ________

Name ______________________

LEVEL II

A. (Self-check) Select the correct forms and write them in the space provided.

1. Brendan looked (calm, calmly) as he left the room. ______
2. The lighthouse is (farther, further) away than it first appeared. ______
3. Better service is ensured if a purchaser has (face-to-face, face to face) dealings with the manufacturer. ______
4. (Fewer, Less) homes have been constructed than ever before. ______
5. Unless data can be assembled (quicker, more quickly), we lose business to our competitors. ______
6. Mr. Burton (sure, surely) made his personal feelings apparent when he announced the policy change. ______
7. Because he forgot your birthday, Matthew felt (bad, badly). ______
8. Mr. Edgerton selected the (later, latter) of the two plans. ______
9. Some small businesses barely exist from (year-to-year, year to year). ______
10. Asked about her health, Aunt Edna said she felt (good, well). ______

Check your answers.

B. Write the correct word in the space provided.

1. Study the directions (careful, carefully) before assembling the model. ______
2. Because of the construction decline, (fewer, less) housing is available. ______
3. Lee thought that she did (good, well) in her interview. ______
4. Honeydew melons taste (good, well) with lemon juice. ______
5. Our office manager will (sure, surely) call for repairs. ______
6. Since its tune-up, the engine runs (smoother, more smoothly). ______
7. Lavonda wasn't (real, really) sure she could attend. ______
8. I hope you won't take this comment (personal, personally). ______
9. Do these peaches taste (bitter, bitterly) to you? ______
10. Your new suit certainly fits you (good, well). ______
11. The new suit looks very (good, well) on you. ______
12. She wanted to debate the question (further, farther). ______
13. He completed the aptitude test (satisfactory, satisfactorily). ______

A. 1. calm, 2. farther, 3. face-to-face, 4. Fewer, 5. more quickly, 6. surely, 7. bad, 8. latter, 9. year to year, 10. well

14. If you write (fewer, less) checks, your service charges will decline. __________
15. Henry feels (sure, surely) that employment will improve. __________
16. It seems (clear, clearly) that few openings will develop. __________
17. Four specialists keyed the lengthy report (perfect, perfectly). __________
18. To reduce costs, they pressed for a settlement (quick, quickly). __________
19. Mr. Turner was (sure, surely) proud of his pilot's license. __________
20. Recovering from his illness, Luis said he felt (good, well). __________

C. Select the correct group of words below. Write its letter in the space provided.

1. (a) coast to coast broadcast
   (b) coast-to-coast broadcast _____
2. (a) well-documented report
   (b) well documented report _____
3. (a) child who is ten-years-old
   (b) child who is ten years old _____
4. (a) ten-year-old child
   (b) ten year old child _____
5. (a) fully certified nurse
   (b) fully-certified nurse _____
6. (a) book that is up to date
   (b) book that is up-to-date _____
7. (a) data-processing service
   (b) data processing service _____
8. (a) arm-twisting tactics
   (b) arm twisting tactics _____
9. (a) last-minute preparations
   (b) last minute preparations _____
10. (a) widely-acclaimed cure
    (b) widely acclaimed cure _____

D. Place commas where needed in the following groups of words.

1. red sports car
2. narrow winding path
3. concise courteous letter
4. snug cheerful apartment
5. imaginative daring designer
6. efficient clerical employee

E. Write sentences using the compound adjectives shown. Be sure that the compound adjectives precede nouns.

EXAMPLE: (up to the minute) Your up-to-the-minute report arrived today.

1. (three year old) ______________________________
2. (once in a lifetime) ______________________________
3. (month by month) ______________________________
4. (out of date) ______________________________
5. (state of the art) ______________________________

Name ____________________

LEVEL III

A. (Self-check) Underline any errors in the following sentences and write their corrected forms in the spaces provided. If a sentence is correct as it is written, write *C*.

EXAMPLE: Elwood is the most unique individual I know. — most nearly unique

1. No solution is more correct than yours. ____________
2. Professor Fugi is the most conscientious teacher I've ever had. ____________
3. She is more conscientious than any teacher I've ever had. ____________
4. We were told to answer the ten last questions. ____________
5. Gomez has the most perfect sales routine in the business. ____________
6. Preston is concerned only with your welfare and happiness. ____________
7. He merely thought you wanted one page copied. ____________
8. Western mountains are more perpendicular than Eastern mountains. ____________
9. San Francisco is the most cosmopolitan city in California. ____________
10. It is more cosmopolitan than any city in the state. ____________

Check your answers.

B. Underline errors and write corrected forms in the spaces provided. If correct, write *C*.

1. Addressing these envelopes is the most endless job in the department. ____________
2. For rapid sale, the 15 last homes were drastically reduced. ____________
3. I would rather sell property for Doris than for any broker in the area. ____________
4. Is it more correct to use an adverb or an adjective in that sentence? ____________
5. Bricklin only produces quality custom cars. ____________
6. Las Vegas is the largest city in Nevada. ____________
7. Las Vegas is larger than any city in Nevada. ____________
8. That encyclopedia is only sold by door-to-door salespeople. ____________
9. Brockton's offers the most complete office service in town. ____________
10. The two first applicants were extremely well-qualified. ____________

A. 1. more nearly correct, 2. C, 3. any other teacher, 4. last ten questions, 5. most nearly perfect, 6. with only, 7. you merely wanted, *or* wanted merely one, 8. more nearly perpendicular, 9. C, 10. any other city

C. ***Review of Levels I, II, III.*** For each sentence below, underline any error. Then write a corrected form in the space provided.

1. It took us over a hour to decipher a nearly unreadable handwritten memo. __________
2. Is Model Z-3 or Model X10 best for our office needs? __________
3. Sandy said that she couldn't barely hear you when you called. __________
4. After the beginning of the year, we anticipate less changes in our recently modified program. __________
5. Hawkins interviewed a Canadian official and an European diplomat concerning the proposed two-year trade program. __________
6. If deliveries can't be made more quicker, we will change carriers. __________
7. Our newly-installed word processing center has productive, timesaving equipment. __________
8. One applicant felt that he had done good on the skills test. __________
9. I like this job better than any job I've ever had. __________
10. We can better judge our inventory once we have conducted our end-of-the-year stock count. __________
11. The designer attempted to create an attractive functional working environment. __________
12. We only try to file necessary paperwork. __________
13. Did you say that the two first rows had empty seats? __________
14. He passed my desk so quick I hardly saw him. __________
15. Dana made a point-by-point comparison of the machines. __________

D. ***Optional Composition.*** Your instructor may ask you to complete this exercise on a separate sheet. Write sentences using the following expressions as adjectives: *five year old, federally funded, fast moving,* and *fewer.* In addition, write sentences using the following words as adverbs: *well, farther, further,* and *only.*

POSTTEST

Underline the correct word.

1. We seem to have (fewer, less) applications than ever before.
2. Please use (a, an) orange marking pen to highlight the report.
3. Mrs. Sherman said she felt (good, well) following her surgery.
4. Erin completed a (page by page, page-by-page) check of the book.
5. The employees liked their (completely-redecorated, completely redecorated) office.

1. fewer, 2. an, 3. well, 4. page-by-page, 5. completely redecorated

CHAPTER 13

Prepositions

OBJECTIVES When you have completed the materials in this chapter, you will be able to do the following:

Level I — *Use objective-case pronouns as objects of prepositions.*
— *Avoid using prepositions in place of verbs and adverbs.*

Level II — *Use correctly eight troublesome prepositions.*
— *Omit unnecessary prepositions and retain necessary ones.*
— *Construct formal sentences that avoid terminal prepositions.*

Level III — *Recognize those words and constructions requiring specific prepositions (idioms).*

PRETEST

Underline the correct word.

1. Speed is important, but proofreading is necessary (to, too).
2. (As, like) I said, all our documents must be accurate.
3. Do you plan (on taking, to take) a two-week vacation?
4. Management and workers alike agreed (to, with) the contract.
5. The printer should be placed (beside, besides) the computer.

LEVEL I

Prepositions are connecting words that show the relationship of a noun or pronoun to another word in a sentence.

Common Use of Prepositions

Here is a list of commonly used prepositions. Notice that prepositions may consist of one word or several.

1. too, 2. As, 3. to take, 4. to, 5. beside

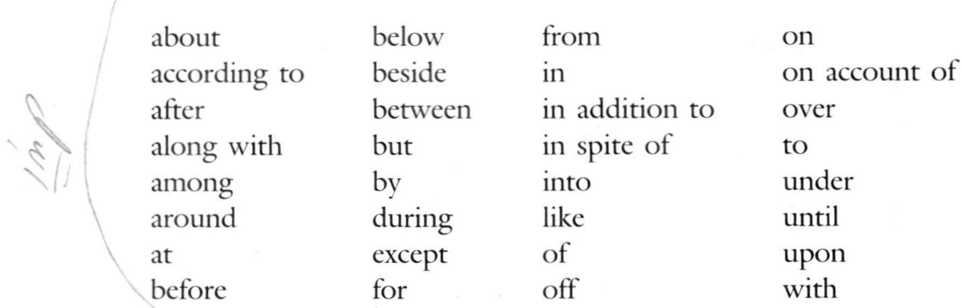

about	below	from	on
according to	beside	in	on account of
after	between	in addition to	over
along with	but	in spite of	to
among	by	into	under
around	during	like	until
at	except	of	upon
before	for	off	with

Objective Case Following Prepositions

As you will recall from Chapter 6, pronouns that are objects of prepositions must be in the objective case.

> Marian, *along with* Jan and *her,* arrived later.
>
> Letters *from* his mother and *them* were forwarded.
>
> Give the account balances *to* Mr. Love and *him.*

To review further, recall that some prepositions — such as *like, between, but,* and *except* — are particularly likely to lead to confusion in determining pronoun case. Consider the following examples.

> Strictly *between you* and *me* (not *I*), the contract is already signed.
>
> Applications from individuals *like* Mr. Sheldon and *him* (not *he*) are rare.
>
> Recommendations from everyone *but them* (not *they*) have arrived.

Fundamental Problems With Prepositions

In even the most casual speech or writing, the following misuses of prepositions should be avoided.

Of* for *have. The verb phrases *should have* and *could have* should never be written as *should of* or *could of.* The word "of" is a preposition and cannot be used in verb phrases.

> Jeremy *should have* (not *should of*) called first.
>
> He *could have* (not *could of*) given some advance notice.

Off* for *from. The preposition *from* should never be replaced by *off* or *off of.*

> My friend borrowed money *from* (not *off of*) me.
>
> Doreen said she got the book *from* (not *off* or *off of*) you.

To* for *too. The preposition *to* means "in a direction toward." Do not use the word *to* in place of the adverb *too,* which means "additionally," "also," or "excessively."

> Dividends are not distributed *to* stockholders unless declared by the directors.
>
> No dividends were declared because profits were *too* small.
>
> Contributions of services will be accepted *too.*

You will recall that the word *to* may also be part of an infinitive construction.

> She is learning *to* program the computer.

Complete the reinforcement exercises for Level I.

Troublesome Prepositions

Be particularly careful to use the following prepositions properly.

Among, between. *Among* is usually used to speak of three or more persons or things; *between* is usually used for two. *Webster's Ninth New Collegiate Dictionary* notes, however, that *between* may be used for more than two persons or things, especially to denote a one-to-one relationship.

The disagreement was *between* Stipchek and his partner.

Supplies were distributed *among* the four divisions.

Behind. Always use the preposition *behind,* rather than the phrase "in back of."

The invoices were found *behind* the desk.

Behind the storage room is the electric panel.

Beside, besides. *Beside* means "next to"; *besides* means "in addition to."

Please sit *beside* me at the assembly.

Besides a preface, you must write an introduction.

Except. The preposition *except,* meaning "excluding" or "but," is sometimes confused with the verb *accept,* which means "to receive."

Everyone *except* Melanie was able to come.
Please *accept* this gift as a token of our appreciation.

In, into. *In* indicates a position or location. *Into* indicates direction or movement to an interior location.

Billing is now done *in* the data processing office. (Preposition *in* indicates location.)

Bring the boxes *into* the storeroom. (Preposition *into* indicates movement to an interior location.)

Some constructions may employ *in* as an adverb preceding an infinitive:

They went *in* to see the manager. (Adverb *in* precedes infinitive *to see.*)

Like. The preposition *like* should be used to introduce a noun or pronoun. Do not use *like* to introduce a clause (a group of words with a subject and a predicate).

The copy looks very much *like* the original. (*Like* used as a preposition.)

It looks *as if* (not *like*) it may rain. (Do not use *like* to introduce the clause *it may rain.*)

As (not *like*) I said earlier, the order was sent. (Do not use *like* to introduce the clause *I said earlier.*)

Using Prepositions Efficiently

Necessary Prepositions

Don't omit those prepositions necessary to clarify a relationship. Be particularly careful when two prepositions modify a single object.

We have every desire *for* and hope *of* an early settlement. (Do not omit *for*.)

What type *of* coupler do you need? (Do not omit *of*.)

Mr. Munoz is unsure *of* where to place the machine. (Do not omit *of*.)

Salaries for temporary positions seem to be higher than *for* permanent positions. (Do not omit *for*.)

When did you graduate *from* high school? (Do not omit *from*.)*

Unnecessary Prepositions

Omit prepositions that are used unnecessarily, particularly the word *of*.

The book fell *off* (not *off of*) the desk.

Leave the package *inside* (not *inside of*) the door.

Both cassettes (not *of the* cassettes) are usable.

All the (not *of the*) memoranda require carbon copies.

Where is the meeting (not *meeting at*)?

She could not help (rather than help *from*) laughing.

Keep the paper near (not *near to*) the printer.

Ending a Sentence With a Preposition

In the past, language authorities warned against ending a sentence (or a clause) with a preposition. In formal writing today most careful authors continue to avoid terminal prepositions. In conversation, however, terminal prepositions are acceptable.

Acceptable usage	Formal usage
What organization is he a member *of*?	*Of* what organization is he a member?
What is the medicine prescribed *for*?	*For* what is the medicine prescribed?
How many forms did you write *on*?	*On* how many forms did you write?
We don't know whom you spoke *to* when you called.	We don't know *to* whom you spoke when you called.

Complete the reinforcement exercises for Level II.

LEVEL III

Idiomatic Use of Prepositions

Every language has idioms (word combinations that are peculiar to that language). These combinations have developed through usage and often cannot be explained rationally. A native speaker usually is unaware of idiom usage until a violation jars his or her ear, such as "He is capable *from* (rather than *of*) violence."

The list below shows words that require specific prepositions to denote precise meanings. This group is just a sampling of the large number of English idioms. Consult a dictionary when you are unsure of the correct preposition to use with a particular word.

acquaint with	You must become *acquainted with* the new equipment.
addicted to	Miss Saguchi was *addicted to* jelly beans.

**See Hot Line Query on p. 176.*

adept in	Are you *adept in* programming?
adhere to	All employees must *adhere to* certain office rules.
agree to (a proposal)	Did they *agree to* the plan for splitting shifts?
agree with (a person)	In this matter I certainly *agree with* you.
angry at (a thing)	Customers are understandably *angry at* the delay.
angry with (a person)	How can you be *angry with* the child?
buy from	You may *buy from* any one of several wholesalers.
capable of	She is *capable of* remarkable accomplishments.
comply with	We must *comply with* governmental regulations.
concur in (an action)	Four countries *concur in* a plan to reduce oil production.
concur with (a person)	Do you *concur with* Andrew in the need for economy?
conform to	These machine parts do not *conform to* specification.
contrast with	The white boat *contrasts* sharply *with* the blue ocean.
correspond to (match)	A bird's wing *corresponds to* a man's arm.
correspond with (to write)	Madge *corresponds with* several distant friends.
desire for	A *desire for* wealth may create greed.
desirous of	Bendix is *desirous of* acquiring Conoco stocks.
differ from (things)	Computer software *differs from* computer hardware.
differ with (person)	I *differ with* you in small points only.
different from	This product is *different from* the one I ordered.
disagree with	Do you *disagree with* him?
expert in	Dr. Rand is an *expert in* electronics.
guard against	*Guard against* infection by covering wounds.
identical with	This house key is *identical with* yours.
independent of	Living alone, the young man was *independent of* his parents.
infer from	I *infer from* your remark that you are dissatisfied.
interest in	Jerry has a great *interest in* personal computers.
negligent of	*Negligent of* his diet, the old man became ill.
oblivious *of* or *to*	McClain was oblivious *of* (or *to*) his surroundings.
plan to (not *on*)	We *plan to* expand the marketing of our products.
prefer to	Do you *prefer to* work a four-day week?
reason with	Mr. Miller tried to *reason with* the unhappy customer.
reconcile with	Checkbook figures must be *reconciled with* bank figures.
reconcile to	He has never become *reconciled to* retirement.
responsible for	William is *responsible for* locking the building.
retroactive to	The salary increase is *retroactive to* last July 1.
sensitive to	Mrs. Choy is unusually *sensitive to* cold.
similar to	Your term paper topic is *similar to* mine.
standing in (not *on*) line	How long have you been *standing in* line?
talk to (to tell something)	The speaker *talked to* the large group.
talk with (exchange of remarks)	After his lecture, the speaker *talked with* club members informally.

Complete the reinforcement exercises for Level III.

HOT LINE QUERIES

QUESTION: Another employee and I are collaborating on a report. I wanted to write this: *Money was lost due to poor attendance.* She says the sentence should read, *Money was lost because of poor attendance.* My version is more concise. Which of us is right?

ANSWER: Most language authorities agree with your coauthor. *Due to* is acceptable when it functions as an adjective, as *Success was due to proper timing.* In this sense, *due to* is synonymous with *attributable to.* However, when *due to* functions as a preposition, as in your sentence, language experts find fault. Your friend is right; substitute *because of.*

QUESTION: What's wrong with saying *Lisa graduated college last year?*

ANSWER: The preposition *from* must be inserted for syntactical fluency. Two constructions are permissible. *Lisa graduated from college* or *Lisa was graduated from college.* The first version is more popular; the second is preferred by traditional grammarians.

QUESTION: Should *sometime* be one or two words in the following sentence? *Can you come over (some time) soon?*

ANSWER: In this sentence you should use the one-word form. *Sometime* means "an indefinite time" *(the convention is sometime in December).* The two-word combination means "a period of time" *(we have some time to spare).*

QUESTION: I saw this printed recently: *Some of the personal functions that are being reviewed are job descriptions, job specifications, and job evaluation.* Is *personal* used correctly here?

ANSWER: Indeed not! The word *personal* means "private" or "individual" (*your personal letters are being forwarded to you*). The word *personnel* refers to employees (*all company personnel are cordially invited*). The sentence you quote requires *personnel.*

QUESTION: Is there any difference between *proved* and *proven*?

ANSWER: As a past participle, the verb form *proved* is preferred (*he has proved his point*). However, the word *proven* is preferred as an adjective form (*that company has a proven record*). *Proven* is also commonly used in the expression *not proven.*

QUESTION: We're writing a letter to our subscribers, and this sentence doesn't sound right to me: *Every one of our subscribers benefit. . . .*

ANSWER: As you probably suspected, the verb *benefit* does not agree with the subject *one.* The sentence should read as follows: *Every one of our subscribers benefits. . . .* Don't let intervening phrases obscure the true subject of a sentence.

QUESTION: In my dictionary I found three ways to spell the same word: *life-style, lifestyle,* and *life style.* Which should I use?

ANSWER: The first spelling shown is usually the preferred one. In your dictionary a second acceptable form may be introduced by the word *also.* If two spellings appear side by side (*ax, axe*), they are equally acceptable.

QUESTION: How should I write *industry wide?* It's not in my dictionary.

ANSWER: A word with the suffix *wide* is usually written solid: *industrywide, nationwide, countrywide, statewide, worldwide.*

Name ____________________

CHAPTER 13 Reinforcement Exercises

LEVEL I

A. (Self-check) Select the correct word and write it in the space provided.

1. Let's share the cost of the trip between (we, us) two. ____________
2. Thomas thought that he (should of, should have) been allowed extra time. ____________
3. Bernstein has (to, too) little patience for that job. ____________
4. Everyone seems to have read the book but (I, me). ____________
5. You might be able to get the lecture notes (off of, from) Kathleen. ____________
6. Should a photocopy be made for Mrs. Korkas or (her, she)? ____________
7. Government, too, has (to, too) consider the effects of inflation. ____________
8. Can you borrow a tent (off, from) the Petersons? ____________
9. With additional study Gregory (could of, could have) earned an A. ____________
10. No one in the group except her and (I, me) will miss the field trip. ____________

Check your answers.

B. Underline any errors you find in the following sentences. Write the correct forms in the spaces provided. Write *C* if the sentence is correct as written.

EXAMPLE: Performers like Mervin and she are crowd pleasers. ____her____

1. No one in the class except he can attend the Saturday session. ____________
2. James could of worked some overtime hours. ____________
3. We got your address off of Tony before he left. ____________
4. Many customers are eager to make appointments with Mr. Jerome or him. ____________
5. Our union said that management's offer was "too little and to late." ____________
6. Mr. Bowman told Andrew and me that we should have read the directions more carefully. ____________

A. 1. us, 2. should have, 3. too, 4. me, 5. from, 6. her, 7. to, 8. from, 9. could have, 10. me

7. It's to soon to tell if the young tree will bear edible fruit. __________

8. Along with Tim and I, Mr. De la Torre will check the computer printout. __________

9. Just between you and me, how many employees will be reassigned? __________

10. You could of attended the premier showing last evening. __________

11. Our manager, together with Tanya and he, helped to complete the transaction. __________

12. If you could of delivered the cassettes earlier, we might have finished on time. __________

13. One can always rely upon friends like Renee and he for assistance in time of need. __________

14. Everyone except him and I received the announcement too late to respond. __________

15. To address the letter properly, you must use information off of their stationery. __________

16. Last year we tried to order supplies off of them too. __________

17. All the checkers except she and he have the holiday off. __________

18. Some of the paper is to long for our everyday use. __________

19. If you could of seen the shipment when it arrived, you would have refused it too. __________

20. Mr. Fenton spoke with Carmen and I about our using computer terminals for information retrieval. __________

Name ______________________

LEVEL II

A. (Self-check) Select the correct word(s).

1. The inheritance will be divided (between, among) all the heirs. ______________
2. Mr. Whitmore moved (in, into) the office next door. ______________
3. Identifying serial numbers are located (inside, inside of) the machines. ______________
4. (Besides, Beside) word processing, the new computer handles our data processing. ______________
5. It looks (like, as if) we'll be working late tonight. ______________
6. You will be billed later if you (except, accept) the shipment. ______________
7. Helen said she felt (like, as) a queen. ______________
8. Has anyone taken the desk (in back of, behind) you? ______________
9. The contracts blew (off, off of) the desk when the door was opened. ______________
10. In the office (beside, besides) mine is data processing. ______________

Check your answers.

B. In the following sentences cross out unnecessary prepositions as well as any other unnecessary words. Insert any necessary prepositions.

EXAMPLES: What type ^of^ wheel bearings are needed?
Where are you going ~~to~~?

1. Both of the mechanics recognized the engine problem immediately.
2. The purchase orders must have been taken off of the desk sometime yesterday.
3. Who can tell me where the meeting is scheduled at?
4. Dr. Forward had a great appreciation and an interest in all applications of computerization.
5. Do you know if all of the orders have been filled?
6. Special printing jobs must be done outside of the office.
7. Only Mr. Wilson knows where those supplies might be stored at.
8. What style clothes is recommended for the formal dinner?
9. Where shall we move the extra desks and chairs to?
10. Daniel's love and interest in photography led to a gratifying career.
11. After the entire stack of boxes tumbled, Randy couldn't help from laughing.
12. I'm not certain where you want me to take this report to.

A. 1. among, 2. into, 3. inside, 4. Besides, 5. as if, 6. accept, 7. like, 8. behind, 9. off, 10. beside

13. Please place the new directories inside of the office.
14. We have been informed that the claim is due on April 15.
15. Did Jill say she graduated high school last year?

C. Write original sentences using these prepositions correctly.

1. (besides) ______________________________
2. (into) ______________________________
3. (except) ______________________________
4. (like) ______________________________
5. (among) ______________________________

D. The following sentences have prepositions that end clauses. Rewrite the sentences so that the prepositions precede their objects.

EXAMPLE: Here is the information you asked about.
Here is the information about which you asked.

1. Whom did you address the letter to? ______________________________
2. Please find the folder you put the letter in. ______________________________
3. What did I come into this room for? ______________________________
4. We have a number of loyal members we can rely upon. ______________________________
5. What salesperson did these brochures come from? ______________________________

Name ______________________

LEVEL III

A. (Self-check) Underline any errors in the use of prepositions in the following sentences, and write a correct form in the space provided. Write *C* if the sentence is correct as written.

1. Al Fernandez is exceptionally adept with woodworking. ______________
2. We find it impossible to comply to the latest safety regulations. ______________
3. In a televised address, the President will talk with the nation at 6 p.m. ______________
4. Lola said that she plans on sleeping late during her vacation. ______________
5. Mrs. Reich's management style is much different than Mr. Haddad's. ______________
6. Ray is very angry at David for divulging the secret. ______________
7. It is difficult to reconcile this new business venture with their recent bankruptcy. ______________
8. Isolated from neighbors, the hermit was independent with local laws. ______________
9. A car very similar with yours is for sale. ______________
10. Richard has little interest with data processing. ______________

Check your answers.

B. Underline any errors in the use of prepositions in the following sentences, and write a correction in the space provided. Write *C* if the sentence is correct as written.

1. Assertion is not identical to truth. ______________
2. Mr. Colotti described how common stock differs with preferred stock. ______________
3. Do you plan on taking your vacation in August? ______________
4. Does Mr. Brady concur with other board members in raising tuition? ______________
5. Have you become acquainted to your new computer yet? ______________
6. That film is much different than what I expected. ______________
7. All procedures must adhere with the company manual. ______________
8. The white letters on the sign do not sufficiently contrast from the yellow background. ______________

A. 1. adept in, 2. comply with, 3. talk to, 4. plans to sleep, 5. different from, 6. angry with, 7. C, 8. independent of, 9. similar to, 10. interest in

9. Is it necessary to hire an interpreter when your company corresponds to Japanese customers? ________

10. Because the franchise is completely standardized, the food and decor in a fast-food restaurant in California may be identical to one in Massachusetts. ________

11. It was necessary to increase parking lot security to guard from auto thefts. ________

12. To conform with departmental procedures, all work must be logged in. ________

13. Brian learned that Ellen was quite angry at him. ________

14. We cannot possibly agree with a contract that we have not yet read. ________

15. The applicant for the position claimed to be an expert on hydraulic systems. ________

C. ***Optional Composition.*** Your instructor may ask you to complete this exercise on a separate sheet. Write sentences using the following expressions: ***oblivious of, adhere to, retroactive to, desirous of, independent of, agree with, identical with, differs from, among, besides,*** and *too.* Use a dictionary if necessary.

POSTTEST

Underline the correct word.

1. The memo was (to, too) long to fit on one page.
2. It looks (like, as if) the company must relocate.
3. Is it necessary for all documents to comply (to, with) the new guidelines?
4. Dividends will be distributed (between, among) stockholders.
5. (Beside, Besides) Ann, who is able to work Saturday?

1. too, 2. as if, 3. with, 4. among, 5. Besides

CHAPTER 14

Conjunctions to Join Equals

OBJECTIVES When you have completed the materials in this chapter, you will be able to do the following:

Level I — *Distinguish between simple and compound sentences.*

— *Punctuate compound sentences joined by* and, or, not, *and* but.

Level II — *Punctuate compound sentences using conjunctive adverbs such as* therefore, however, *and* consequently.

— *Punctuate sentences using parenthetical (interrupting) adverbs such as* therefore, however, *and* consequently.

Level III — *Recognize correlative conjunctions such as* either . . . or, not only . . . but also, *and* neither . . nor.

— *Use parellel construction in composing sentences with correlative conjunctions.*

PRETEST

Insert commas or semicolons to punctuate the following sentences correctly.

1. Sales on the West Coast have increased therefore we are assigning more sales representatives to that area.
2. It is important however that we also continue to cover all other sales territories adequately.
3. Eleanor Uyeda prefers to remain in Fullerton but Wanda Deen is considering the San Diego area.
4. As many as 20 agents will move nevertheless the transition must be made smoothly.

Underline the letter of the sentence that is more effective.

5. (a) Not only is this copier faster but it also is cheaper than the other.
   (b) This copier is not only faster but also cheaper than the other.

1. increased; therefore, 2. important, however, 3. Fullerton, 4. move; nevertheless, 5. b

Conjunctions are connecting words. They may be separated into two major groups: those that join grammatically equal words or word groups and those that join grammatically unequal words or word groups. This chapter will focus on those conjunctions that join equals. Recognizing conjunctions and understanding their patterns of usage will, among other things, enable you to use commas and semicolons more appropriately.

LEVEL I

Coordinating Conjunctions

Coordinating conjunctions connect words, phrases, and clauses of equal grammatical value or rank. The most common coordinating conjunctions are *and, or, but,* and *nor.* Notice in these sentences that coordinating conjunctions join grammatically equal elements.

We think your action is *illogical, unfair,* and *arbitrary.* (Here the word *and* joins equal words.)

Give serious thought *to your letters* and *to reader reaction.* (Here *and* joins equal phrases.)

Mr. Freeman opens the mail, but *Miss Dunaway fills the orders.* (Here *but* joins equal clauses.)

Phrases and Clauses

A group of related words without a subject and a verb is called a *phrase.* You are already familiar with verb phrases and prepositional phrases. It is not important that you be able to identify the other kinds of phrases (infinitive, gerund, participial), but it is very important that you be able to distinguish phrases from clauses.

The alarm was coming from another part of the building.

phrase phrase phrase

A group of related words including a subject and a verb is a *clause.*

We interviewed three applicants, and we decided to hire Mr. Lee.

clause clause

Karen is interested in a job in marketing, but she wants to travel also.

clause clause
phrase phrase

Salaries begin at $25,000 annually, and they can reach over $50,000.

clause clause

Clauses may contain phrases within them, as illustrated in the last sentence.

Simple and Compound Sentences

A simple sentence has one independent clause, that is, a clause that can stand alone. A compound sentence has two or more independent clauses.

We agreed to lease the equipment. (Simple sentence.)

Our Travel Services Department planned the sales trip, but some salespeople also made private excursions. (Compound sentence.)

Punctuating Compound Sentences

When coordinating conjunctions join clauses in compound sentences, a comma precedes the conjunction unless the clauses are very short (four or fewer words in each clause).

> We can ship the merchandise by air, *or* we can ship it by rail.
>
> Ship by air *or* ship by rail. (Clauses are too short to require a comma.)

Do not use commas when coordinating conjunctions join compound verbs, objects, or phrases.

> The bank will notify you of each transfer, or it will send you a monthly statement. (Comma used because *or* joins two independent clauses.)
>
> The bank will notify you of each transfer or will send you a monthly statement. (No comma needed because *or* joins the compound verbs of a single independent clause.)
>
> Thomas Edison said that colleges should not have to choose between lighting their buildings or enlightening their students. (No comma needed because *or* joins the compound objects of a prepositional phrase.)
>
> Stockholders are expected to attend the meeting or to send in their proxies. (No comma needed because *or* joins two infinitive phrases.)
>
> Analyze all your possible property risks, and protect yourself with insurance. (Comma needed to join two independent clauses; the subject of each clause is understood to be *you*.)

Complete the reinforcement exercises for Level I.

LEVEL II

Conjunctive Adverbs

Conjunctive adverbs may also be used to connect equal sentence elements. Because conjunctive adverbs are used to effect a transition from one thought to another, and because they may consist of more than one word, they have also been called *transitional expressions*. The most common conjunctive adverbs follow.

accordingly	in fact	on the other hand
consequently	in the meantime	that is
furthermore	moreover	then
hence	nevertheless	therefore
however	on the contrary	thus

In the following compound sentences, observe that conjunctive adverbs join clauses of equal grammatical value. Note that semicolons (*not* commas) are used before conjunctive adverbs that join independent clauses. Commas should immediately follow conjunctive adverbs of two or more syllables. Note also that the word following a semicolon is not capitalized — unless, of course, it is a proper noun.

> Electricians rewired the equipment room; *nevertheless,* fuses continued to blow.
>
> Some machines require separate outlets; *consequently,* new outlets were installed.
>
> Equipment expenditures are very great this quarter; *on the other hand,* new equipment will reduce labor costs.

Complex equipment requires operators who are specialists; *thus* we must train operators to become specialists.

Competition among computer manufacturers is intensive; *hence* prices may decrease sharply.

Generally, no comma is used after one-syllable conjunctive adverbs such as *hence, thus,* and *then* (unless a strong pause is desired).

Distinguishing Conjunctive Adverbs From Parenthetical Adverbs

Many words that function as conjunctive adverbs may also serve as parenthetical (interrupting) adverbs that are employed to effect transition from one thought to another. Use semicolons *only* with conjunctive adverbs that join independent clauses. Use commas to set off parenthetical adverbs that interrupt the flow of a sentence.

Jackson is, *however,* a fine administrator.

Jackson is a fine administrator; *however,* he is a poor fund raiser.

The Federal Reserve System, *moreover,* is a vital force in maintaining a sound banking system and a stable economy.

The Federal Reserve System is a vital force in maintaining a sound banking system; *moreover,* it is instrumental in creating a stable economy.

We believe, *on the other hand,* that sales will increase soon.

We believe that sales will increase soon; *on the other hand,* costs will be going up also.

Complete the reinforcement exercises for Level II.

LEVEL III

Other Conjunctions

Correlative Conjunctions

We have studied thus far two kinds of conjunctions used to join grammatically equal sentence elements: coordinating conjunctions (used to join equal words, phrases, and clauses) and conjunctive adverbs (used to join grammatically equal clauses in compound sentences). Correlative conjunctions form the third and final group of conjunctions that join grammatically equal sentence elements.

Correlative conjunctions are always paired: *both . . . and, not only . . . but (also), either . . . or, neither . . . nor.* When greater emphasis is desired, these paired conjunctions are used instead of coordinating conjunctions.

Your glasses are on the counter *or* on the table.

Your glasses are *either* on the counter *or* on the table. (More emphatic.)

In using correlative conjunctions, place them so that the words, phrases, or clauses being joined are parallel in construction.

Parallel: He was working *either* in Scottsdale *or* in Phoenix.

Not Parallel: *Either* he was working in Scottsdale *or* in Phoenix.

Parallel: She was *not only* gracious *but also* kind.
Not Parallel: She was *not only* gracious, *but* she was *also* kind.

Parallel: I have *neither* the time *nor* the energy for this.
Not Parallel: I *neither* have the time *nor* the energy for this.

Additional Coordinating Conjunctions

At Level I you studied the four most commonly used coordinating conjunctions: *and, or, nor,* and *but*. Three other coordinating conjunctions should also be mentioned.

The words *yet* and *for* may function as coordinating conjunctions, although they are infrequently used as such.

We have only two hours left, *yet* we hope to finish.

The weary traveler was gaunt and ill, *for* his journey had been long and arduous.

The word *so* is sometimes informally used as a coordinating conjunction. In more formal contexts the conjunctive adverbs *therefore* and *consequently* should be substituted for the conjunction *so*.

Informal: The plane leaves at 2:15, *so* you still have time to pack.
Formal: The plane leaves at 2:15; *therefore,* you still have time to pack.

Complete the reinforcement exercises for Level III.

HOT LINE QUERIES

QUESTION: Please help me decide which *maybe* to use in this sentence: *He said that he (maybe, may be) able to help us.*

ANSWER: Use the two-word *may be,* which is the verb form. *Maybe* is an adverb that means "perhaps" (*maybe she will call*).

QUESTION: At the end of a typewritten line, is it acceptable to type part of an individual's name on one line and carry the rest to the next line?

ANSWER: Full names may be divided between the first and last names or after the middle initial. For example, you could type *John R.* on one line and *Williamson* on the next line. Do not, however, separate a short title and a surname (such as *Mr./Williamson*), and do not divide a name (such as *William/son*).

QUESTION: What should the verb in this sentence be? *There (has, have) to be good reasons . . .*

ANSWER: Use the plural verb *have,* which agrees with the subject *reasons*. In sentences that begin with the word *there,* look for the subject after the verb.

QUESTION: Does *Ms.* have a period after it? Should I use this title for all women in business today?

ANSWER: *Ms.* is considered an abbreviation of *mistress,* formed by combining and shortening *Miss* and *Mrs.* Therefore, it does have a period following it. Some women in business prefer to use *Ms.,* presumably because it is a title equal to *Mr.* Neither title reveals one's marital status. Many other women, however, prefer to use *Miss* or *Mrs.* as titles. It's always wise, if possible, to determine the preference of the individual.

QUESTION: I just typed this sentence: *He was given a new title in lieu of a salary increase.* I went to my dictionary to check the spelling of *in lieu of,* but I can't find it. How is it spelled and what does it mean?

ANSWER: The listing in the dictionary is under *lieu,* and it means "instead of." Many authorities today are recommending that such foreign phrases be avoided. It's easier and clearer to say "instead of."

QUESTION: Can you help me with the words *averse* and *adverse?* I've never been able to straighten them out in my mind.

ANSWER: *Averse* is an adjective meaning "disinclined" and generally is used with the preposition *to* (*the little boy was averse to bathing; she is averse to statistical typing*). *Adverse* is also an adjective, but it means "hostile" or "unfavorable" (*adverse economic conditions halted the company's growth; the picnic was postponed because of adverse weather conditions*). In distinguishing between these two very similar words, it might help you to know that the word *averse* is usually used to describe animate (living) objects.

QUESTION: What should I write: *You are our No. 1 account,* or *You are our number one account?* Should anything be hyphenated?

ANSWER: Either is correct, but I prefer *No. 1* because it is more easily recognizable. No hyphen is required.

Name ______________________

CHAPTER 14 **Reinforcement Exercises**

LEVEL I

A. (Self-check) Indicate whether the following sentences are punctuated correctly (*C*) or incorrectly (*I*).

EXAMPLE: It rained most of the morning, but stopped in the afternoon when the sun began to shine. ___I___

1. The value-added tax is quite popular in Europe, but it has received little support in this country. ______
2. I did not expect a profit, and did not fear a loss. ______
3. Listen well, and look carefully. ______
4. Word processing specialists must possess excellent English skills, and they must be skilled at keyboarding. ______
5. Thank you for applying for admission, and for sending us your data sheet. ______
6. The concert did not begin until 8 p.m., but a large crowd began to gather at noon. ______
7. Ms. Phillips types and Mrs. Rogers edits. ______
8. We find it necessary to increase the prices of our packaging film, and the prices of our entire line of paper products. ______
9. Personnel Director Berman will be interviewing applicants Monday and Tuesday, and will make a decision on the appointment by Friday. ______
10. The city of Bombay originally rested on seven islands, but the islands were joined by landfill long ago. ______

Check your answers.

B. A simple sentence has one independent clause. A compound sentence has two or more independent clauses. Indicate with a check mark whether the following sentences, all of which are punctuated correctly, are simple or compound. Hint: A sentence is not compound unless the words preceding and following a conjunction form independent clauses. If these groups of words could not stand alone as sentences, the sentence is not compound.

	Simple	Compound
1. Mr. Thomas wrote a travel report, and he shared its information with other members of the staff.	______	______
2. Mr. Thomas wrote a travel report and shared its information with other members of the staff.	______	______

A. 1. C, 2. I, 3. I, 4. C, 5. I, 6. C, 7. C, 8. I, 9. I, 10. C

	Simple	Compound
3. We will allow you our discount of 10 percent and also a cash rebate of over $50 for each purchase.	______	______
4. The recently constructed corporate headquarters contained attractive executive offices, but the structure had few support facilities for employees.	______	______
5. The recently constructed corporate headquarters contained attractive executive offices but few support facilities for employees.	______	______
6. Management trainees are sent to all our branch offices in this country and to some of the branch offices in South America and Europe.	______	______
7. We will consider the information already submitted or any other information collected in the near future.	______	______
8. Fill in all the answers on the application, and send the form to the personnel director.	______	______
9. Send copies of the project report to me and to other management personnel in our three subsidiaries.	______	______
10. Supplies for three offices arrived today, but most of our order will not arrive until later.	______	______

C. Insert commas where appropriate in the following sentences. Then, in the space provided, indicate the number of commas you have added for each sentence. If no comma is needed, write *0*.

EXAMPLE: Kevin attended classes on Monday, but he went to the beach on Tuesday. ___1___

1. This is merely my opinion and I'm not sure you will agree with it. ______
2. Mrs. Sokol authorized the expenditure and directed the purchasing agent to place an order immediately. ______
3. Mr. Peterson was not pleased with the delay but he did not seem to be angry with the vendor. ______
4. Please transcribe this letter and mail it. ______
5. I will try to attend today's meeting but I'm not sure I can also attend Friday's. ______
6. Annuities for all contributors may accumulate yearly or may be withdrawn at regular intervals over a five-year period. ______
7. Proverbs are often short in length but they are usually long in experience. ______
8. Raw materials and supplies are available but machinery and equipment must be replaced before production can begin. ______
9. Consider the alternatives and act accordingly. ______
10. You may be interested in a career in this country or you may be interested in working abroad. ______

Name ______________________

LEVEL II

A. (Self-check) In the following sentences selected adverbs and conjunctions have been italicized. Using the letters below, indicate what punctuation should precede and follow the italicized words. In addition, insert the punctuation in each sentence.

(a) ; ________ , (c) , ________ (e) no punctuation
(b) ; ________ (d) , ________ ,

EXAMPLE: Too many salespeople missed the seminar; *therefore*, attendance will be mandatory in the future. a

1. Our Reprographics Department is currently understaffed; *thus* we are behind on our production schedule. ______
2. We are, *however*, able to make single copies quickly. ______
3. The bill of lading did not match the order; *consequently*, the shipment was refused. ______
4. Property may be insured in excess of its actual value; *however*, damages will be paid for no more than the actual loss. ______
5. Kelly did, *nevertheless*, pick up the printed copies she needed immediately. ______
6. Mrs. Arnold appears to be best qualified; *on the other hand*, Mr. Percy has excellent recommendations. ______
7. Jeanette considered the possibility of changing jobs *but* was unwilling to accept the risks involved. ______
8. Kevin, *on the other hand*, changed jobs whenever the urge impelled him. ______
9. Our Accounts Receivable Department has written to you three times; *however*, we have had no response to our letters. ______
10. Your account is now three months overdue; *hence* we have only one alternative left open to us. ______

Check your answers.

B. In the following sentences selected adverbs and conjunctions have been italicized. Using the letters below, indicate what punctuation should precede and follow the italicized words. In addition, insert the punctuation in each sentence.

(a) ; ________ , (c) , ________ (e) no punctuation
(b) ; ________ (d) , ________ ,

EXAMPLE: Some loans must be secured; *therefore*, the borrower must supply collateral. a

1. Early America was greatly influenced by royalist England; *in fact*, the White House was originally called the "President's Palace." ______

A. 1. b, 2. d, 3. a, 4. a, 5. d, 6. a, 7. e, 8. d, 9. a, 10. b

(a) ; ________ , (c) , ________ (e) no punctuation
(b) ; ________ (d) , ________ ,

2. Microwave relay stations have reduced telephone costs *moreover* cable and satellite circuits may reduce costs even more. ______
3. We are faced *nevertheless* with unusually expensive communication costs. ______
4. The current interest rate seems extremely high *but* may rise even higher. ______
5. Insurance works under the law of averages *thus* increased losses will send the average cost of insurance premiums upward. ______
6. The car came with an automatic transmission *nevertheless* it provided better-than-average gas mileage. ______
7. We are *moreover* pleased with its maneuverability and handling. ______
8. A new directory will be released later in the month *in the meantime* use the old book and the information service. ______
9. Automobile repair costs are skyrocketing *consequently* car insurance costs are rising sharply. ______
10. Please place your order immediately *or* you will not be eligible for the discount. ______
11. Members of our management staff *moreover* are interested in hiring a consultant to train customer personnel on the new equipment. ______
12. Information concerning equipment used in business offices is needed *therefore* we are conducting a survey. ______
13. Over 3,000 questionnaires will be mailed to business organizations *thus* we will need a postal permit for metered mail. ______
14. We are currently using envelopes made from kraft paper *and* find that some of our deliveries are arriving in damaged condition. ______
15. Servco has produced *on the other hand* a tool with remarkable safety features and excellent ease of handling. ______
16. The company gave each employee a holiday bonus *therefore* Christmas checks were considerably larger this year. ______
17. This apprenticeship program *on the contrary* combines classroom instruction with on-the-job training. ______
18. The sessions for business managers start on Tuesday *but* the seminars for sales representatives do not begin until Wednesday. ______

C. Write compound sentences using the conjunctions shown below.

1. *consequently* ____

____

2. *but* ____

____

3. *nevertheless* ____

____

Name ______________________________

LEVEL III

A. (Self-check) Select the more effective version of each of the following pairs of sentences. Write its letter in the space provided. Study the construction of the sentences so that you can rewrite sentences in the exercises that follow.

1. (a) Either she sent the letter on Monday or on Tuesday.
   (b) She sent the letter either on Monday or on Tuesday. ______
2. (a) Mr. Kinsman is not able to represent us and neither is Mrs. Bragg.
   (b) Neither Mr. Kinsman nor Mrs. Bragg is able to represent us. ______
3. (a) Our objectives are both to improve customer relations and increasing sales.
   (b) Our objectives are both to improve customer relations and to increase sales. ______
4. (a) She neither called nor explained her absence.
   (b) Neither did she call nor explain her absence. ______
5. (a) This work order must be completed by Friday, so you may have to work late Thursday.
   (b) This work order must be completed by Friday; therefore, you may have to work late Thursday. ______
6. (a) Our new copier is not only faster but also less expensive.
   (b) Not only is our new copier faster, but it also is less expensive. ______
7. (a) Neither did the staff finish the proposals nor the contracts.
   (b) The staff finished neither the proposals nor the contracts. ______
8. (a) He has had no formal education, yet he is very well-read.
   (b) He has had no formal education; yet he is very well-read. ______
9. (a) A three-hour time difference separates us; so you should call immediately.
   (b) A three-hour time difference separates us; therefore, you should call immediately. ______
10. (a) You must either telephone or telegraph him immediately.
    (b) Either you must telephone or telegraph him immediately. ______

Check your answers.

B. Which of these sentence pairs is more effective?

1. (a) Either give the time card to Tina Chang or to me.
   (b) Give the time card either to Tina Chang or to me. ______
2. (a) Our travel counselor will both plan your trip and make your reservations.
   (b) Our travel counselor will both plan your trip and reservations will be made. ______

A. 1. b, 2. b, 3. b, 4. a, 5. b, 6. a, 7. b, 8. a, 9. b, 10. a

3. (a) We have checked every figure carefully; yet the totals do not balance.
   (b) We have checked every figure carefully, yet the totals do not balance. ______

4. (a) Not only does a product carry an expressed warranty, but it also carries an implied warranty.
   (b) A product carries not only an expressed warranty but also an implied warranty. ______

5. (a) We must receive either your payment or a reason why you cannot pay.
   (b) Either we must receive your payment, or you must give us a reason why you cannot pay. ______

C. Rewrite the following sentences to make them more effective.

1. Either bankruptcy can be declared by the debtor or it can be requested by the creditors.

   ____

   ____

2. Neither the staff was happy with the proposed cutbacks in class offerings, and nor were the students. ______________________________

   ____

3. Not only do banks use computers to sort checks, but they also use computers for disbursing cash automatically. ______________________________

   ____

D. ***Optional Composition.*** Your instructor may ask you to complete this exercise on a separate sheet. Write sentences that illustrate the following: a simple sentence, a compound sentence, a parenthetical adverb, and a pair of correlative conjunctions. Write three compound sentences using different conjunctive adverbs. Label each sentence.

POSTTEST

Add commas or semicolons to the following sentences.

1. The cost of our raw materials is increasing consequently the price of our product must also increase.
2. We are convinced nevertheless that our products will continue to be competitive in today's market.
3. We are searching for other suppliers and we are also trying to reduce transportation costs.
4. One supplier is located in the state of Washington however we have been unable to find anyone closer.

Underline the letter of the sentence that is more effective.

5. (a) Neither can we ship the printer or the computer until April 1.
   (b) We can ship neither the printer nor the computer until April 1.

1. increasing; consequently, 2. convinced, nevertheless, 3. suppliers, 4. Washington; however, 5. b

CHAPTER 15

Conjunctions to Join Unequals

OBJECTIVES When you have completed the materials in this chapter, you will be able to do the following:

Level I — *Distinguish among phrases, dependent clauses, and independent clauses.*
— *Expand dependent clauses into complete sentences.*

Level II — *Punctuate correctly introductory and terminal dependent clauses.*
— *Punctuate parenthetical, essential, and nonessential dependent clauses.*

Level III — *Recognize simple, compound, complex, and compound-complex sentences.*
— *Convert simple sentences into a variety of more complex patterns.*

PRETEST

Insert appropriate commas in the following sentences. Mark *C* if correct.

1. When you finish work tomorrow remember that you must back up all files.
2. If possible we will stop work a little early on Friday.
3. The employee who submits the best suggestion will win the bonus trip.
4. We understand that Jenny Jones who works in Legal Services will be leaving next month.
5. Although several applicants passed the test no one has been hired yet.

LEVEL I

Subordinating Conjunctions

In Chapter 14 (pp. 183–194), we studied conjunctions that joined equal sentence elements such as words, phrases, and clauses. Such equal sentence parts can be joined by coordinate conjunctions (*and, or, nor, but*), conjunctive adverbs (such as *therefore, however, consequently*), and correlative conjunctions (*either . . . or*).

1. tomorrow, 2. possible, 3. C 4. Jones, Services, 5. test,

Now let's talk about joining unequal sentence elements such as independent clauses and dependent clauses. To join such unequal sentence parts, we use subordinating conjunctions. A list of the most common subordinating conjunctions follows.

after	because	since	when
although	before	so that	where
as	if	that	whether
as if	in order that	unless	while
as though	provided	until	

You should become familiar with this list of conjunctions, but do not feel that you must at all times be able to recall every subordinating conjunction. Generally you can recognize a subordinating conjunction by the way it limits or subordinates the clause it introduces. In the clause *because he always paid with cash,* the subordinating conjunction *because* limits the meaning of the clause it introduces. The clause is incomplete and could not stand alone as a sentence.

Independent and Dependent Clauses

Main clauses that can stand alone are said to be *independent.* They have subjects and verbs and make sense by themselves.

Clauses that cannot stand alone are said to be *dependent.* They have subjects and verbs, but they depend upon other clauses for the completion of their meaning. Dependent clauses are often introduced by subordinating conjunctions.

Independent or Main Clauses:

Business writing should be concise. (One main clause)

Business writing should be concise, and it should be clear as well. (Two main clauses)

Mr. Lee writes many memos, but Mrs. Sims writes more letters. (Two main clauses)

Dependent Clauses:

When Mr. Lee writes memos, he signs only his initials. (Dependent clause precedes the main clause.)

Since Mrs. Sims works with customers, she writes many letters. (Dependent clause precedes the main clause.)

Business letters are important because they represent the company. (Dependent clause, *because they represent the company,* comes after the main clause.)

N.B. Dependent clauses should never be written or punctuated as if they were complete sentences.

Relative Pronouns

Although classified as pronouns, the words *who, whom, whose, which,* and *that* actually function as conjunctions when they introduce dependent clauses. *Who* and *whom* are used to refer to human antecedents. *Which* is used to refer to nonhuman antecedents, and *whose* and *that* may refer to either human or nonhuman antecedents.

He is the student *who* can program the computer.

The first orientation program, *which* begins October 2, is filled.

The car *that* you described is parked over there.

Complete the reinforcement exercises for Level I.

LEVEL II

Punctuation of Sentences With Dependent Clauses

Business writers are especially concerned with clarity and accuracy. A misplaced or omitted punctuation mark can confuse a reader by altering the meaning of a sentence. The following guidelines for using commas help ensure clarity and consistency in writing. Some professional writers, however, take liberties with accepted conventions of punctuation, particularly in regard to comma usage. These experienced writers may omit a comma when they feel that such an omission will not affect the reader's understanding of a sentence. Beginning writers, though, are well advised to first develop skill in punctuating sentences by following traditional guidelines.

Introductory Dependent Clauses

Use a comma after a dependent (subordinate) clause that precedes an independent clause.

Before they left the office, they finished the project.

Until he returns, we cannot continue.

When you are ready to start, let me know.

Use a comma after an introductory dependent clause even though the subject and verb may not be stated.

As [it is] expected, the shipment is overdue.

If [it is] possible, send a replacement immediately.

When [they are] printed, your brochures will be distributed.

Terminal Dependent Clauses

Generally, a dependent clause introduced by a subordinating conjunction does not require a comma when the dependent clause falls at the end of a sentence.

They finished the project *before* they left the office.

We cannot continue *until* he returns.

Let me know *when* you are ready to start.

If, however, the dependent clause at the end of a sentence interrupts the flow of the sentence and sounds as if it were an afterthought, a comma should be used.

I know the canceled check was returned, *although* I cannot find it now.

We will ship the goods within the week, *if* that is satisfactory with you.

Parenthetical Clauses

Within a sentence, dependent clauses that interrupt the flow of a sentence and are unnecessary for the grammatical completeness of the sentence are set off by commas.

The motion, *unless* there is further discussion, will be tabled until our next meeting.

At our next meeting, *provided* there is a quorum, the motion will be reconsidered.

Relative Clauses

Dependent clauses introduced by relative pronouns such as *who, that,* and *which* may be essential (restrictive) or nonessential (nonrestrictive).

Essential Clauses. An essential clause is needed to identify the noun to which it refers; therefore, no commas should separate this clause from its antecedent.

Any student *who missed the test* must make it up. (Dependent clause needed to identify which students must make up the test.)

Parking permits *that were issued in the fall* must be validated for the spring. (Dependent clause needed to identify which permits must be validated.)

Nonessential Clauses. A nonessential clause supplies additional information that is not needed to identify its antecedent; therefore, commas are used to separate the nonessential information from the rest of the sentence. Notice that *two* commas are used to set off internal nonessential dependent clauses.

Amy Curtis, *who missed the exam,* must make it up. (Dependent clause: the antecedent of the clause, Amy Curtis, is clearly identified.)

Lot C parking permits, *which were issued in the fall,* must be validated for the spring. (Dependent clause: the antecedent of the clause is clearly identified.)

> N.B. Careful writers use the word *that* for essential clauses and the word *which* for nonessential clauses. Dependent clauses introduced by *which* require commas.

Punctuation Review

Let's briefly review three common sentence patterns and their proper punctuation.

	(Independent clause), +	and or nor but	+ (Independent clause).	(Comma used when a coordinating conjunction joins independent clauses.)
	(Independent clause); +	therefore, consequently, however, nevertheless,	+ (Independent clause).	(Semicolon used when a conjunctive adverb joins independent clauses.)
Since If As When	(Dependent clause),	+	(Independent clause).	(Comma used after a dependent clause introduced by a subordinate conjunction.)

Complete the reinforcement exercises for Level II.

Sentence Variety

To make their writing interesting, good writers strive for variety in sentence structure. Notice the monotony of a paragraph made up entirely of simple sentences.

> The first American industrial revolution started in 1820. It ended in 1850. During this period Congress provided high tariffs. The tariffs protected American products. The tariffs spurred American business. The population grew. Scores of American people moved from farms. They sought employment in the cities.

Compare the following version of this paragraph, which uses independent clauses and other structures to achieve greater sentence variety.

> The first American industrial revolution started in 1820, and it ended in 1850. During this period Congress provided high tariffs, which protected American products and spurred American business. As the population grew, scores of American people moved from farms to the cities, where they sought employment.

Recognizing the kinds of sentence structures available to writers and speakers is an important step toward achieving effective expression. Let's review the three kinds of sentence structures that you have been studying and include a fourth category as well.

Kind of sentence	Minimum requirement	Example
Simple	One independent clause	The American industrial revolution started in 1820.
Compound	Two independent clauses	The American industrial revolution started in 1820, and it ended in 1850.
Complex	One independent clause and one dependent clause	The American industrial revolution, which started in 1820, ended in 1850.
Compound–complex	Two independent clauses and one dependent clause	The American industrial revolution, which started in 1820, ended in 1850; however, a second industrial revolution began about 1870.

Developing the ability to use a variety of sentence structures to facilitate effective communication takes practice and writing experience. Start sharpening your skills with the reinforcement exercises for Level III.

HOT LINE QUERIES

QUESTION: Can the word *that* be omitted from sentences? For example, *She said [that] she would come.*

ANSWER: The relative pronoun *that* is frequently omitted in conversation and casual writing. For absolute clarity, however, skilled writers include it.

QUESTION: Is there some rule about putting periods in organization names that are abbreviated? For example, does *IBM* have periods?

ANSWER: When the names of well-known business, educational, governmental, labor, and other organizations or agencies are abbreviated, periods are normally not used to separate the letters. Thus, no periods would appear in IBM, ITT, UCLA, AFL-CIO, YWCA, AMA. The names of radio and television stations and networks are also written without periods: Station WJR, KNX-FM, PBS, WABC-TV. Geographical abbreviations, however, generally do require periods: U.S.A., U.S.S.R., S.A. The two-letter state abbreviations recommended by the U.S. Postal Service require no periods: NY, OH, CA, MI, NJ, OR, MA, and so on.

QUESTION: As a command, which is correct: *lay down* or *lie down*?

ANSWER: Commands are given in the present tense. You would never tell someone to *closed the door* because commands are not given in the past tense. To say *lay down* (which is the past tense form of *lie*) is the same as saying *closed the door*. Therefore, use the present tense: *lie down*.

QUESTION: In this sentence which word should I use? *Your order will be sent to you in the (later or latter) part of the week.*

ANSWER: Use *latter*. The word *latter* designates the second of two persons or things. In addition, *latter* can be used to mean "further advanced in time or sequence," or *latter* can be used to contrast with *former*. In your sentence, the *latter* part of the week contrasts with the *former* part of the week.

QUESTION: We're having a sale on *nonChristmas* items. Should a hyphen follow *non?* In my dictionary the prefix *non* is not hyphenated when it is joined to other words.

ANSWER: A hyphen is not used when a prefix is joined to most words: *nonessential, prewar, unwelcome, anticlimax*. A hyphen is used, however, when a prefix is joined to a proper (capitalized) noun: *non-Christmas, pre-Columbian, un-Christian, anti-American*.

QUESTION: I have a lot of trouble with verbs in sentences like this: *He is one of the 8 million Americans who (has or have) a drinking problem.*

ANSWER: You're not alone. Make your verb agree with its antecedent (*Americans*). One easy way to work with sentences like this is to concentrate on the clause that contains the verb, *Of the 8 million Americans who have a drinking problem, he is one.*

Name ______________________

CHAPTER 15 **Reinforcement Exercises**

LEVEL I

A. (Self-check) Indicate whether the following word groups are phrases (*P*), independent clauses (*I*), or dependent clauses (*D*). (Remember that phrases do not have both subjects and verbs.)

EXAMPLE: in the spring of the year ___P___

1. when you consider how much time we spent ______
2. clerks and secretaries worked together ______
3. at the crack of dawn to finish studying ______
4. as he stated earlier in the lecture ______
5. she answered immediately ______
6. recently they acquired an option to purchase the property ______
7. before anyone had an opportunity to examine it carefully ______
8. during the middle of the five-year fiscal period from 1980 through 1985 ______
9. unless the personnel department rejects John's application ______
10. our new pricing schedule takes effect January 1 ______

Check your answers.

B. Indicate whether the following word groups are phrases (*P*), independent clauses (*I*), or dependent clauses (*D*). For the clauses, underline the subjects once and the verbs twice.

EXAMPLE: until we are able to assess the damage ___D___

1. as you complete the research ______
2. in order that students may attend ______
3. many businesses sell services rather than products ______
4. on the last line of the contract ______
5. after he complimented Miss Ross's work ______
6. she swerved just in time ______
7. might have been considered ______
8. since Charles began working as a marketing representative ______
9. Division Manager Kelsey analyzed the data ______
10. during our lunch hour last week ______

A. 1. D, 2. I, 3. P, 4. D, 5. I, 6. I, 7. D, 8. P, 9. D, 10. I

C. After each sentence write the correct word in the space provided.

1. We're looking for a person (which, that) we can train. ______________
2. Is this the horse (who, that) broke his leg? ______________
3. The IRS, (who, which) audits only 2 percent of all income tax returns, is choked with paperwork. ______________
4. General Electronics is known as a company (who, that) emphasizes customer service. ______________
5. I have a friend (who, which) cannot study alone. ______________

D. Sort this group of words into three lists and write them below: *and, however, if, but, moreover, although, nor, because, consequently, or, thus, since*

Coordinating conjunctions	Conjunctive adverbs	Subordinating conjunctions

E. Write the following complete sentences. Remember that clauses must contain subjects and verbs.

1. A sentence using *and* to connect two independent clauses.

____

____

2. A sentence using *but* to connect two independent clauses.

____

____

3. A sentence using *because* to introduce a dependent clause.

____

____

4. A sentence using *although* to introduce a dependent clause.

____

____

5. A sentence using *after* to introduce a dependent clause.

____

____

Name ____________________

LEVEL II

A. (Self-check) Where appropriate, insert commas in the following sentences. In the space provided after each sentence, indicate the number of commas you have added to that sentence. Do not add any commas that you cannot justify.*

EXAMPLE: After we hiked to the summit, we pitched our tent. ___1___

1. Tony Molino who recently took out a life insurance policy wanted more security for his family. ______
2. As predicted interest rates continue to climb throughout this period of rampant inflation. ______
3. Supplies for all office equipment which includes the word processing machines are now stored in Room 20. ______
4. A magazine that is featuring the newest copying machines is now on the newsstands. ______
5. Annette Ridgeway who was the first salesperson to reach the quota earned a considerable bonus. ______
6. Any salesperson who sells more than the weekly quota will receive a bonus. ______
7. If possible send the report that shows your current sales figures compared with last year's. ______
8. The latest production model unless it is altered drastically looks as if it will be a winner. ______
9. Please consider our budget deficit before you make a decision. ______
10. A profit-sharing plan for employees is now available although I believe the announcement will not be made until next week. ______

Check your answers.

B. Where appropriate, insert commas in the following sentences. In the space provided after each sentence, indicate the number of commas that you added. Be prepared to discuss the reason for the commas you use.

1. Joseph Farrell who recently called for an appointment had to cancel that appointment. ______
2. A salesman who recently called for an appointment had to cancel that appointment. ______
3. If you have any further questions please contact Mr. Brown. ______

**In the punctuation exercises, punctuation marks have been added in the smaller typeface that is used for answers throughout the Instructor's Edition of* Business English. *The punctuation marks that the students should be adding can be distinguished from those marks already present by their lighter appearance. Regular punctuation and answer punctuation are presented side by side for comparison: ; ; , , . .*

A. 1. (2) Molino, policy, 2. (1) predicted, 3. (2) equipment, machines, 4. (0) 5. (2) Ridgeway, quota, 6. (0) 7. (1) possible, 8. (2) model, drastically, 9. (0) 10. (1) available,

4. We have received a directive to hold all shipments although I do not know why. ______
5. I will edit and process the Rayco order tomorrow morning if that meets with your approval. ______
6. When completed the newly printed forms will be used for billing. ______
7. All the information on my personal résumé which I typed myself fills just one page. ______
8. Although you said my order was shipped ten days ago I have not yet received it. ______
9. The warranty that you refer to in your recent letter covers only merchandise brought to our shop for repair. ______
10. Justin Edwards who works in the Traffic Department received last month's merit award. ______
11. A secretary who joined our staff only two months ago received this month's merit award. ______
12. Zone Improvement Program codes which are better known as zip codes are designed to expedite the sorting and delivery of mail. ______
13. I would like to give your suggestion more thought when I am not quite so preoccupied. ______
14. The Senate will surely when it convenes in its regular session take up the defense issue. ______
15. Before you make a decision consider carefully our strained financial condition. ______
16. No additional payments may be made from the revolving fund if I understand the stipulations correctly. ______
17. In order that we may complete the mailing quickly the address list has been entered into the computer. ______
18. In the coming fiscal year provided enough funds are available we hope to expand our employee recreation program. ______
19. The clerk who receives the orders also sets the prices and makes the initial calculations. ______
20. The completed paperwork that includes all calculations is then sent to the billing typist. ______

Name ______________________

LEVEL III

A. (Self-check) Indicate the structure of the following sentences by writing the appropriate letter in the spaces provided:

a - Simple sentence c - Complex sentence
b - Compound sentence d - Compound-complex sentence

EXAMPLE: We expect to receive the price list shortly. ___a___

1. The advertising manager suggested a new marketing campaign. ______
2. Since it passed the controversial ordinance, the city council has been besieged by calls. ______
3. A decision had to be made soon; therefore, a managers' meeting was scheduled for Monday. ______
4. We have no supplies, and other departments face a similar problem. ______
5. Allen was offered a sales position in Grand Rapids; therefore, he eagerly made plans to travel to Michigan, where he looked forward to beginning his sales career. ______
6. The bank will charge a service fee unless you write fewer checks. ______
7. The cost of the product increased, but sales continued to climb. ______
8. Although the letter was concise, its message was clear; moreover, it promoted goodwill. ______
9. Alison Stewart, Dee Frome, and Mike Guitterez will be transferred. ______
10. Because pictures are worth a thousand words, your report should include photos or graphics. ______

Check your answers.

B. Rewrite the following groups of simple sentences into *one* sentence for each group. Add coordinating conjunctions, conjunctive adverbs, and subordinating conjunctions as needed to create more effective complex, compound, and compound-complex sentences.

EXAMPLE: Baskin-Robbins needed an executive assistant. It advertised in local newspapers. It finally hired a recent graduate. The graduate had excellent skills. After advertising for an executive assistant in local newspapers, Baskin-Robbins finally hired a recent graduate who had excellent skills.

1. Rusty was recently hired as a word processing specialist. She will work for DuPont. DuPont is located in Wilmington, Delaware. ______________________

____

____

A. 1. a, 2. c, 3. b, 4. b, 5. d, 6. c, 7. b, 8. d, 9. a, 10. c

2. Carmen needed a car to drive to school and work. She bought a used VW. However, the VW soon needed a new transmission. This made Carmen very unhappy. ______________

____

____

3. Radio Moscow is the Soviet version of the Voice of America. Radio Moscow hopes to enliven its broadcasts. It added jazz and rock music recordings. The recordings were made in Russia. ______________

____

____

____

4. Jerry Eichhorn recently finished his business degree. He is looking for employment in New Jersey. New Jersey is Jerry's home. ______________

____

____

5. Vicki started working in the mail room at Sunkist. She hopes eventually to work into management. ______________

____

____

C. ***Optional Composition.*** Your instructor may ask you to complete this exercise on a separate sheet. Write sentences that illustrate the following: a simple sentence, a compound sentence, a complex sentence, and a compound-complex sentence. Write sentences that begin with the following subordinating conjunctions: *if, when, as,* and *since.* In addition, write sentences in which *who* is used to introduce an essential clause and again to introduce a nonessential clause. Label each sentence.

POSTTEST

Insert appropriate commas in the following sentences. Mark *C* if the sentence is correct.

1. If the printer is available send it immediately to our Wichita branch office.
2. When necessary we make rush shipments of products that we have in our immediate inventory.
3. The demonstration by Jeremy Jenkins who represents DataTech Products will be Friday.
4. Any manager or employee who is unable to attend the Friday demonstration should call me.
5. Since many employees are interested in spreadsheet programs they will be discussed first.

1. available, 2. necessary, 3. Jenkins, Products, 4. C 5. programs,

Name ____________________

UNIT 4 REVIEW **Chapters 12–15 (Self-Check)**

Begin your review by rereading Chapters 12 through 15. Then test your comprehension of those chapters by completing the exercises that follow. Compare your responses with those provided at the end of this review.

LEVEL I

In the blank provided, write the letter of the word or phrase that correctly completes each of the following sentences.

1. I've never seen a (a) worse, (b) worst printing job than this. ______
2. In comparing matrix printers with impact printers, we concluded that matrix printers were (a) fastest, (b) faster. ______
3. This is (a) a, (b) an example of what I meant. ______
4. The technician (a) could have, (b) could of repaired the equipment if he had had the parts. ______
5. The weather was (a) to, (b) too moist for the paint to dry. ______
6. We are fortunate to have exceptional employees like Thomas and (a) him, (b) he. ______
7. We're seeking a bright young person (a) which, (b) whom we can train. ______
8. The group of words *if you will write us* is a(n) (a) phrase, (b) independent clause, (c) dependent clause. ______

In the following group of sentences, selected words have been underscored. Using the letters below, indicate what punctuation should precede and what should follow the underscored words.

(a) , ________ (c) ; ________ (e) no punctuation
(b) , ________ , (d) ; ________ ,

9. Fran came to Los Angeles in May <u>but</u> moved to Spokane in July. ______
10. Jeffrey might be assigned to work in our legal office <u>or</u> he might be assigned to our administrative headquarters. ______
11. Stop at the crosswalk <u>and</u> look both ways. ______

LEVEL II

Write the letter of the word or phrase that correctly completes each sentence.

12. Before we proceed any (a) further, (b) farther with this matter, I must consult my attorney. ______
13. The search was conducted (a) house to house, (b) house-to-house. ______

14. If you have (a) less, (b) fewer than ten items, you use the quick-check lane. ______

15. Mr. Jefferson said that we had done the work (a) satisfactorily, (b) satisfactory. ______

16. What paper is left must be divided (a) among, (b) between the three typists. ______

17. One of the printers must be moved (a) into, (b) in the outer office. ______

In the following sentences, selected words have been underscored. Using the letters below, indicate what punctuation should precede and what should follow the underscored words.

(a) , ________ (c) ________ , (e) no punctuation
(b) , ________ , (d) ; ________ ,

18. Miss Daily's secretarial service was an immediate success consequently she is considering opening a second office. ______

19. In the meantime we learned that many others felt the same way. ______

20. The employee who asked for a transfer will be moving to Atlanta. ______

21. Send all your checks to Jerry Daniels who is in charge of contributions. ______

22. As reported sales figures for the entire corporation have dropped. ______

LEVEL III

Write the letter of the word or phrase that correctly completes each sentence.

23. Los Angeles is larger than (a) any other city, (b) any city on the West Coast. ______

24. Examine carefully the (a) 50 first, (b) first 50 pages of the booklet. ______

25. Despite her meager income, Sally remained independent (a) of, (b) from her parents. ______

26. You will find that the test questions are not very different (a) than, (b) from some of the review questions. ______

27. The union asked that the salary increase be retroactive (a) to, (b) from the first of the year. ______

In the following sentences selected words have been underscored. Using the letters below, indicate what punctuation should precede and follow the underscored words.

(a) , ________ (c) ________ , (e) no punctuation
(b) , ________ , (d) ; ________ ,

28. When you called our office last week I was unable to locate the information you requested. ______

29. I was unable to locate the information you requested when you called our office last week. ______

30. Sales in your district have risen markedly moreover service requests are decreasing. ______

1. a, 2. b, 3. b, 4. a, 5. b, 6. a, 7. b, 8. c, 9. c, 10. a, 11. c, 12. a, 13. a, 14. b, 15. a, 16. a, 17. a, 18. d, 19. c, 20. c, 21. a, 22. c, 23. a, 24. b, 25. a, 26. b, 27. a, 28. c, 29. c, 30. d

UNIT FIVE

Punctuating Sentences

CHAPTER 16

Commas

OBJECTIVES When you have completed the materials in this chapter, you will be able to do the following:

Level I — *Correctly place commas in series, direct address, and parenthetical expressions.*

— *Use commas correctly in punctuating dates, addresses, geographical items, and appositives.*

Level II — *Place commas correctly in punctuating independent adjectives, verbal phrases, and prepositional phrases.*

— *Use commas correctly in punctuating independent, introductory, terminal, and nonessential clauses.*

Level III — *Use commas correctly in punctuating degrees, abbreviations, and numerals.*

— *Use commas to indicate omitted words, contrasting statements, clarity, and short quotations.*

PRETEST

Insert appropriate commas in the following sentences.

1. Our records Mr. Thomas indicate that your order was received May 3 and shipped May 6.
2. That manufacturer has plants in Akron Ohio and in Denver Colorado.
3. The attorney had reason to believe by the way that the judge was not impartial and might be biased against this case.
4. Insurance rates at this time are not expected to rise but they may begin to go up after the first of the year.
5. Although tired employees preferred the evening not the morning in-service training programs.

When you talk with a friend, you are probably unaware of the "invisible" commas, periods, and other punctuation marks that you are using. In conversation your pauses and voice inflections punctuate your thoughts and clarify your meaning. In writing, however, you must use a conventional set of symbols, punctuation marks, to help your reader understand your meaning.

---

1. records, Mr. Thomas, 2. Akron, Ohio, Denver, 3. believe, way, 4. rise, 5. tired, evening, morning,

Over the years we have gradually developed a standardized pattern of usage for all marks of punctuation. This usage has been codified (set down) in rules that are observed by writers who wish to make their writing as precise as possible. As noted earlier, some professional writers may deviate from conventional punctuation practices. In addition, some organizations, particularly newspapers and publishing houses, maintain their own style manuals to establish a consistent "in-house" style.

The punctuation guidelines presented in this book represent a consensus of punctuation styles that are acceptable in business writing. Following these guidelines will enable you to write with clarity, consistency, and accuracy.

LEVEL I

Basic Comma Guidelines

The most used and misused punctuation mark, the comma, indicates a pause in the flow of a sentence. *Not all sentence pauses, however, require commas.* It is important for you to learn the standard rules for the use of commas so that you will not be tempted to clutter your sentences with needless, distracting commas. Here are the guidelines for basic comma usage.

Series

Commas are used to separate three or more equally ranked (coordinate) elements (words, phrases, or short clauses) in a series. A comma before the conjunction ensures separation of the last two items. No commas are used when conjunctions join all the items in a series.

A special consultant planned the office lighting, color, furnishings, and layout. (Series of words.)

Marvella conducted the research, organized the data, and wrote the report. (Series of phrases.)

Mrs. Horton is the manager, Mr. Travis is the personnel manager, and Miss Zavala is the executive assistant. (Series of clauses.)

Mr. Crews asked that all proper nouns and numbers and formulas be verified. (No commas needed when conjunctions are repeated.)

Direct Address

Words and phrases of direct address are set off with commas.

You must agree, *Mr. Lee,* that Luis has done outstanding work.

I respectfully request, *sir,* that I be transferred.

Parenthetical Expressions

Parenthetical words, phrases, and clauses may be used to create transitions between thoughts. When these expressions interrupt the flow of a sentence and are unnecessary for its grammatical completeness, they should be set off with commas. Here are examples of commonly used parenthetical expressions.

accordingly	hence	namely
all things considered	however	needless to say
as a matter of fact	in addition	nevertheless
as a result	incidentally	no doubt

as a rule	in fact	of course
at the same time	in my opinion	on the contrary
by the way	in other words	on the other hand
consequently	in the first place	otherwise
for example	in the meantime	therefore
furthermore	moreover	under the circumstances

In addition, your typing skills are excellent. (At beginning of sentence.)

This report is not, *however,* one that must be classified. (Inside sentence.)

You have checked with other suppliers, *no doubt.* (At end of sentence.)

The words in question are set off by commas only when they are used parenthetically and actually interrupt the flow of a sentence.

However the vote goes, we will abide by the result. (No comma needed after *however.*)

There is *no doubt* that our selling techniques must be revamped. (No commas needed to set off *no doubt.*)

Dates, Addresses, and Geographical Items

When dates, addresses, and geographical items contain more than one element, the second and succeeding elements are normally set off by commas. Study the following illustrations.

Dates:

On January 3 we opened for business. (No comma needed for one element.)

On January 3, 1985, we opened for business. (Two commas set off second element.)

On Monday, January 3, 1985, we opened for business. (Commas set off second and third elements.)

In June, 1983, the reorganization was effected. (Commas set off second element.)

Note: In June 1983 the reorganization was effected. (This alternate style is acceptable in writing the month and year only.)

Addresses:

Send the battery to Mr. Chun Wong, 1639 East 69 Street, Cleveland, Ohio 44116, before Tuesday. (Commas are used between all elements except the state and zip code, which are in this special instance to be considered a single unit.)

Geographical Items:

He moved from Nashville, Tennessee, to Chicago, Illinois. (Two commas set off the state unless it appears at the end of the sentence.)

N.B. In separating cities and states and dates and years, many writers remember the initial comma but forget the final one, as in *My friend from Birmingham, Alabama, called.*

Or, *The treaty was signed July 17, 1976, and ratified later.*

Appositives

You will recall that appositives rename or explain preceding nouns or pronouns. An appositive that provides information not essential to the identification of its antecedent should be set off by commas.

Debbie Robinson, *the Datamax sales representative,* is here. (The appositive adds nonessential information; commas set it off.)

The sales representative *Debbie Robinson* is here to see you. (The appositive is needed to identify which sales representative has arrived; therefore, no commas are used.)

One-word appositives do not requre commas.

My husband Kevin sometimes uses my computer.

Complete the reinforcement exercises for Level I.

LEVEL II

Comma Guidelines

At this level we will review comma usage guidelines that you studied in previous chapters, and we will add one new guideline for the punctuation of prepositional phrases.

Independent Adjectives

Separate two or more adjectives that equally modify a noun (Chapter 12).

An *industrious, ambitious* student came to see me.

Introductory Phrases

Verbal phrases (Chapter 11) that precede main clauses should be followed by commas.

To qualify for the position, you must have two years' experience.

Starting on Monday, all sales orders must be in triplicate.

One or more introductory prepositional phrases totaling five or more words should be followed by a comma.

In the spring of the year, our thoughts may be diverted from academics.

For a period of six months, a new employee is on probation.

Introductory prepositional phrases of fewer than five words require *no* commas.

In 1986 that stock reached its highest price. (Short prepositional phrase requiring no comma.)

In some instances it will be necessary to increase our price. (Short prepositional phrase requiring no comma.)

N.B. Do *not* insert unnecessary commas around prepositional phrases, especially short introductory phrases, such as the two shown above.

Nonessential Phrases

Use commas to set off phrases that interrupt the flow of a sentence with information not needed for the grammatical completeness of the sentence.

Blanca Baray, *coming to us from Venezuela,* has joined our customer service branch.

Safety procedures for all employees, *in view of recent government directives,* must be reviewed. (Unneeded information interrupts the flow of the sentence.)

Do *not* use commas to set off prepositional phrases that contain essential information and that do not interrupt the sentence.

Sales for our branches *during the month of February* have improved. (No commas needed. Prepositional phrases tell when sales improved.)

We do not *at this time* anticipate any unusual expenses. (No commas needed. Prepositional phrase tells when no unusual expenses are expected.)

Independent Clauses

When a coordinating conjunction (Chapter 14) joins independent clauses, use a comma before the coordinating conjunction, unless the clauses are very short.

We may have Paul Dean work on that project, *or* we may ask Valerie Lieu.

Introductory Clauses

Dependent clauses that precede independent clauses are followed by commas.

When you have finished, please return the style manual.

If you need help, please call me in the afternoon.

Since we need more clerks, we will begin advertising.

Terminal Dependent Clauses

Use a comma before a dependent clause at the end of a sentence only if the dependent clause is an afterthought.

Please return the style manual *when you have finished.* (No comma needed)

I plan to leave at 3:30, *if that meets with your approval.* (Dependent clause added as an afterthought.)

Nonessential Clauses

Use commas to set off clauses that are used parenthetically or that supply information unneeded for the grammatical completeness of a sentence.

An increase in employee benefits, *as you can well understand,* must be postponed until profits improve.

We received a letter from Anne Diga, *who is now living in Anchorage, Alaska.*

Do *not* use commas to set off clauses that contain essential information.

A student *who is studying English* certainly needs an up-to-date dictionary. (No commas are necessary because the italicized clause is essential; it tells what student needs an up-to-date dictionary.)

Complete the reinforcement exercises for Level II.

Comma Guidelines

Degrees and Abbreviations

Degrees following individuals' names are set off by commas. Abbreviations such as *Jr.* and *Sr.* are also set off by commas unless the individual prefers to omit the commas.

Elizabeth Truez, M.D., has a flourishing practice.

John T. O'Dell, Jr., is frequently confused with John T. O'Dell, Sr.

We have retained Carson McQueen, Esq., to represent us.

Only Gregory Stoddard Jr. is unable to participate. (Individual prefers to omit commas.)

The abbreviations *Inc.* and *Ltd.* are set off by commas if the company's legal name includes the commas.

Blackstone & Smythe, Inc., exports goods worldwide. (Notice that two commas are used if *Inc.* appears in the middle of a sentence.)

Shoes Inc. operates at three locations in Tampa. (Legal name does not include comma before *Inc.*)

Numerals

Unrelated figures appearing side by side should be separated by commas.

A total of 150, 1990 graduates attended the reception.

Numbers of more than three digits require commas.

1,760 47,950 6,500,000

However, calendar years and zip codes are written without commas within the numerals.

Calendar years:	1776	1975	1984
Zip codes:	02116	45327	90265

Telephone numbers, house numbers, decimals, page numbers, serial numbers, and contract numbers are also written without commas within the numerals.

(202) 786-6301	347-0551	(Telephone numbers)
20586 Victory Avenue		(House number)
.98651	.0050	(Decimal numbers)
p. 3561	p. 1055	(Page numbers)
36-5710-1693285763		(Serial number)
No. 359063420		(Contract number)

Omitted Words

A comma is used to show the omission of words that are understood.

Last summer we hired twelve employees; this summer, three employees. (Comma shows omission of *we hired* after *summer.*)

Contrasting Statements

Commas are used to set off contrasting or opposing expressions. These expressions are often introduced by such words as *not, never, but,* and *yet.*

The nominating committee selected Mr. Durell, not Mr. Monroe, as its representative. (Two commas set off contrasting statement that appears in the middle of a sentence.)

Our budget for equipment this year is reduced, yet quite adequate.

The greater the bonus to salespeople, the greater the resulting sales. (One comma sets off contrasting statement that appears at the end of a sentence.)

Clarity

Commas are used to separate words repeated for emphasis and words that may be misread if not separated.

Mr. Long said it was a very, very complex contract.

Whoever goes, goes at his own expense.

No matter what, you know you have our support.

Short Quotes

A comma is used to separate a short quote from the rest of a sentence. If the quotation is divided into two parts, two commas are used.

Mrs. Lara said, "The deadline for the McBride contract is June 6."

"The deadline for the McBride contract," said Mrs. Lara, "is June 6."

N.B. Here's a good rule to follow in relation to the comma: When in doubt, leave it out!

Complete the reinforcement exercises for Level III.

HOT LINE QUERIES

QUESTION: My boss always leaves out the comma before the word *and* when it precedes the final word in a series of words. Should the comma be used?

ANSWER: Although some writers omit that comma, present practice favors its use so that the last two items in the series cannot be misread as one item. For example, *The departments participating are Engineering, Accounting, Personnel, and Human Resources.* Without that final comma, the last two items might be confused as one item.

QUESTION: Should I use a comma after the year in this sentence? *In 1986 we began operations.*

ANSWER: No. Commas are not required after short introductory prepositional phrases unless confusion might result without them. If two numbers, for example, appear consecutively, a comma would be necessary to prevent confusion: *In 1986, 156 companies used our services.*

QUESTION: Are these three words interchangeable? *assure, ensure,* and *insure.*

ANSWER: Although all three words mean "to make secure or certain," they are not interchangeable. *Assure* refers to persons and may suggest setting someone's mind at rest (*let me assure you that we are making every effort to locate it*). *Ensure* and *insure* both mean "to make secure from loss," but only *insure* is now used in the sense of protecting or indemnifying against loss (*the building and its contents are insured*).

QUESTION: It seems to me that the word *explanation* should be spelled as *explain* is spelled. Isn't this unusual?

ANSWER: Many words derived from root words change their grammatical form and spelling. Consider these: *maintain, maintenance; repeat, repetition; despair, desperate, desperation; pronounce, pronunciation.*

QUESTION: Is *appraise* used correctly in this sentence? *We will appraise stockholders of the potential loss.*

ANSWER: No. Your sentence requires *apprise,* which means "to inform or notify." The word *appraise* means "to estimate" (*he will appraise your home before you set its selling price*).

QUESTION: Is an apostrophe needed in this sentence? *The supervisor('s) leaving early on Thursday prevented us from finishing the job by Friday.*

ANSWER: The apostrophe is needed: *the supervisor's leaving. . . . The word leaving* is a verbal noun (a gerund), and its modifier must be possessive. Other examples are these: *the boy's whistling, the lion's roaring, my friend's driving.*

QUESTION: Which word is correct in this sentence? *The officer (cited, sited) me for speeding.*

ANSWER: Your sentence requires *cited,* which means "to summon" or "to quote." *Site* means "a location," as in *a building site. Sight* means "a view" or "to take aim," as in *The building was in sight.*

Name ____________________

CHAPTER 16 **Reinforcement Exercises**

LEVEL I

A. (Self-check) In the sentences below insert necessary commas. Then for each sentence write in the space provided the number of commas you inserted.

EXAMPLE: We believe, on the contrary, that our budget is too low. 2

1. Saturday February 4 1991 is the most important date in the history of our company. ____
2. Hong Kong is on the other hand one of the most densely populated areas in the world. ____
3. Please see the large selection of trunks briefcases airplane luggage, and other travel items in our store. ____
4. Patti lived in Bloomington Illinois before she began working in Seattle Washington. ____
5. Your student Jim Farwell called this morning. ____
6. Judith Simpson your business English student also called. ____
7. Prices for our products on the contrary did not keep pace with increased production costs. ____
8. Your car Mr. Takeda is not properly registered. ____
9. There can be no doubt that such practices are widespread. ____
10. Organize your thoughts and jot down some notes and then dictate the letter from your notes. ____

Check your answers.

B. Insert necessary commas in the sentences below. Then for each sentence write in the space provided the number of commas that you inserted.

1. As a matter of fact several students asked the same question. ____
2. Send the package to Mrs. J. D. McKay 4692 Palm Drive Miami Florida 30021 as soon as possible. ____
3. Cynthia Felix the former office manager now has a similar job in Nashville Tennessee. ____
4. We would like of course to have personal letters sent to all the donors. ____

---

1. (3) Saturday, February 4, 1991, 2. (2) is, hand, 3. (3) trunks, briefcases, airplane luggage, 4. (3) Bloomington, Illinois, Seattle, 5. (0) 6. (2) Simpson, student, 7. (2) products, contrary, 8. (2) car, Mr. Takeda, 9. (0) 10. (0)

5. The document was recorded on Tuesday March 21 1980 in Athens Georgia.
6. We feel however that a job transfer would be appropriate.
7. I understand that your brother Keith is their marketing director.
8. It is a pleasure to announce that interest on your investment account at this bank will now be credited every three months.
9. For you Mrs. Treadwell we have a three months' subscription to *Forbes*.
10. Hector Vargas joined the staff in December 1984.
11. It is necessary consequently for you to pay the return postage.
12. Terry Thomas who is a student at Mercer Community College is studying office technology.
13. Under the circumstances we must make flight reservations immediately.
14. The special fares by the way are available only until July 1.
15. Tanya Collins is president Troy Schumacher is vice president and Sherry Gonzalez is secretary.
16. I wonder Ms. Gilford when we may visit the San Antonio Texas resort hotels.
17. My cousin Paul will arrive Monday July 17 from Columbus Ohio.
18. Bennie Porter the chief security officer reported a disturbance at 1:30 a.m.
19. We must as a matter of fact analyze the entire document cycle.
20. There is no doubt in my mind about his competency and integrity.
21. Our latest catalog contains exceptional selections of jewelry china and linens.
22. Incidentally do you feel that we should get an outside opinion?
23. It appears Mr. and Mrs. Ford that you owe additional taxes.
24. I see that your friend Elizabeth was recently hired.
25. Adam Adler the eminent San Francisco architect studied our needs developed a plan and designed our office complex.

Name ______________________

LEVEL II

A. (Self-check) Insert any necessary commas. Then for each sentence write in the space provided the number of commas that you inserted.

1. Jeremy made several constructive imaginative suggestions. ______
2. Production interruptions no matter what the cause must be eliminated. ______
3. In 1983 the company enacted a program of energy conservation. ______
4. As soon as Anna typed the letter I proofread it and mailed it. ______
5. Gus's new computer which he uses for both word and data processing has become an obsession. ______
6. Beginning on the 15th of June the interest on your savings will be nontaxable. ______
7. Mr. Johnson attended the conference in London and he then traveled to Spain to vacation. ______
8. The work in this office is strictly confidential as I am sure you are well aware. ______
9. The secretary who answers the telephone sounds very alert and responsive. ______
10. When you have completed this exercise you are to check your answers. ______

Check your answers.

B. Insert any necessary commas. For each sentence write in the space provided the number of commas that you inserted.

1. If we could reorganize several branches we could develop a more productive profitable operation. ______
2. The happy carefree students had just completed their examinations although many had to leave immediately for their jobs. ______
3. Whether you do or do not buy please feel free to seek our advice. ______
4. We are looking for a stable reliable individual who is interested in growing with our organization. ______
5. Grace Washington who is the head of our telephone order service takes care of more customers than any other salesperson. ______
6. Refusing to release complete control Mr. Southard continued to act as a consultant to the new chairman of the board. ______
7. Our current liability insurance in view of the new law that went into effect April 1 needs to be increased. ______

---

1. (1) constructive, 2. (2) interruptions, cause, 3. (0) 4. (1) letter, 5. (2) computer, processing, 6. (1) June, 7. (1) London, 8. (1) confidential, 9. (0) 10. (1) exercise,

8. Some companies have designed excellent voice mail systems but other organizations are using impersonal systems that frustrate and irritate callers. _____

9. It was a privilege to show you our new offices and we look forward to serving you in the near future. _____

10. In the fall the sports scene is dominated by football. _____

11. Having misplaced her keys Kerry had to retrace her day's activities. _____

12. You have purchased from us often and your payments in the past have always been prompt. _____

13. Before a policy is issued a prospective policyholder is thoroughly investigated. _____

14. In our company a prospective policyholder is thoroughly investigated before a policy is issued. _____

15. As Mr. Harris predicted the energetic resourceful sales representative was most successful. _____

16. Although it appears to be a small share of our total sales the loss of the Tampa territory would negatively affect our profits. _____

17. Lynda Lee who recently bought a sports car has received three speeding tickets in the past six weeks. _____

18. Before we announce this sale to the general public we are inviting our charge account customers to a one-day presale. _____

19. You are probably concerned about your increased insurance rates but you don't know where to find adequate coverage at reduced rates. _____

20. The contracts that were finished during the early summer must be revised and resubmitted for consideration at the fall board meeting. _____

21. Planning for the cold months ahead your gas company has developed a plan to equalize your monthly bills. _____

22. We hope that the new year will be prosperous for you and that we may have many more opportunities to serve you. _____

23. At a meeting of our advertising committee we decided to renew our contract for one-page advertisements in your magazine. _____

24. We do not at this time see any reason for continuing this inefficient profitless practice. _____

25. When you place your next order please use our toll-free number. _____

Name ____________________

LEVEL III

A. (Self-check) Insert necessary commas in the following sentences. For each sentence write in the space provided the number of commas that you added.

1. What it is is a matter of principle. ______
2. The first tract of homes will be available May 15; the second September 1. ______
3. "I am having your policy amended" said Mrs. Bennet "and you will receive the paperwork soon." ______
4. In the fall we will need six operators; in the spring eight. ______
5. Mark Simonton CPA listed the firm's assets at $873 500. ______
6. At least 16 1992 Chevy vans must be serviced. ______
7. Policy No. 2176800394 has been issued in your name. ______
8. We were expecting Miss Weber not Mr. Allen to conduct the audit. ______
9. "The contest was developed with the help of many well-known people in education " said Dr. Weems. ______
10. The octogenarians had known each other for a long long time. ______

Check your answers.

B. Insert necessary commas in the following sentences. For each sentence write in the space provided the number of commas that you added.

1. "After this case" said Kim Franker "my next assignment is in Akron." ______
2. Did you know that on July 23 16 additional workers will be hired? ______
3. On January 1 your Policy No. 8643219 will expire. ______
4. Francisco Torres Sr. was born in 1897 and died in 1980. ______
5. On paper diets often sound deceptively simple. ______
6. The longer we keep the funds invested the greater will be the interest. ______
7. Major responsibility for the loan lies with the signer; secondary responsibility with the cosigner. ______
8. That task must be reserved for experienced never inexperienced employees. ______
9. Professor Marcus said "All extra-credit assignments are due May 1." ______
10. In short employees must be more considerate of others. ______
11. Jeff Brady Ph.D. and Dominic Corloni M.D. spoke at the opening session. ______
12. Toyota management was worried because 231 1992 Camrys had to be recalled. ______

---

1. (1) is, 2. (1) second, 3. (2) amended," Bennet, 4. (1) spring, 5. (3) Simonton, CPA, $873,500
6. (1) 16, 7. (0) 8. (2) Weber, Allen, 9. (1) education," 10. (1) long,

13. We prefer rigid diskettes not floppies as our storage medium. _____
14. What it was was an international power struggle. _____
15. Half of the payment for the shipment is due on delivery; the balance in six weeks. _____
16. Although bored students managed to stay awake during the lecture. _____
17. Whatever it is it is not very amusing. _____
18. In Room 201 32 computers and 16 printers are operating. _____
19. Cooperation not criticism is what is needed. _____
20. "Frankly" said Brian "I don't really understand his motivation." _____
21. Our government has approved over $5000000 in defense spending. _____
22. Lynn Craig L.V.N. and Annette Juarez R.N. both work at St. Elizabeth's Hospital. _____
23. Foreign Service Level 6 secretaries are eligible for promotion after 12 months of probation; Level 5 secretaries after 18 months. _____
24. Whatever is is right. _____
25. The number of workers this year is greatly reduced yet remains adequate. _____

C. ***Optional Composition.*** Your instructor may ask you to complete this exercise on a separate sheet. This chapter presents many guidelines for using commas. Select ten guidelines that you consider most important, and write original sentences to illustrate their use. Identify each guideline.

POSTTEST

Insert appropriate commas in the following sentences.

1. Your letter Mrs. Youngblood should describe the merchandise and announce the beginning of our fall clothing sale.
2. The manager thinks on the other hand that all service calls must receive prior authorization and that current service contracts must be honored.
3. Professor Connie Jo Clark Ph.D. and Pat King CPA have been asked to speak at our Chicago Illinois conference.
4. When trained all employees in this company should be able to offer logical effective advice to customers.
5. If you are unsure you may ask Mrs. Carlson not Mr. Ray for additional information.

1. letter, Mrs. Youngblood, 2. thinks, hand, 3. Clark, Ph.D., King, CPA, Chicago, Illinois, 4. trained, logical, 5. unsure, Carlson, Ray,

CHAPTER 17

Semicolons and Colons

OBJECTIVES When you have completed the materials in this chapter, you will be able to do the following:

Level I
- *Use semicolons correctly in punctuating compound sentences.*
- *Use semicolons when necessary to separate items in a series.*

Level II
- *Distinguish between the proper and improper use of colons to introduce listed items.*
- *Correctly use colons to introduce quotations and explanatory sentences.*

Level III
- *Distinguish between the use of commas and semicolons preceding expressions such as* namely, that is, *and* for instance.
- *Understand why semicolons are sometimes necessary to separate independent clauses joined by* and, or, nor, *and* but.
- *Use colons appropriately and be able to capitalize words following colons when necessary.*

PRETEST

Insert appropriate semicolons, colons, and commas in the following sentences.

1. Small businesses often lack credit opportunities therefore the owners of these businesses must raise capital privately.
2. We have engaged as speakers the following individuals Kathleen Stewart Moraine Valley Community College Roietta Fulgham American River College and Kathy Green Phoenix College.
3. Speakers for the morning session are now scheduled speakers for the afternoon session have not yet been arranged.
4. The programming committee however must proceed with plans for the entire conference.
5. Although the committee had many cities from which to choose we decided to limit the selection to the following namely San Francisco, Denver, or New Orleans.

---

1. opportunities; therefore, 2. individuals: Stewart, College; Roietta Fulgham, College; Green, 3. scheduled; 4. committee, however, 5. choose, following; namely,

Most ideas are contained in separate sentences. Mature writers occasionally, however, combine two closely related ideas into a compound sentence with the use of a semicolon (;). The semicolon tells the reader to think of these ideas together.

The semicolon is a stronger punctuation mark than a comma, which signifies a pause; but the semicolon is not as strong as a period, which signifies a complete stop. Understanding the use of the semicolon will help you avoid fundamental writing errors, such as the *comma splice* (separating two independent clauses with a comma) and the *run-on sentence* (running two independent clauses together without punctuation).

WARNING! Don't overuse the semicolon. Most independent clauses will end with periods. Join clauses together only when the combined idea improves comprehension.

LEVEL I

Basic Uses of the Semicolon

Independent Clauses Separated by Conjunctive Adverbs

You have already learned that independent clauses separated by a conjunctive adverb or a transitional expression (Chapter 14) require a semicolon. Here are some review examples.

A company can make no profit until it recovers its costs; *therefore,* most companies use a cost approach in pricing. (Semicolon separates two independent clauses joined by the conjunctive adverb *therefore.*)

Advertising is aimed at increasing sales; *thus* an advertising policy must be formulated with that objective. (Semicolon separates two independent clauses joined by the conjunctive adverb *thus.*)

Remember that a comma is used after a conjunctive adverb or transitional expression of more than one syllable. Remember, too, that the word following a semicolon is not capitalized unless it is a proper noun.

Independent Clauses Without a Coordinating Conjunction or a Conjunctive Adverb

Two or more closely related independent clauses not separated by a conjunctive adverb or a coordinating conjunction (*and, or, nor, but*) require a semicolon.

The licensing company is called the *franchisor;* the dealer is called the *franchisee.*

Our inside teller service closes early; the outside teller service remains open until 6 p.m.

As you learned in Chapter 3, a serious punctuation error results when separate independent clauses are joined by only a comma (a comma splice) or without any punctuation whatever (a run-on sentence).

Comma splice:	Our inside teller service closes early, the outside teller service remains open until 6 p.m.
Run-on sentence:	Our inside teller service closes early the outside teller service remains open until 6 p.m.

Series Containing Internal Commas or Complete Thoughts

Semicolons are used to separate items in a series when one or more of the items contains internal commas.

> Only the company branches in Wilmington, Delaware; Atlanta, Georgia; and Cincinnati, Ohio, are showing substantial profits.
>
> Attending the conference were Teresa Caruana, executive vice president, Ridgeway Industries; Martin Manheim, president, Servex Corporation; and Joyce Moran, program director, Club Mediterranean.

Semicolons are used to separate three or more serial independent clauses.

> The first step consists of surveying all available information related to the company objective so that an understanding of all problems can be reached; the second step involves interviewing consumers, wholesalers, and retailers; and the third step consists of developing a research design in which the actual methods and procedures to be used are indicated.

A series of short independent clauses, however, may be separated by commas.

> Ease of handling is excellent, passenger comfort is certainly above average, and fuel consumption is the lowest of all cars tested.

Complete the reinforcement exercises for Level I.

LEVEL II

Basic Uses of the Colon

Formally Listed Items

Use a colon after an independent clause introducing a formal list of items — whether listed vertically or horizontally. A formal list is usually introduced by such words as *the following, as follows, these,* or *thus.* A colon is also used when words like these are implied but not stated.

> Some of the most commonly used manufacturers' discounts are *the following:* trade, cash, quantity, and seasonal. (Formal list with introductory expression stated.)
>
> Our business is considering several private mail services: United Parcel, National Post Office, and Independent Postal Service of America. (Formal list with introductory expression only implied.)
>
> *These* are a few of the services that a correspondent bank performs for other banks:
>
> 1. Collecting checks, payments, and other credit instruments
> 2. Accepting letters of credit and travelers' checks
> 3. Making credit investigations

Do not use a colon unless the list is introduced by an independent clause. Often, lists function as sentence complements or objects. Because the statement introducing the list is not complete, no colon should be used. It might be easiest to remember that lists introduced by verbs or prepositions require no colons (because the introductory statement is incomplete). Another instance when no colon is used is when an intervening sentence falls between the introductory statement and the list.

Three courses in this program are accounting, business English, and Computer Science 22. (No colon is used because the introductory statement is not complete; the list is introduced by a *to be* verb and functions as a complement to the sentence.)

The recommended instructors were Professor Loncorich, Ms. Harned, and Dr. Konishi. (No colon is used because the introductory statement is not an independent clause; the list functions as an object of the preposition *to*.)

Purchase orders are being sent to the following companies. The supplies are needed immediately.

IBM	A.B. Dick
Exxon	Wang

Quotations

Use a colon to introduce long one-sentence quotations and quotations of two or more sentences.

> Consumer advocate Sandra Hersh said: "Historically, in our private-enterprise economy, consumers determine what and how much is to be produced through their purchases in the marketplace; hence the needs of consumers are carefully monitored by producers."

Incomplete quotations not interrupting the flow of a sentence require no colon, no comma, and no initial capital letter.

> The River Walk area of San Antonio is sometimes described as "the Venice of the Southwest."

Explanatory Sentences

Use a colon to separate two independent clauses if the second clause explains, illustrates, or supplements the first.

> The company's newly elected directors were immediately faced with a perplexing dilemma: they had to choose between declaring bankruptcy and investing additional funds in an attempt to recoup previous losses.
>
> The applicants for the position all exhibited one common trait: they were achievers who accepted nothing less than success.

Complete the reinforcement exercises for Level II.

LEVEL III

Special Considerations in Using Semicolons and Colons

Introductory Expressions Such as *namely, for instance, that is*

When introductory expressions (such as *namely, for instance, that is,* and *for example*) are used immediately following independent clauses, they may be preceded by either commas or semicolons. Generally, if the words following the introductory expression appear at the end of the sentence and form a series or an independent clause, use a semicolon before the introductory expression. If not, use a comma.

Use semicolons

Numerous fringe benefits are available to employees; *namely,* injury compensation, life insurance, health insurance, dental care, and vision care. (A semicolon is used because *namely* introduces a series at the end of the sentence.)

Salaries of most government employees are determined by the General Schedule; *for example,* typists are classified GS-2 or GS-3. (A semicolon is used because *for example* introduces an independent clause.)

Use commas

We must consider petroleum emergency measures, *for example,* a standby gasoline rationing plan. (A comma is used because *for example* introduces neither a series nor an independent clause.)

N.B. Notice that a comma follows *namely, for instance, that is,* and *for example* when these words are used as introductory expressions.

These same introductory expressions (*namely, for instance,* etc.) may introduce parenthetical words within sentences. Usually, commas punctuate parenthetical words within sentences. If the parenthetical words thus introduced are punctuated by internal commas, however, use dashes or parentheses. (Dashes and parentheses will be treated in detail in Chapter 18.)

Use commas

The biggest health problems facing workers, *namely,* drug abuse and alcoholism, cost American industry over $10 billion a year.

Use dashes

The pursuit of basic job issues — *for instance,* wages, job security, and working conditions — has been the main concern of American workers.

Independent Clauses With Coordinating Conjunctions

Normally, a comma precedes a coordinating conjunction (*and, or, nor, but*) when it joins two independent clauses. If either of the independent clauses contains an additional comma, however, the reader might be confused as to where the second independent clause begins. For this reason many writers prefer to use a semicolon, instead of the normally expected comma, to separate independent clauses when either independent clause contains a comma.

Use comma

We have considered your suggestions carefully, and it appears that they have considerable merit. (Comma precedes coordinating conjunction because no additional punctuation appears within either clause.)

Use semicolon

On the basis of Comptroller Macon's recommendation, we have considered your suggestions carefully; and it appears that they have considerable merit. (Semicolon precedes coordinating conjunction because a comma appears within one of the independent clauses.)

Other Uses of the Colon

a. After the salutation of a business letter

Dear Mr. Jameson: Gentlemen: Dear Mike:

b. In expressions of time to separate hours from minutes

2:45 p.m. 12:01 a.m.

c. Between titles and subtitles

HOW: A Handbook for Office Workers

d. Between place of publication and name of publisher

> Guffey, Mary Ellen. *Essentials of Business Communication.* Boston: PWS-KENT Publishing Company, 1991.

Capitalization Following Colons

Do not capitalize the initial letter of words or of phrases listed following a colon unless the words so listed are proper nouns or appear as a vertical array.

> The four Cs of effective letter writing are the following: clarity, courtesy, conciseness, and correctness.
>
> These cities will receive heavy promotional advertising: Omaha, Lincoln, Sioux City, and Council Bluffs.
>
> To be legally enforceable, a contract must include at least four elements:
> 1. Mutual assent of all parties
> 2. Parties who are competent
> 3. A consideration
> 4. A lawful purpose

Note: Generally, no punctuation follows incomplete statements listed vertically.

Do not capitalize the first letter of an independent clause following a colon if that clause explains or supplements the first one (unless, of course, the first word is a proper noun).

> You will be interested in our new savings plan for one special reason: it allows you to invest up to $2,500 in a tax-free account.

Capitalize the first letter of an independent clause following a colon if that clause states a formal rule or principle.

> In spacing colons, typists should always observe the following rule: A colon should be followed by two spaces.

For a quotation following a colon, capitalize the initial letter of each complete sentence.

> Commenting on the importance of incorporation, historians Krooss and Gilbert said: "A strong case can be made by the proposition that the increased use of the corporation was the most important institutional innovation of the century. The corporate form permeates American business."

A Final Word

Semicolons are wonderful punctuation marks when used carefully and knowingly. After reading this chapter, though, some students are guilty of semicolon overkill. They begin to string together two — and sometimes even three — independent clauses with semicolons. Remember to use semicolons in compound sentences *only* when two ideas are better presented together. Forget about joining three independent clauses with semicolons — too unconventional and too difficult to read. In most instances, independent clauses should end with periods.

Complete the reinforcement exercises for Level III.

HOT LINE QUERIES

QUESTION: Here's a sentence we need help with: *We plan to present the contract to whoever makes the lowest bid.* My supervisor recommends *whoever* and I suggest *whomever.* Which of us is right?

ANSWER: Your supervisor. The preposition *to* has as its object the entire clause (*whoever makes the lowest bid*). Within that clause, *whoever* functions as the subject of the verb *makes;* therefore, the nominative case form *whoever* should be used.

QUESTION: When I list items vertically, should I use a comma or semicolon after each item? Should a period be used after the final item? For example,

Please inspect the following rooms and equipment:
1. *The control room*
2. *The power transformer and its standby*
3. *The auxiliary switchover equipment*

ANSWER: Do not use commas or semicolons after items listed vertically, and do not use a period after the last item in such a list. However, if the listed items are complete sentences or if they are long phrases that complete the meaning of the introductory comment, periods may be used after each item.

QUESTION: Is there a plural form of *plus and minus?*

ANSWER: The plural form is *pluses* (or *plusses*) and *minuses* (*consider all the pluses and minuses before you make a decision*).

QUESTION: I'm setting up advertising copy, and this sentence doesn't look right to me: *This line of fishing reels are now priced. . . .*

ANSWER: Your suspicion is correct. The subject of the verb in this sentence is *line;* it requires the singular verb *is.*

QUESTION: I wonder if the possessive is correctly expressed in this sentence that I'm transcribing: *I appreciate the candor of both you and Neil in our conversation.* Shouldn't both *you* and *Neil* be made possessive?

ANSWER: No. It would be very awkward to say *your and Neil's candor.* It's much better to use the *of* construction thus avoiding the awkward double possessive.

QUESTION: Is this a double negative: *We can't schedule the meeting because we have no room available?*

ANSWER: No, this is not regarded as a double negative. In grammar a double negative is created when two negative adverbs modify a verb, such as *can't hardly, won't barely,* or *can't help but.* Avoid such constructions.

Name ______________________

CHAPTER 17 **Reinforcement Exercises**

LEVEL I

A. (Self-check) For each of the following sentences, underline any errors in punctuation. Then in the space provided, write the correct punctuation mark plus the word preceding it. Write *C* if the sentence is correct.

EXAMPLE: Breeding and raising horses can be profitable, consequently, large sums are being invested. ___profitable;___

1. Horse breeding has become a big business and investors are supplying large sums for thoroughbreds. ______________
2. Most thoroughbreds are sold as yearlings it is usually one year before they can race. ______________
3. Investors' expectations are high therefore, competitive bidding for breeding animals is brisk. ______________
4. Some investors use thoroughbred horses as tax shelters, these investors "write off" the expenses of maintaining the horses. ______________
5. Mr. Marks invested, Mrs. Hiram was interested, and Mr. Phipps declined. ______________
6. Important breeding is being conducted at the Peachtree Ranch, Rome, Georgia; the Blue Meadows Ranch, Lexington, Kentucky; and the Flag Is Up Ranch, Buellton, California. ______________
7. Stallions yield the highest prices; but mares can also be extremely expensive. ______________
8. The average auction price has tripled in the last five years profits from breeding have climbed even faster. ______________
9. Several investors may form a syndicate to buy a good horse, the syndicate then shares expenses and spreads risks. ______________
10. Horse breeding can be an exciting and profitable venture, thus many investors are choosing horses over stocks and bonds. ______________

Check your answers.

B. Add any necessary commas or semicolons to the following sentences. (Do not add periods.) In the spaces provided write the number of punctuation marks you inserted. Write *C* if a sentence is correct as written.

EXAMPLE: New equipment was ordered eight weeks ago; delivery is expected within two weeks. ___1___

A. 1. business, 2. yearlings; 3. high; 4. shelters; 5. C 6. C 7. prices, 8. years; 9. horse; 10. venture;

1. Small automobiles were being sold rapidly therefore the dealership was expanded. ______
2. Dr. Paulson scheduled appointments every thirty minutes he was assisted by an experienced nurse. ______
3. Buildings swayed lights flickered and dishes rattled. ______
4. Serving on the panel are Paige Baker marketing director Trinity Sales Evelyn Katusak sales supervisor Broome Products and Timony Miank market analyst Lansing Enterprises. ______
5. Several members of the staff are near the top of their salary ranges we may have to reclassify their jobs before recommending them for increases. ______
6. Your account is now several months past due consequently it is not possible for us to grant you further extensions. ______
7. It is a pleasure to send you a copy of our booklet on office furniture we hope you will find it useful. ______
8. Every Christmas we hire a number of temporary office workers hence I am writing to you to make this announcement of job openings to your students. ______
9. Jeremy worked Jennifer supervised and Jean entertained. ______
10. Newspaper advertising is effective in reaching a large metropolitan area television advertising is aimed at national or local audiences. ______
11. General Dynamics hired 2,400 new employees last year it plans to hire even more next year. ______
12. The response to our small advertisement in the classified section was minimal thus we must place a larger advertisement in the real estate section. ______
13. We are opening a branch office in Ventura and we hope we will be able to serve your needs from that office in the future. ______
14. An independent accounting firm is conducting a standard audit of our organization consequently we are asking you to check the enclosed statement for accuracy. ______
15. Speakers for the afternoon session include Ms. Jana Webb executive vice president Artistic Designs Professor Linda Scher-Padilla Department of Office Administration Los Angeles City College and Dr. Jane Mangrum director of research Miami Industries. ______
16. Our new Instant Cash checking service allows you to write a check for more than the balance in your checking account we transfer funds automatically to your account. ______
17. Employment opportunities are available in hospitals banks and insurance companies however training is often required. ______
18. Such training nevertheless can usually be completed in six to ten months thus you can begin earning wages in less than a year. ______
19. If you open your account immediately your first 500 checks will be supplied free moreover you will receive a bonus gift if you are among our first 50 customers. ______
20. Three participating institutions are Lima Technical College Lima Ohio Antelope Valley College Lancaster California and Concordia College Moorhead Minnesota. ______

Name ____________________

LEVEL II

A. (Self-check) For each of the following sentences, underline any errors in punctuation. Then in the space provided, write the correct punctuation plus the preceding word. If a colon should be omitted, write *Omit colon*. Write *C* if the sentence is correct.

EXAMPLE: Special invitations were sent to: President Owens, Vice President Spears, and Treasurer Avery. ___Omit colon___

1. The most outstanding speakers at the national convention were: Judy Dresser, Cathy Grant, and Carol Engel. ____________
2. Our trip last summer included visits to the following historical sites: Mount Vernon, Virginia; Gettysburg, Pennsylvania; and Concord, Massachusetts. ____________
3. Supplies from these companies are needed immediately. They must be ordered today:

Microm	Moore Paper Products
IBM	Dysan, Inc.

   ____
4. The representative from Creative Computing said; "Minicomputers are defined as computers costing between $5,000 and $400,000. They are used primarily for process control or for business, scientific, and communication applications." ____________
5. The switchboard supervisor solved her transportation problem: she now rollerskates from one switchboard location to another very quickly. ____________
6. The new computer was introduced as: "the tool of the century." ____________
7. We have requests for information from three local companies: Sterling Laboratories, Putnam Brothers, and Data Control. ____________
8. Because of the urgency of the problem, we have sent Express messages to: Evelyn Dobson, Mary Ringle, and Connie Clark. ____________
9. The most commonly observed holidays are the following: Thanksgiving, Labor Day, Christmas, July Fourth, and New Year's Day. ____________
10. Arriving late for class, the student offered a convincing excuse: her car had run out of gas three miles away. ____________

Check your answers.

A. 1. Omit colon 2. C 3. today. 4. said: 5. C 6. Omit colon 7. C 8. Omit colon 9. C 10. C

B. For the following sentences, add any necessary but missing punctuation marks. For each sentence indicate in the space provided the number of necessary additions you have made. Mark *C* if the sentence is correct as it stands.

EXAMPLE: Shipments of computer components will be sent to Dallas, Sacramento, Cleveland, and Zurich. 4

1. The most commonly typed documents were letters memoranda and short reports. ______
2. Japan faces a serious economic threat its dependence upon oil imports endangers its future economic growth. ______
3. The usual minicomputer system includes these components central processing unit main memory and peripheral equipment. ______
4. Addressing the convention, the Secretary of the Treasury said "Inflation, unemployment, growth, energy, and the balance of payments are interrelated. Our governmental policies must address all our diverse economic objectives together." ______
5. The records of the following employees will be reviewed for salary evaluation Please send the records by October 1

   Vicki Torres Julie Mauer
   Tony Watkins Ivan Krakowski ______

6. The balance sheet is a statement of assets liabilities and owner's equity. ______
7. Included in our introductory offer are the following colored manila folders self-closing envelopes and erasable ballpoint pens. ______
8. Energy in this country is supplied from a number of sources oil natural gas coal nuclear fission and hydropower. ______
9. For graduation you must complete courses in mathematics, accounting, English, management, and computer science. ______
10. The law of supply and demand can function only under the following condition: producers must know what consumers want. ______
11. Professor Charlotte Cohen asked that research reports contain the following parts introduction body summary and bibliography. ______
12. Additional costs in selling the house are title examination, title insurance, transfer tax, preparation of documents, and closing fee. ______
13. Tom Hamilton described his information processing system in this way "The video display has interactive programming. Salespeople find it very easy to use. They follow the program by reading the screen and providing the information required." ______
14. In addition to drilling holes, a good electric drill will also enable you to sand rough surfaces, grind compounds, and polish surfaces. ______
15. Business letters generally include four parts date, inside address, body, and closing. ______

Name ______________________________

LEVEL III

A. (Self-check) Indicate whether the following sentences are punctuated and capitalized correctly. Use *C* for correct and *I* for incorrect.

1. The local community youth program attracted several employees as volunteers; namely, Pam Wheeler, Benita Washington, Sid Daily, and Samar Hillo. ______
2. Foreign Service secretaries may be assigned to a number of foreign countries; for example, India, Brazil, Finland, and France. ______
3. Daily newspapers in the United States, of which there are approximately 1,800, have a combined circulation of 65 million; and daily papers that publish Sunday editions, of which there are about 700, have a combined circulation of over 52 million. ______
4. The meeting started promptly at 1:15 p.m. and ended at 3:45 p.m. ______
5. Many banks now offer automated transfers from savings to checking accounts, that is, money may be kept in an interest-bearing savings account until needed. ______
6. All secretaries are urged to observe the following rule: When in doubt, consult the company style manual. ______
7. The writer of a research report should include a variety of references; for example, books, periodicals, government publications, and newspapers. ______
8. Mr. Dyson considered naming his book *Successful Investing; A Complete Guide to the Financial Future.* ______
9. For the opening session of the convention, the keynote speaker will be systems analyst Norma Patterson; and for the afternoon general membership meeting, the speaker will be NASA representative Judith R. Rice. ______
10. Loans may be repaid according to one of the following plans: the annual plan, the semiannual plan, the quarterly plan, or the weekly plan. ______

Check your answers.

B. For the following sentences, add any necessary but missing punctuation marks. For each sentence indicate in the space provided the number of necessary additions you have made. Mark *C* if correct.

EXAMPLE: If she completes the proposal, Ms. Upchurch will fly to Washington on Tuesday; if not, she will leave on Thursday. 3

1. When searching for employment consider a number of job sources for instance private employment agencies state agencies classified advertisements school placement services friends and relatives. ______
2. Because of his extended service abroad Edward Mautz was selected to head our export division and because of her outstanding sales experience Barbara Malom was selected to head our marketing division. ______

A. 1. C, 2. C, 3. C, 4. C, 5. I, 6. C, 7. C, 8. I, 9. C, 10. C

3. Ms. Epstein remarked that the plural forms of nearly all nouns are shown in her favorite dictionary namely *The American Heritage Dictionary.* ______

4. One of the titles I'm considering for my book is *Dictation Techniques A Complete Guide for the Word Originator.* ______

5. Some punctuation marks require a great deal of instruction and practice for example commas colons and semicolons. ______

6. Three times have been designated for the interviews Thursday at 630 p.m. Friday at 330 p.m. and Monday at 10 a.m. ______

7. An author, composer, or photographer may protect his or her product with a government-approved monopoly namely a copyright. ______

8. Our school operates on the quarter system that is the school year is divided into four equal quarters. ______

9. Ms. Valdez enjoyed her current position as sales representative very much but when a competing company offered her a substantial increase in salary she found it very tempting. ______

C. ***Optional Composition.*** Your instructor may ask you to complete this exercise on a separate sheet. Write three original sentences illustrating basic uses of semicolons. Write three original sentences illustrating basic uses of colons. Write one sentence using ***namely*** with a semicolon preceding it. Compose a list arranged vertically and introduced by an independent clause requiring a colon. Label each of the preceding sentences.

POSTTEST

Add appropriate semicolons, colons, and commas.

1. Most students prefer morning classes consequently we schedule many courses before noon.
2. The following instructors have been chosen to represent their schools at the professional meeting Marian Geering Niagara County Community College Deborah Kitchin Heald Business College and Paul Murphey Southwest Wisconsin Technical College.
3. All morning sesions will begin at 9 a.m. all afternoon sessions will commence at 1 p.m.
4. Since little time remains we are forced to choose from among the top vendors for example IBM, Wang, or Texas Instruments.
5. We feel however that more time should be allowed for major equipment decisions.

---

1. classes; consequently, 2. meeting: Geering, College; Kitchin, College; Murphey, 3. 9 a.m.; 4. remains, vendors; for example, 5. feel, however,

CHAPTER 18

Other Punctuation

OBJECTIVES When you have completed the materials in this chapter, you will be able to do the following:

Level I
- *Use periods to correctly punctuate statements, commands, indirect questions, and polite requests.*
- *Use periods to correctly punctuate abbreviations, initials, and numerals.*
- *Use question marks and exclamation points correctly.*

Level II
- *Recognize acceptable applications of the dash.*
- *Use parentheses to deemphasize material.*
- *Explain when to use commas, dashes, or parentheses to set off nonessential material.*
- *Correctly punctuate and capitalize material set off by parentheses and dashes.*

Level III
- *Correctly use double and single quotation marks.*
- *Correctly place other punctuation marks in relation to quotation marks.*
- *Use brackets and underscores (italics) appropriate.*

PRETEST

Insert appropriate punctuation in the following sentences.

1. Will you please send certificates to Wanda Allenton and Paula Brin
2. Miss Lee Mrs Adams and Mr Simon have been appointed to the FCC committee.
3. San Francisco Los Angeles and Phoenix these are the only cities receiving automobiles f o b
4. The chapter entitled Telecommunication Today was the best one in the book Current Office Technology.
5. Did Professor Scholl say There will be no class Tuesday

---

1. Brin. 2. Lee, Mrs. Adams, Mr. 3. Francisco, Angeles, Phoenix — these f.o.b. 4. "Telecommunication Today" *Current Office Technology* 5. say, "There Tuesday"?

Uses for the Period

To Punctuate Sentences

Use a period at the end of a statement, a command, an indirect question, or a polite request. Although it may have the same structure as a question, a polite request ends with a period.

James was promoted to a position with increased salary and responsibilities. (Statement.)

Send our latest catalog and price list to them. (Command.)

Marilyn asked whether we had sent the price list. (Indirect question.)

Would you please send me your brochure and introductory sample. (Polite request.)

To Punctuate Abbreviations and Initials

Use periods after initials and after most abbreviations. The periods may be omitted, however, after well-known abbreviations like *ID, CPA, IQ, RSVP, GNP, UPS,* and *TV*. The periods may also be omitted after abbreviations for certain fraternal, business, and governmental organizations (*VFW, YMCA, AAA, CIA, UCLA*). For ease in reading, the periods are generally used in abbreviations written with small letters (*p.m., c.o.d., f.o.b.,* and *i.e.*). Consult a good reference manual or an up-to-date dictionary for guidance in using periods with abbreviations.

The c.o.d. shipment was received this morning at 11:45 a.m. (Note that only one period is used after an abbreviation at the end of a sentence.)

Mr. and Mrs. L. P. Peterson, Jr., invited Dr. and Mrs. V. O. Perez to the concert.

Officials from the FCC were greeted in the VIP lounge at JFK when they arrived in New York.

We elected our representative, i.e., Professor Susan Uchida.

To Punctuate Numerals

For a monetary sum use a period (decimal point) to separate dollars from cents.

The two items in question, $13.92 and $98, were both charged in the month of October.

Use a period (decimal point) to mark a decimal fraction.

Although a moderate voter turnout was predicted, only 18.6 percent of registered voters actually voted.

Uses for the Question Mark

To Punctuate Direct Questions

Use a question mark at the end of a direct question.

What qualities are necessary for a person to become a successful administrator?

Have you compiled the figures requested by Techdata, Inc.?

N.B. To distinguish between a polite request and a direct question, examine the statement carefully. A polite request (actually a polite *command*) asks the reader to perform a specific action and is usually answered by an action rather than a verbal response. For example, *Will you mail your check in the enclosed envelope.* The reader is expected to send the check, not merely answer *Yes* or *No.*

To Punctuate Questions Appended to Statements

Place a question mark after a question that is appended to a statement. Use a comma to separate the statement from the question.

> We have already placed an order for additional office supplies, haven't we?
>
> Contributions should be collected from individual departments, don't you think?

To Indicate Doubt

A question mark within parentheses may be used to indicate a degree of doubt about some aspect of a statement.

> The accounting department needs two(?) temporary clerks.
>
> A beginning salary of $2,500(?) per month is possible.

Uses for the Exclamation Point

To Express Strong Emotion

After a word, phrase, or clause expressing strong emotion, use an exclamation point. In business writing, however, exclamation points should be used sparingly.

> Impossible! We understood the deadline to be tomorrow.
>
> What a day! Will 5 p.m. never come?
>
> It is incredible that the timer is still working after such punishment!

Do not use an exclamation point after mild interjections, such as *oh* and *well.*

> Well, it seems we have little choice in the matter.

If no exclamation point is available on a typewriter, a typist may construct one by typing an apostrophe, backspacing, and then typing a period.

Complete the reinforcement exercises for Level I.

Uses for the Dash

The dash is a legitimate and effective mark of punctuation when used according to accepted conventions. As an emphatic punctuation mark, however, the dash loses effectiveness when it is overused. On a keyboard the dash is constructed by typing two successive hyphens (without spacing before, between, or after the hyphens). Study the following suggestions for and illustrations of appropriate uses of the dash.

To Set off Parenthetical Elements

Within a sentence parenthetical elements are usually set off by commas. If, however, the parenthetical element itself contains internal commas, use dashes (or parentheses) to set it off.

> Sources of raw materials — farming, mining, fishing, and forestry — are all dependent upon energy.
>
> Four efficient secretaries — Priscilla Alvarez, Vicki Evans, Yoshiki Ono, and Edward Botsko — received cash bonuses for outstanding performance in their departments.

To Indicate an Interruption

An interruption or abrupt change of thought may be separated from the rest of a sentence by a dash.

> The shipment will be on its way — you have my word — by Wednesday.
>
> Send the diskettes by Friday — no, we must have them sooner.

Sentences with abrupt changes of thought or with appended afterthoughts can usually be improved through rewriting.

To Set off a Summarizing Statement

Use a dash (not a colon) to separate an introductory list from a summarizing statement.

> Variety of tasks, contact with people, opportunity for advancement — these are what I seek in a job.
>
> Running, hiking, and reading — those are Rudy's favorite pastimes.

To Attribute a Quotation

Place a dash between a quotation and its source.

> "English is the language of men ever famous and foremost in the achievements of liberty." — John Milton
>
> "A man has no worse enemy than himself." — Cicero

Uses for Parentheses

To Set off Nonessential Sentence Elements

Generally, there are three ways to punctuate nonessentia! sentence elements: (1) with commas, to make the lightest possible break in the normal flow of a sentence; (2) with dashes, to emphasize the enclosed material; and (3) with parentheses, to deemphasize the enclosed material.

> One of the blueprints, which appears on page 7, shows the internal structure of the engine clearly. (Normal punctuation.)
>
> One of the blueprints — which appears on page 7 — shows the internal structure of the engine clearly. (Dashes emphasize enclosed material.)
>
> One of the blueprints (which appears on page 7) shows the internal structure of the engine clearly. (Parentheses deemphasize enclosed material.)

Explanations, references, and directions are often enclosed in parentheses.

> The bank's current business hours (10 a.m. to 3 p.m.) will be extended in the near future (to 6 p.m.).
>
> We recommend that you use hearing protectors (see our comment on p. 618) when using this electric drill.

Additional Considerations

If the material enclosed by parentheses is embedded within another sentence, a question mark or exclamation point may be used where normally expected. Do not, however, use a period after a statement embedded within another sentence.

> We have tickets to "The Chorus Girl" (have you seen it?) on the evening of March 9. (A question mark concludes a question enclosed by parentheses and embedded in another sentence.)
>
> The fire alarm sounded (but no one responded!) during the middle of our final exam. (An exclamation mark concludes an exclamation enclosed by parentheses and embedded in another sentence.)
>
> An air conditioner cools space (this will be discussed in detail in the next chapter) by removing heat from it. (A period is not used at the end of a statement that is enclosed by parentheses and embedded in another sentence.)

If the material enclosed by parentheses is not embedded in another sentence, use whatever punctuation is required.

> The dot matrix printer appears to be the least expensive printer. (See the appendix for a comparison of printers and prices.)
>
> In fewer than ten years, the price of that article has tripled. (Who would have thought it possible?)

In sentences involving expressions within parentheses, a comma, semicolon, or colon that would normally occupy the position occupied by the second parenthesis is then placed after that parenthesis.

> When I return from my trip (in late June), I will begin work on the feasibility study. (Comma follows parenthesis.)
>
> Your application for a credit card has been received before the deadline (November 1); however, you did not supply two financial references. (Semicolon follows parenthesis.)

Complete the reinforcement exercises for Level II.

Uses for Quotation Marks

To Enclose Direct Quotations

Double quotation marks are used to enclose direct quotations. Unless the exact words of a writer or speaker are being repeated, however, quotation marks are not employed.

"Education, engineering, and scientific communities are welcoming computer-based data banks," said Paul Murphey, information consultant. (Direct quotation enclosed.)

Susan Dunn said that the data base consisted of six different categories ranging from home information to electronic mail. (Indirect quotation requires no quotation marks.)

Capitalize only the first word of a direct quotation.

"The office staff," said Mrs. Rogers, "has now reached its full complement." (Do not capitalize the word *has*.)

To Enclose Quotations Within Quotations

Single quotation marks (apostrophes on the typewriter) are used to enclose quoted passages cited within quoted passages.

Sharon Miles remarked, "In business writing I totally agree with Aristotle, who said, 'A good style must, first of all, be clear.' " (Single quotation marks within double quotation marks.)

To Enclose Short Expressions

Slang, words used in a special sense, and words following *stamped* or *marked* are often enclosed within quotation marks.

Cheryl thought her Christmas bonus was "out of sight." (Slang.)

Federal Reserve Banks are called "bankers' banks." (Words used in a special sense.)

In computer terminology a "bit" is the smallest unit of measure in a computer word. (Word used in a special sense.)

The package was stamped "Handle with Care." (Words following *stamped*.)

To Enclose Definitions

Quotation marks are used to enclose definitions of words or expressions. The word or expression being defined should be underscored or set in italics.

The Latin word *ergo* means "therefore" or "hence."

Businessmen use the term *working capital* to indicate an "excess of current assets over current debts."

To Enclose Titles

Quotation marks are used to enclose titles of literary and artistic works, such as magazine and newspaper articles, chapters of books, movies, television shows, poems, lectures, and songs. Names of books, magazines, pamphlets, and newspapers, however, are set in italics (underscored) or typed in all capital letters.

Students find the chapter entitled "Persuasive Letters" from *Writing for the World of Work* very helpful.

One source of information for your term paper might be the magazine article "Cross-Training of Key Personnel," which appeared in *Newsweek* recently.

Additional Punctuation Considerations

Periods and commas are always placed inside closing quotation marks, whether single or double. Semicolons and colons are, on the other hand, always placed outside quotation marks.

Betty Pearman said, "I'm sure the package was marked 'Fragile.' "

The article is entitled "Bad Business of Banks," but we can't locate the magazine in which it appeared.

The contract stipulated that "both parties must accept arbitration as binding"; therefore, the decision reached by the arbitrators is final.

Three dates have been scheduled for the seminar listed as "Telecommunications Today": April 1, May 3, and June 5.

Question marks and exclamation points may go inside or outside closing quotation marks, as determined by the form of the quotation.

Jeanette said, "How may I apply for that position?" (Quotation is a question.)

"The next time," fumed Mr. Bradley, "please inform us in advance!" (Quotation is an exclamation.)

Do you know who it was who said, "Money is more trouble than it's worth"? (Incorporating sentence asks question; quotation does not.)

I can't believe the check was stamped "Insufficient Funds"! (Incorporating sentence is an exclamation; quotation is not.)

When did the manager say, "Who wants to reserve a summer vacation?" (Both incorporating sentence and quotation are questions. Use only one question mark inside the quotation marks.)

Uses for Brackets

Within quotations, brackets are used by writers to enclose their own inserted remarks. Such remarks may be corrective, illustrative, or explanatory. Brackets are also used within quotations to enclose the word *sic,* which means *thus* or *so*. This Latin form is used to emphasize the fact that an error obvious to all actually appears *thus* in the quoted material.

"A British imperial gallon," reported Miss Sedgewick, "is equal to 1.2 U.S. gallons [4.54 liters]."

"The company's reorganization program," wrote President Theodore Bailey, "will have its greatest affect [*sic*] on our immediate sales."

Uses for the Underscore (Italics)

The underscore (underline) is used to indicate words that would be italicized in printed works. Italics are normally used for titles of books, magazines, newspapers, and other complete works published separately, as we have already mentioned. In addition, words under discussion in the sentence and used as nouns are italicized or underscored.

Creative Financing, the latest book of author Thomas Manley, was favorably reviewed in *The Wall Street Journal.*

Two of the most frequently misspelled words are *calendar* and *separate.* (Words used as nouns.)

Complete the reinforcement exercises for Level III.

HOT LINE QUERIES

QUESTION: We can't decide whether the period should go inside quotation marks or outside. At the end of a sentence, I have typed the title "Positive Vs. Negative Values." The author of the document I'm typing wants the period outside because she says the title does not have a period in it.

ANSWER: In the U.S., typists and printers have adopted a uniform style: when a period or comma falls at the same place quotation marks would normally fall, the period or comma is always placed inside the quotation marks — regardless of the content of the quotation. In Britain a different style is observed.

QUESTION: I'm not sure where to place the question mark in this sentence: *His topic will be "What Is a Good Health Plan (?)"* Does the question mark go inside the quotation marks? Too, should a comma precede the title of the talk?

ANSWER: First, the question mark goes inside the quotation mark because the quoted material is in the form of a question. Be sure that you do not use another end punctuation mark after the quotation mark. Second, do not use a comma preceding the title of the topic because the sentence follows normal subject-verb-complement order. No comma is needed to separate the verb and the complement.

QUESTION: Is it correct to say *Brad and myself were chosen . . . ?*

ANSWER: No. Use the nominative case pronoun *I* instead of *myself.*

QUESTION: What salutation should I use when addressing a letter to Sister Mary Elizabeth?

ANSWER: The salutation of your letter should be *Dear Sister Mary Elizbeth.* For more information on forms of address, consult a good dictionary or reference manual.

QUESTION: Is anything wrong with saying *someone else's car?*

ANSWER: Although it sounds somewhat awkward, the possessive form is acceptable. The apostrophe is correctly placed in *else's.*

QUESTION: I've looked in the dictionary but I'm still unsure about whether to hyphenate *copilot.*

ANSWER: The hyphen is no longer used in most words beginning with the prefix *co* (*coauthor*, *cocounsel*, *codesign*, *cofeature*, *cohead*, *copilot*, *costar*, *cowrite*). Only a few words retain the hyphen (*co-anchor*, *co-edition*, *co-official*). Check your dictionary for usage. In reading your dictionary, notice that centered periods are used to indicate syllables (*co·work·er*); hyphens are used to show hyphenated syllables (*co-own*).

QUESTION: Can you tell me what sounds strange in this sentence and why? *The building looks like it was redesigned.*

ANSWER: The word *like* should not be used as a conjunction, as has been done in your sentence. Substitute *as if* (*the building looks as if it was redesigned*).

Name ______________________________

CHAPTER 18 Reinforcement Exercises

LEVEL I

A. (Self-check) In the spaces provided after each sentence, indicate whether a period, question mark, or exclamation point is needed. Use the symbol. If no additional punctuation is required, write *0*.

EXAMPLE: May I have your answer by return mail^ ___.___

1. Would you give me your latest price figure for a ream of 16-pound bond paper ______
2. What an amazingly complex situation this has become ______
3. There is no reason for retaining these files, is there ______
4. Has anyone checked to see if the mail has been distributed ______
5. Send for your complimentary brochure today ______
6. Help! Smoke is coming from my keyboard ______
7. Juanita asked if she should come in at 7 a.m. to complete the work for Techtronics, Inc. ______
8. Oh, I don't believe we should worry about it at this time ______
9. I wonder whether I am to store this letter on magnetic media ______
10. Will you please keep one copy and return the other to me ______

Check your answers.

B. In the following sentences all punctuation has been omitted. Insert commas, periods, question marks, colons, and exclamation points. The words have extra space between them so that punctuation may be inserted. Use a caret (^) to indicate your insertion. Periods and commas may be placed inside the caret. In the space at the right, indicate the number of punctuation marks you inserted. Consult a reference manual or a dictionary for abbreviation style if necessary.

EXAMPLE: Will you please add Mr^. T^. G^. Skaggs^, Jr^.^, to the address list^. ___7___

1. Abbreviations such as misc and attn are generally not used in business correspondence ______
2. Very common abbreviations like a m and p m may appear in business correspondence ______
3. Only one awardee was selected i e Dr Ellen Anderson ______

A. 1. . 2. ! 3. ? 4. ? 5. . 6. ! 7. 0 8. . 9. . 10. .

4. You did place an ad in the classified section didn't you
5. It was Miss Jenkins not Mrs Reed who was to receive the c o d shipment
6. What a dilemma the latest F C C regulations have created
7. Stop Don't touch that switch
8. Deliver the signed contracts to Mr C P Ryan before 5 p m
9. If I B M offers a full-service contract we would be interested
10. What a fine day for lunch in the park
11. Darren asked if most automobiles were delivered f o b Detroit
12. Please accept my congratulations on the completion of your M B A
13. Ms J S Neighbors has been appointed consultant for educational services to the A F L - C I O
14. He often uses the abbreviations *e g* and *i e* in his dictation
15. Will you please R S V P before Friday September 30
16. Some authorities wonder if the I Q of school-age children is affected by T V
17. Has the erroneous charge of $45 95 been removed from my account
18. The following individuals have agreed to serve Dr Lyn Clark Ms Deborah Kitchin and Prof Marilyne Hudgens
19. Lt Gen Maxwell asked if he could serve in West Germany
20. Why we have not heard from either the C E O or the C F O is a mystery to me
21. We are scheduled to meet at 8 p m aren't we
22. Among the speakers are Michael Hartman M D and Gail Nemire R N (*Don't forget the commas!*)
23. Will you please send me the latest bulletin showing the G N P for the past ten years
24. Only one member of our staff received an award i e Professor Renee R Cornell
25. Wow I have finally finished this exercise

Name ______________________________

LEVEL II

A. (Self-check) Write the letter of the correctly punctuated sentence in the space provided.

1. (a) Reading, traveling, and jogging: these are my favorite activities.
   (b) Reading, traveling, and jogging — these are my favorite activities.
   (c) Reading, traveling, and jogging; these are my favorite activities. ______

2. (a) "Civilization and profits go hand in hand." — Calvin Coolidge
   (b) "Civilization and profits go hand in hand," Calvin Coolidge
   (c) "Civilization and profits go hand in hand": Calvin Coolidge ______

3. (a) I was forty minutes late (would you believe it) to the final exam.
   (b) I was forty minutes late (would you believe it?) to the final exam.
   (c) I was forty minutes late (would you believe it) to the final exam? ______

4. (Emphasize parenthetical element.)
   (a) Currently our basic operating costs: rent, utilities, and wages, are 10 percent higher than last year.
   (b) Currently our basic operating costs (rent, utilities, and wages) are 10 percent higher than last year.
   (c) Currently our basic operating costs — rent, utilities, and wages — are 10 percent higher than last year. ______

5. (a) Loading and unloading disks (see page 23 in the manual) must be done carefully.
   (b) Loading and unloading disks, see page 23 in the manual, must be done carefully.
   (c) Loading and unloading disks: see page 23 in the manual, must be done carefully. ______

6. (a) Recently you applied for a position (legal secretary); however, you did not indicate for which branch your application is intended.
   (b) Recently you applied for a position; (legal secretary) however, you did not indicate for which branch your application is intended.
   (c) Recently you applied for a position (legal secretary;) however, you did not indicate for which branch your application is intended. ______

7. (Emphasize)
   (a) Sales, sales, and more sales: that's what we need to succeed.
   (b) Sales, sales, and more sales — that's what we need to succeed.
   (c) Sales, sales, and more sales; that's what we need to succeed. ______

8. (Demphasize)
   (a) Three Washington cities — Seattle, Everett, and Tacoma — are competing for the large industrial complex.
   (b) Three Washington cities, Seattle, Everett, and Tacoma, are competing for the large industrial complex.
   (c) Three Washington cities (Seattle, Everett, and Tacoma) are competing for the large industrial complex. ______

Check your answers.

A. 1. b, 2. a, 3. b, 4. c, 5. a, 6. a, 7. b, 8. c

B. Insert dashes or parentheses in the following sentences. In the space provided after each sentence, write the number of punctuation marks you inserted. Count each parenthesis and each dash as a single mark.

EXAMPLE: (Emphasize.) That line of peripheral equipment—printers, modems, and screens, etc.—is clearly aimed at the microcomputer market. 2

1. (Deemphasize.) The modernized production of Shakespeare's "As You Like It" have you read the reviews? will be opening here very shortly. ____
2. Fingerprints, mug shots, and arrest records these are now stored on microforms by law enforcement officers. ____
3. "Do not squander time, for that is the stuff life is made of." Benjamin Franklin ____
4. (Emphasize.) Three branch assistant managers Augusta Jones, James Redman, and Candi Herman will be promoted this month. ____
5. (Deemphasize.) Three branch assistant managers Augusta Jones, James Redman, and Candi Herman will be promoted this month. ____
6. (Deemphasize.) As soon as you are able to make an appointment try to do so before December 30 ,we will process your insurance forms. ____
7. Quality copies, low cost, ease of operation, compact design what more could a customer want in an economical office copy machine? ____
8. Funds for the project will be released on the following dates see Section 12.3 of the original grant: January 1, March 14, and June 30. ____
9. (Deemphasize.) Although toy factories are heavily concentrated in three locations New York, Chicago, and Boston, the largest single manufacturer is located in Hawthorne, California. ____
10. The warranty period for this electrical appliance is limited to sixty 60 days. ____

C. Using three different forms of punctuation, correctly punctuate the following sentence. In the space provided explain how the three methods you have employed differ.

1. Numerous considerations all of which are fully described in our report prompted the closure of the outlet.
2. Numerous considerations all of which are fully described in our report prompted the closure of the outlet.
3. Numerous considerations all of which are fully described in our report prompted the closure of the outlet.

Explanation: ______________________________

Name ______________________

LEVEL III

A. (Self-check) Indicate whether the following statements are True (*T*) or False (*F*).

1. Quotation marks are used to enclose the exact words of a writer or speaker. ______
2. The names of books, magazines, pamphlets, and newspapers may be underscored or enclosed in quotation marks. ______
3. Periods and commas are always placed inside closing quotation marks. ______
4. Parentheses are used by a writer to enclose his own remarks inserted into a quotation. ______
5. A quotation within a quotation is shown with a single quotation mark. ______
6. Semicolons and colons are always placed inside closing quotation marks. ______
7. On a typewriter the underscore is used to emphasize words that would be italicized in printed copy. ______
8. If both a quotation and its introductory sentence are questions, use a question mark before the closing quotation marks. ______
9. The word *sic* is used to show that a quotation is free of errors. ______
10. A single quotation mark is typed by using the apostrophe key. ______

Check your answers.

B. Many, but not all, of the following sentences contain direct quotations. None of the sentences has any punctuation. Insert all necessary punctuation.

EXAMPLE: The word asset means "an item of monetary value."

1. In our five-year projections said the general manager we plan to expand marketing and distributing to the East Coast
2. Careful speakers use the word mad to mean insane
3. Graham's chapter entitled Drawing the World Together appeared in the book Global Links
4. Did Mr Cruz say Where are the printers that need repair
5. One of the turbines wrote Mr Haller has to [*sic*] little torque
6. Melissa said that she hoped we would call her if we needed assistance
7. Although he was somewhat worried about the interview Jerry told his friends that he was cool
8. The postal worker said Shall I stamp your package Fragile
9. A chain-mail suit for deep-sea divers is described in an article entitled A Jawbreaker for Sharks which appeared in National Geographic
10. The expression persona non grata means one who is not acceptable

---

A. 1. T, 2. F, 3. T, 4. F, 5. T, 6. F, 7. T, 8. T, 9. F, 10. T

11. After banging on the elevator doors repeatedly Mrs Lowe shouted Please help us
12. Has anyone seen the extra copy of the sheet music for Rhapsody in Blue
13. The title of the article is Automation in the Office however the author may rewrite the title later
14. Our copy machine said the sales representative will reproduce charts books and large-size originals
15. Some writers confuse the word principal with principle

C. Insert all necessary punctuation. These sentences review Levels I, II, and III.

1. Wait Don't you have your keys with you
2. Eating studying and working these are Mike's principal activities
3. (Deemphasize.) Regular cleaning of the tape head see Chart 2 in the operating manual is necessary for best performance
4. (Emphasize.) Two of our best researchers Darlene McClure and Judith Ehresman were hired by our competitor
5. (Deemphasize.) Stereo systems for cars these include amplifiers tape decks speakers and FM receivers have blossomed into a lucrative specialty market
6. (Direct quote.) Was it President Martin who said What can't be cured must be endured
7. The word copyright literally means right to copy
8. Evelyn Taylor wrote the chapter entitled The Structure of the State Court System which appeared in Remedies at Law
9. The envelope marked Confidential was delivered to the wrong office
10. (Direct quote.) Did Alicia say Where is our supply of ribbons

D. ***Optional Composition.*** Your instructor may ask you to complete this exercise on a separate sheet. Write original sentences to illustrate the following: a period with an abbreviation, a question mark to end a direct question, an exclamation point, a dash to set off parenthetical elements, parentheses around deemphasized material, quoted material following a brief introduction, quotation marks enclosing a title, and brackets.

POSTTEST

Insert necessary punctuation.

1. Will you please send me a copy of the book entitled Office Careers Today
2. Why did we receive this envelope marked Confidential
3. The only guests who have not sent RSVPs are Miss Lee Mrs. Gold and Mr Sims
4. The word principal was misused in the chapter entitled Writing Persuasive Letters
5. Did Professor Miles say How many students expect to miss the test Friday

---

1. Office Careers Today. 2. "Confidential"? 3. Lee, Mrs. Gold, Mr. Sims. 4. principal "Writing Persuasive Letters." 5. say, "How Friday?"

Name ________________

UNIT 5 REVIEW **Chapters 16–18 (Self-Check)**

First, review Chapters 16 through 18. Then, test your comprehension of those chapters by completing the exercises that follow and comparing your responses with those shown at the end of the review.

LEVEL I

Use the letters below to indicate how the italicized words in the following sentences should be punctuated.

(a) , __________ (c) __________ , (e) no punctuation
(b) , __________ , (d) ; __________ ,

1. Under no circumstances *Mr. Greenwood* will your complaints be disregarded. _____
2. *However* the matter is resolved, the goodwill of the customer is paramount. _____
3. Our Sales Department is concerned with the financing *delivery* and installation of our products. _____
4. A student *who studies diligently and masters the principles* will score well on the examination. _____
5. Our management team feels *on the other hand* that they must hold the line on benefits and salaries. _____
6. The sales representative *Walter S. Anderson* presented a thorough report. _____

Select (a), (b), or (c) to indicate the correctly punctuated sentence.

7. (a) Some of the equipment is stored in the warehouse other equipment is now in transit.
   (b) Some of the equipment is stored in the warehouse, other equipment is now in transit.
   (c) Some of the equipment is stored in the warehouse; other equipment is now in transit. _____
8. (a) Seminar participants are arriving from Denver, Colorado, Miami, Florida, and Baltimore, Maryland.
   (b) Seminar participants are arriving from Denver, Colorado; Miami, Florida; and Baltimore, Maryland.
   (c) Seminar participants are arriving from Denver; Colorado; Miami; Florida; and Baltimore; Maryland. _____
9. (a) Investments should turn a profit; however, security is also important.
   (b) Investments should turn a profit, however, security is also important.
   (c) Investments should turn a profit; however security is also important. _____
10. (a) Would you please send the shipment c.o.d.
    (b) Would you please send the shipment c.o.d.?
    (c) Would you please send the shipment cod? _____

Select (a), (b), or (c) to indicate the correctly punctuated sentence.

11. (a) We were expected to send an R.S.V.P., weren't we?
    (b) We were expected to send an RSVP, weren't we?
    (c) We were expected to send an RSVP weren't we? _____

12. (a) Wow! A total of 89.9 percent of the voters approved!
    (b) Wow, a total of 89 point 9 percent of the voters approved!
    (c) Wow. A total of 89.9 percent of the voters approved! _____

13. (a) We are evaluating three printers; matrix, impact, and laser.
    (b) We are evaluating three printers: matrix, impact, and laser.
    (c) We are evaluating three printers, matrix, impact, and laser. _____

14. (a) Thus far, we have received brochures from Xerox, IBM, and Wang.
    (b) Thus far, we have received brochures from, Xerox, IBM, and Wang.
    (c) Thus far, we have received brochures from: Xerox, IBM, and Wang. _____

15. (a) Mr. Jenkins said, "We used to depend upon fixed-rate mortgages."
    (b) Mr. Jenkins said: "We used to depend upon fixed-rate mortgages."
    (c) Mr. Jenkins said; "We used to depend upon fixed-rate mortgages." _____

16. (a) Three of the most populous states: Illinois, New York, and California, will receive extra federal funding.
    (b) Three of the most populous states — Illinois, New York, and California — will receive extra federal funding.
    (c) Three of the most populous states, Illinois, New York, and California, will receive extra federal funding. _____

17. (a) Cameras, VCRs, and projectors — these are only some of the products we carry.
    (b) Cameras, VCRs, and projectors: these are only some of the products we carry.
    (c) Cameras, VCRs, and projectors, these are only some of the products we carry. _____

18. *Emphasize*:
    (a) Only three products: cameras, VCRs, and camcorders account for 70 percent of our total sales.
    (b) Only three products — cameras, VCRs, and camcorders — account for 70 percent of our total sales.
    (c) Only three products (cameras, VCRs, and camcorders) account for 70 percent of our total sales. _____

19. (a) The three Texas cities selected are Houston, Fort Worth, and Dallas.
    (b) The three Texas cities selected are: Houston, Fort Worth, and Dallas.
    (c) The three Texas cities selected are — Houston, Fort Worth, and Dallas. _____

20. *Deemphasize:*
    (a) A pilot project — refer to page 6 of the report — may help us justify the new system.
    (b) A pilot project, refer to page 6 of the report, may help us justify the new system.
    (c) A pilot project (refer to page 6 of the report) may help us justify the new system. _____

Select (a), (b), or (c) to indicate the correctly punctuated sentence.

21. (a) In short employees must be extremely courteous.
    (b) In short — employees must be extremely courteous.
    (c) In short, employees must be extremely courteous. ______

22. (a) The aim of our company is to build, not destroy, customer goodwill.
    (b) The aim of our company is to build: not destroy, customer goodwill.
    (c) The aim of our company is to build, not destroy customer goodwill. ______

23. (a) Only one department has submitted its report on time, namely the Legal Department.
    (b) Only one department has submitted its report on time, namely, the Legal Department.
    (c) Only one department has submitted its report on time: namely, the Legal Department. ______

24. (a) The location of the convention has been narrowed to three sites, namely, New Orleans, Chicago, and San Francisco.
    (b) The location of the convention has been narrowed to three sites; namely, New Orleans, Chicago, and San Francisco.
    (c) The location of the convention has been narrowed to three sites; namely New Orleans, Chicago, and San Francisco. ______

25. (a) The computer was producing "garbage," that is, the screen showed gibberish.
    (b) The computer was producing "garbage"; that is, the screen showed gibberish.
    (c) The computer was producing "garbage;" that is, the screen showed gibberish. ______

26. (a) A cartel is defined as a "group of companies acting to control prices."
    (b) A "cartel" is defined as a 'group of companies acting to control prices.'
    (c) A *cartel* is defined as a "group of companies acting to control prices." ______

27. (a) *The Office,* a magazine which publishes much automation data, recently featured an article entitled *Coping With Copiers.*
    (b) *The Office,* a magazine which publishes much automation data, recently featured an article entitled "Coping With Copiers."
    (c) "The Office," a magazine which publishes much automation data, recently featured an article entitled *Coping With Copiers.* ______

28. (a) "An ombudsman, said Mr. Sirakides, is an individual hired by management to investigate and resolve employee complaints."
    (b) "An ombudsman," said Mr. Sirakides, "Is an individual hired by management to investigate and resolve employee complaints."
    (c) "An ombudsman," said Mr. Sirakides, "is an individual hired by management to investigate and resolve employee complaints." ______

29. (a) Who was it who said, "A penny saved is a penny earned."?
    (b) Who was it who said, "A penny saved is a penny earned?"
    (c) Who was it who said, "A penny saved is a penny earned"? ______

30. (a) Did the office manager really say, "Stamp this package 'Confidential'?"
(b) Did the office manager really say, "Stamp this package 'Confidential' "?
(c) Did the office manager really say, "Stamp this package "Confidential"? ______

Hot Line Review

Write the letter of the word or phrase that correctly completes each sentence.

31. Every measure has been taken to (a) ensure, (b) insure your satisfaction. ______
32. Because few policyholders were (a) appraised, (b) apprised of the deficit, no action was taken. ______
33. My partner and (a) I, (b) me, (c) myself have signed an agreement. ______
34. Have you ever been (a) cited, (b) sited, (c) sighted for a speeding violation? ______
35. Give the extra paper to (a) whoever, (b) whomever needs it most. ______

---

1. b, 2. c, 3. b, 4. c, 5. b, 6. c, 7. c, 8. b, 9. a, 10. a, 11. b, 12. a, 13. b, 14. a, 15. a, 16. b, 17. a, 18. b, 19. a, 20. c, 21. c, 22. a, 23. b, 24. b, 25. b, 26. c, 27. b, 28. c, 29. c, 30. b, 31. a, 32. b, 33. a, 34. a, 35. a

UNIT SIX

Writing With Style

CHAPTER 19

Capitalization

OBJECTIVES When you have completed the materials in this chapter, you will be able to do the following:

Level I — *Distinguish between common and proper nouns for purposes of capitalization.*
— *Decide when to capitalize proper adjectives and when not to.*

Level II — *Use proofreading marks in properly capitalizing personal titles, numbered items, and points of the compass.*
— *Correctly capitalize departments, divisions, committees, government terms, product names, and literary titles.*

Level III — *Identify and capitalize appropriate words in quotes, rules, phrases, and enumerated items.*
— *Apply special rules in capitalizing personal titles and proper nouns with common noun elements.*

PRETEST

Underline any letters that should be capitalized in the sentences below.

1. Last spring mother took classes in history, computer technology, english, and psychology.
2. The american chemical society will meet in the st. louis room of the hilton hotel on march 25.
3. After receiving a bachelor's degree from humboldt state university, sharon became assistant to the personnel manager at bank of america.
4. Our company president and vice president met with several supervisors on the west coast last week.
5. The internal revenue service requires corporations to fill out form 1350 before the april 15 deadline.

Rules governing capitalization reflect conventional practices; that is, they have been established by custom and usage. By following these conventions, a writer, among other things, tells a reader what words are important. In earlier times writers capitalized most

1. Mother English 2. American Chemical Society St. Louis Room Hilton Hotel March 3. Humboldt State University Sharon Bank of America 4. West Coast 5. Internal Revenue Service Form 1350 April

nouns and many adjectives at will; few conventions of capitalization or punctuation were then consistently observed. Today most capitalization follows definite rules that are fully accepted and practiced at all times.

Within many larger organizations, capitalization style may be prescribed in a stylebook. Dictionaries are also helpful in determining capitalization practices, but they do not show all capitalized words. To develop skill in controlling capitals, study the rules and examples shown in this chapter.

LEVEL I

Basic Rules of Capitalization

Proper Nouns

Capitalize proper nouns, including the *specific* names of persons, places, schools, streets, parks, buildings, religions, holidays, months, nicknames, agreements, and so forth. Do *not* capitalize common nouns that make *general* reference.

Proper nouns	Common nouns
Jackson Turner	a young man on the basketball team
Mexico, Canada	neighboring countries of the U.S.
Cypress College, Ohio University	a community college and a university
Stoner Avenue Park	a picnic in the park
Catholic, Presbyterian	representatives of two religions
Empire Room, Royal Inn	a room in the hotel
Veterans Day, Easter	on these holidays
Golden Gate Bridge	a bridge over the bay
Chrysler Building	the building in the city
House of Representatives, Senate	components of government
January, February, March	first three months of the year
the Windy City, the Big Apple	nicknames of cities
Stipulation of Interest Agreement	an agreement between companies

Proper Adjectives

Capitalize most adjectives that are derived from proper nouns.

Victorian furniture	Socratic method
Danish pastry	British thermal unit
Keynesian economics	Roman numeral
Arabic alphabet	Greek symbols

Do not capitalize those few adjectives originally derived from proper nouns that have become common adjectives (without capitals) through usage. Consult your dictionary when in doubt.

mandarin collar	homburg hat
french fries	china dishes
manila folder	diesel engine
india ink	charley horse

Beginning of Sentence

Capitalize the first letter of a word beginning a sentence.

Inventory and sales data can be beamed from microwave towers.

Geographic Locations

Capitalize the names of *specific* places such as states, cities, mountains, valleys, lakes, rivers, oceans, and geographic regions. Capitalize *county* and *state* when they follow the proper nouns.

Oregon, Washington, Idaho
Oklahoma City, Salt Lake City
San Fernando Valley
Lake Michigan, Salton Sea
Broward County, Cook County (*but* the city of Chicago, the county of Cook, the state of Colorado)

Rogue River, Mississippi River
Atlantic Ocean, Indian Ocean
New England, Texas Panhandle
European Community (EC)
New York State

Organization Names

Capitalize the principal words in the names of all business, civic, educational, governmental, labor, military, philanthropic, political, professional, religious, and social organizations.

Professional Secretaries International
National Association of Letter Carriers
Peace Corps
Federal Aviation Administration
Screen Actors Guild

Arthritis Foundation
San Diego Unified School District
Communications Satellite Corporation
National Park Service
The Ohio River Company*

Generally, do *not* capitalize *company, association, board,* and other shortened name forms when they are used to replace full organization names. If these shortened names, however, are preceded by the word *the* and are used in formal or legal documents (contracts, bylaws, minutes, etc.), they may be capitalized.

Did you know that the *company* will pay certain medical benefits? (Informal document.)

The Treasurer of the *Association* is herein authorized to disburse funds. (Formal document.)

Academic Courses and Degrees

Capitalize specific academic degrees and course titles. Do not capitalize references to general academic degrees and subject areas.

Professor Waxman, Ph.D., is scheduled to offer Psychology 104 in the spring.

Mr. Jones, who holds bachelor's and master's degrees, teaches conversational French.

Becky expects to enroll in Keyboarding I, Office Administration 32, and Accounting 28.

My most interesting classes are history, business management, and psychology.

**Capitalize* the *only when it is part of an organization's official name (as it would appear on the organization's stationery).*

Seasons

Do not capitalize seasons unless they are personified (spoken of as if alive).

> Last winter we drew lots for summer vacations.
> "Come, Winter, with thine angry howl . . . ." — Burns

Complete the reinforcement exercises for Level I.

LEVEL II

Rules of Capitalization

Titles of People

a. Capitalize personal titles when they precede names.

Aunt Gertrude	Budget Director Magee
Councilman Mendler	Mayor Bradley
Commander Howard Rogers	President Morales

b. Capitalize titles in addresses and closing lines.

Mr. Kenneth Miller	Very sincerely yours,*
Executive Vice President, Planning	
Energy Systems Technology, Inc.	
8907 Canoga Avenue	Patricia Barr
Canoga Park, CA 91371	Sales Supervisor

c. Capitalize titles of high government rank or religious office.

the President of the U.S.	our Governor, Thurston Lee
the Pope's visit	Stanislaw Dimitri, Premier
the Senator from Pennsylvania	an audience with the Queen
the Chief Justice	the Secretary of State

Notice that titles of high rank or office are capitalized when they precede a name, follow a name, or replace a name.

d. Do not capitalize titles following names.

> Leon Jones, president of Atlas Chemical Company
> Rose Valenzuela, supervisor, Word Processing Center
> Davonne Adams, office manager

e. Do not capitalize titles appearing alone.

> The president of that company was made chairman of the board.
> Refer the problem to the vice president or personnel manager.

f. Do not capitalize titles when they are followed by appositives.†

> Our cost accountant, Mona Chase, submitted her revised figures.

g. Do not capitalize family titles used with possessive pronouns.

my mother	our aunt
his father	your cousin

**In the complimentary close only the first word is capitalized.*

†You will recall that appositives rename or explain previously mentioned nouns or pronouns.

But do capitalize titles of close relatives when they are used without pronouns.

Please call Father immediately.

N.B. The capitalization of *business* titles can be summarized in one rule: Capitalize business titles *only* when they precede personal names and are not followed by appositives, as *Personnel Director Roslyn Katz.*

Numbered and Lettered Items

Capitalize nouns followed by numbers or letters (except in page, paragraph, line, and verse references).

Gate 69, Flight 238	FHA Form 2900-4	Building I-63-B
Invoice No. 15891	Volume II, Appendix A	Medicare Form 72T
page 6, line 12	State Highway 5	Supplement No. 3

Points of the Compass

Capitalize *north, south, east, west,* and their derivatives when they represent *specific* regions. Do not capitalize the points of the compass when they are used in directions or in general references.

the Middle East, the Far East	heading east on the turnpike
the Midwest, the Pacific Northwest	to the west of town
the East Coast, the West Coast	eastern Maine, western Illinois
Easterners, Southerners	southern Georgia
Northern Hemisphere	

Departments, Divisions, and Committees

Capitalize the names of departments, divisions, or committees within your own organization. Outside your organization capitalize only *specific* department, division, or committee names.

Sue works in our Communications Services Department.

Dr. Nguyen is director of the Northeast Division of Barco.

Send your employment application to their personnel department.

Grievances are referred to our Personnel Practices Committee.

A steering committee has not yet been named.

Governmental Terms

Do not capitalize the words *federal, government, nation,* or *state* unless they are part of a specific title.

Neither the state government nor the federal government would fund the proposal.

The Federal Trade Commission regulates advertising in all the states.

Product Names

Capitalize product names only when they represent trademarked items. Except in advertising, common names following manufacturers' names are not capitalized.

Coca-Cola	Whirlpool washer	Paper-Mate pen
DuPont Teflon	Sears vacuum cleaner	Kodak camera
Ray-Ban sunglasses	IBM computer	Levi 501 jeans

Literary Titles

Capitalize the principal words in the titles of books, magazines, newspapers, articles, movies, plays, songs, poems, and reports. Do *not* capitalize articles (*a, an, the*), short conjunctions (*and, but, or, nor*), and prepositions of fewer than four letters (*in, to, by, for,* etc.) unless they begin or end the title.

> Fowler's *The King's English* (Book.)
> Clark and Clark's *HOW: A Handbook for Office Workers* (Book.)
> Gershwin's "An American in Paris" (Symphonic tone poem.)
> "How to Get the Most From a Placement Service" (Magazine article.)

Complete the reinforcement exercises for Level II.

LEVEL III

Rules of Capitalization

Beginning Words

In addition to capitalizing the first word of a complete sentence, capitalize the first words in quoted sentences, independent phrases, enumerated items, and formal rules or principles following colons.

> Calvin Coolidge said, "The business of America is business." (Quoted sentence.)
>
> No, not at the present time. (Independent phrase.)
>
> Micrographics allow us many options:
> 1. Fonts
> 2. Forms
> 3. Logotypes
>
> Our office manager responded with his favorite rule: Follow the company stylebook for correct capitalization. (Rule following colon.)

Celestial Bodies

Capitalize the names of celestial bodies such as Jupiter, Saturn, and Neptune. Do not capitalize the terms *earth, sun,* or *moon* unless they appear in a context with other celestial bodies.

> Where on earth did you find that ancient typewriter?
>
> Venus and Mars are the closest planets to Earth.

Ethnic References

Terms that relate to a particular culture, language, or race are capitalized.

In Hawaii, Oriental and Western cultures merge.

Both English and Hebrew are spoken by Jews in Israel.

Plural Proper Nouns With Common Noun Elements

When a common noun element is used to describe two or more proper nouns, do not capitalize the common noun.

Smith has traveled extensively across both the Atlantic and Pacific *oceans.*

Coal shipments are sent via the Ohio and Mississippi *rivers.*

Congress is considering both the Long and Brooks *acts.*

Words Following *marked* and *stamped*

Capitalize words that follow the words *marked* and *stamped.*

For greater care in transport, the package was stamped "Fragile."

That bill was marked "Paid in Full" on September 15.

Special Uses of Personal Titles and Terms

a. Generally, titles are capitalized according to the specifications set forth earlier. However, when a title of an official appears in that organization's minutes, bylaws, or other official document, it may be capitalized.

The Controller will have authority over college budgets. (Appearing in bylaws.)

By vote of the stockholders, the President is empowered to implement a stock split. (Appearing in Annual Report.)

b. When the words *ex, elect, late,* and *former* are used with capitalized titles, they are not capitalized.

The projections of ex-Vice President Baldwin have proven exceedingly accurate.

Mayor-elect Cortazzo addressed the city council.

The President appointed former Secretary of Labor James Watson to the commission.

c. Titles other than *sir, ladies,* and *gentlemen* are capitalized when used in direct address.

May I ask, Doctor, what the prognosis is?

You, gentlemen, are well aware of the gravity of the situation.

Complete the reinforcement exercises for Level III.

HOT LINE QUERIES

QUESTION: I don't know how to describe the copies made from our copy machine. Should I call them *Xerox* copies or something else?

ANSWER: They are *Xerox* copies only if made on a Xerox copier. Copies made on other machines may be called *xerographic* copies, *machine* copies, or *photocopies.*

QUESTION: In the doctor's office where I work, I see the word *medicine* capitalized, as in *the field of Medicine.* Is this correct?

ANSWER: No. General references should not be capitalized. If it were part of a title, as in the Northwestern College of *Medicine*, it would be capitalized.

QUESTION: I work for the National Therapy Association. When I talk about *the association* in a letter, should I capitalize it?

ANSWER: No. When a shortened form of an organization name is used alone, it is generally not capitalized. In formal or legal documents (contracts, bylaws, printed announcements), it may be capitalized.

QUESTION: I work for a state agency, and I'm not sure what to capitalize or hyphenate in this sentence: *State agencies must make forms available to <u>non-English speaking</u> applicants.*

ANSWER: Words with the prefix *non* are usually not hyphenated (*nonexistent, nontoxic*). But when *non* is joined to a word that must be capitalized, it is followed by a hyphen. Because the word *speaking* combines with *English* to form a single-unit adjective, it should be hyphenated. Thus, the expression should be typed *non-English-speaking applicants.*

QUESTION: When we use a person's title, such as *business manager,* in place of a person's name, shouldn't the title always be capitalized?

ANSWER: No. Business titles are capitalized only when they precede an individual's name, as in *Business Manager Smith.* Do not capitalize titles when they replace an individual's name: *Our business manager will direct the transaction.*

QUESTION: How do you spell *marshal,* as used in the Grand Marshal of the Rose Parade?

ANSWER: The preferred spelling is with a single *l: marshal.* In addition to describing an individual who directs a ceremony, the noun *marshal* refers to a high military officer or a city law officer who carries out court orders (*the marshal served papers on the defendant*). As a verb, *marshal* means "to bring together" or "to order in an effective way" (*the attorney marshaled convincing arguments*). The similar-sounding word *martial* is an adjective and means "warlike" or "military" (*martial law was declared after the riot*).

Name ______________________________

CHAPTER 19 **Reinforcement Exercises**

LEVEL I

A. (Self-check) In the following sentences, use proofreading marks to correct errors you find in capitalization. Use three short lines (≡) under a lowercase letter to indicate that it is to be changed to a capital letter. Draw a diagonal (/) through a capital letter you wish to change to a lowercase letter. Indicate at the right the total number of changes you have made in each sentence.

EXAMPLE: The Bandit Henry McCarthy was also known as Billy the kid. ___2___

1. One of the World's largest trading businesses is the japanese sumimoto corporation. ______
2. Born in Cook county, Wilson grew up in the state of Ohio. ______
3. All Ford Motor Company Cars and Light Trucks carry a Warranty. ______
4. Isaac Bantu is studying spanish, accounting, Management, and Keyboarding. ______
5. Use India ink to make dark headings on the manila folders. ______
6. Pelee island is located on the canadian side of lake erie. ______
7. Regulations of the Occupational Safety and health administration resulted in costly expenses for our Company. ______
8. Salt lake city, in the State of Utah, was founded by Brigham Young and a small Party of Mormons in 1847. ______
9. All sales representatives of the Company met in the Sheraton room of the Red lion motor inn. ______
10. Both the Senate and the house passed consumer protection laws. ______

Check your answers.

B. Use proofreading marks to correct any capitalization errors in these sentences. Indicate the total number of *changes* at the right. If no changes are needed, write *0*.

A. 1. world's, Japanese, Sumimoto Corporation (4); 2. County (1); 3. cars, light trucks, warranty (4); 4. Spanish, management, keyboarding (3); 5. india (1); 6. Island, Canadian, Lake Erie (4); 7. Health Administration, company (3); 8. Lake City, state, party (4); 9. company, Room, Lion Motor Inn (5); 10. House (1)

1. Because he was interested in Computer Technology, Craig took computer mathematics I, general physics I, and computer circuitry II. ______
2. Representatives from the methodist, presbyterian, baptist, and catholic faiths will hold a Conference in St. petersburg beach, florida. ______
3. Rex Mackey was sent to our Kansas city branch office for the Month of March, but he hopes to return in April. ______
4. The newspaper reports that Joe Fujimoto, ph.d., has joined your Company. ______
5. Increasing coal shipments have affected business for The Ohio River Company. (The word *the* is part of the company name.) ______
6. Last Fall Ms. Adams took out a policy with the Prudential life insurance company. (The word *the* is part of the company name.) ______
7. Work schedules will have to be adjusted in november for veterans day. ______
8. All company representatives gathered in atlantic city in the zenith room of the holiday inn for the spring sales meeting. ______
9. The windy city is attractive to many local Tourists as well as to european and canadian visitors. ______
10. Professor Daruty employed the socratic method of questioning students to elicit answers about Business Management. ______
11. After driving through New York state, we stayed in New York city and visited the Empire State building. ______
12. Although mimeograph copies are cheaper, xerox copies are much easier to produce. ______
13. Mr. Randolph completed the requirements for a bachelor's degree at the Massachusetts institute of technology. ______
14. The report contained some roman numerals and many greek symbols in the engineering equations. ______
15. Last spring my political science class visited the tishman building in westwood village. ______

Name ____________________

LEVEL II

A. (Self-check) Use proofreading marks to correct errors you find in capitalization. Indicate at the right the total number of changes you make.

EXAMPLE: General manager Harold Gross was promoted to Vice President. ___3___

1. Henry Davis, supervisor of our legal department, traveled to the east coast over the holidays. ______
2. Please consult figure 52D in appendix B for instructions in computing the depreciation of equipment. ______
3. We will ask sales manager Sperazza to be chairman of an investigation committee. ______
4. Both mother and aunt grace received Timex Watches as Christmas gifts. ______
5. The fishing industry in the Pacific northwest is affected by recent federal regulations. ______
6. Our business manager and our vice president attended a seminar in southern Illinois. ______
7. My Uncle recommended that I read the article entitled "how management is guided by research." ______
8. Address the envelope to Ms. Maria Velez, director, employee services, Omega Corporation, 304 Hilyard Street, Eugene, Oregon. ______
9. The president met with the newly appointed secretary of defense to discuss defense appropriations. ______
10. Centron Oil Company, with headquarters in western Texas, distributes its products throughout the entire northern hemisphere. ______

Check your answers.

B. Use proofreading marks to correct errors in the sentences below. Indicate the number of changes you make for each sentence.

1. Harley Lee, vice president of Manufacturers trust company, asked his Executive Assistant to direct the united way office contributions. ______

A. 1. Legal Department, East Coast (4); 2. Figure, Appendix (2); 3. Sales Manager (2); 4. Mother, Aunt Grace, watches (4); 5. Northwest (1); 6. (0); 7. uncle, How Management Is Guided by Research (6); 8. Director, Employee Services (3); 9. President, Secretary of Defense (3); 10. Northern Hemisphere (2)

2. My sister, my cousin, and I will fly to visit mother, father, and uncle Eduardo over the Spring holidays. ______

3. Marcia Morrow, formerly with our office products department, recently published *Word processing from infancy through the 90s.* ______

4. When the president, the secretary of state, and the secretary of labor traveled to the State of Kentucky, stringent security measures were effected. ______

5. You will find a discussion of keynesian economics in volume II on page 71, starting with line 11. ______

6. The Sales Manager of Datacom, who wrote a manual for sales representatives, conducted a training session in the city of Logansport. ______

7. Our director of purchasing, Harvey Gross, ordered Victor Calculators and Sony Recorders. ______

8. The letter is addressed to Paul Jorgensen, director of research and development, blum corporation, p.o. box 58, gulfport, florida 33707. ______

9. May Co.'s ad featured Royal Manor Dishes and teflon-coated pans. ______

10. Overtime compensation for Carmen Corregas was referred to our industrial relations department. ______

11. Susan searched for levi 501 jeans at the westside pavilion ______

12. Franklin became an assistant to the administrator of the Governor Bacon Health center, which is operated by the department of health and social services of the State of Delaware. ______

13. Business Manager Edward Davis devised a procedure for expediting Purchase Orders from Area D Offices. ______

14. Douglas ordered a big mac, french fries, and a coca-cola for lunch. ______

15. A midwesterner who enjoys sunshine, Evans travels south each Winter to vacation in Southern Georgia. ______

16. David Kane is now supervising our entire gulf coast division. ______

17. As stated in part II of the Contract, massachusetts general insurance company pays claims related to injuries only. ______

18. The new Datonics model 100 cellular phone will be demonstrated at the national office products show at the bonaventure hotel next fall. ______

Name ____________________

LEVEL III

A. (Self-check) Use proofreading marks to indicate necessary changes. Write the total number of changes at the right.

EXAMPLE: Mercury, Venus, earth, and Mars are Dense and solid. 2

1. Your check was stamped "insufficient funds" and returned. ____
2. The guiding principle of capitalization is this: capitalize *specific* names and references, but do not capitalize *general* references. ____
3. Both the Pacific and Atlantic Oceans are main thoroughfares of Commerce. ____
4. The Late President Theodore Roosevelt is remembered for his initiation of policies to conserve american natural resources. ____
5. The most frequently typed documents in an Attorney's office are the following:
   1. affidavits
   2. wills and trusts
   3. briefs ____
6. Spacecraft from earth have recently been sent to the planets of Mars, Jupiter, and Venus. ____
7. Oversupply of american dollars causes the dollar's value to decline compared with the german mark, the swiss franc, the japanese yen, and the french franc. ____
8. We have Ex-Councilman Lupus and Mayor-Elect Lanham scheduled for the Memorial day festivities. ____
9. Do you think, Sir, that the figures for the bid could be ready before Friday? ____
10. Our Organization's bylaws state the following: "The Secretary of the Association will submit an agenda two weeks before each meeting." ____

Check your answers.

B. Use proofreading marks to indicate necessary changes. Write the total number of changes at the right.

A. 1. Insufficient Funds (2); 2. Capitalize (1); 3. oceans, commerce (2); 4. late, American (2); 5. attorney's, Affidavits, Wills, Briefs (4); 6. Earth (1); 7. American, German, Swiss, Japanese, French (5); 8. ex-Councilman, Mayor-elect, Day (3); 9. sir (1); 10. organization (1)

1. Although the Sun was hot, the company Vice President went ahead with his scheduled outdoor speech. ______
2. Would you like a ride home? yes, thank you very much. ______
3. A New York Advertising Agency prepared a series of advertisements with greetings in dutch, hebrew, french, and italian. ______
4. Both the Potomac and Patuxent Rivers flow into Chesapeake bay. ______
5. Please take the file marked "budget" to the Business Manager's office. ______
6. The Minutes of the last meeting show that the Vice President acting on behalf of the President conducted the meeting despite the lack of a quorum. ______
7. Governor-Elect Hudson sat beside Ex-Mayor Benedict and senator Waller at the morning Ceremony. ______
8. How much, professor, does the Final Exam count? ______
9. Some of the factors I am considering in seeking a job are the following:
   1. income
   2. geographical location
   3. job security ______
10. Benjamin Disraeli provided England with its National motto when he said, "something will turn up." ______

C. ***Optional Composition.*** Your instructor may ask you to complete this exercise on a separate sheet. Write six original sentences that contain at least 20 properly capitalized words.

POSTTEST

Underline any letter that should be capitalized.

1. Both the president and the personnel manager were fluent in spanish and english.
2. Judy studied english literature, accounting, and sociology at pasadena city college.
3. The engineers will meet in the san marino room of the red lion inn next thursday.
4. Although we ordered a model 500 sony calculator, we received a model 400 calculator.
5. My mother, my father, and uncle michael will spend the easter holidays with us.

---

1. Spanish English 2. English Pasadena City College 3. San Marino Room Red Lion Inn Thursday
4. Model 500 Sony Model 400 5. Uncle Michael Easter

CHAPTER 20

Numbers

OBJECTIVES When you have completed the materials in this chapter, you will be able to do the following:

Level I — *Correctly choose between figures or word forms to express general numbers, money, and numbers beginning sentences.*

— *Express dates, clock time, addresses, and telephone numbers appropriately.*

Level II — *Use the correct form in writing related numbers, consecutive numbers, periods of time, and ages.*

— *Use the correct form in expressing numbers in conventional phrases, with abbreviations and symbols, and as round numbers.*

Level III — *Express correctly weights, measures, and fractions.*

— *Use the correct form in expressing percentages, decimals, and ordinals.*

PRETEST

Examine the expression of numbers in the following sentences. Should word or figure form be used? Underline any incorrect form and write an improved form in the blank provided. For example, which is preferred: *$10* or *ten dollars*?

1. On the fifth of September at five p.m., our 1st computer left the assembly line. ____________________
2. When she reached 21 years of age, she assumed ownership of over fifty acres of property in two states. ____________________
3. Please take three dollars to pick up one hundred three-cent stamps at the post office. ____________________
4. Of the twenty cars we had available on May 2nd, we have only four cars left today. ____________________
5. The art treasure measures only nine inches by twelve inches, but it is said to be worth nearly two million dollars. ____________________

1. 5th 5 p.m. first 2. twenty-one 50 acres 3. $3 100 4. 20 cars May 2, 4 cars 5. 9 by 12 inches $2 million

Just as capitalization is governed by convention, so is the expression of numbers. Usage and custom determine whether numbers are to be expressed in the form of a figure (for example, 5) or in the form of a word (for example, *five*). Numbers expressed as figures are shorter and more easily comprehended, yet numbers used as words are necessary in certain instances. The following guidelines are observed in expressing numbers that appear in written *sentences.* Numbers that appear in business communications — such as invoices, statements, purchase orders — are always expressed as figures.

LEVEL I

Basic Guidelines for Expressing Numbers

General Rules

The numbers *one* through *ten* are generally written out as words. Numbers above *ten* are written as figures.

> The jury consisted of *nine* regular members and *one* alternate.
>
> Gift taxes are imposed by *49* states.

Numbers that begin sentences are written as words. If a number involves more than two words, however, the sentence should be rewritten so that the number no longer falls at the beginning.

> *Twenty-three* investors provided capital for the down payment.
>
> A total of *320* distributors agreed to market the product. (Not: *Three hundred twenty* distributors agreed to market the product.)

Money

Sums of money $1 or greater are expressed as figures. If a sum is a whole dollar amount, most business writers omit the decimal and zeros (whether or not the amount appears with fractional dollar amounts).

> Although he budgeted only *$20,* Mike spent *$34.50* for the gift.
>
> A monthly statement showing purchases of *$7.13, $10, $43.50, $90,* and *$262.78* was sent.

Sums less than $1 are written as figures that are followed by the word *cents.* If they are part of sums greater than $1, use a dollar sign and a decimal instead of the word *cents.*

> Lisa said she had only *65 cents* with her.
>
> Supplies for the project were listed as $1.35, *$.99,* $2.80, $1, and *$.40.*

Dates

In dates, numbers that appear after the name of the month are written in cardinal figures (*1, 2, 3,* etc.). Those that stand alone or appear before the name of a month are written in ordinal figures (*1st, 2d, 3d,* etc.*).

> The meeting is scheduled for *October 5* in our office.
>
> On the *2d* day of January and again on the *18th,* we called for service.

**Many writers today are using the more efficient* 2d *and* 3d *instead of* 2nd *and* 3rd.

N.B. Cardinal numbers may be expressed in word (*one, two, three*) or figure (*1, 2, 3*) style. Ordinal numbers may also be expressed in word (*first, second, third*) or figure (*1st, 2d, 3d*) style. As you study these guidelines, be alert to suggestions in using word or figure style.

In business documents dates generally take the following form: month, day, year. An alternative form, used primarily in military and foreign correspondence, begins with the day of the month.

The contract was originally signed *25 June 1989*.

Some business organizations also prefer the military date style for its clarity, since it separates the numerical date of the month from the year.

Clock Time

Figures are used when clock time is expressed with *a.m.* or *p.m.* Omit the colon and zeros with whole hours. When exact clock time is expressed with *o'clock,* either figures or words may be used.

The first shift starts at *8 a.m.,* and the second begins at *3:30 p.m.*

At *four* (or *4*) *o'clock* completed documents are distributed.

Addresses and Telephone Numbers

Except for the number *One,* house numbers are expressed as figures.

805 Fiske Avenue
27321 Riverside Drive
One Wilshire Boulevard
1762 Cone Street

Street names that involve the number *ten* or a lower number are written entirely as words. In street names involving numbers greater than *ten,* the numeral portion is written as figures. If no compass direction (*North, South, East, West*) separates a house number from a street number, the street number is expressed in ordinal form (*– st, – d, – th*).

503 Second Street
11901 Ninth Avenue
2320 West 11 Street
613 North 102 Avenue
327 39th Avenue (Use *th* when no compass direction separates house number and numerical portion of street name.)

Telephone numbers are expressed with figures. When used, the area code is placed in parentheses preceding the telephone number.

Please call us at *(213) 828-1100* for further information.

You may reach me at *(805) 685-4321, Ext. 281,* after 9:30 a.m.

Complete the reinforcement exercises for Level I.

Guidelines for Expressing Numbers

Related Numbers

Numbers are related when they are used primarily within the same reference. All related numbers should be expressed as the largest number is expressed. Thus if the largest number is greater than *ten,* all the numbers should be expressed as figures.

On Monday *three* students signed up, on Tuesday *four* students enrolled, and on Thursday *nine* additional students registered.

Only *3* companies out of *147* neglected to return the survey form.

Of the *35* documents processed, *9* letters and *3* memoranda were urgent.

Unrelated numbers within the same reference are written as words or figures according to the general guidelines presented earlier in this chapter.

The *two* studies included *22* employees working in *three* separate offices.

The *two* bridges carry at least *10,000* cars during the *four* hours of peak traffic.

Consecutive Numbers

When two numbers appear consecutively and both modify a following noun, readers may misread the numbers because of their closeness. The writer should (a) rewrite the expression or (b) express one number in word form and the other in figure form. Use word form for the number that may be expressed in the fewest number of words. If both numbers have an equal count, spell out the first number and place the second one in figures.

We offered to publish *400 thirty*-page brochures. (*Use word form for the number that may be expressed in the fewest words.*)

The economist divided the era into *four 25*-year periods.

Please purchase *thirty 4-inch* galvanized nails for the job. (*Use word form for the first number since both have an equal word count.*)

Periods of Time

Periods of time are generally expressed in word form. However, figures may be used to achieve special emphasis in expressing business concepts such as discount rates, interest rates, warranty periods, credit terms, loan periods, and payment terms.

Word form

Congress has regulated minimum wages for over *forty-five* years.

We agreed to keep the book for only *fifteen* days.

Figure form (business concept)

The warranty period is limited to *2* years.

For payment within *30* days, a cash discount is provided.

Ages

Ages are generally expressed in word form unless the age appears immediately after a name or is expressed in exact years and months.

When he was *forty-one,* Mr. Selnig became the company's president.

Grace Siebold, *63,* plans to retire in four years.

The child was adopted when he was *3* years and *8* months old.

Numbers Used in Conventional Phrases, With Abbreviations, and With Symbols

Numbers used in conventional phrases are expressed as figures.

page 4	Policy 04-168315	Area Code 213
Room 14	Volume 5	Section 16
Option 3	Form 1040	Public Law 96-221

Numbers used with abbreviations are expressed as figures.

Apt. 16	Serial No. 265188440	Nos. 199 and 202
Ext. 245	Account No. 286-32-5891	Social Security No. 135-52-2016

Notice that the word *number* is capitalized and abbreviated when it precedes a number. Notice, too, that no commas are used in serial, account, and policy numbers.

The use of symbols (such as #, %, ¢) is usually avoided in contextual business writing (sentences). In other business documents where space is limited, however, symbols are frequently used. Numbers appearing with symbols are expressed as figures.

15%   44¢   #10 nails   2/10, n/60

Round Numbers

Round numbers are approximations. They may be expressed in word or figure form, although figure form is shorter and easier to comprehend.

Almost *400* (or *four hundred*) employees signed the petition.

At last count we had received about *20* (or *twenty*) reservations.

For ease of reading, round numbers in the millions or billions should be expressed with a combination of figures and words.

The President asked for a budget cut of *$8 billion.*

In its lawsuit IBM made available to the government *69 million* documents.

Nearly *1.5 million* imported cars were sold last year.

Complete the reinforcement exercises for Level II.

LEVEL III

Guidelines for Expressing Numbers

Weights and Measurements

Weights and measurements are expressed as figures.

A microfiche card measures *4 by 6 inches.*

Our specifications show the weight of the printer to be *7 pounds 9 ounces.*

The truck needed *21 gallons* of gasoline and *2 quarts* of oil.

In sentences the nouns following weights and measurements should be spelled out (for example, 21 *gallons* instead of 21 *gal.*). In business forms or in statistical presentations, however, such nouns may be abbreviated.

9′ × 12′   10#   7 oz.   30 sq. yds.   2 lb.   12 qt.

Fractions

Simple fractions are expressed as words. If a fraction functions as a noun, no hyphen is used. If it functions as an adjective, a hyphen separates its parts.

Over *three fourths* of the students attended the lecture. (Fraction used as a noun.)

A *two-thirds* majority is needed to carry the measure. (Fraction used as an adjective.)

N.B. A fraction immediately followed by an *of* phrase usually functions as a noun and is therefore not hyphenated. For example, *About one third of the cars were defective.*

Complex fractions appearing in sentences may be written either as figures or as a combination of figures and words.

The microcomputer will execute a command in *1 millionth* of a second. (Combination of words and figures is easier to comprehend.)

Flight records revealed that the emergency system was activated 13/200 of a second after the pilot was notified. (Figure form is easier to comprehend.)

Mixed fractions (whole numbers with fractions) are always expressed by figures.

The desks were expected to be *35¼* inches long, not *35½* inches. (Notice that no space follows a whole number and a typewriter key fraction.)

The envelope measured *3 5/8* inches by *6 1/2* inches. (Notice that fractions that must be typed with slashes are separated from their related whole numbers.)

When fractions that are constructed with slashes appear with typewriter key fractions, be consistent by using the slash construction for all the fractions involved.

Percentages and Decimals

Percentages are expressed with figures that are followed by the word *percent.* The percent sign (%) is used only on business forms or in statistical presentations.

Interest rates have been as low as *6½* percent and as high as *19* percent.

The report states that *52* percent of the workers joined the union.

Decimals are expressed with figures. If a decimal does not contain a whole number (an integer) and does not begin with a zero, a zero should be placed before the decimal.

Daryl Thomas set a record when he ran the race in *9.86* seconds. (Contains a whole number.)

Close examination revealed the settings to be *.005* inch off. (Begins with a zero.)

Less than *0.1* percent of the operating costs will be borne by taxpayers. (Zero placed before decimal that neither contains a whole number nor begins with a zero.)

Ordinals

Although ordinal numbers are generally expressed in word form (*first, second, third,* etc.), three exceptions should be noted: (1) figure form is used for dates appearing before a month or appearing alone, (2) figure form is used for street names involving numbers greater than *ten,* and (3) figure form is used when the ordinal would require more than two words.

Most ordinals
The company is celebrating its *fortieth* anniversary.
Before the *eighteenth* century, spelling was not standardized.
Of 237 sales representatives, Joanna ranked *second* in total sales.
Frank Collier represents the *Twenty-ninth* Congressional District.
Dates
Your payment must be received by the *30th* to qualify for the cash discount.
On the *2d* of June we will begin construction.
Streets
A traffic light was installed on *Second* Street.
The customer service division has been moved to *35th* Street.
Larger ordinals
Our bank ranks *103d* in terms of capital investments.

Complete the reinforcement exercises for Level III.

HOT LINE QUERIES

QUESTION: I'm never sure when to hyphenate numbers, such as *thirty-one.* Is there some rule to follow?

ANSWER: When written in word form, the numbers *twenty-one* through *ninety-nine* are hyphenated. Numbers are also hyphenated when they form compound adjectives and precede nouns (*ten-year-old* child, *16-story* building, *four-year* term, *30-day* lease).

QUESTION: I've always been confused by *imply* and *infer.* Which is correct in this sentence: *We* (*imply* or *infer*) from your letter that the goods are lost.

ANSWER: In your sentence use *infer. Imply* means "to state indirectly." *Infer* means "to draw a conclusion" or "to make a deduction based on facts " A listener or reader *infers.* A speaker or writer *implies.*

QUESTION: When fractions are written as words, why are they hyphenated sometimes and not hyphenated other times?

ANSWER: Most writers do not hyphenate a fraction when it functions as a noun (*one fourth of the letters*). When a fraction functions as an adjective, it is hyphenated (*a one-third gain in profits*).

QUESTION: Should I put quotation marks around figures to emphasize them? For example, *Your account has a balance of "$2,136.18."*

ANSWER: Certainly not! Quotation marks are properly used to indicate an exact quotation, or they may be used to enclose the definition of a word. They should not be used as a mechanical device for added emphasis.

QUESTION: I'm an engineer, and we have just had a discussion in our office concerning spelling. I have checked the dictionary, and it shows *usage.* Isn't this word ever spelled *useage?*

ANSWER: No. The only spelling of *usage* is without the internal *e.* You are probably thinking of the word *usable,* which does have a variant spelling — *useable.* Both forms are correct, but *usable* is recommended for its simplicity. Incidentally, if the word *usage* can be replaced by the word *use,* the latter is preferred (*the use* [*not usage*] *of carbon paper is declining*).

QUESTION: How should I spell the word *lose* in this sentence? *The employee tripped over a* (*lose* or *loose*) *cord.*

ANSWER: In your sentence use the adjective *loose,* which means "not fastened," "not tight," or "having freedom of movement." Perhaps you can remember it by thinking of the common expression *loose change,* which suggests unattached, free coins jingling in your pocket. If you *lose* (*mislay*) some of those coins, you have less money and fewer *o*'s.

Name ______________________

CHAPTER 20 **Reinforcement Exercises**

LEVEL I

A. (Self-check) Choose (a) or (b) to complete the following sentences.

1. We are able to finish only (a) 11, (b) eleven letters by noon. ______
2. (a) 15, (b) Fifteen applicants responded to the advertisement. ______
3. The office will reopen on the (a) 14th, (b) fourteenth of June. ______
4. Duplicating this brochure will cost (a) 4 cents, (b) $.04 per page. ______
5. Ellen has collected (a) $20.00, (b) $20 for the gift. ______
6. His address is listed as (a) Three, (b) 3 Meadowlark Drive. ______
7. Financial institutions are clustered on (a) Seventh, (b) 7th Avenue. ______
8. Send the letter to (a) 320 27th Street, (b) 320 27 Street. ______
9. She said that a ream of paper would cost (a) $6, (b) six dollars. ______
10. We plan to meet at (a) 9:00 a.m., (b) 9 a.m. ______

Check your answers.

B. Assume that the following phrases appear in business correspondence. Write the preferred forms in the spaces provided. If a phrase is correct as shown, write *C*.

EXAMPLE: 8930 23 Avenue — 8930 23d Avenue

1. fourteen clerks ______
2. Tenth Street ______
3. $.09 per issue ______
4. 7 memoranda ______
5. June ninth ______
6. 5th Avenue ______
7. $6.59, 98 cents, and $30.00 ______
8. the eighteenth of September ______
9. 9:00 p.m. ______
10. eight o'clock ______
11. thirty-three desks ______
12. January 22d ______

A. 1. a, 2. b, 3. a, 4. a, 5. b, 6. b, 7. a, 8. a, 9. a, 10. b

13. 12655 32d Street ______
14. 12655 West 32d Street ______
15. two executives ______
16. twenty-four dollars ______
17. 7 Hampton Square ______
18. 1 Hampton Square ______
19. sixty-six rooms ______
20. 7 o'clock ______
21. (military style) April 15, 1983 ______
22. 2742 8th Street ______
23. six thirty p.m. ______
24. the fourth of May ______
25. one hundred dollars ______
26. ninety cents ______
27. 18307 Eleventh Street ______
28. 18307 North Eleventh Street ______
29. 50 states ______
30. 2 batteries ______

C. Rewrite these sentences correcting any errors you note.

1. On January thirteenth Alex submitted the following petty cash disbursements: $1.80, 99 cents, $3.00, and 9 cents. ______

2. Elizabeth moved from seventeen sixteen Sunset Drive to one Bellingham Court. ______

3. 24 branch banks compose the Federal Reserve System. ______

4. On the 28 of January, we made at least 3 calls to your office. ______

5. If you have only thirty dollars, why are you considering the model that costs $49.99? ______

6. Regular work breaks are scheduled at 10:00 a.m. and again at 3:30 p.m. ______

7. We expect to continue operations through the thirtieth, but we may be forced to close by the twenty-second. ______

8. 362 contracts had been signed before the June 1st deadline. ______

Name ______________________

LEVEL II

A. (Self-check) Select (a) or (b) to complete each of the following sentences.

1. We are working on (a) three 16-page, (b) 3 sixteen-page booklets. _____
2. Mrs. Walker has worked there for (a) twenty-seven, (b) 27 years. _____
3. A seminar on investing is being held in (a) Room Two, (b) Room 2. _____
4. Of the 650 envelopes sent, (a) nine, (b) 9 were returned. _____
5. Although she is only (a) 21, (b) twenty-one, Miss Love was appointed manager. _____
6. Current sales have reached (a) $2 million, (b) $2,000,000. _____
7. Have you completed your IRS Form (a) Ten Forty, (b) 1040? _____
8. About (a) 350, (b) three hundred fifty letters were addressed today. _____
9. The short-term loan covers a period of (a) 60, (b) sixty days. _____
10. The serial number on my typewriter is (a) 85056170, (b) 85,056,170. _____

Check your answers.

B. For the following sentences underscore any numbers or words that are expressed inappropriately. For sentences with inappropriate forms, write the correct forms in the spaces provided. If a sentence is correct as written, write *C*.

EXAMPLE: We need 16 29-cent stamps to complete the mailing. sixteen

1. The advisory committee is composed of 17 members, of whom five are supervisors, three are consultants, and nine are technicians. ______________
2. Please order five hundred two-page snapout carbon sets. ______________
3. Over the next 10 years we expect to see an increased need for clerical workers. ______________
4. Before microfilming, the 26,000,000 documents filled nine rooms. ______________
5. The following policy Nos. are listed for John Daley: No. 1355801 and No. 1355802. ______________
6. Model 8,400 costs $10,000 and can be leased for $275 a month. ______________
7. A revolutionary new light bulb will reduce the demand for electricity by 8,000,000,000 kilowatt-hours per year. ______________
8. Of the 65 typed pages, nine pages have minor revisions and six pages require heavy revision. ______________

A. 1. a, 2. a, 3. b, 4. b, 5. b, 6. a, 7. b, 8. a (preferred), 9. a, 10. a

9. John Edwards, forty-one, and Maria Gomez, thirty-three, were interviewed for the two executive positions. ______

10. On page twenty-two of Volume two, the total sales are listed at nearly $22 million. ______

11. All three electrical appliances have warranties limited to ninety days. ______

12. The total book club membership of eight hundred thousand received the four bonus books. ______

13. Only 43 of the 57 staff members could attend the two training sessions. ______

14. Approximately thirty positions will be reclassified before June 15. ______

15. When she is 21 years old, Ms. Enrico will inherit $1.3 million. ______

16. It took 12 inspection teams to review and rewrite thirty thousand pages of deeds, options, leases, and bills of sales. ______

17. The old man was 93 years old, but he said he felt as if he were fifty-three. ______

18. With 4 pickups daily, the delivery service serves two thousand employees in 45 departments. ______

C. Assume that the following phrases appear in business correspondence. Write the preferred forms in the spaces provided. If a phrase is correct as shown, write *C*.

1. four rooms with eleven typewriters and fifteen desks ______
2. two fifty-four pound weights ______
3. loan periods of sixty days ______
4. Martha Diamond, fifty-eight, and John Diamond, sixty-one ______
5. Account No. 362,486,012 ______
6. three point two billion dollars ______
7. Room Five ______
8. seventeen years ______
9. ninety-one books ______
10. about two hundred guests ______
11. four point four million people ______
12. Section three point two ______
13. three hundred twelve-cent stamps ______
14. fourteen months ______
15. warranty period of two years ______
16. approximately one hundred fifty people ______

Name ______________________________

LEVEL III

A. (Self-check) Choose (a) or (b) to complete the following sentences.

1. Operators watch a screen that measures (a) 11″ × 11″, (b) 11 by 11 inches. ______
2. Over (a) four fifths, (b) 4/5 of the workers approved the pact. ______
3. The profit margin is expected to be (a) 16 percent, (b) 16%. ______
4. Next year marks this company's (a) 25th, (b) twenty-fifth anniversary. ______
5. Newspaper advertising accounts for about (a) one third, (b) one-third of all advertising dollars. ______
6. The company warehouses are now located on (a) Sixty-second, (b) 62d Street. ______
7. We need a rug measuring (a) 9 by 12 feet, (b) nine by twelve feet. ______
8. Maintenance costs are only (a) 0.5, (b) .5 percent above last year's. ______
9. Did you order (a) five, (b) 5 quarts of oil? ______
10. The elevator stops at the (a) 14th, (b) fourteenth floor. ______

Check your answers.

B. Rewrite the following sentences with special attention to appropriate number usage.

1. The microfiche reader is ten and three-quarters inches long, four and one-half inches wide, and three inches high. ______________________________

____

2. Up to 2,000,000 tourists visit the public rooms in the White House each year. ______________

____

____

3. Even our most precise instrument cannot measure more closely than 0.005 inch. ______________

____

____

4. I'm looking for a briefcase word processing machine that weighs less than ten pounds and is no more than twelve inches long and two inches deep. ______________________________

____

____

5. Approximately 3/4 of every dollar contributed goes to charity. ______________________________

____

____

A. 1. b, 2. a, 3. a, 4. b, 5. a, 6. b, 7. a, 8. a, 9. b, 10. b

6. In the 23d Congressional District, only 1/3 of the potential voters are registered. ________

7. Our college ranks one hundred seventh in terms of its endowment. ________

8. Invoices that are paid before the tenth will receive a two percent cash discount. ________

9. At least seven tenths of the members attended the May tenth meeting when we approved the budget of thirty-five thousand dollars. ________

10. In the year 2,001 our nation will celebrate its two hundred twenty-fifth anniversary. ________

11. A stock that costs fifty dollars a share and pays four dollars in dividends will yield an eight percent return. ________

C. ***Optional Composition.*** Your instructor may ask you to complete this exercise on a separate sheet. Select ten number rules from this chapter. Write sentences illustrating each rule. Label each rule.

POSTTEST

Underline numbers that are expressed inappropriately. Write corrected forms in the space provided.

1. It took the IRS seven years to collect the 750,000 dollars owed by the 2 companies. ________
2. Before the third of the month, we had received seventeen calls regarding the bicycle advertised for twenty dollars. ________
3. The department had eighteen employees, and they shared four telephones, ten file cabinets, and seven computers. ________
4. Professor Yeoman reported that five hundred students enrolled, an increase of ten percent over last year. ________
5. We will need three hundred nine-page calendars before December 1st. ________

1. $750,000 two 2. 3d or 3rd 17 $20 3. 18 4. 500 10 percent 5. 300 nine-page December 1

CHAPTER 21

Effective Sentences

OBJECTIVES When you have completed the materials in this chapter, you will be able to do the following:

Level I
— *Eliminate wordy phrases and redundant words.*
— *Use the active voice in writing efficient sentences.*
— *Compose unified sentences by avoiding excessive detail and extraneous ideas.*

Level II
— *Write clear sentences using parallel construction for similar ideas.*
— *Place words, phrases, and clauses close to the words they modify.*
— *Avoid ambiguous pronoun references such as* this, that, *and* which.

Level III
— *Achieve emphasis by subordinating secondary ideas to primary ideas.*
— *Recognize and use concrete words instead of abstract words.*
— *Use transitional expressions (such as* therefore, however, *and* for example*) to develop coherency between thoughts.*

PRETEST

Rewrite the following sentences to rectify problems in parallelism, redundancy, modification, reference, conciseness, and coherence.

1. In view of the fact that we are moving, we are not renewing the contract. ____________

   ____

2. By totaling every column separately, the error was quickly located. ____________

   ____

3. Lisa had to empty the cash register, count the cash, and the doors had to be locked.

   ____

4. I would like your final decision by June 1. ____________

   ____

5. The new computer is for the desk in the outer office, which was delivered yesterday.

   ____

---

1. Since we are moving, we are not renewing the contract. 2. By totaling every column separately, we located the error quickly. 3. Lisa had to empty the cash register, count the cash, and lock the doors. 4. I would like your decision by June 1. 5. The new computer, which was delivered yesterday, is for the outer office.

Business people value efficient, economical writing that is meaningful and coherent. Wordy communication wastes the reader's time; unclear messages confuse the reader and are counterproductive. In the business world, where time is valuable, efficient writing is demanded. You can improve your writing skills by emulating the practices of good writers. Most good writers begin with a rough draft that they revise to produce a final version. This chapter will show you how to revise your rough draft sentences to make them more efficient, clear, emphatic, and coherent.

LEVEL I

Writing Efficient Sentences

Revising Wordy Phrases

Sentences are efficient when they convey a thought directly and economically — that is, in the fewest possible words. Good writers excise all useless verbiage from their writing. Some of our most common and comfortable phrases are actually full of "word fat"; when examined carefully, these phrases can be pared down considerably.

Wordy phrases	Efficient substitutes
at the present time at this point in time	now
due to the fact that	because
for the purpose of in connection with	for
in spite of the fact that	even though
in the amount of	for
in the event that	if
in the near future	soon
in the neighborhood of	about
in terms of	regarding
in view of the fact that	since
with a view to	to
with reference to with regard to	about

Notice that the revised versions of the following wordy sentences are more efficient.

Wordy: *Due to the fact that* fire damaged our warehouse, we must delay some shipments.

More efficient: *Because* fire damaged our warehouse, we must delay some shipments.

Wordy: Please send your check *in the amount of* $45.

More efficient: Please send your check *for* $45.

Wordy: We expected *in the neighborhood of* 25 applicants.

More efficient: We expected *about* 25 applicants.

Eliminating Redundant Words

Words that are needlessly repetitive are said to be "redundant." Business writers can achieve greater efficiency (and thus more effective sentences) by eliminating redundant words or phrases.

Redundant: The examples shown in Figure 2 illustrate letter styles.
More efficient: Figure 2 shows letter styles.
Redundant: The seminar covers only the fundamental basics.
More efficient: The seminar covers only the basics (or, only the fundamentals).
Redundant: As a rule, we generally approve all such requests.
More efficient: We generally approve all such requests.
Redundant: The committee cooperated together to settle the issue.
More efficient: The committee cooperated to settle the issue.

Using the Active Voice

Sentences that use active verbs are more economical — and, of course, more direct — than those using passive verbs. (See Chapter 8 for a review of passive and active voices.)

Passive: Your account *has been credited* with your recent payment.
Active: We *credited* your account with your recent payment.
Passive: At our next meeting your request *will be considered.*
Active: At our next meeting we *will consider* your request.
Passive: Our Office Products Division was informed by you that you want an office copier.
Active: You *informed* our Office Products Division that you want an office copier.

Writing Unified Sentences

A sentence is unified if it contains only closely related ideas. When extraneous or unrelated ideas appear in a sentence, they confuse the reader. Sentences lacking unity can be improved by excising the extraneous ideas or by shifting the unrelated ideas to separate sentences.

Lacks unity: It is easy for you to do your Christmas shopping, and we offer three unique catalogs.
Improved: Because we offer three unique catalogs, it is easy for you to do your Christmas shopping.
Lacks unity: I certainly appreciate the time you spent with me in our interview last week, and I am enrolling in a computer science course this summer.
Improved: I certainly appreciate the time you spent with me last week. Because of our interview, I am enrolling in a computer science course this summer.
Lacks unity: Retailers must have a system of inventory control, and they must keep current on reorders.
Improved: To be able to keep current on reorders, retailers must have a system of inventory control.

The inclusion of excessive detail can also damage sentence unity. If many details are necessary for overall clarity, put them in an additional sentence.

Excessive detail: One of the nation's leading suppliers of pure bottled water mails thousands of computerized statements every month, along with a variety of inserts including overdue payment notices and pieces that are meant to be advertising and promotions, which became very costly in terms of both cash flow and personnel time.

Improved: One of the nation's leading suppliers of pure bottled water mails thousands of monthly computerized statements, overdue notices, and promotional information. This mailing operation has become costly and time consuming.

Excessive detail: A report can be important, but it may not be effective or be read because it is too long and bulky, which will also make it more difficult to distribute, to store, and to handle, as well as increasing its overall cost.

Improved: An important report may be ineffective because it is too long. Its bulk may increase its cost and make it difficult to read, handle, distribute, and store.

Complete the reinforcement exercises for Level I.

LEVEL II

Writing Clear Sentences

Clear sentences are those that immediately convey their central thought. Good writers achieve sentence clarity by the use of parallel construction, the avoidance of misplaced modifiers, and the use of unambiguous pronoun references.

Developing Parallel Construction

Sentence clarity can be improved by expressing similar ideas with similar grammatical structures. For example, if you are listing three ideas, do not use *ing* words for two of the ideas and a *to* verb for the third idea: *reading, eating, and studying* (not *to study*). Use nouns with nouns, verbs with verbs, phrases with phrases, and clauses with clauses. In the following list, use all verbs: *the machine sorted, stamped, and counted* (not *and had a counter*). For phrases, the wording for all parts of the list should be matched: *safety must be improved in the home, in the classroom, and on the job* (not *and for office workers*).

Faulty: Steel filing cabinets are best for durability, ease of cleaning, and they resist fire better.

Improved: Steel filing cabinets are best for durability, ease of cleaning, and fire resistance. (Matches nouns.)

Faulty: The new shredder-compactor helped us save money, reduce pollution, and paper could be recycled.

Improved: The new shredder-compactor helped us save money, reduce pollution, and recycle paper. (Matches verb-noun construction.)

Faulty: Composing, revising, and then to retype — these are necessary steps in report writing.

Improved: Composing, revising, and retyping — these are necessary steps in report writing. (Matches *ing* nouns.)

Avoiding Misplaced Modifiers

As you will recall, modifiers are words, phrases, or clauses that limit or restrict other words, phrases, or clauses. To be clear, modifiers must be placed carefully so that the words modified by them are obvious. When a modifier is placed so that it does not appear to be modifying the word or words intended to be modified, that modifier is said to be *misplaced*. In Chapter 11 introductory verbal modifiers were discussed. An introductory verbal modifier is sometimes misplaced simply by being at the beginning of the sentence. Consider how the introductory verbal modifier makes the following sentence nonsensical: *Walking down the street, the building was the tallest I had ever seen.* After all, the building is not doing the walking. In positions other than the beginning of a sentence, misplaced modifiers may also damage sentence clarity.

Faulty: We provide a map for all visitors *reduced to a one-inch scale.*

Improved: For all visitors we provide a map *reduced to a one-inch scale.*

Faulty: Employees did not hear the alarm *working busily on the rush printing job.*

Improved: Employees *working busily on the rush printing job* did not hear the alarm.

Faulty: You can install these wall pockets on flat surfaces *with screws or double-foam tape.*

Improved: *With screws or double-foam tape,* you can install these wall pockets on flat surfaces.

Improving Pronoun References

Sentence confusion results from the use of pronouns without clear antecedents. Be particularly careful with the pronouns *this, that, which,* and *it.* Confusion often results when these pronouns have as their antecedents an entire clause; such confusion can usually be avoided by substituting a noun for the pronoun or by following the pronoun with a clarifying noun (or nouns).

Faulty: Installation of a computerized billing system has improved our cash flow and reduced our accounts receivable. *This* helps our entire operation run more efficiently and profitably.

Improved: Installation of a computerized billing system has improved our cash flow and reduced our accounts receivable. *The new system* helps our entire operation run more efficiently and profitably.

Faulty: We have a policy of responding to customer inquiries and orders on the same day they are received. *That* keeps us busy and keeps our customers satisfied.

Improved: We have a policy of responding to customer inquiries and orders on the same day they are received. *That policy* keeps us busy and keeps our customers satisfied.

Faulty: Our engineering projects require work on thousands of details that need constant updating and access to technical data, supplies, and references, *which* is why an open office design allowing team interaction is essential.

Improved: Our engineering projects require work on thousands of details that need constant updating and access to technical data, supplies, and references. *These needs* explain why an open office design allowing team interaction is essential.

Complete the reinforcement exercises for Level II.

LEVEL III

Writing Emphatic and Coherent Sentences

In your writing you can achieve emphasis and coherence by using clause subordination, concrete words, and effective transitions.

Emphasis Through Subordination

Subordination is a technique used by skillful writers to show the relationship between unequal ideas. Appropriate emphasis can be achieved by using subordinate conjunctions, such as *if, because, since,* and *when,* and relative pronouns, such as *who, which,* and *that,* to introduce secondary ideas or incidental information. Principal ideas should appear in independent clauses, and less important ideas in subordinate or dependent clauses.

Principal idea: Compucorp recently entered the microcomputer market.
Secondary idea: Compucorp is a division of Intel.
Sentence: Compucorp, which is a division of Intel, recently entered the microcomputer market.

Principal idea: Your account is now three months overdue.
Secondary idea: You have been a good customer in the past.
Sentence: Although you have been a good customer in the past, your account is now three months overdue.

Principal idea: A credit card holder is not liable for more than $50 in unauthorized purchases.
Secondary idea: The credit card holder must give notice to the issuer of the card.
Sentence: If a credit card holder gives notice to the issuer of the card, the holder is not liable for more than $50 in unauthorized purchases.

Emphasis Through the Use of Concrete Words

As you know, concrete words (see Chapter 4) refer to specific persons, places, concepts, and actions. They bring to mind sharp images and arouse strong feelings. Abstract words, such as *honesty, freedom,* and *utilization,* because they refer to general ideas, do not call forth immediate sensory reactions or feelings. Use concrete words and constructions to make your writing emphatic, persuasive, and unambiguous.

Abstract: Your shipment will be sent *soon.*
Concrete: Your shipment will be sent *October 1.*
Abstract: Our candidate won by a *substantial margin.*
Concrete: Our candidate won by a *2-to-1 margin.*
Abstract: The *utilization of computer capabilities* helped us reduce costs.
Concrete: *Computerized filing and billing* helped us reduce costs.
Abstract: The Model DC-161 copier produces your first copy *quickly.*
Concrete: The Model DC-161 copier produces your first copy *in five seconds.*

When an abstract word is necessary, its meaning can often be enhanced by the addition of clarifying words.

Abstract: During the hearing, no one questioned Mr. Turner's *loyalty.*
Concrete: During the hearing, no one questioned Mr. Turner's *loyalty to the company.*

Coherence Through the Use of Transitional Words or Phrases

Orderly and consistent development of ideas leads to coherency. Coherence between sentences can be attained by the use of transitional expressions such as *therefore, in this way, in addition, for example, however, moreover, for this reason,* and *on the other hand.* These words and phrases serve as flags to signal the reader that ideas are being contrasted or amplified. Notice that in the following sentences transitional words and phrases help the reader connect successive ideas.

We have improved customer services as a result of spending less time on clerical chores. *Moreover,* we reduced storage charges for shipments held up because of incorrect documentation.

Our company stands ready to help you in the event of loss or damage to your microfilm records. *For example,* we have salvaged thousands of feet of muddied, tangled rolls of microfilm after floods.

A blank endorsement enables anyone in possession of a check to cash it. A special endorsement, *on the other hand,* enables only a specific person to negotiate the check.

When the federal government purchases goods on a cost-plus contract, it requires detailed accounting reports. *In this way,* it can monitor the production operations and costs.

Complete the reinforcement exercises for Level III.

HOT LINE QUERIES

QUESTION: I just typed this sentence: *You will see in our manual where multiple bids must be obtained.* Somewhere from my distant past I seem to recall that *where* should not be used this way. Can you help me?

ANSWER: You're right. *Where* should not be substituted for the relative pronoun *that.* In your sentence, use *that.* A similar faulty construction to be avoided is the use of *while* for *although* (*although* [not *while*] *I agree with his position, I disagree with his procedures*).

QUESTION: When the company name *Halperin, Inc.,* appears in the middle of a sentence, is there a comma following *Inc.*?

ANSWER: Current authorities recommend the following practice in punctuating *Inc.:* If the legal company name includes a comma preceding *Inc.,* then a comma should follow *Inc.* if it is used in the middle of a sentence. (*We received from Kent, Inc., its latest catalog.*)

QUESTION: Where should the word *sic* be placed when it is used?

ANSWER: *Sic* means "thus" or "so stated," and it is properly placed immediately following the word or phrase to which it refers. For example, *The kidnappers placed a newspaper advertisement that read, "Call Monna [sic] Lisa." Sic* is used within a quotation to indicate that a quoted word or phrase, though inaccurately spelled or used, appeared thus in the original. *Sic* is italicized and placed within brackets.

QUESTION: Which is correct: *I feel* (*bad* or *badly*)?

ANSWER: *Bad* is an adjective meaning "not good" or "ill." *Badly* is an adverb meaning "harmfully," "wickedly," or "poorly." Your sentence appears to require *bad* (*I feel ill*), unless you mean that your sense of touch is impaired (*I feel poorly*).

QUESTION: Should I capitalize *oriental* rug?

ANSWER: Yes. Adjectives derived from proper nouns are capitalized (*French* dressing, *German* shepherd, *Danish* furniture). Very well-known adjectives, however, are not capitalized (*pasteurized* milk, *venetian* blinds, *french* fries, *china* plates).

QUESTION: In a business report is it acceptable to write the following: *Most everyone agrees . . .* ?

ANSWER: In this construction *most* is a shortened form of *almost*. Although such contractions are heard in informal speech, they should not appear in business writing. Instead, use the longer form: *Almost everyone agrees . . . .*

Name ____________________

CHAPTER 21 Reinforcement Exercises

LEVEL I

A. (Self-check) In the following sentences, inefficient phrases have been underlined. In the space provided after each sentence, suggest a more efficient substitute for each underlined phrase.

EXAMPLE: In the event that the alarm sounds, please leave in an orderly manner. If

1. In view of the fact that you have not responded to our letters, we have no alternative. ____________
2. We must at the present time send your account to our collection agency. ____________
3. Due to the fact that a strike has temporarily closed our factory, deliveries are delayed. ____________
4. We find it necessary to inform all customers with regard to delivery delays. ____________
5. In the event that you are unable to attend, please notify us at once. ____________
6. We have received your check in the amount of $450. ____________
7. In spite of the fact that production costs are rising, we have tried to maintain our current pricing schedule. ____________
8. We find that we must at this point in time reconsider our prices. ____________
9. For the purpose of more efficient record-keeping, we will begin writing invoices in triplicate. ____________
10. If the estimate is in the neighborhood of $100 or less, the repair can be made immediately. ____________

Check your answers.

B. Rewrite the following sentences to eliminate redundancies.

EXAMPLE: Her solution made absolutely perfect sense.
Her solution made perfect sense.

1. Tim's report appears to contain all the basic essentials. ____________

____

A. 1. Since, 2. now, 3. Because, 4. about, 5. If, 6. for, 7. Even though, 8. now, 9. For, 10. about

2. Our modern office equipment is up-to-date in every feature. ____________________

3. Any pages with corrections that are visible to the eye must be retyped. ____________________

4. In an explanation at the beginning of the article, the author explained his position. ________

C. Make the following sentences more efficient and more direct by using the active voice.

EXAMPLE: The invoice was sent by our organization ten days ago.
We sent the invoice ten days ago.

1. Better service is received by our customers who read the instruction booklet. ____________________

2. Your order is now being processed by our Shipping Department. ____________________

3. Apparently my account was not credited by you with my check for $35. ____________________

4. A charge account has been opened for you by us at our store. ____________________

D. The following sentences lack unity. Improve them by reorganizing the ideas or by shifting extra details to separate sentences.

EXAMPLE: We are installing a centralized dictation system, and our current transcription production is days behind schedule. Because we are installing a centralized dictation system, we are days behind in our current transcription production.

1. The keynote speaker will be Dr. Jay S. Cook, and vendors will display their products following the keynote address. ____________________

2. We have placed a lien against your property and your payment is 60 days past due, which explains the lien. ____________________

3. We are one of the nation's largest office products distributors, and you can save 15 to 50 percent on your word processing supplies for your office which we supply to our 260,000 customers who are satisfied from coast to coast because we have been in business for the past twenty years satisfying our customers. ____________________

Name ______________________

LEVEL II

A. (Self-check) In the sentences below, the underlined words illustrate the following: (a) faulty parallel construction, (b) faulty phrase placement, and (c) faulty pronoun reference. After each sentence, write the letter that best indicates the sentence fault.

EXAMPLE: Our objectives are to increase production, reduce costs, and improving the quality of our work. ___a___

1. We use a four-part delivery ticket, with three copies made in various weights; this is the basis of our billing system. ______
2. Aluminum construction is lightest, wood is cheapest, and the strongest is steel. ______
3. Please complete the enclosed questionnaire sent to typical families concerning detergent preferences. ______
4. Our new billing system totals all balances, gives weekly reports, and statements are printed. ______
5. Centralized inspection in one area and floor inspection along the assembly line improve product quality; it is useful when precise standards must be met. ______
6. Automatic cash transfers can be made only on the written authority of the customer from a checking account. ______
7. Computing, coding, recording, and storage — these are functions of data processing. ______
8. The three basic elements of a computer are input, processor, and output units, which can be obtained in a variety of configurations. ______
9. The next time you travel for business or for pleasure, charge everything to your credit card in the United States. ______
10. Our objectives are to make our stock profitable, to operate efficiently, and developing good employee relations. ______

Check your answers.

B. Rewrite the following sentences so that they demonstrate parallel construction.

1. The job description lists these duties: answering the telephone, making appointments, and data must be collected for reports. ______________________________

____

2. This department requires more personnel, better facilities, and our equipment should be up-to-date. ______________________________

____

A. 1. c, 2. a, 3. b, 4. a, 5. c, 6. b, 7. a, 8. c, 9. b, 10. a

3. Business letters should be written concisely, clearly, and with accuracy. ____________

____

____

4. In filing, the use of color can increase productivity significantly by providing faster retrieval, reducing the number of lost files, and improvement of employee morale. ____________

____

____

C. Rewrite these sentences to remedy misplaced modifiers.

1. The customer wrote a check for his purchase with insufficient funds. ____________

____

____

2. Any person may recover damages from the manufacturer of a product who is injured by a product. ____________

____

____

3. Victor Office Products announced a three-in-one calculator that will help you solve your calculation problems in Peoria, Illinois. ____________

____

____

4. Since we installed insulation, we have saved up to 25 percent on our heating costs in our attic and walls. ____________

____

____

D. Rewrite the following sentences avoiding faulty pronoun references.

1. Mrs. Valdez suggested that we try a four-day work week on an experimental basis for one month. *That* received considerable employee support. ____________

____

____

2. Our Reprographics Division produces thousands of company letterheads, booklets, and brochures; *this* demands expert equipment and personnel. ____________

____

____

3. Our equipment is outmoded, production is costly, and orders are slow, *which* is why we are forced to cut back. ____________

____

____

Name ______________________

LEVEL III

A. (Self-check) After each of the following sentences, write *T* (for true) or *F* (for false).

1. Appropriate subordination of secondary ideas is a technique of skillful writers. ______
2. The word *therefore* might be used as a transition between related ideas. ______
3. *Implementation* is an example of a concrete word. ______
4. The word *although* may be used to introduce a principal idea in an independent clause. ______
5. Transitional expressions serve as flags to signal changes in the presentation of ideas. ______
6. The use of concrete words makes writing more persuasive and emphatic. ______
7. Coherency is achieved when sentences and their parts are related logically. ______
8. Principal ideas should appear in independent clauses. ______
9. *Utilization* is an example of an abstract word. ______
10. Abstract words are as effective as concrete words. ______

Check your answers.

B. Shown below are sets of principal ideas and secondary ideas. For each set, write a sentence combining, with appropriate emphasis, both ideas.

	Principal idea	Secondary idea
1.	Massey, Inc., has contracted with a Japanese firm to produce electrical components.	Massey, Inc., has been in operation in the U.S. for over eighty years.
2.	Congress has given the Food and Drug Administration additional authority over the years.	The FDA was established in 1906.
3.	Phoenix Tires, Inc., has been making tires and fan belts for fifty-five years.	Phoenix Tires offers its products under the brand name of Wearwell.

A. 1. T, 2. T, 3. F, 4. F, 5. T, 6. T, 7. T, 8. T, 9. T, 10. F

C. Rewrite the following sentences making the italicized words concrete. Supply any information needed.

EXAMPLE: Our organization is improving *conservation.*

Our organization is improving conservation of natural gas, electricity, and paper supplies.

1. We will send your order *as soon as possible.* ______________________

2. When we have further information, we will *contact* you. ______________________

3. This course includes English *fundamentals.* ______________________

4. Survey Associates questioned a *consumer* about a *product.* ______________________

5. Our employees enjoy much *freedom.* ______________________

D. ***Optional Composition.*** Your instructor may ask you to complete this exercise on a separate sheet. Write four original sentences that use the following transitional expressions to develop coherence: *therefore, however, consequently,* and *in addition.* Write a sentence with a misplaced modifier; then show how it can be remedied. Label all sentences.

POSTTEST

Rewrite the following sentences to correct problems in parallelism, redundancy, modification, reference, conciseness, and coherence. Check your responses with your instructor.

1. We are at this point in time ready to sign a contract. ____________________

   ____

2. Speeding down the highway, the brakes were suddenly applied. ____________________

   ____

3. First and foremost, you must reserve a meeting room. ____________________

   ____

4. All sales reports must be complete, concise, and written with accuracy. ____________________

   ____

5. Our benefit package is appealing to older employees with both dental and vision care services. ____________________

   ____

---

1. We are now ready to sign a contract. 2. Speeding down the highway, the driver suddenly applied the brakes. 3. First, you must reserve a meeting room. 4. All sales reports must be complete, concise, and accurate. 5. Our benefit package with both dental and vision care services is appealing to older employees.

Name ______________________

UNIT 6 REVIEW **Chapters 19–21 (Self-Check)**

First, review Chapters 19 through 21. Then test your comprehension of those chapters by completing the exercises that follow. Compare your responses with those shown at the end of the review.

LEVEL I

Select (a) or (b) to describe the group of words that is more acceptably expressed.

	(a)	(b)	
1.	(a) courses in Business Law, Spanish, and Sociology	(b) courses in business law, Spanish, and sociology	_____
2.	(a) living in Ventura county	(b) living in Ventura County	_____
3.	(a) the State of Ohio	(b) the state of Ohio	_____
4.	(a) during summer vacation	(b) during Summer vacation	_____
5.	(a) a victorian home	(b) a Victorian home	_____
6.	(a) the 22d of June	(b) the twenty-second of June	_____
7.	(a) twenty dollars	(b) $20	_____
8.	(a) on 11th Street	(b) on Eleventh Street	_____
9.	(a) on December 15th	(b) on December 15	_____
10.	(a) at this point in time	(b) now	_____
11.	(a) about	(b) with reference to	_____
12.	(a) in the near future	(b) soon	_____

LEVEL II

Select (a) or (b) to describe the group of words that is more acceptably expressed.

	(a)	(b)	
13.	(a) your Aunt and Uncle	(b) your aunt and uncle	_____
14.	(a) travel east on Highway 10	(b) travel East on Highway 10	_____
15.	(a) our manager, Joe Lopez	(b) our Manager, Joe Lopez	_____
16.	(a) their receiving department	(b) their Receiving Department	_____
17.	(a) a message from Mia Cook, Sales Director	(b) a message from Mia Cook, sales director	_____
18.	(a) a message from Sales Director Cook	(b) a message from sales director Cook	_____

19. (a) for the next two years (b) for the next 2 years _____

20. (a) 2 twenty-five page booklets (b) two 25-page booklets _____

21. (a) three computers serving 14 offices (b) 3 computers serving 14 offices _____

Each of the following sentence illustrates one of these sentence faults:

(a) faulty parallel construction (such as *running, walking, and to ride*)
(b) faulty phrase placement (phrase not close to words it modifies)
(c) faulty pronoun reference (pronoun such as *this, that, it* lacking clear antecedent)

Write the letter that describes the sentence fault in each of the next three sentences.

22. We installed fabric divider panels in the office to provide privacy, reduce sound, and they made the office more attractive. _____

23. Michelle stood at the lectern on the stage looking at the audience with a blank mind and a dry mouth. _____

24. Poor ventilation, inadequate light, and hazardous working conditions were cited in the complaint. It must be improved before negotiations continue. _____

(On a separate sheet of paper, rewrite the above sentences to rectify their faults.)

LEVEL III

Select the correct group of words below and write its letter in the space provided.

25. (a) our chief executive officer, Mr. Spiros (b) our Chief Executive Officer, Mr. Spiros _____

26. (a) U.S. Vice President-Elect (b) U.S. Vice President-elect _____

27. (a) a package stamped "photographs" (b) a package stamped "Photographs" _____

28. (a) our 28th anniversary (b) our twenty-eighth anniversary _____

29. (a) less than 0.1 percent (b) less than .1 percent _____

30. (a) 4 quarts of ice cream (b) four quarts of ice cream _____

31. (a) a 10% return (b) a 10 percent return _____

32. (a) on his 20th birthday (b) on his twentieth birthday _____

Hot Line Review

Write the letter of the word or phrase that correctly completes each sentence.

33. May I (a) imply, (b) infer from your remark that you will not be able to attend the meeting? _____

34. We'll have to (a) reupholster, (b) re-upholster the chair. ______

35. The workmen wore (a) lose, (b) loose clothing. ______

36. (a) Almost, (b) Most everyone will be watching the series on TV. ______

37. I know you felt (a) badly, (b) bad about the error. ______

---

1. b, 2. b, 3. b, 4. a, 5. b, 6. a, 7. b, 8. a, 9. b, 10. b, 11. a, 12. b, 13. b, 14. a, 15. a, 16. a, 17. b, 18. a, 19. a, 20. b, 21. a, 22. a, 23. b, 24. c, 25. a, 26. b, 27. b, 28. b, 29. a, 30. a, 31. b, 32. b, 33. b, 34. a, 35. b, 36. a, 37. b

APPENDIX 1

Developing Spelling Skills

Why Is English Spelling So Difficult?

No one would dispute the complaint that many English words are difficult to spell. Why is spelling in our language so perplexing? For one thing, our language has borrowed many of its words from other languages. English has a Germanic base upon which a superstructure of words borrowed from French, Latin, Greek, and other languages of the world has been erected. For this reason, its words are not always formed by regular patterns of letter combinations. In addition, spelling is made difficult because the pronunciation of English words is constantly changing. Today's spelling was standardized nearly 300 years ago, but many words are pronounced differently today than they were then. Therefore, pronunciation often provides little help in spelling. Consider, for example, the words *sew* and *dough.*

What Can Be Done to Improve One's Spelling?

Spelling is a skill that can be developed, just as adding, subtracting, multiplying, dividing, typing, and other skills can be developed. Because the ability to spell is a prerequisite for success in business and in most other activities, effort expended to acquire this skill is effort well spent.

Three traditional approaches to improving spelling have met with varying degrees of success.

1. Rules or Guidelines

The spelling of English words is consistent enough to justify the formulation of a few spelling rules, perhaps more appropriately called guidelines, since the generalizations in question are not invariably applicable. Such guidelines are, in other words, helpful but not infallible.

2. Mnemonics

Another approach to improving one's ability to spell involves the use of mnemonics or memory devices. For example, the word *principle* might be associated with the word *rule,* to form in the mind of the speller a link between the meaning and the spelling of *principle.* To spell *capitol*, one might think of the *dome* of the capitol building and focus on the *o*'s in both words. The use of mnemonics can be an effective device for the improvement of spelling only if the speller makes a real effort to develop the necessary memory hooks.

3. Rote Learning

A third approach to the improvement of spelling centers on memorization. The word is studied by the speller until it can be readily reproduced in the mind's eye.

The 1-2-3 Spelling Plan

Proficiency in spelling is not attained without concentrated effort. Here's a plan to follow in mastering the 400 commonly misspelled words included in this appendix. For each word, try this 1-2-3 approach.

1. Is a spelling guideline applicable? If so, select the appropriate guideline and study the word in relation to that guideline.
2. If no guideline applies, can a memory device be created to aid in the recall of the word?
3. If neither a guideline nor a memory device will work, the word must be memorized. Look at the word carefully. Pronounce it. Write it or repeat it until you can visualize all its letters in your mind's eye.

Before you try the 1-2-3 plan, become familiar with the six spelling guidelines that follow. These spelling guidelines are not intended to represent all the possible spelling rules appearing in the various available spelling books. These six guidelines are, however, among the most effective and helpful of the recognized spelling rules.

Guideline 1: Words Containing *ie* or *ei*

Although there are exceptions to it, the following familiar rhyme can be helpful.

(a) Write *i* before *e*
(b) Except after *c*,
(c) Or when sounded like *a*
As in *neighbor* and *weigh*.

Study these words illustrating the three parts of the rhyme.

(a) *i* before *e*		(b) except after *c*	(c) or when sounded like *a*
achieve	grief	ceiling	beige
belief	ingredient	conceive	eight
believe	mischief	deceive	freight
brief	niece	perceive	heir
cashier	piece	receipt	neighbor
chief	shield	receive	reign
convenient	sufficient		their
field	view		vein
friend	yield		weight

Exceptions: These exceptional *ei* and *ie* words must be learned by rote or with the use of a mnemonic device.

caffeine	height	seize
either	leisure	sheik
financier	neither	sleight
foreigner	protein	weird

Guideline 2: Words Ending in *e*

For most words ending in an *e*, the final *e* is dropped when the word is joined to a suffix beginning with a vowel (such as *ing, able,* or *al*). The final *e* is retained when a suffix beginning with a consonant (such as *ment, less, ly,* or *ful*) is joined to such a word.

Final *e* dropped	Final *e* retained
believe, believing	arrange, arrangement
care, caring	require, requirement
hope, hoping	hope, hopeless
receive, receiving	care, careless
desire, desirable	like, likely
cure, curable	approximate, approximately
move, movable	definite, definitely
value, valuable	sincere, sincerely
disperse, dispersal	use, useful
arrive, arrival	hope, hopeful

Exceptions: The few exceptions to this spelling guideline are among the most frequently misspelled words. As such, they deserve special attention. Notice that they all involve a dropped final *e*.

acknowledgment	ninth
argument	truly
judgment	wholly

Guideline 3: Words Ending in *ce* or *ge*

When *able* or *ous* is added to words ending in *ce* or *ge,* the final *e* is retained if the *c* or *g* is pronounced softly (as in *change* or *peace*).

advantage, advantageous	change, changeable
courage, courageous	service, serviceable
outrage, outrageous	manage, manageable

Guideline 4: Words Ending in *y*

Words ending in a *y* that is preceded by a consonant normally change the *y* to *i* before all suffixes except those beginning with an *i.*

Change *y* to *i* because *y* is preceded by a consonant	Do not change *y* to *i* because *y* is preceded by a vowel
accompany, accompaniment	employ, employer
study, studied, studious	annoy, annoying, annoyance
duty, dutiful	stay, staying, stayed
industry, industrious	attorney, attorneys
carry, carriage	valley, valleys
apply, appliance	
try, tried	**Do not change *y* to *i* when adding *ing***
empty, emptiness	accompany, accompanying
forty, fortieth	apply, applying
secretary, secretaries	study, studying
company, companies	satisfy, satisfying
hurry, hurries	try, trying

Exceptions: day, daily; dry, dried; mislay, mislaid; pay, paid; shy, shyly; gay, gaily.

Guideline 5: Doubling a Final Consonant

If one-syllable words or two-syllable words accented on the second syllable end in a single consonant preceded by a single vowel, the final consonant is doubled before the addition of a suffix beginning with a vowel.

Although complex, this spelling guideline is extremely useful and therefore well worth mastering. Many spelling errors can be avoided by applying this guideline.

One-syllable words	Two-syllable words
can, canned	acquit, acquitting, acquittal
drop, dropped	admit, admitted, admitting
fit, fitted	begin, beginner, beginning
get, getting	commit, committed, committing
man, manned	control, controller, controlling
plan, planned	defer, deferred (BUT deference*)
run, running	excel, excelled, excelling
shut, shutting	occur, occurrence, occurring
slip, slipped	prefer, preferring (BUT preference*)
swim, swimming	recur, recurred, recurrence
ton, tonnage	refer, referring (BUT reference*)

Here is a summary of conditions necessary for application of this guideline:

1. The word must end in a single consonant.
2. The final consonant must be preceded by a single vowel.
3. The word must be accented on the second syllable (if it has two syllables).

Words derived from *cancel, offer, differ, equal, suffer,* and *benefit* are not governed by this guideline because they are accented on the first syllable.

Guideline 6: Prefixes and Suffixes

For words in which the letter that ends the prefix is the same as the letter that begins the main word (such as in *dis-similar*), both letters must be included. For words in which a suffix begins with the same letter that ends the main word (such as in *cool-ly*), both letters must also be included.

Prefix	Main word	Main word	Suffix
dis	satisfied	accidental	ly
ir	responsible	incidental	ly
il	literate	clean	ness
mis	spell	cool	ly
mis	state	even	ness
un	necessary	mean	ness

On the other hand, do not supply additional letters when adding prefixes to main words.

Prefix	Main word
dis	appoint (not di*ss*appoint)
dis	appearance
mis	take

Perhaps the most important guideline one can follow in spelling correctly is to use the dictionary whenever in doubt.

**Because the accent shifts to the first syllable, the final consonant is not doubled.*

400 Most Frequently Misspelled Words*
(Divided into 20 lists of 20 words each)

List 1

1. absence
2. acceptance
3. accessible
4. accidentally
5. accommodate
6. accompaniment
7. accurately
8. accustom
9. achievement
10. acknowledgment
11. acquaintance
12. acquire
13. across
14. actually
15. adequately
16. admitted
17. adolescence
18. advantageous
19. advertising
20. advice, advise

List 2

21. afraid
22. against
23. aggressive
24. all right
25. almost
26. alphabetical
27. already
28. although
29. amateur
30. among
31. amount
32. analysis
33. analyze
34. angel, angle
35. annoyance
36. annual
37. answer
38. apologized
39. apparent
40. appliance

List 3

41. applying
42. approaches
43. appropriate
44. approximately
45. arguing
46. argument
47. arrangement
48. article
49. athlete
50. attack
51. attendance, attendants
52. attitude
53. attorneys
54. auxiliary
55. basically
56. beautiful
57. before
58. beginning
59. believing
60. benefited

List 4

61. biggest
62. breath, breathe
63. brief
64. business
65. calendar
66. capital, capitol
67. career
68. careless
69. carrying
70. cashier
71. ceiling
72. certain
73. challenge
74. changeable
75. chief
76. choose, chose
77. cloths, clothes
78. column
79. coming
80. committee

List 5

81. companies
82. competition
83. completely
84. conceive
85. conscience
86. conscientious
87. conscious
88. considerably
89. consistent
90. continuous
91. controlling
92. controversial
93. convenience
94. council, counsel
95. cylinder
96. daily
97. deceive
98. decision
99. define
100. dependent

List 6

101. description
102. desirable
103. destroy
104. development
105. difference
106. dining
107. disappearance
108. disappoint
109. disastrous
110. discipline
111. discussion
112. disease
113. dissatisfied
114. distinction
115. divide
116. doesn't
117. dominant
118. dropped
119. due
120. during

**Compiled from lists of words most frequently misspelled by students and business people.*

List 7

121. efficient
122. eligible
123. embarrass
124. encourage
125. enough
126. environment
127. equipped
128. especially
129. exaggerate
130. excellence
131. except
132. exercise
133. existence
134. experience
135. explanation
136. extremely
137. familiar
138. families
139. fascinate
140. favorite

List 8

141. February
142. fictitious
143. field
144. finally
145. financially
146. foreigner
147. fortieth
148. forty, fourth
149. forward, foreword
150. freight
151. friend
152. fulfill
153. fundamentally
154. further
155. generally
156. government
157. governor
158. grammar
159. grateful
160. guard

List 9

161. happiness
162. hear, here
163. height
164. heroes
165. hopeless
166. hoping
167. huge
168. humorous
169. hungry
170. ignorance
171. imaginary
172. imagine
173. immediately
174. immense
175. importance
176. incidentally
177. independent
178. indispensable
179. industrious
180. inevitable

List 10

181. influential
182. ingredient
183. initiative
184. intelligence
185. interest
186. interference
187. interpretation
188. interrupt
189. involve
190. irrelevant
191. irresponsible
192. island
193. jealous
194. judgment
195. kindergarten
196. knowledge
197. laboratory
198. laborer
199. laid
200. led, lead

List 11

201. leisurely
202. library
203. license
204. likely
205. literature
206. lives
207. loneliness
208. loose, lose
209. losing
210. luxury
211. magazine
212. magnificence
213. maintenance
214. manageable
215. maneuver
216. manner
217. manufacturer
218. marriage
219. mathematics
220. meant

List 12

221. mechanics
222. medicine
223. medieval
224. mere
225. miniature
226. minutes
227. mischief
228. misspell
229. mistake
230. muscle
231. mysterious
232. naturally
233. necessary
234. Negroes
235. neighbor
236. neither
237. nickel
238. niece
239. ninety
240. ninth

List 13

241. noticeable
242. numerous
243. obstacle
244. occasionally
245. occurrence
246. off
247. offered
248. official
249. omitted
250. operate
251. opinion
252. opportunity
253. opposite
254. organization
255. origin
256. original
257. paid
258. pamphlet
259. parallel
260. particular

List 14

261. passed, past
262. pastime
263. peaceable
264. peculiar
265. perceive
266. performance
267. permanent
268. permitted
269. persistent
270. personal, personnel
271. persuading
272. phase, faze
273. philosophy
274. physical
275. piece
276. planned
277. pleasant
278. poison
279. political
280. possession

List 15

281. possible
282. practical
283. precede
284. preferred
285. prejudice
286. preparation
287. prevalent
288. principal, principle
289. privilege
290. probably
291. proceed
292. professor
293. prominent
294. proving
295. psychology
296. pursuing
297. quantity
298. quiet, quite
299. really
300. receipt

List 16

301. receiving
302. recognize
303. recommend
304. reference
305. referring
306. regard
307. relative
308. relieving
309. religious
310. reminiscent
311. repetition
312. representative
313. requirement
314. resistance
315. responsible
316. restaurant
317. rhythm
318. ridiculous
319. sacrifice
320. safety

List 17

321. satisfying
322. scenery
323. schedule
324. science
325. secretaries
326. seize
327. sense, since
328. sentence
329. separation
330. sergeant
331. serviceable
332. several
333. shining
334. shoulder
335. significance
336. similar
337. simply
338. sincerely
339. site, cite
340. source

List 18

341. speak, speech
342. specimen
343. stationary, stationery
344. stopped
345. stories
346. straight, strait
347. strenuous
348. stretch
349. strict
350. studying
351. substantial
352. subtle
353. succeed
354. success
355. sufficient
356. summary
357. suppose
358. surprise
359. suspense
360. swimming

List 19

361. syllable
362. symbol
363. symmetrical
364. synonymous
365. technique
366. temperament
367. temperature
368. tendency
369. than, then
370. their, there
371. themselves
372. theories
373. therefore
374. thorough
375. though
376. through
377. together
378. tomorrow
379. tragedies
380. transferred

List 20

381. tremendous
382. tried
383. truly
384. undoubtedly
385. unnecessary
386. until
387. unusual
388. useful
389. using
390. vacuum
391. valuable
392. varies
393. vegetable
394. view
395. weather, whether
396. weird
397. were, where
398. wholly, holy
399. writing
400. yield

APPENDIX 2

Developing Vocabulary Skills

If you understand the meanings of many words, you can be said "to have a good vocabulary." Words are the basis of thought. We think with words, we understand with words, we communicate with words.

A large working vocabulary is a significant asset. It allows us to use precise words that say exactly what we intend. In addition, we understand more effectively what we hear and read. A large vocabulary also enables us to score well on employment and intelligence tests. Lewis E. Terman, who developed the Stanford-Binet IQ tests, believes that vocabulary is the best single indicator of intelligence.

In the business world, where precise communication is extremely important, surveys show a definite correlation between size of vocabulary and level of management. Skilled workers, in the majority of cases, have larger vocabularies than unskilled workers. Supervisors know more words than the workers they direct, and executives have larger vocabularies than employees working for them.

Having a good vocabulary at our command doesn't necessarily assure our success in life, but it certainly gives us an advantage. Improving your vocabulary will help you expand your options in an increasingly complex world.

Vocabulary can be acquired in three ways: accidentally, incidentally, and intentionally. Setting out intentionally to expand your word power is, of course, the most efficient vocabulary-building method. One of the best means of increasing your vocabulary involves the use of 3-by-5 cards: when you encounter an unfamiliar word, write it on a card and put the definition of the word on the reverse side of the card. Just five to ten minutes of practice each day with such cards can significantly increase your vocabulary.

Your campaign to increase your vocabulary can begin with the 20 lists of selected business terms and words of general interest included in this unit. You may already know partial definitions for some of these words. Take this opportunity to develop more precise definitions for them. Follow these steps in using the word lists:

1. Record the word on a 3-by-5 card.

2. Look up the word in your dictionary. Compare the dictionary definitions of the word with the definition alternatives shown after the word in your copy of *Business English*. Select the correct definition, and circle its letter in your textbook. (The definitions provided in your textbook are quite concise but should help you remember the word's most common meaning.)

3. On the reverse side of your card, write the phonetic spelling of the word and the word's part of speech. Then write its definition using as much of the dictionary definition as you find helpful. Try also to add a phrase or sentence illustrating the word.

4. Study your 3-by-5 cards often.
5. Try to find ways to use your vocabulary words in your speech and writing.

List 1

1. adjacent = (a) previous, (b) similar, (c) overdue, (d) nearby ______
2. ambivalence = having (a) uncertainty, (b) ambition, (c) compassion, (d) intelligence ______
3. belligerent = (a) overweight, (b) quarrelsome, (c) likable, (d) believable ______
4. contingent = (a) conditional, (b) allowable, (c) hopeless, (d) impractical ______
5. decadent = in a state of (a) repair, (b) happiness, (c) decline, (d) extreme patriotism ______
6. entitlement = (a) label, (b) tax refund, (c) screen credit, (d) legal right ______
7. equivalent = (a) subsequent, (b) identical, (c) self-controlled, (d) plentiful ______
8. paramount = (a) foremost, (b) high mountain, (c) film company, (d) insignificant ______
9. plausible = (a) quiet, (b) acceptable, (c) notorious, (d) negative ______
10. unilateral = (a) powerful, (b) harmonious, (c) one-sided, (d) indelible ______

List 2

1. affluent = (a) rich, (b) slippery, (c) persistent, (d) rebellious ______
2. autocrat = one who (a) owns many cars, (b) is self-centered, (c) has power, (d) collects signatures ______
3. benevolent = for the purpose of (a) religion, (b) doing good, (c) healing, (d) violence ______
4. entrepreneur = (a) business owner, (b) traveler, (c) salesperson, (d) gambler ______
5. impertinent = (a) stationary, (b) bound to happen, (c) obsolete, (d) rude and irreverent ______
6. imprudent = (a) unwise, (b) crude, (c) vulnerable, (d) lifeless ______
7. mediator = one who seeks (a) overseas trade, (b) profits, (c) safe investment, (d) peaceful settlement ______
8. preponderance = (a) thoughtful, (b) exclusive right, (c) superiority, (d) forethought ______
9. recipient = (a) receiver, (b) respondent, (c) voter, (d) giver ______
10. reprehensible = (a) obedient, (b) independent, (c) blameworthy, (d) following ______

List 3

1. affable = (a) cheap, (b) pleasant, (c) strange, (d) competent ______
2. consensus = (a) population count, (b) attendance, (c) tabulation, (d) agreement ______
3. criterion = (a) standard, (b) command, (c) pardon, (d) law ______
4. diligent = (a) gentle, (b) industrious, (c) prominent, (d) intelligent ______
5. hydraulic = operated by means of (a) air, (b) gasoline, (c) liquid, (d) mechanical parts ______
6. hypothesis = (a) triangle, (b) promulgate, (c) highest point, (d) theory ______
7. phenomenon = (a) imagination, (b) rare event, (c) appointment, (d) clever saying ______
8. reticent = (a) silent, (b) strong-willed, (c) inflexible, (d) disagreeable ______
9. sanctuary = a place of (a) healing, (b) refuge, (c) rest, (d) learning ______
10. stimulus = something that causes (a) response, (b) light, (c) pain, (d) movement ______

List 4

1. beneficiary = one who (a) receives a license, (b) creates goodwill, (c) receives proceeds, (d) makes friends ______
2. constrain = (a) restrict, (b) filter, (c) use, (d) inform ______
3. corroborate = (a) contradict, (b) recall, (c) erode, (d) confirm ______
4. dun (n) = a demand for (a) legal action, (b) payment, (c) credit information, (d) dividends ______
5. equitable = (a) fair, (b) profitable, (c) similar, (d) clear ______
6. fluctuate = (a) rinse out, (b) magnetic field, (c) pricing schedule, (d) swing back and forth ______
7. indolent = (a) self-indulgent, (b) lazy, (c) pampered, (d) uncertain ______
8. nullify = (a) disappear, (b) imitate, (c) invalidate, (d) enhance ______
9. obsolete = (a) ugly, (b) outmoded, (c) audible, (d) scant ______
10. stabilize = to make (a) pleasant, (b) congenial, (c) traditional, (d) firm ______

List 5

1. arbitrate = (a) decide, (b) construct, (c) conquer, (d) ratify ______
2. coalition = (a) deliberation, (b) allegiance, (c) adherence, (d) alliance ______
3. collate = (a) assemble, (b) denounce, (c) supersede, (d) uninformed ______
4. conglomerate = combination of (a) executives, (b) companies, (c) investments, (d) countries ______

5. franchise = (a) fictitious reason, (b) right, (c) obligation, (d) official announcement ______
6. logistics = (a) speculations, (b) analytic philosophy, (c) reasonable outcome, (d) details of operation ______
7. proxy = authority to (a) act for another, (b) write checks, (c) submit nominations, (d) explain ______
8. subsidiary = (a) below expectations, (b) country dominated by another, (c) company controlled by another, (d) depressed financial condition ______
9. termination = (a) end, (b) inception, (c) identification, (d) evasive action ______
10. virtually = (a) absolutely, (b) precisely, (c) almost entirely, (d) strictly ______

List 6

1. affiliate = (a) trust, (b) attract, (c) effect, (d) join ______
2. alter = (a) table for religious ceremony, (b) solitary, (c) attribute, (d) modify ______
3. boisterous = (a) vociferous, (b) masculine, (c) cheerful, (d) brusque ______
4. configuration = (a) stratagem, (b) foreign currency, (c) form, (d) comprehension ______
5. conveyance = (a) vehicle, (b) transformation, (c) baggage, (d) consortium ______
6. infringe = (a) ravel, (b) decorative border, (c) encroach, (d) frivolous ______
7. jurisdiction = (a) science of law, (b) enunciation, (c) justice, (d) authority ______
8. nonpartisan = (a) unbiased, (b) antisocial, (c) ineffective, (d) untenable ______
9. parity = (a) price index, (b) justice under law, (c) plenitude, (d) equality of purchasing power ______
10. usury = (a) method of operation, (b) implementation, (c) illegal interest, (d) customary ______

List 7

1. anonymous = (a) multiplex, (b) powerless, (c) vexing, (d) nameless ______
2. cartel = (a) combination to fix prices, (b) ammunition belt, (c) partnership to promote competition, (d) placard ______
3. conjecture = (a) coagulation, (b) gesticulation, (c) guesswork, (d) connection ______
4. disparity = (a) unlikeness, (b) separation, (c) lacking emotion, (d) repudiation ______
5. environment = (a) urban area, (b) zenith, (c) surroundings, (d) latitude ______

6. impetus = (a) oversight, (b) stimulus, (c) hindrance, (d) imminent ______

7. portfolio = a list of (a) books, (b) security analysts, (c) corporations, (d) investments ______

8. quiescent = (a) presumptuous, (b) latent, (c) immoderate, (d) volatile ______

9. surrogate = (a) substitute, (b) accused, (c) authenticate, (d) suspend ______

10. tariff = (a) marsupial, (b) announcement, (c) ship, (d) duty ______

List 8

1. accrue = (a) conform, (b) accumulate, (c) diminish, (d) multiply ______

2. amortize = (a) pay off, (b) reduce, (c) romance, (d) kill ______

3. commensurate = (a) infinitesimal, (b) erroneous, (c) reliable, (d) proportional ______

4. consortium = (a) configuration, (b) partnership or association, (c) royal offspring, (d) rental property ______

5. discernible = (a) perceptive, (b) pretentious, (c) recognizable, (d) dissident ______

6. frugal = (a) thrifty, (b) wasteful, (c) judicious, (d) profligate ______

7. pecuniary = (a) rudimentary, (b) eccentric, (c) financial, (d) distinctive ______

8. retract = (a) disavow, (b) reorganize, (c) reciprocate, (d) hide ______

9. scrutinize = (a) cheerfully admit, (b) baffle, (c) persist, (d) examine carefully ______

10. tenacious = (a) falling apart, (b) holding on, (c) immobile, (d) chagrined ______

List 9

1. amiable = (a) contumacious, (b) impetuous, (c) feasible, (d) congenial ______

2. credible = (a) plausible, (b) deceitful, (c) religious, (d) tolerant ______

3. defendant = one who (a) sues, (b) answers suit, (c) judges, (d) protects ______

4. dissipate = (a) accumulate, (b) partition, (c) liquify, (d) scatter or waste ______

5. incentive = (a) impediment, (b) support, (c) motive, (d) remuneration ______

6. innocuous = (a) harmless, (b) injection, (c) facetious, (d) frightening ______

7. oust = (a) install, (b) instigate, (c) shout, (d) expel ______

8. pittance = (a) tiny amount, (b) tithe, (c) abyss, (d) pestilence ______

9. plaintiff = one who (a) defends, (b) is sad, (c) sues, (d) responds ______

10. superfluous = (a) extraordinary, (b) very slippery, (c) shallow, (d) oversupplied ______

List 10

1. adroit = (a) ideal, (b) resilient, (c) witty, (d) skillful ______
2. derogatory = (a) minimal, (b) degrading, (c) originating from, (d) devious ______
3. escrow = (a) international treaty, (b) public registration, (c) licensed by state, (d) type of deposit ______
4. facsimile = (a) principle, (b) prototype, (c) exact copy, (d) counterfeit ______
5. inordinate = (a) unwholesome, (b) excessive, (c) unimportant, (d) treacherous ______
6. logical = (a) reasoned, (b) irrelevant, (c) lofty, (d) intricate ______
7. malfeasance = (a) prevaricate, (b) injurious, (c) superstitious, (d) misconduct ______
8. noxious = (a) pernicious, (b) unusual, (c) pleasant, (d) inconsequential ______
9. résumé = (a) budget report, (b) minutes of meeting, (c) photo album, (d) summary of qualifications ______
10. spasmodic = (a) paralyzing, (b) intermittent, (c) internal, (d) painful ______

List 11

1. animosity = (a) happiness, (b) deep sadness, (c) hatred, (d) study of animals ______
2. caveat = (a) headwear, (b) warning, (c) neckware, (d) prerogative ______
3. conscientious = (a) meticulous, (b) productive, (c) cognizant, (d) sophisticated ______
4. cosmopolitan = (a) provincial, (b) multicolored, (c) heavenly, (d) worldly ______
5. decipher = (a) preclude, (b) decode, (c) demise, (d) reproach ______
6. euphemism = (a) religious discourse, (b) facial expression, (c) figurative speech, (d) inoffensive term ______
7. fraudulent = (a) loquacious, (b) candid, (c) deceitful, (d) despotic ______
8. peripheral = (a) supplementary, (b) imaginary, (c) visionary, (d) supernatural ______
9. pungent = (a) knowledgeable, (b) wise religious man, (c) acrid, (d) vulnerable ______
10. requisite = (a) essential, (b) demand, (c) skillful, (d) discreet ______

List 12

1. ad valorem = (a) esteemed, (b) genuine, (c) recompense, (d) proportional ______
2. carte blanche = (a) white carriage, (b) credit terms, (c) full permission, (d) geographical expression ______
3. de facto = (a) prejudicial, (b) actual, (c) valid, (d) unlawful ______

4. esprit de corps = (a) group enthusiasm, (b) strong coffee, (c) central authority, (d) government overturn ______

5. modus operandi = (a) method of procedure, (b) practical compromise, (c) business transaction, (d) flexible arbitration ______

6. per capita = per unit of (a) income, (b) population, (c) birth, (d) household ______

7. per diem = (a) daily, (b) weekly, (c) yearly, (d) taxable ______

8. prima facie = (a) self-taught, (b) apparent, (c) principal, (d) artificial effect ______

9. status quo = (a) haughty demeanor, (b) steadfast opinion, (c) position of importance, (d) existing condition ______

10. tort = (a) rich cake, (b) extended dream, (c) wrongful act, (d) lawful remedy ______

List 13

1. acquit = (a) discharge, (b) pursue, (c) interfere, (d) impede ______

2. annuity = (a) yearly report, (b) insurance premium, (c) tuition refund, (d) annual payment ______

3. complacent = (a) appealing, (b) self-satisfied, (c) sympathetic, (d) scrupulous ______

4. contraband = (a) discrepancy, (b) opposing opinion, (c) smuggled goods, (d) ammunition ______

5. insolvent = (a) uncleanable, (b) unexplainable, (c) bankrupt, (d) unjustifiable ______

6. malicious = marked by (a) good humor, (b) ill will, (c) great pleasure, (d) injurious tumor ______

7. negligent = (a) careless, (b) fraudulent, (c) unlawful, (d) weak ______

8. nominal = (a) enumerated, (b) beneficial, (c) extravagant, (d) insignificant ______

9. rescind = (a) consign, (b) oppose, (c) repeal, (d) censure ______

10. stringent = (a) rigid, (b) expedient, (c) compliant, (d) resilient ______

List 14

1. affirm = (a) business organization, (b) validate, (c) elevate, (d) encircle ______

2. exonerate = (a) commend, (b) declare blameless, (c) banish, (d) emigrate ______

3. expedite = (a) elucidate, (b) get rid of, (c) amplify, (d) rush ______

4. hamper (v) = (a) impede, (b) delineate, (c) release, (d) assuage ______

5. implement (v) = (a) suppress, (b) ameliorate, (c) carry out, (d) attribute ______

6. induce = (a) teach, (b) construe, (c) persuade, (d) copy ______

7. obliterate = (a) obstruct, (b) prevent, (c) minimize, (d) erase ______

8. quandary = a state of (a) doubt, (b) certainty, (c) depression, (d) apprehension ______

9. surmount = (a) hike, (b) overcome, (c) interpret, (d) specify ______

10. veracity = (a) truthfulness, (b) swiftness, (c) efficiency, (d) persistence ______

List 15

1. aggregate = constituting a (a) hostile crowd, (b) word combination, (c) total group, (d) sticky mass ______

2. ambiguous = (a) peripatetic, (b) uncertain, (c) enterprising, (d) deceptive ______

3. amend = (a) alter, (b) pray, (c) praise, (d) utter ______

4. apportion = (a) sanction, (b) ratify, (c) estimate, (d) divide ______

5. collaborate = (a) scrutinize, (b) cooperate, (c) surrender, (d) accumulate ______

6. ingenuity = (a) innocence, (b) torpor, (c) cleverness, (d) self-composure ______

7. irretrievable = not capable of being (a) sold, (b) identified, (c) explained, (d) recovered ______

8. lenient = (a) liberal, (b) crooked, (c) benevolent, (d) explicit ______

9. retrench = (a) dig repeatedly, (b) curtail, (c) reiterate, (d) enlighten ______

10. trivial = (a) composed of three parts, (b) momentous, (c) paltry, (d) economical ______

List 16

1. audit = (a) examine, (b) speak, (c) exchange, (d) expunge ______

2. arrears = (a) old-fashioned, (b) gratuity, (c) overdue debt, (d) option ______

3. curtail = (a) obstruct, (b) restore, (c) rejuvenate, (d) abbreviate ______

4. encumber = (a) grow, (b) substantiate, (c) burden, (d) illustrate ______

5. exemplify = (a) segregate, (b) divulge, (c) illustrate, (d) condone ______

6. extension = (a) unusual request, (b) prolonged journey, (c) haphazard results, (d) extra time ______

7. fortuitous = (a) accidental, (b) courageous, (c) radical, (d) assiduous ______

8. innovation = (a) reorganization, (b) occupancy, (c) introduction, (d) solution ______

9. syndicate = (a) union of writers, (b) council of lawmakers, (c) group of symptoms, (d) association of people ______

10. venture = (a) speculative business transaction, (b) unsecured loan, (c) stock split, (d) gambling debt ______

List 17

1. acquiesce = (a) gain possession of, (b) confront, (c) implore, (d) comply ______

2. enumerate = (a) articulate, (b) list, (c) enunciate, (d) see clearly ______

3. erratic = (a) pleasurable, (b) wandering, (c) exotic, (d) serene ______

4. expedient = serving to promote (a) fellowship, (b) one's self-interests, (c) good of others, (d) speedy delivery ______

5. feasible = (a) auspicious, (b) profuse, (c) reasonable, (d) extraneous ______

6. literal = (a) exact, (b) devout, (c) apropos, (d) noticeable ______

7. lucrative = (a) providential, (b) swift, (c) pleasant, (d) profitable ______

8. negotiable = (a) essential, (b) adequate, (c) transferable, (d) economical ______

9. nonchalant = (a) dull, (b) cool, (c) unintelligent, (d) sagacious ______

10. reconcile = (a) settle or resolve, (b) calculate, (c) modify, (d) remunerate ______

List 18

1. byte = (a) dental occlusion, (b) computer storage, (c) digits processed as a unit, (d) type font ______

2. disk = (a) magnetic storage medium, (b) print wheel, (c) computer belt, (d) program ______

3. execute = (a) eradicate, (b) inquire, (c) oppose, (d) carry out ______

4. memory = (a) printer logic, (b) computer storage, (c) automatic printout, (d) software ______

5. menu = list of (a) parts, (b) selections, (c) serial numbers, (d) vendors ______

6. microfiche = sheet of (a) computer printouts, (b) microimages, (c) reduced digits, (d) tiny cards ______

7. program = (a) alphabetical list, (b) computer log, (c) coded instructions, (d) microprocessor ______

8. prompt (n) = (a) reminder, (b) on time, (c) function, (d) format ______

9. retrieve = (a) acquiesce, (b) instruct, (c) remove code, (d) recover information ______

10. software = (a) equipment, (b) programs, (c) plastic component, (d) solid-state semiconductor ______

List 19

1. apprehensive = (a) knowledgeable, (b) fearful, (c) reticent, (d) autonomous ______

2. circumspect = (a) cautious, (b) uncertain, (c) cooperative, (d) frugal ______

3. collateral = (a) revenue, (b) secret agreement, (c) book value, (d) security for a loan ______

4. insinuation = (a) disagreeable proposal, (b) indirect suggestion, (c) elucidating glimpse, (d) flagrant insult ______

5. liaison = (a) legal obligation, (b) treaty, (c) connection between groups, (d) quarantine ______

6. procrastinate = (a) predict, (b) reproduce, (c) postpone, (d) advance ______

7. ratification = the act of (a) confirming, (b) reviewing, (c) evaluating, (d) inscribing ______

8. renovate = (a) renegotiate, (b) restore, (c) supply, (d) deliver ______

9. saturate = to fill (a) slowly, (b) dangerously, (c) as expected, (d) to excess ______

10. vendor = (a) seller, (b) manufacturer, (c) tradesman, (d) coin collector ______

List 20

1. abhorrent = (a) disagreeable, (b) attractive, (c) valueless, (d) adducible ______

2. appraisal = (a) general information, (b) certification, (c) estimation, (d) approval ______

3. collusion = (a) secret agreement, (b) direct conflict, (c) partial exclusion, (d) original artwork ______

4. commingle = (a) socialize, (b) mix, (c) separate, (d) communicate ______

5. dissolution = (a) intemperance, (b) soluble, (c) unsolvable, (d) separation ______

6. ensue = (a) change subtly, (b) relinquish, (c) track down, (d) follow immediately ______

7. rejuvenate = to make (a) youthful, (b) slender, (c) sturdy, (d) impregnable ______

8. stipulation = (a) permission, (b) requirement, (c) rejection, (d) concurrence ______

9. subsidy = (a) scholarship, (b) financial assistance, (c) payment due, (d) unacknowledged payment ______

10. tenuous = (a) flimsy, (b) indecisive, (c) cautious, (d) firm ______

APPENDIX 3

Writing Paragraphs

Instructor: Please see pp. 355–356 for suggestions regarding the use of Appendixes 3, 4, and 5.

The basic unit in writing is the sentence. All sentences have subjects and predicates (verbs), as discussed in Chapter 3. All sentences should be complete. Broken-off parts of sentences, called fragments (p. 25), should not be punctuated as if they were complete. Techniques for writing effective sentences are presented in Chapter 21.

The next unit in writing is the paragraph. In business writing, a paragraph is one or more sentences that express an idea. A paragraph may be complete in just one sentence if that sentence expresses a complete thought. No additional sentences may be required. Usually, however, additional sentences are needed to amplify and explain the initial idea. If the paragraph is composed of several sentences, all should relate to the primary idea.

Combining effective sentences into good paragraphs is a writing skill that must be developed through instruction and practice, just as keyboarding skill is developed through instruction and practice. Beginning writers often find it helpful to follow a plan that gets them started in creating effective paragraphs. Here's a simple plan that may help you write like a professional:

PRO plan for paragraph development

1. Primary idea
2. Related sentence
3. Other sentences

PRO Plan for Paragraph Development

Primary Idea

Write a sentence that clearly states the main idea of your paragraph. If possible, summarize everything that you want to include in the paragraph.

Sentence 1: The sales staff will discuss several items at its meeting on Tuesday, September 30, in the staff conference room at 2 p.m.

Related Sentence

Write a second sentence that adds an idea directly related to your first sentence. Try to repeat a key word or idea from the first sentence.

Sentence 2: At the *meeting* a new plan for sales quotas and bonuses will be presented.

Notice that the second sentence amplifies the first sentence by giving additional information about the meeting. The second sentence also repeats the word *meeting*, contained in the previous sentence. Such repetition helps the reader move from one thought to the next.

Other Sentences

Add additional sentences, if needed, to expand and clarify the primary idea.

> *Sentence 3:* *In addition,* we will discuss the restructuring of some sales territories.
>
> *Sentence 4:* *This restructuring* is necessary to enable us to serve our rapidly increasing number of customers.

Achieving Paragraph Coherence

Effective paragraphs are coherent; that is, they hold together. Coherence is a quality of good writing that does not happen accidentally. It is consciously achieved through effective organization and through skillful use of three devices.

Repetition of Key Ideas or Key Words

Repeating a key word or key thought from the first sentence or from the preceding sentence helps guide a reader from one thought to the next. This redundancy is necessary to build cohesiveness into writing. In the examples above, the word *meeting* is repeated in the second sentence. In the fourth sentence above, the word *restructuring* is repeated to promote coherence. Repetition may consist of repeating a key idea stated somewhat differently, rather than using the same words.

> *Example:* The modern athlete has learned that improvements in equipment, training, and techniques continue to expand the limits of human performance. Westinghouse has learned that the *same principle* works in the office.

In the above example the words *same principle* repeat a key idea from the previous sentence without actually reusing the identical words. Notice, too, how the second sentence uses the same grammatical structure as the first sentence and repeats the verb *has learned.* Such balancing helps the reader see that the thoughts in both sentences are meant to be parallel.

Use of Pronouns That Refer Clearly to Their Antecedents

Pronouns such as *this, that, they, these,* and *those* help connect the thoughts in one sentence to the thoughts in a previous sentence. Often it's better to make the pronoun into an adjective joined with its antecedent to ensure that the reference is absolutely clear. In Sentence 4 of the preceding example, the word *this* is coupled with *restructuring* to remind the reader that *restructuring* was mentioned earlier.

Be very careful in using pronouns. A pronoun without a clear antecedent can be most annoying. The reader doesn't know precisely to what the pronoun refers.

> *Faulty:* The library now has thousands of individualized programs and systems software packages. *This* will be useful to many users.
>
> *Improved:* The library now has thousands of individualized programs and systems software packages. *This new service* will be useful to many users.

Use of Transitional Expressions

One of the most effective ways to achieve paragraph coherence is through the use of transitional expressions. These expressions act as road signs: they indicate where the message is headed, and they help the reader anticipate what is coming. Some common transitional expressions follow:

although	furthermore	moreover
as a result	hence	nevertheless
consequently	however	of course
for example	in addition	on the other hand
for this reason	in this way	therefore

Other words that act as connectives are *first, second, after, meanwhile, next, after all, instead, specifically, thus, also, likewise, as,* and *as if.*

Writing Concise Paragraphs

Concise writing is prized in business. Time is money, and time wasted reading wordy messages represents money lost. Writing concisely is far more difficult than writing profusely without concern for brevity. In writing to a friend, Blaise Pascal, the philosopher for whom a computer language is named, apologized for the length of his letter. He said if he had had more time, the letter would have been shorter.

Most messages can be condensed and improved through conscious effort and revision. Three techniques for concise writing follow.

Avoid Wasted Words and Phrases

Be constantly alert for ways to boil down your writing. Making phrases into adjectives and adverbs eliminates unnecessary words.

Wordy: The speaker who is giving the keynote address . . .
Improved: The keynote speaker . . .
Wordy: We have on a few occasions . . .
Improved: We have occasionally . . .
Wordy: In the meeting that was held at 10 o'clock . . .
Improved: In the 10 o'clock meeting . . .
Wordy: Leave your car in one of the lots that is marked for parking.
Improved: Leave your car in one of the marked parking lots.
Wordy: On a day that was cold and windy . . .
Improved: On a cold and windy day . . .

Avoid Wasted Sentences

Combine sentences that relate to the same subject and can be stated economically in one sentence.

Wordy: The seminar will be held at the Hilton Hotel. It is scheduled to begin at 2 p.m.
Improved: The seminar will begin at 2 p.m. at the Hilton Hotel.
Wordy: Your new sales rep is Jeffrey Lee. He will be visiting you in July.
Improved: Jeffrey Lee, your new sales rep, will visit you in July.

Wordy: I would like to order 4 dozen ribbon cartridges. Please send them immediately.

Improved: Please send me 4 dozen ribbon cartridges immediately.

Reduce Dependence on Expletives

Expletives are words like *it, there,* and *here.* We often use them in English to fill in a sentence. Although expletives are not grammatically incorrect, they usually weaken a thought with meaningless words. Notice how much stronger and cleaner the following sentences are when they are rewritten to avoid dependence upon expletives.

Wordy: There is a free booklet that describes our services.
Improved: A free booklet describes our services.
Wordy: It is an investment offering safety and high returns.
Improved: The investment offers safety and high returns.
Wordy: There were several changes to be made in the report.
Improved: Several changes were to be made in the report.

Rewriting Paragraphs

One of the best ways to develop writing skills is to compare an improved version of a message with a poorly written one. Analyzing the improved version will help you understand what changes were made and why. Compare these two versions of the same message.

Wordy, Inefficient Message

You may be interested in applying for a new position within the company. The Personnel Department has a number of jobs available immediately. The positions are at a high-level. Employees who are currently working may apply immediately. There are jobs in marketing as well as some in personnel and some in production. Come to the Personnel Department. We have a book showing the qualifications for all company positions. Many of the jobs are now open. Interviews will have to be scheduled within the next two weeks.

Analysis. The first sentence does not give a clear summary of the total paragraph. No effort was made in the second sentence to connect it to the first. Many words are wasted with prepositional phrases that could be condensed into adjectives. Little use is made of transitional expressions to guide the reader through the message.

Improved Version

The Personnel Department has a number of high-level positions for which current employees may apply. These positions, which are in marketing, personnel, and production, must be filled immediately. Therefore, interviews will be scheduled within the next two weeks. If you are interested in applying for one of these positions, come to the Personnel Department to see the list and read the qualifications.

Analysis. The first sentence of the improved version summarizes the primary idea of the paragraph. The second sentence repeats the word *positions* and also uses *these* to strengthen the bond between the two sentences. The third sentence employs the transitional expression *therefore* to inform the reader that the following information results from the previous. The fourth sentence, beginning with *If you are interested,* adds additional needed information. However, this sentence might be separated from the previous paragraph and used to form a paragraph by itself. One-sentence paragraphs in business writing are frequently used to introduce or conclude messages.

Notice how much more efficient *high-level positions* is instead of *positions at a high level.* Note, too, that *employees who are currently working* becomes *current employees.* And the expletive *There (are)* is eliminated.

APPLICATION EXERCISES

Instructor: Solutions for most of these paragraphs are provided in the transparency packet.

3–1. On a separate sheet, revise the following poorly written paragraph.

Miss Tania Adams is our new District sales rep for the Southwest. When she visits your store, she will be able to demonstrate one of our new products. This product is a new copier. This new copier will validate numbers for projects. Miss Adams will be able, at the time of her visit, to discuss with you techniques for making your photocopying operations better. It is important to make your photocopying operations accountable. It will do this for you. Miss Adams will visit the store that you own on March 12.

3–2. On a separate sheet, revise the following poorly written paragraph.

There is a National Computer Conference. It will be held October 10–13. It will feature products, seminars, and films. The film forum includes films and videotapes showing the latest advancements in micro technology. The conference will also have professional development seminars. Over 650 manufacturers will demonstrate their new products. These manufacturers are from all over the world. It is in Las Vegas.

3–3. Revise the following poorly written paragraph. It suffers from wordiness, reliance upon expletives (*There is* . . .), vague pronouns (*this, they*), poor organization, and many other faults.

As you probably already know, this company (Tektronics, Inc.) will be receiving new microcomputers shortly. There will be a demonstration of them April 18, which is a Tuesday. We felt this was necessary because this new system is so different from our previous equipment. It will be from 9 to 12 a.m. in the morning. This will show employees how the computers work. They will learn about the disk operating system of the computer, and this should be helpful to nearly everyone. There will be information about word processing, which should be beneficial to our secretaries. For all you people who work with payroll, there will be information about the new data base program. We can't show everything the system will do at this one demo, but for these three areas there will be some help at the Tuesday demo. Oh yes, Charlene Ruley will be presenting the demonstration. She is the representative from Computers, Inc.

3–4. Assume that you work in the Human Resources Department of Bank of America. You must write an announcement describing a special program of classes for your employees. Use the following information to write a concise one-paragraph announcement.

Explain that Bank of America will reimburse any employee the full cost of tuition and books if that employee attends classes. Describe the plan. Skyline Community College, in cooperation with Bank of America, will offer a group of courses (for college credit) at very convenient locations for our employees. Actually, the classes will be offered at our downtown and East Bay branches. Tell employees that they should call Jean Fujimoto at Ext. 660 if they are interested. You'd better mention the tuition: $60 for a semester course. Explain that we (Bank of America) are willing to pay these fees because we value education highly. Employees must call Jean before September 1 to enroll in fall classes. However, make it clear that employees must receive a grade of C or higher before they are eligible for reimbursement of course and book fees. It might be a good idea to attach a list of the courses and the times that they will be offered.

3–5. Construct your own coherent, efficient paragraph, using the skeletal information that follows.

1. It is important to use good telephone techniques.
2. Answer promptly.
3. Identify yourself.
4. Eliminate the need for repetition. Listen carefully.
5. Be considerate.
6. Transfer calls only if you have to.

Mini-essays. Choose one or more of the following topics. Write a well-organized, coherent paragraph using this pattern of development:

a. Begin with an introductory sentence stating your primary idea or argument.
b. Discuss three or four supporting arguments. Illustrate each with an example. Use transitions to get from one idea to the next.
c. End with a concluding statement that ties in with your opening.

3–6. Local high school graduates should attend ____insert name of your school____.

3–7. Returning adults should attend ____insert name of your school____.

3–8. Working as a checkout clerk (or use title of a job you have held) can be a valuable employment experience.

3–9. Specialty catalogs are becoming more elaborate and more numerous.

3–10. A job search often begins with the want ads.

3–11. Buying a new (or used) car is difficult.

APPENDIX 4

Writing Informational Memorandums

Functions

Memorandums (memos) are forms of internal communication; that is, they deliver information within an organization. In most companies more memorandums are written than letters addressed outside the organization.

Memos explain policies, procedures, and guidelines; they make announcements, request information or action; and they respond to requests. They serve as reminders, and they provide a written record of decisions, telephone conversations, and meetings. In short, memos are a vital means of conducting business within an organization.

Characteristics

Well-considered memos have the following qualities:

1. They begin with *To, From, Date,* and *Subject*.
2. They cover just one topic.
3. They are written informally.
4. They are concise.

Memos, as you can see, have much in common with paragraphs. Both memos and paragraphs are written concisely and cover just one topic. Although memos relate to just one topic, they may contain more than one paragraph because the subject generally has different aspects that are best treated in separate paragraphs.

Many organizations have printed memorandum paper for interoffice messages. Using a standardized memo format benefits both the sender and the receiver of memos. The format forces the sender to organize his thoughts in order to compose the subject line. It also enables the receiver to comprehend at a glance the identity of the sender and the subject of the message. Moreover, the *To, From, Date,* and *Subject* lines are invaluable when filing and retrieving memos.

Writing Plan

Subject line: Summarizes memo contents
Opening: Tells reader purpose of memo
Body: Provides background information; expands subject
Closing: Requests action or summarizes message

Subject Line

The most important part of a memo is the subject line. It should summarize the contents of the memo in concise language. But it shouldn't be so brief that it makes no sense. The subject line *Revised Procedures* is probably meaningless to a reader. An improved subject line might read *Revised Procedures for Applying for Authorized Dental Benefits.*

A subject line is like a newspaper headline. It should attract attention, create a clear picture, and present an accurate summary. It should not be a complete sentence and should rarely occupy more than one line. Cramming comprehensive information into one dense line is a challenge that many writers enjoy because it tests their word and organizational skills.

Some writers prefer to write the subject line after they have written a first draft of the memo.

Opening

An informational memo should open directly by stating the main reason for writing. The opening may issue a polite command, make a request, or ask a question. For example, a memo that seeks information might begin, *Please answer the following questions regarding the conference you are offering October 1.* A memo that requests action might open with *Please begin research on the possibility of initiating a summer internship program.* For specific information a memo might open with a question, such as, *Can your department complete the printing of our personnel announcement by January 15?*

The first paragraph may consist of only one sentence if that is all that is required to explain the purpose of the memo. However, if additional statements are needed, use the PRO plan to write a unified paragraph.

Body

Arrange in logical order explanations and amplification of the primary idea of the memo. If a considerable amount of information is involved, use a separate paragraph for each topic, being ever mindful of the need for brevity.

Often the information in a memo lends itself to enumeration. Numbered sentences or paragraphs emphasize ideas and help the reader comprehend quickly. If you use a numbered list, be sure to keep the numbered items parallel; that is, write the items so that they use the same grammatical construction. For example, the following list lacks parallel form:

Our future plans include the following:

1. Increasing service profits
2. Expanding our sales force
3. Enlargement of our showrooms

By changing the last item in the list to *Enlarging our showrooms,* all the items have the same form and are more effective and pleasing to the reader.

The tone of memos is informal. Don't be self-conscious about using personal pronouns (*I, me, we*), contractions, and conversational language.

Closing

End the memo with a request for action or with a summary. If action on the part of the reader is sought, spell out that action clearly. A vague request, such as *Please order supplies soon,* is ineffective because the reader may not understand exactly what is to be done. A better request might be worded, *Please order 50 reams of 20-pound bond paper before October 15.*

It is unnecessary to conclude memos with goodwill statements such as those found in letters to customers. Also omitted are the complimentary close and typed signature. Memos are usually initialed (not signed) by the writer next to his or her typed name at the top of the memo. The writer may, however, write a signature at the end of the memo.

Model 1: *Effective Memo*

TO: Pharmacy Staff

FROM: J. W. Lee, Comptroller JWL

DATE: November 3, 19xx

SUBJECT: ANNUAL PHARMACY INVENTORY SCHEDULED JUNE 2

Please be prepared to exhibit stored inventory items as well as shelf stocks in our annual inventory, which will be conducted by Inventory Incorporated on June 2.

Inventory Incorporated is an independent firm that specializes in taking pharmacy inventories. We've hired this Philadelphia-based firm to assist us in conducting an accurate and objective count of our pharmacy stocks. At the completion of its work, Inventory Incorporated will supply us with a statement certifying the amounts for our records.

In addition to the officials from Inventory Incorporated, we've invited representatives from our CPA firm, Williams & Larson, to observe the inventory.

Since this is the first inventory that we've had done by an outside firm, I'm asking that every pharmacist and pharmacy clerk cooperate fully with the officials from Inventory Incorporated and with the visitors from Williams & Larson.

Analysis. The subject line announces the main idea of the memo. The first sentence explains why the memo is being written. Notice that this first sentence also summarizes the contents of the memo but does so in a complete sentence with more information than in the subject line. The body of the memo supplies additional information about the inventory. Transitional words (*in addition, since*) help build coherence into the message. A conversational tone is suggested in the use of personal pronouns and the contractions *we've* and *I'm*.

Model 2: *Ineffective Memo*

TO: Department Heads

FROM: Jerry Munson, Business Manager

DATE: January 4, 19xx

SUBJECT: COPY MACHINE

Our front office, as you know, has a copy machine that we allow all staff members to use.

Please be advised that service and supply costs are rising astronomically. The number of copies being made can be monitored; the total copies we can determine. What we don't know is who is making all the copies. And the machine seems to need servicing nearly every month. It was just serviced last Friday.

Please be advised that in the near future a new machine will be installed. The new machine will be controlled by a meter. There will be meters given to department heads only. Inform your staff members herewith that copies should be made only for office work and only with the meter—which you will control.

We know how much everyone has come to depend upon this copy machine. Perhaps some tasks should be duplicated by other means.

Analysis. This memo fails in nearly every category. First, the subject line does not summarize the memo. The first sentence starts out weakly; it should state why the memo is being written. Background information is presented haphazardly instead of in a logical progression describing the conditions leading up to the need for purchase of a meter-controlled copier.

Reading the memo is difficult because it lacks organization and transitions to promote coherence. In addition, the tone of the memo is poor. Instead of being conversational, it sounds preachy. Expressions like "please be advised" and "inform herewith" are too formal. The memo is wordy and could be condensed, retaining only the essential facts. Finally, this memo does not end with a clear statement of what action, if any, is desired.

Model 3: *Memo With Enumeration*

TO: Museum Couriers

FROM: Ann Davert, Curator

DATE: March 15, 19xx

SUBJECT: RESPONSIBILITIES OF COURIERS ESCORTING MUSEUM OBJECTS

Here is a list of guidelines to be observed by museum couriers when they escort museum objects.

Because the museum is about to embark on an extensive program of national artwork exchange, we feel that couriers should be aware of the following important responsibilities:

1. Keep your mission confidential. Do not discuss it with colleagues or individuals outside the museum. Do not discuss it with fellow travelers.

2. Know what you are escorting. Read the condition report. Examine the object. Observe the packing.

3. Travel alone. If you are planning a vacation with family or others after you have completed your mission, they must travel on separate aircraft and join you after your official responsibilities have ended.

4. Observe the loading and unloading of the shipment. Accompany the shipment to and from the airport.

5. Stay in touch with the museum staff while at the airport.

6. Accompany and supervise the shipment to the borrower's premises. Agree on a moderate speed limit before leaving the airport.

7. Supervise the installation of the object.

In escorting museum objects in future missions, please follow the preceding guidelines. Your primary concern should always be the safety of the shipment. Please see me if you have specific questions that I may answer.

Analysis. The first sentence states why the memo is being written. Since the content of the memo lends itself to enumeration, items are numbered. The numbered paragraphs are particularly effective because the items are parallel; they all begin with verbs and are written as commands.

APPLICATION EXERCISES

4–1. Rewrite Model 2, the ineffective memo shown on pp. 333–334. The analysis following it should help you see its weaknesses and point the way to improvements. Add any facts that you think are needed to produce a coherent message.

4–2. Rewrite the following ineffective memo. Revise the list using enumerated sentences or paragraphs. Be sure your list is parallel.

TO: All staff members

FROM: Douglas Dorff

DATE: Current

SUBJECT: COPIER RULES

Some of you missed the demonstration of the operation of our new Ziod X copier last week. I thought you might appreciate receiving this list of suggestions from the salesperson when she gave the demonstration. This list might also be helpful to other employees who saw the demo but didn't take notes and perhaps can't remember all these pointers. It's sometimes hard to remember how to operate a machine when you do it infrequently. Here's what she told us to do. There are two paper loading trays. Load 8½-x-11-inch or 8½-x-14-inch paper in the two loading trays. The paper should curve upward in the tray. You should take your copy and feed it into the machine face up. However, if you have small sheets or book pages or cut-and-pasted copy, lift the copier door and place your copy face down on the glass.

Before you begin, select the number of copies to be made by pressing the touch selector panel. Don't push too hard. If copies become jammed, open the front door and see where the paper got stuck in the feed path. Remove jammed paper. Oh yes, your meter must be inserted before the machine will operate. Make only as many copies as you really need.

If you or any of your staff members need a private demonstration, I'd be happy to oblige sometime.

4–3. You are vice president, Customer Services Division, Milwaukee Breweries. Write a memo to Layne Zant, supervisor, Customer Services. Ask Layne to draft a form letter that can be sent to groups requesting plant tours. In your memo, explain that the brewery has always encouraged tour groups to see our home plant brewery. We cannot sponsor tours at this time because of extensive remodeling. We are also installing a computer-controlled bottling system. Tours are expected to resume in September. You need a form letter that can be sent to all groups but that can be personalized for individual responses. You need the letter draft by Monday, April 6. The letter should build good customer relations, a primary goal of our tour policy. The letter might enclose a free product coupon and a brochure picturing our operations. Tell Layne to add any information that he feels would improve the letter.

4–4. You are supervisor, Publication Services, Rike's Department Store. Write a memo to Lynn Baker, manager, Housewares Department. You have received a request for publication of her sales promotion scheduled for July 1. You would like to begin work on this campaign, but you can't because you need answers to some questions. If you receive answers to all your questions by May 15, you could get a rush draft of the promotional letter to her by May 20. That may be cutting it very close to complete all the work before the July sale, but you'll try to meet her schedule. Most of the questions you have for Lynn relate to the form letter to charge customers. You're not sure what she wants to emphasize. She also didn't mention the usual one-week presale for preferred customers. Is there such a period for charge customers? Another question you have about the letter is this: Does she want to use the formal or informal store stationery? Should we promote one particular item in the letter? If so, what item? How soon before the event does she want the letter to be sent out? It might be a good idea for the letter to go out over her signature. How does that sound? Tell Lynn that you have assigned Anne Mason to prepare the advertising layouts. Anne is a new but very promising graphics designer. Anne may have questions and would like to be able to call Lynn whenever necessary.

4–5. Play the part of Tiffany Lopez, manager of the office staff at Data Services. In a memo inform the office staff of the upcoming Christmas party you are organizing. Data Services will pay for a holiday luncheon. Choose a local restaurant. Decide on the time of the luncheon party. Do you want a gift exchange? (Staff members seemed to enjoy the gift exchange in the past.) All members of the office staff are invited. They don't have to pay, but you must know how many will be attending so that you can make reservations at the restaurant by December 15. Perhaps you should avoid the word *Christmas* in your memo; some staff members don't observe it.

APPENDIX 5

Writing Informational Business Letters

Functions

Business letters are forms of external communication; that is, they deliver information to individuals outside an organization.

Business letters request information, respond to requests, make claims, seek adjustments, order merchandise, sell merchandise, recommend individuals, develop goodwill, and achieve many other goals. Business correspondence may be divided into three broad categories: (1) good news or neutral letters, (b) bad news letters, and (c) persuasive letters. In this unit we will be most concerned with the first category, writing good news or neutral letters.

Characteristics

Well-written business letters reflect the 4 Cs. That is, they are (1) concise, (2) clear, (3) correct, and (4) courteous. Let's consider each of these characteristics.

Conciseness

Concise letters save the reader's time by presenting information directly. Avoid these faults: (a) wordy phrases (such as *in addition to the above* and *in view of the fact that;* (b) excessive use of expletives (such as *There are four reasons* or *It is a good plan*); (c) long lead-ins (such as *This letter is to inform you that* or *I am writing this letter to*); needless adverbs (such as *very, definitely, quite, extremely,* and *really*); and old-fashioned expressions (such as *attached please find* and *pursuant to your request*).

Clarity

Business letters are clear when they are logically organized and when they present enough information for the reader to understand what the writer intended. Informational letters are usually organized deductively: the main idea comes first. Clarity can be enhanced by including all necessary information. Some authorities estimate that one third of all business letters are written to clarify previous correspondence. To ensure that your letters are clear, put yourself in the reader's position and analyze what you have written. What questions may the reader ask? Does your information proceed logically from one point to another? Are your sentences and paragraphs unified and coherent?

Correctness

Two aspects of correctness are accuracy of facts and accuracy of form. In regard to facts, good business writers prepare to write by gathering relevant information. They collect supporting documents (previous letters, memos, and reports), they make inquiries, they jot down facts, and they outline the message. Correct letters require thorough preparation. In the same manner, correct letters require careful proofreading and attention to form. Typographical errors, spelling irregularities, and grammatical faults distract the reader and damage the credibility of the writer. Correct business letters also follow one of the conventional formats, such as block, modified block, or simplified style, as shown on pp. 347–349.

Courtesy

You develop courtesy in business letters by putting yourself in the place of the reader. Imagine how you would like to be treated and show the same consideration and respect for the individual receiving your message. The ideas you express and the words used to convey those ideas create an impression on the reader. Be alert to words that may create a negative feeling, such as *you claim, unfortunately, you neglected, you forgot, your complaint,* and so forth. Create a positive feeling by presenting your message from the point of view of the reader. Try to use the word *you* more than the words *I* and *we*. Create a positive tone in business letters by using conversational language. Think of your reader as if he or she were across from you and you were having a friendly chat. Avoid formal, pretentious, and stuffy language, such as *the undersigned is pleased to grant your request.* In your business messages, you can develop goodwill toward your company and toward yourself by putting yourself in the place of the reader, by developing a friendly tone, and by using conversational language.

Writing Plan

Most business letters have three parts: opening, body, and closing. What information belongs in each of these parts?

Opening

The opening of a business letter may include a subject line that refers to previous correspondence or summarizes the content of the message. A subject line should make sense but should not be a complete sentence; it is not followed by a period.

The first sentence of a business letter that requests or delivers information should begin directly with the main idea. If you are asking for information, use one of two approaches. Ask the most important question first, such as *Do you have available a two-bedroom cottage on Devil's Lake for the week of July 8–15?* A second approach involves beginning with a summary statement, such as *Please answer the following questions regarding. . . .* If the letter delivers information, begin with the most important information first, such as *Yes, we have available a two-bedroom cottage on Devil's Lake for . . . ,* or *Here is the information you requested regarding. . . .* Most informational business letters should *not* begin with an explanation of why the letter is being written.

Body

The body of the letter provides explanations and additional information to clarify the first sentence. Use a separate paragraph for each new idea, being careful to strive for concise style.

If the message lends itself to enumeration, list the items. Be certain, of course, to construct the list so that each item is parallel (see pp. 186, 290 and 332).

Think about the individual reading your message. Will that person understand what you are saying? Have you included enough information? What may seem perfectly clear to you may not be so evident to your reader. In responding to requests, don't hestitate to include more information than was requested — if you feel it would be helpful.

Maintain a friendly, conversational, and positive tone.

Closing

Business letters that demand action should conclude with a specific request, including end dating if appropriate. That is, tell the reader when you would like the request complied with and, if possible, provide a reason. For example, *Please send me this information by June 1 so that I can arrange my vacation.*

Letters that provide information may end with a summary statement or a pleasant, forward-looking thought. For example, *I hope this information helps you plan your summer vacation.* Business organizations may also use the closing to promote products and services.

Avoid ending your letters with mechanical phrases, such as *If I can be of further service, don't hestitate to call upon me,* or *Thanks for any information you can provide.* Find a fresh way to show appreciation or to express your desire to be of service.

Model 1: Information Request

April 17, 19xx

Koniki Image Systems
5592 Buckeye Drive
Milpitas, CA 95035

Gentlemen:

Does your company manufacture a microfiche reader/printer that uses removable cartridge carriers but can also read microfiche film?

As controller of a very active accounting department at Valley Receiving Hospital, I need a reader/printer that is more flexible than our current DataPro Model RX. Every year we film over 1.7 million patient billing records, and we are now using cartridges. Some of our older records, however, are on microfiche. At present I am looking for a reliable system that uses cartridge carriers but that can also read our older film. If you have such a system, please answer the following questions:

1. Do you have a heavy-duty model that can handle our workload?
2. Does your model use toner, and if so, how messy is the refilling process?
3. Are other hospitals currently using your model?

Please send me answers to these questions before May 1, when I will be comparing the models of various vendors. If your model seems to meet our requirements, perhaps we can schedule a demonstration in June.

Sincerely yours,

Jeffry T. Autori
Controller

Analysis. Notice that the letter begins directly by asking the most important question first. The body includes explanation of the needs of the writer, as well as additional questions. The letter closes with end dating and a forward-looking statement.

Model 2: Information Response

Dear Mr. Autori:

SUBJECT: YOUR APRIL 15 LETTER REQUESTING READER/PRINTER INFORMATION

Yes, we produce a heavy-duty microfilm reader/printer that reads both cartridge film and microfiche film.

Our Model SNY-RP 30AU is used throughout the world in both manufacturing and service industries where record storage is critical. We are particularly proud of its durability; many users go 12 months or more with no service calls at all. Let me answer your specific questions.

1. Workload: Our Model SNY-RP can produce up to 50,000 copies annually, reading and printing both microfiche and cartridge film.
2. Toner: Our unique toner case enables the user to replace toner without dirtying hands or clothing.
3. Users: Brigham and Women's Hospital in Boston and Our Lady of Angels in Los Angeles are both using our new reader/printer with excellent results.

Enclosed is additional literature describing the Model SNY-RP. I would be happy to arrange a demonstration for you and your staff at your convenience. Call me at (818) 346-0012.

Cordially,

Analysis. This letter begins directly by answering the most important question first. The body provides additional information arranged logically and coherently. It closes with extra information and a forward-looking thought.

Model 3: Order Letter

Ladies and Gentlemen:

Please send by UPS the following items shown in your June catalog:

4	#24-39	Anti-static desk pads @19.95	$ 79.80
1	#25-02	Surge protector @ 59.90	59.90
2	#24-93	Multiple outlet strips @ 49.95	99.90
	Total		$239.60

Please add tax and shipping costs. Charge to Visa credit card 4990-3359-2280-1490 (expiration date 4/xx). I would appreciate receiving these computer supplies before May 1.

Sincerely,

Model 4: Routine Claim Letter

Ladies and Gentlemen:

Please replace my Model 6100 Suki printer or return the purchase price of $479.99.

I purchased a Model 6100 from J & L Distributors in North Hollywood on May 5. Copies of the purchase documents and warranty are enclosed. During the past four months, the printer has been in your service shop for repair on three different occasions. The paper feed mechanism has jammed several times, and the ribbon take-up reel still does not function properly. I have been without a printer for a total of 38 days.

When the printer is working, the copies are beautiful. However, I feel that this particular machine is defective. Therefore, I would like either a replacement or a refund of my purchase price. Please send me authorization to exchange my Model 6100 for a new printer or a check for $479.99 by October 1.

Sincerely yours,

APPLICATION EXERCISES

5–1. ***Information Request.*** Rewrite the following poorly expressed information request. Handwrite or type your letter on good-quality paper using modified block style and mixed punctuation. This is a personal business letter; follow the format shown in Figure 4 on p. 350, inserting your own address in the return address block. Remember that this letter is poorly written. Improve it!

Ms. Mary E. Burns, Manager
Rainbow Resort
1100 West Brannan Island Road
Isleton, CA 95641

Dear Mary E. Burns:

I saw an advertisement recently in *Sunset* magazine where Rainbow Resorts rents houseboats. My family and I (there are three kids and my wife and me) would like to take a vacation on a houseboat from July 17 through July 24 in the California Delta area. We've never done this before but it sounds interesting.

Please send me any information you may have. I'll have to make my vacation plans soon.

I have no idea how much this might cost. If we rent a houseboat, my wife wants to know do you provide bedding, dishes, pots and pans, and the like? I'm wondering about navigating a houseboat. Will I have to take a course or training on how to operate it? It may be too difficult for me to run. How far can we travel in the Delta area in one of your houseboats? What if we decide to stay on more than one week? I actually have two weeks of vacation, but we may want to travel in our RV part of the time. Does insurance come with the rental fee? My kids want to know if it has TV.

Yours,

Dennis Murphy

5–2. ***Information Response.*** Assume you are Mary E. Burns. Write a response to Mr. Murphy's letter, shown in Exercise 5–1. Use block style and open punctuation. Tell Mr. Murphy that the rental fee, which is $175 per day or $1,000 per week, does include insurance. You have a houseboat available for July 17 through 24, but definite reservations must be made for that time and for the week following, if Mr. Murphy decides to stay two weeks. Your houseboats can travel about 100 miles on the inland waterways of the Delta. Rainbow Resort provides bedding, dishes, and kitchenware. Yes, each houseboat has a TV set. You also provide an AM/FM radio and a stereo cassette player. Your houseboats accommodate four to ten people, and you require a deposit of $500 for a one-week reservation. Reservations must be received by June 1 to ensure a July vacation. Your houseboats are easy to operate. No special training is required, but you do give each operator about 30 minutes of instruction.

Send Mr. Murphy a brochure describing Rainbow Resorts and the memorable holiday he and his family can enjoy. The scenery and attractions are good.

5–3. ***Information Request.*** Assume you are Ginger Guzman, vice president, Personnel Operations, Trinity Corporation. You are planning a training seminar for 250 of your employees at the Sheraton East Hotel, Seventh and Main Streets, Richmond, Virginia 23260. Using modified block style with mixed punctuation, write to Ellen Hunter, conference manager, for information. Your event is scheduled for Friday, January 16, from 9 a.m. to 1:30 p.m. You need four conference rooms that can seat at least 65 people each. These rooms must have audiovisual equipment, including a 35 mm slide projector, viewing screen, and a public address system. You wonder if the conference rooms have a lectern, rostrum, or stage. You are very concerned about air conditioning, acoustics, and the noise level in the conference rooms, but you'll have to inspect this personally if the hotel seems to be able to accommodate your group at a reasonable cost. Inquire about scheduling a lunch from 12:30 to 1:30. What are the menu choices and costs per person? Because you want your employees to sit together at lunch, a banquet room for 250 is necessary. Inquire about parking and fees. Give a deadline for receiving this information. You would like to begin publicizing the training seminar May 15. Don't forget to ask about the cost of the conference rooms.

5–4. ***Order Letter.*** Assume you are Grace Petro, manager, Coast Federal Savings. You need to order office supplies immediately as your stocks are very low. Using block style and open punctuation, write to Office Supply Company, 344 North Ninth Street, DeKalb, Illinois 60115. Order 12 reams of bond paper, Order No. 3590, at $4.80 per ream; 3 boxes of continuous form computer paper, Order No. 290-C, at $23.90 per box; and 2 boxes of twin window envelopes, Order No. 385-E, at $24.30 per box. You're ordering from the fall sale catalog, and prices may have changed. You'd like this order charged to your company's account. Oh yes, you would also like 3 anti-glare mesh filters, Order No. 4443, at $25.90 each. (These are helpful in reducing glare from computer monitors.) Have these items shipped by prepaid parcel post. Instruct the supply house to add shipping charges and tax.

5–5. ***Routine Claim.*** Write a personal business letter in response to the following problem. For your home office you ordered a combination telephone/answering machine called the Execudyne Remote 2010. Instead of troublesome cassette tapes, the Execudyne used solid-state micro chips to record both incoming and outgoing messages. It had many attractive features, and you were eager to try it. When it arrived, however, you plugged it in and discovered that an irritating static sound interfered with every telephone call you made or received. Eventually you discovered that the static occurred only when the fluorescent light fixtures over your desk were turned on. When the lights were on, the telephone picked up static, making telephone calls impossible. You returned the telephone January 15 by UPS surface mail to ElectroWare, Inc., the mail order supplier from whom you purchased the unit. You still have a copy of the invoice, which states that merchandise may be returned for any reason within 30 days after purchase. You also have the UPS receipt proving that you returned it. However, your MasterCharge statement (No. 5390-3390-2219-0002) has not shown a credit for the return. Both your February and March statements show no credit for $188.90. You're wondering what happened. Did ElectroWare receive the returned telephone? Why hasn't your account been credited? If they did not receive the machine, you want UPS to trace it. Write to ElectroWare, Inc., 22121 Crystal Creek Boulevard, Bothell, Washington, 98021. You have complied with their instructions regarding returning merchandise, and you want them to credit your account. You do not want another telephone/answering machine.

5–6. ***Information Response.*** A friend of yours who lives in another city asks you to describe your course of study and your school. Write a personal business letter to your friend describing the courses you are taking and the degree, certificate, or vocational goal to which they lead. You may have to do some research to provide good information. Describe the more important courses. What kinds of jobs are open to an individual who completes this program? Why are you taking it? Would you recommend your school? Why or why not? Include any information in which you think your friend will be interested.

APPENDIX 6

Letter Parts and Styles

The first impression a letter makes upon its reader often determines whether that letter will actually be read, and it also may determine the reader's reaction to the contents of the letter. Therefore, business letter writers must, in addition to composing well-written sentences and paragraphs, be able to communicate their thoughts in efficient, appropriate letter form.

Parts and Styles

Letter Parts and Placement

Figure 1 on page 347 illustrates the parts of a business letter.

1. ***Letterhead.*** A business letter is usually typed on 8½-by-11-inch printed letterhead paper displaying the name, address, and telephone number of the organization sending the letter.

2. ***Dateline.*** The date is typed two spaces below the last line of the letterhead or 2 inches from the top edge of the paper (line 13). Use whichever method produces the lower placement.

3. ***Address Block.*** The address of the organization receiving the letter is typed singlespaced at the left margin. The number of lines left blank between the dateline and the address depends upon the size of the body of the letter, the size of type (the pitch) used, and the length of the typing lines. Generally, three to nine lines are left blank after the dateline.

4. ***Attention Line.*** An attention line is used to direct a letter to a specific individual or department within an organization. The attention line may be typed two lines below the address block, or it may be typed immediately below the organization name within the address block. The attention line is often underlined to draw attention to it. A colon following the word *attention* is optional.

5. ***Salutation.*** The letter greeting, or salutation, is typed two spaces below the last line of the address block or the attention line (if used). The letter may be addressed to an individual (*Dear Bud* or *Dear Mr. Kelly*) or to an organization (*Gentlemen* or *Ladies and Gentlemen* if you know women are in management). Although an attention line may be used, the letter is still officially addressed to the organization; hence the salutation should be directed to the organization (e.g., *Gentlemen*).

6. ***Subject and Reference Line.*** A brief indication of the subject of the letter may be typed two spaces below the salutation. This subject line is often entirely in capitals with a colon following the word *SUBJECT*. Instead of (or in addition to) a subject line, some businesses use a reference line to cite a policy, order, file, or account number. If a reference line is used, it is aligned two spaces below the dateline and begins with the words *Re* or *IN RE*.

7. *Body.* Most business letters are typed single-spaced, with double spacing between paragraphs.

8. *Complimentary Close.* Typed two spaces below the last line of the letter, the complimentary close may be formal (*Very truly yours*) or informal (*Sincerely yours* or *Cordially yours*).

9. *Organization Name.* If an organization name is used after the complimentary close, the name should be typed entirely in capitals two spaces below the complimentary close.

10. *Author, Title, and Department.* The author of the letter needs space to sign his or her name; therefore, three blank lines (four typewriter carrier returns) should be left above the typed name of the author. If short, the author's title or department may appear on the same line as the author's name. If long, they should be typed immediately below the author's name.

11. *Reference Initials.* The initials of the typist are typed two spaces below the author's name and title. If the author chooses to include his or her initials in the reference initials line, the author's initials should appear before the typist's (e.g., EM:mef).

12. *Enclosure (or Attachment) Notation.* If an enclosure (or attachment) accompanies the letter, a notation to that effect is typed two spaces below the reference initials. This notation reminds the typist to insert the enclosure in the envelope, and it reminds the letter receiver to look for the enclosure (or attachment). The notation may be spelled out (*Enclosure, Attachment*), or it may be abbreviated (*Enc., Att.*). It may indicate the number of enclosures or attachments, and it may also identify an enclosure specifically (*Enclosure: Copy of Invoice 6309*).

13. *Copy Notation.* If copies of a business letter have been made for other individuals, a *c* notation is typed one or two spaces below the enclosure notation (if used). A colon following *c* is optional.

Letter Styles

You should be familiar with at least three business letter styles: block, modified block, and simplified.

Figure 1 on p. 347 shows a letter typed in block style. All its lines begin at the left margin.

Figure 2 on p. 348 illustrates modified block letter style. The dateline, reference line (if used), complimentary close, organization name (if used), author's name, and title begin at the center of the page. The first line of each paragraph may begin at the left margin or may be indented five or ten spaces. All other lines begin at the left margin.

Figure 3 on p. 349 illustrates simplified style, introduced by the Administrative Management Society. All lines begin at the left margin. Notice that a subject line, typed in all caps, replaces the salutation. A triple space precedes and follows the subject line. Instead of a complimentary closing or company name, the author's name and title are typed in all capitals five carrier returns below the last line of the letter body.

In addition to these three letter styles, you should be able to use the personal business letter style, shown in Figure 4 on p. 350. This style is appropriate when you write your own business letter on plain paper. Notice that the writer's address appears above the date in the upper right corner, replacing a printed letterhead.

Punctuation Styles

The phrase *punctuation style* refers to the punctuation marks used after the salutation and the complimentary close in a business letter. Most organizations use *mixed punctuation.*

1 — **TECHNICAL DESIGNS, INC.**

1505 Fifth Avenue
Seattle, WA
(206) 628-3149

2 — September 30, 19XX

3 — Pacific Resources, Inc.
1160 Bishop Street
Honolulu, HI 96813

4 — Attention Ms. Alicia Chavez

5 — Ladies and Gentlemen

6 — SUBJECT: OFFICE LETTER STYLE

7 — Our office prefers the block letter style, as shown in this letter. Notice that all lines begin at the left margin. This is a popular style among our correspondence secretaries because it requires no tabular stops for indentions. With the block letter style, we use open punctuation for its efficiency.

Many of the letter writers within our organization use the company name after the complimentary close. When it is included, it is typed entirely in capitals two spaces below the complimentary close.

I am enclosing samples of our intracompany stationery and memorandum forms for you. I will also send stationery samples to your colleagues, Ms. Schultz and Mr. Farmer.

8 — Sincerely yours

9 — TECHNICAL DESIGNS, INC.

10 — Eric Mann, Consultant
Community Services Department

11 — EM:mef

12 — Enc.

13 — c Ms. Laura Schultz
Mr. Andrew Farmer

1. Letterhead, 2. Dateline, 3. Address Block, 4. Attention Line, 5. Salutation, 6. Subject Line, 7. Body, 8. Complimentary Close, 9. Organization Name, 10. Author, Title, and Department, 11. Reference Initials, 12. Enclosure Notation, 13. Copy Notation

FIGURE 1 Business Letter: Block Style, Open Punctuation

FIRST SOUTHERN BANK OF ORLANDO

350 Park Avenue, North
Winter Park, Florida 32789

January 16, 19xx

Mrs. Janet Miller
Aimes Advertising Agency
115 North Lakemont Avenue
Winter Park, FL 32792

Dear Mrs. Miller:

SUBJECT: MARCH AND APRIL STATEMENT STUFFERS

To be able to include your advertising as stuffers in our March statements, I need a letter from you stating the number of stuffers and a copy of the proposed stuffer.

In our telephone call you said that you would like stuffers included in both the March and April statements. Do you want the stuffers to be included in just the Winter Park statements or in the University Boulevard branch statements as well?

I am sending a copy of this letter to Andrew Tilley, our operations manager, so that he may advise me regarding the necessary steps for approval of your request. If approval is granted, you may count on 2,000 checking accounts and 1,300 savings accounts.

Please send me a copy of the proposed stuffer, as well as the other information requested above, by February 1 so that we can meet your schedule.

Sincerely yours,

Gary P. Williams

Gary P. Williams
Vice President and Manager

mef

c Andrew Tilley

FIGURE 2 Business Letter: Modified Block Style, Mixed Punctuation

DATATECH
International, Inc.

4038 Candlewood Drive
Lakewood, California 90714
Telephone: (213) 925-9021

February 12, 19xx

Professor Clara J. Smith
Office Occupations Department
North Seattle Community College
9600 College Way North
Seattle, WA 98103-3599

YOUR INQUIRY REGARDING LETTER STYLES

In response to your letter regarding a survey your college is conducting, I am happy to send you this letter illustrating the letter style we prefer.

Our organization prefers this simplified letter style for many reasons. First, it is efficient and easy for our secretaries to produce. Second, it eliminates the problem of choosing a salutation that is appropriate for the receiver. In many instances we're not certain whether to send a letter addressed to "Gentlemen" or "Ladies" or both. Other times we don't know whether to address a letter to "Mr." or "Ms." This letter style eliminates uncertainty regarding salutations.

We are pleased to participate in your survey and would appreciate receiving a copy of your final report.

Elizabeth R. St. James

ELIZABETH R. ST. JAMES, MANAGER, CUSTOMER RELATIONS

mef

FIGURE 3 Business Letter: Simplified Style

5849 West Seventh Avenue
Eugene, OR 97405
February 20, 19xx

Dr. Sharon Miles, Director
Oregon Institute of Legal Studies
18002 South Molalla Avenue
Oregon City, OR 97045

Dear Dr. Miles:

Please send me information regarding your training program in paralegal studies.

I saw your advertisement in the Daily Register January 21, and I would like additional information. Could you answer the following questions for me:

1. May students with an associate's degree enter your program?

2. How long would it take a full-time student to complete the paralegal program?

3. Is financial aid available?

4. Do you offer summer classes?

5. Do you help graduates find employment?

I would appreciate answers to these questions before March 15 so that I may plan my summer and my future training program.

Sincerely,

Amy Lee

Amy Lee

FIGURE 4 Personal Business Letter: Modified Block Style, Mixed Punctuation

In this style a colon follows the salutation, and a comma follows the complimentary close. Some organizations prefer the more efficient *open punctuation* style, especially if their letter style is *block*. In open punctuation style, no punctuation follows the salutation or the complimentary close; these lines are, in other words, left "open." Regardless of the punctuation style that is selected, sentences in the body of the letter are punctuated normally.

Mixed punctuation	Open punctuation
Dear Mrs. Gasparian:	Dear Mrs. Gasparian
Cordially yours,	Cordially yours

Many businesses provide employees with style manuals that show preferred letter and punctuation styles. Other businesses allow workers to choose the styles that they prefer.

INDEX

Note to the Instructor: This index applies only to the text of the student edition of *Business English*. The instructor's supplementary material appears separately.